WATERFRONT BLUES

WATERFRONT BLUES

The rise and fall
of Liverpool's dockland

BRIAN TOWERS

For my grandmother
'Lizzie' Towers
(1895–1966)

By the same author: *The Representation Gap: Change and Reform in the British and American Workplace* (Oxford University Press, 1997)

Waterfront Blues: The Rise and Fall of Liverpool's Dockland

Copyright © Brian Towers, 2011

First published in 2011 by
Carnegie Publishing Ltd,
Carnegie House,
Chatsworth Road,
Lancaster LA1 4SL
www.carnegiepublishing.com

British Library Cataloguing-in-Publication data
A catalogue record for this book is available from the British Library

ISBN 978-1-85936-179-5

Designed and typeset by Carnegie Book Production, Lancaster
Printed and bound in the UK by Short Run Press, Exeter

Contents

List of tables

Editor's preface

S ADLY, the author of this book, Brian Towers, passed away, not long after the editing process on his manuscript had begun. The staff at Carnegie Publishing were naturally shocked at the news, and all of our best wishes and commiserations go out to his family, academic colleagues and friends.

Before Brian's death the publishing process had begun upon its long and winding course. A favourable academic referee's report had already been secured, leading to the publisher's enthusiastic acceptance of the manuscript. In the usual, time-honoured manner the next stage was to have been a period of on-going discussion and dialogue relating to the editing of the manuscript for publication. As always in such situations, queries of fact and interpretation would have been referred back to the author for clarification or amendment, while publishers and editors usually see it as their preserve to niggle about authors' idiosyncrasies of style, grammar and syntax. The often slow and occasionally tortuous work of editing would eventually have led to an agreed text to offer to the public in the form of the final book.

With the support of Brian's family it was agreed that his book presented such an important and valuable contribution that the process should continue, and that the book should be published posthumously. Brian had already agreed to my suggested amendments to his Introduction and first chapter, and had already incorporated many of the comments of the academic referee. The broad parameters of the editing process had also been agreed.

Nevertheless, it has been a daunting task to undertake the editing work without being able to refer queries or comments to the author for adjudication. However, armed with Brian's many, well-catalogued box files of notes and original sources, and buoyed by the knowledge that he had been more than happy with the small sample of editing he had seen, it was decided that we should press on.

I have tried to retain Brian's style of writing as much as possible, and have consulted his notes only to answer queries of fact. I have not altered any of his broad interpretations. The text has been sanctioned by Brian's daughter Susan and his grandson Ali – who also kindly and diligently compiled the index – and I hope that the published book will find approval from reviewers and readers alike.

Alistair C. Hodge, publisher/editor

Author's preface and acknowledgements

I HAVE BEEN WORKING ON THIS BOOK, on and off, for almost ten years. One explanation for this length of time has been the demands of other work, but another is that it is my first attempt at writing what is essentially a mixture of labour and social history over a period of nearly 300 years. That, for someone not trained in the methods and approaches used by professional historians, has been daunting. I have also tried to write a book that will be read by those who lived and/or worked along the waterfront or those who find the stories and memories of those who did (their parents and grandparents perhaps) of compelling interest.

As well as the time it took to complete this book, it has had an even longer gestation, its inspiration having very deep roots. Part of it comes from my still vividly remembered childhood, on Scotland Road, during and after the Second World War. Although I have not lived in Liverpool for any length of time since I was eighteen, and though my trips back have not been that frequent – except for the many more recent ones in the preparation of this book – in my case there is much truth in the old adage that 'you can take the boy out of Liverpool ...'

Well beyond childhood and the years of growing up into an adult, another recent inspiration for writing the book was the 1995–98 labour dispute at Seaforth Docks. Among other things, this helped to put the history of life for working people on the Liverpool waterfront in context. What also struck supporters and observers in 1995–98 was some re-awakening of the old community spirit of the old waterfront, though by this late date almost all of the people had gone, along with their houses, tenements and courts under the hammers and bulldozers of the demolition gangs. The waterfront became, though on a limited scale and for a brief time, something more than a folk memory as the dockers marched, in the old familiar way, from Myrtle Street by the Philharmonic, down to St George's Plateau.

The big transport strike of 1911, when 60,000 were out, was an important milestone in Liverpool's 'electric social history'.[1] Such a turbulent story is worth resurrecting and preserving in the celebration of the city's 800-year history. Liverpool's civic founding has also been marked in print, notably in three major publications in the years 1907, 1957 and 2006.[2] Liverpool is also a UNESCO World Heritage Site and, in 2008, celebrated its year as a European Capital of

Culture. Yet with all of these accolades, and the worthy anniversary volumes, a continuous history of Liverpool's waterfront – its workers, its families, its communities – has not been written. This book, hopefully, begins to fill that gap.

The best people to write this history would have been those who lived and worked through it, the 'forgotten men [and women] at the bottom of the pyramid' as Roosevelt so memorably put it. But conducting research, writing books and reports, even letters, are activities which are the preserve of the well educated, the privileged and the comfortably off. The poor do have more interesting things to say than we, but they were not called the working classes, by the Victorians, for nothing. Particularly in the early decades of the industrial era, their time was taken up with simple survival; they lacked the leisure time, the education or the resources to do much more. A book such as this must, therefore, mostly draw heavily on the written contributions and testimonies of those who studied and observed the work and life of the waterfront, with some exceptions, without experiencing it directly.

Fortunately, there are also some who lived it at first hand who have been inspired to write their memoirs and reflections. Perhaps the most vivid, personal account is that of Pat O'Mara,[3] in his recently re-published memoirs. O'Mara went to school in Seel Street, then a down-at-heel slum district that had seen better times; Dr Duncan, Liverpool's Medical Officer of Health, was born and brought up there before he went off to study medicine. Besides poverty, O'Mara was witness to sectarianism, rioting, looting and unemployment in the early years of the twentieth century, recording it all with an unsentimental, even caustic gaze. Other contributions of a similar kind are usually much shorter. Notable among these are Johnnie Woods' and Terry Cooke's accounts of growing up in Scotland Road between the wars and Joan Boyce's direct experience of the traumas of the evacuees in the Second World War.[4] Bryan Perrett, though a military historian, actually grew up in Liverpool during the last war, and this experience strengthens and illuminates his detailed account of the Blitz and the Battle of the Atlantic.[5] Autobiographies can also give us much, including that of Jack Jones,[6] the reforming General Secretary of the Transport and General Workers' Union, who in his early chapters recalls his formative experiences of growing up at Garston, where he worked for a while on the docks before becoming a union official. Another is Eric Heffer's,[7] a Liverpool MP, once a trade union representative on the waterfront though not a docker.

James Sexton,[8] who could claim to have built up, if not founded, Liverpool's National Union of Dock Labourers, was also a sailor on sailing ships and then a docker, before swiftly rising to prominence in the union and, later, as an MP. His story is a mixture of acute, often sardonic observations as well as some self-justification, but essential reading for all that. Beyond Liverpool, Jack Dash,[9] the legendary unofficial leader of the London men, has left us with a detailed, wryly humorous account of the long influence of the unofficial movement on the docks, not just in London. Parallel to this are Robert Roberts' two classic, compulsive accounts of life viewed from a corner shop in the Salford slums before the Great War.[10] Here and there, too, I have been unable to resist the temptation, but only in notes, to use my own experience to confirm or augment the experiences of others. One detailed oral history source should also be cited here. Transcripts of the interviews of those of all ages and both sexes, who lived and worked through the Blitz years were kindly made available by Lorraine Chesters, formerly assistant curator at the Museum of Liverpool Life.[11]

Given the naturally limited direct accounts of life and labour along the waterfront, the few academic works that draw on direct experience have been invaluable. Notable among these is the work of Caradog Jones and his colleagues,[12] at Liverpool University between the wars, detailing the lives and homes of Liverpool people under the stresses of mass long-term unemployment. More recent work on the experience of the 1930s is that of Sam Davies and his colleagues[13] as well as Pat Ayers' vivid first-hand study of Athol Street's community life up to the 1980s.[14] For the experience of the seamen in the Second World War an analytical, though lively source, laced with incisive comments of the men themselves, and a mine of information, is Tony Lane[15] who has also given us his affectionate short account of his adopted city, cited earlier.

Other academic works provided the greater part of the book's narrative and analytical spine. These sources are cited throughout. But some, the most used, deserve a special mention here. For the economic history of Liverpool Francis Hyde[16] has been the standard text. For early accounts of dock labour Eric Taplin's[17] books have been essential. There is also the fascinating, two-volume international and comparative study of port labour, by port and theme, of Sam Davies and his colleagues.[18] For developments up to the 1970s and 1980s, Phillips and Whiteside,[19] David Wilson[20] and Michael Jackson[21] are the main sources. Coates and Topham's[22] encyclopaedic, always lively, even exciting study of the emergence of the TGWU has been a much used source, as has Lavalette and Kennedy's short work on the 1995–98 dispute.[23]

For earlier times, including the construction of the docks from 1715 to Seaforth's opening in 1972, Nancy Ritchie-Noakes'[24] study has no rival. Her work is complemented by Adrian Jarvis'[25] biographical and other studies, adding much to the story of the docks in the fleshing-out of the major contributions of Jesse Hartley and George Lyster in the construction of the still largely existing dock estate. For the impact of the Irish on the waterfront, including those fleeing the Potato Famine, the most detailed source is Frank Neal. He also describes the role of sectarianism, and the desperate suffering and experience of the poor, not least the Irish.[26] Philip Waller's[27] tracing of the interaction between politics and sectarianism over 75 years was also frequently turned to for good, analytical overviews and lively, entertainingly critical views of personalities. A last mention must also be given here to the excellent, detailed, informative account by Peter Turnbull and his colleagues[28] of the traumatic period during which the National Dock Labour Board was abolished and the TGWU called a national strike, including an analysis of the aftermath of that strike's historic failure for those still working on the waterfront. Peter, an old friend and colleague, also read the typescripts of chapters 13 and 14, offering detailed comments, extra information, and some factual corrections. These were especially helpful even though any remaining errors and omissions remain mine.

Some of the people whose works are mentioned here have also helped directly in the writing of the book through direct personal contact. Their knowledge, advice and encouragement were essential. These include Bill Cooke and his colleagues at Wayne State University, Detroit and Geraldine Healy and her then colleagues at the University of Hertfordshire where I gave presentations to seminars as the book proceeded. Other individuals, whose writings have already been noted, include Adrian Jarvis, John Murden, Frank Neal, David Sapsford, Eric Taplin, and Peter Turnbull. Rory Miller and Rogan Taylor of the University of Liverpool were also helpful with their advice.

Adrian Jarvis deserves a special acknowledgement for providing an early typescript of his as yet unpublished work, 'A History of the Port of Liverpool', upon which I have drawn. I am also grateful for his careful, detailed reading of my own manuscript. I have incorporated almost all of his many factual corrections, additions and amplifications, especially those relating to the early chapters.

The librarians at Liverpool University's Sydney Jones Library were always helpful. The archives and curators of Liverpool's William Brown Library (David Stoker, Roger Hull and David Webster), the Crosby Library (Andrew Lee Hart, Mark Sargant and Angela Willis) and the curators of the Liverpool Maritime Museum archive gave their time and access to their collections of photographs. James King of Warwick University's Modern Records Centre suggested a useful lead on tracing strike incidence, on Merseyside, during the Second World War. Lifette Rimmer, an hydrographer at Associated British Ports, Southampton, shared with me her expert knowledge of the tidal advantages of that fine, natural harbour.

The following gave interviews about their experiences of working on the docks: John Docherty, Graham Farrell (including providing photographs) Geoff Liddy and Richard Williams. Special mention also needs to be given to Bob Richie, a former shop steward and dismissed Torside employee who I first met in Scotland in 1995. He was the source of invaluable information and observation over most of the book's writing, complementing the written sources and other interviews. His unique collection of memorabilia, photographs and videos has also been donated to the Maritime Museum. Interviews also included that of Bill Hunter, a 'retired' activist and author and Eric Leatherbarrow, Corporate Affairs Director at Peel Ports Ltd, now owners of the Mersey docks, whose experience goes back to before the 1989 dispute.

Bishop Tom Williams, formerly parish priest at St Anthony's, Scotland Road (many of whose priests died in nineteenth-century cholera epidemics) was also helpful, including introducing me to his brother, Richard, an ex-docker mentioned above. Another Williams, Ken, formerly of the Royal Navy in the Second World War, was also insightful on the experience of that time. Then there was Dave Williams, an employee of Tate & Lyle, who provided a brief but informative chance interview in the company's car park off the Dock Road! Paul Unger, a Liverpool-based journalist, also gave me his time for a useful discussion of Liverpool's modern development, including the rescue of the Mersey from silt and pollution.

More basically, my accommodation needs in Liverpool were latterly met by my old friends Ivor and Lise Roberts though, over most of the period of researching and writing, I enjoyed the warmth, help, and good value accommodation of the Augustine Sisters of Park House, Seaforth, in their new role as hoteliers! Of special mention are Sisters Carmel and Marian who maintain, with great cheerfulness, their order's long traditions of care and hospitality. They, from my first stay, treated me as a friend, as did their staff, Irene Akery, John McEwan, Alice Bell and Jack Murphy — all with family connections to the docks. I must also thank Judy Rose, another old friend who, at several difficult times, brought an untidy, handwritten, and crudely edited manuscript to a final, pristine fruition.

More formally, the text of this book has been amplified and illustrated by photographs from copyrighted collections made available through the co-operation of the Merseyside Maritime Museum and the Record Office of the Liverpool Central Library. Acknowledgement for permission to reproduce the photographs is given below each caption. Many thanks to everyone who helped.

Brian Towers
Southport,
November 2008

From 'Black Spot on the Mersey'[1] to European Capital of Culture

If the map of England were shaded to represent the rates of mortality of last quarter in the registration districts, the eye, travelling from the lighter south to the darker north would be instantly drawn to a spot of portentous darkness on the Mersey.

(Registrar General, 1866)[2]

Notwithstanding some attention to outlying areas, Liverpool it seems is following the pattern of Glasgow, the last British city to enjoy European City of Culture status in 1990: a rapidly regenerating and gentrifying urban core surrounded by a ring of intensely disadvantages areas.

(John Belchem, 2006)[3]

T HE STORY of Liverpool and its waterfront can be told in several ways, their ups and downs narrated from very different viewpoints through time. Almost three hundred years have passed since Liverpool's first, pioneering dock was opened in 1715. Over those three centuries there have been many highlights, including times of rapid economic expansion, during which there was great prosperity, albeit never well distributed through the population. There have also been blemishes, from the abominations of the slave trade to the Victorian public health horrors highlighted by social reformers such as the Registrar General, quoted above, and the country's first medical officer of health, Dr Henry Duncan.

Liverpool has always been a place of paradoxes: great civic pride among its influential merchant class alongside insecurity and poverty of existence for casually employed and frequently unemployed dock workers; imaginative corporate governance of the port and its finances alongside sub-standard housing and sanitation for the wider population; prosperity alongside great poverty, enormous fluctuations and variations of economic wealth, and periods of great and widespread distress.

The economic fortunes of the city have waxed and waned. At the time Duncan and the Registrar General were rattling Victorian consciences about issues

1

of public health, mortality and poverty, mercantile Liverpool was still in the ascendancy. Since the mid-eighteenth century trade had grown steadily until by the mid-nineteenth century – by some criteria at least – Liverpool was challenging London as the most important port of empire. A century further on, when its imperial status had long gone, Liverpool was still prospering; its manufacturing base moved towards a major expansion during the long post-war boom of the 1950s and 1960s. Then the age-old over-dependence on trade finally seemed to be a thing of the past; even auto manufacturing plants – Ford, Vauxhall and British Leyland – were confident of a permanent presence on Merseyside. But the lifeblood of Liverpool – its port – was ailing, and all of a sudden everything seemed to go horribly wrong. For a generation the news from Liverpool was mostly bad: there were long-term trends such as the shift of British trade towards Europe which Liverpool, on the west coast, was ill-placed to cater for; there was, of course, the shift to transatlantic air traffic; and ever-larger container ships preferred to berth in deep-water harbours; suddenly Liverpool's largely Victorian docks were either too small or too inefficient, or both.

But Liverpool is known for its resilience. Today Liverpool remains among the poorest places in Britain, yet there has undoubtedly been something of a renaissance of the city, and the fortunes of the port are rising once more, in terms both of tonnage and profits.

Liverpool's urban experience is unusual, if not unique. Many towns have rivers at their heart, yet few have turned their gaze so completely outwards towards the sea. In Tudor and early Stuart times Liverpool had been little more than a small village and a little port that was of similar size and importance to several others on the west coast of England. Yet by the time Thomas Steers built that first dock early in the eighteenth century, it was already the third port in England, with a population of perhaps 10,000. As it underwent its great transformation into a great maritime city it began to look outwards. The boggy plain of south-west Lancashire, with its poor soil and worse communications, was at least a physical if not a psychological barrier to Liverpool's integration with its rural hinterland. Instead, Liverpool looked outwards: to the ocean and to distant lands with which its prosperity was inextricably linked. And Liverpool's waterfront – that ribbon of reclaimed land, docks and warehouses – was at the forefront; it was a boundary, a frontier; it was a riverine staging post to a new world beyond the Mersey Bar and the horizon. When in Liverpool, one is almost always drawn towards the waterfront: in part because it is visible from the hills further inland, but mainly because three centuries and more of overseas maritime trade have oriented the city's outlook almost exclusively in that direction.

Thus the waterfront of Liverpool is at the heart and soul of the city, and of its story. And those who worked there were in the front line of that story: from Mersey flats, Lancashire 'nobbys' and coastal shipping to slave ships and cargo vessels of all types and sizes. To understand Liverpool is to understand the waterfront, and vice versa.

Where does one begin to tell that story?

Some physical as well as psychological echoes survive. These include what is perhaps the best publicised, guilty aspect of its past. Liverpool's long and prominent involvement in the slave trade remains a shaming part of Liverpool's and other ports' histories with which they are coming to some terms with exhibitions, including Liverpool's permanent exhibition in the Maritime Museum, expanded in 2007. The slave trade, an abomination in itself, was more so in the context of its final years. Ships were still leaving Liverpool to trade in human cargo along the west coast of Africa even as the 'enlightenment' was in its full, final flowering, including in Liverpool itself. Slaves were being transported, via the infamous, deadly 'middle passage', to the Caribbean and North America even as Toussaint l'Ouverture was proclaiming the first black republic inspired by the ideals of the Paris revolutionaries. At the same time the other revolutionaries, in America, were building their own new country on first principles, the rights to life, liberty and the pursuit of happiness: except, of course, if you were black or red. In Liverpool, the slave traders even campaigned against abolition. Liverpool was the 'Black Spot on the Mersey' in more ways than one. Nor did the 'middle passage', so far away in the waters of the Atlantic, provide a daily, guilty reminder of this odious traffic. Even the African people who had long been a feature of Liverpool's waterfront, were, for the most part, the descendants of those West African sailors who had been recruited to help man Liverpool's ships.

There are still some physical reminders along the waterfront, too, of that sweet substance of Liverpool's shameful, trading past, even though these brick and concrete temples to profit were constructed long after Liverpool's and Britain's involvement in human trafficking and human bondage was finally extinguished. Tate & Lyle's concrete silo is still there. Inside, the size of two football pitches, it held raw cane sugar, until the company pulled the plug in 1981. Now the cylindrical storage tanks nearby hold molasses and vegetable oil. The silo is used for dry bulk products, such as grain, another staple of Liverpool trade. Tate's now employ about fifty on Merseyside when once the Love Lane refinery, about a mile and a half to the south, used to have work for several thousand.

The Tate & Lyle silo starts on the Dock Road, opposite Huskisson Dock, stretching to Derby Road in the east. The dock, opened in 1852 and still working, is named after William Huskisson, once President of the Board of Trade and a Liverpool MP. He was, famously, the world's first celebrity casualty of the railway age: accidentally and fatally mown down by none other than Robert Stephenson's *Rocket* in the presence of the prime minister, the Duke of Wellington, at the opening of the railway in 1830 (there is a prominent memorial to him in St James's cemetery under the shadow of the tower of the Anglican cathedral, as well as a more modest one upon the site of the accident itself). In modern Liverpool the Huskisson Dock is more famous, and still talked about, as the dock where the 7,500-ton SS *Malakand* was berthed in the first week of May 1941. Somehow a damaged, hydrogen-filled barrage balloon appears to have fallen upon the ship, catching fire. Incendiaries contributed to the conflagration on the ship and nearby warehouses, and despite several days' heroic efforts by firefighters and the ship's crew, the fire made its way to the ship's 1,000-ton cargo of high explosives. The massive explosion took Huskisson No. 2 Branch Dock with it as well as the nearby Overhead Railway station. Astonishingly, none of those fighting the blaze was killed, although four people on the Dock Road lost their lives from falling ships' plates, one of which landed an astonishing 2½ miles away.

Further down the Dock Road, even more massive than Tate & Lyle's silo, is the Stanley Dock tobacco warehouse, once the biggest of its kind in the world but now looking more like a semi-derelict northern Dartmoor, with smashed window panes and ageing brickwork. Yet it still dominates Stanley and Collingwood docks and, once a week, comes back from the dead. Every Sunday morning its ground floor is vibrant with noisy, crowded life, a giant latter day 'Paddy's Market'[4] reviving old memories – at least for a few.

Tobacco and cane sugar were still lucrative commodities for Liverpool well into our own times. Today, however, tobacco has lost much of its grip on the British, and Tate & Lyle offers little physical to remind Liverpudlians of its historic cane sugar connections with the city. The demolition of its almost iconic refinery in Love Lane, Vauxhall, was one of the enduring images of Alan Bleasdale's celebrated TV drama *Boys from the Blackstuff*, broadcast in the same decade. The year the refinery went – 1981 – was also the year when Toxteth's youth hit the world's headlines with riots, destruction and burning.

Those desperate times, which were marked especially by chronic mass unemployment – in scope not seen in Liverpool since the 1930s and thought to have gone for ever – were not easily predicted in the 1960s. The Mersey Docks and Harbour Board was even bullish. The North End was still full of ships as the tonnage passing through Liverpool was at its then highest ever level. Even the South End of the dock system had enough work, and was making enough money to cover its face. Elsewhere, large-scale manufacturing, including of cars, was transforming job prospects as the 'new' industries, such as pharmaceuticals, established earlier, were contributing to the heady optimism.

By 1965 it looked as though the old times were gone for ever. New businesses, and an increasingly manufacturing industrial base stimulated further the move away from the old trading and shipping sectors. Yet the legacy of the past lived on. In the nineteenth century most Liverpudlians, certainly of the city centre, had lived in deep poverty, with occasional visits of destitution. In time, though, they got clean piped water, efficient sanitation, and better housing, the first two delivered with energy and some enthusiasm ahead of all other Victorian cities, by James Newlands, the first municipal engineer, whose achievements at least match those of Liverpool's pioneering, first medical officer of health Dr Duncan. Dr Duncan was celebrated enough to have a pub named after him in St John's Lane, the other side of the St John's Gardens at the back of St George's Hall. Housing, the third of the holy trinity, would take much longer than water and sanitation, even into our own times. In this area, too, Liverpool's record was creditable, despite the scale of the problems made much worse by the damage and the loss of housing in the Second World War, although some maintained that the housing was so poor that in this respect, though no other, the Luftwaffe actually did Liverpool a favour.

Adequate pay to achieve a household living income was, in the old days as now, another essential ingredient making for decent lives. Good pay was closely linked to strong, high membership of trade unions, recognised by the employers. Liverpool had union recognition on the docks as early as 1911, ahead of other ports and other industries. Yet that union's long-serving and long-suffering General Secretary, James Sexton, got little credit for his major role in building the organisation. The National Union of Dock Labourers, its members mostly on Merseyside (the building of the 'Liverpool Union', as it became known in London), was largely down to Jimmy Sexton, though he was not shy in boasting about it. But Liverpool's dockers, even more than those of Birkenhead, rarely put their trust in their union officials. They put that into their 'union', which meant those who worked alongside them, in the hold or the warehouse, in the grain silo or 'heaving' coal for ships. They struck readily over victimisation or for the exclusive employment of union men, identified by the wearing of the 'button'. They would also strike over pay or recognition, straightforward issues dear to the hearts of full-time officials though they naturally insisted that any striking had to be official, orderly, even disciplined. That discipline was not easy for freewheeling dockers, even with their traditional solidarity. Yet with pay they were normally not at odds with their officials who, inevitably, had to compromise.

But what really divided the dockers from their officials was the casual system. To a man, the officials wanted to get rid of the system of casual employment of labour. This included James Sexton, which increased his unpopularity. Ernest Bevin, the 'Dockers' QC', was able to ride his own disapproval, given his other considerable achievements. Many dockers liked the casual system for the freedom they said it gave them, especially the younger men, even if Ernie Bevin saw it, rather, as the freedom to starve. So it was not surprising that the first serious attempt to end casual labour did not come until 1947, building on Bevin's compulsory introduction of permanent employment as wartime Minister of Labour. That attempt failed and it took another twenty years to end a system that dockers clung to like an old flame; they even struck against its abolition.[5] By those days pay, already greatly improved relative to other workers, had become more stable with permanent employment.

Working conditions, though, took longer to become even adequate. As late as the ending of casualism, by Lord Devlin in 1967, he was instructing the National Dock Labour Board (Attlee's 1947 creation) to survey and, by implication, improve dockers' facilities in the eighty or so ports under its control – the so-called 'Scheme' ports. Dock work remained one of the most dangerous of jobs, as hazardous as going down the mines. Cargo handling was still loose, manual and dangerous. It would need to be palletised, mechanised and put into containers before the accident statistics would improve significantly. Those innovations would mostly make the job safer, but less varied and less interesting. They also involved drastic job losses, with many fewer dockers being required than before. The dockers were not opposed to containerisation as such, but to its impact upon their livelihoods. Like the Luddites 150 years before, the dockers suffered from a bad press.

The dockers were prone to strike action, with the Liverpool men often in the national vanguard. Dockers ranked high in the strike statistics, rivalled only by the miners, the car workers and the shipyard men. They had to be. There were strong forces forever lined up against them; among these the employers, always putting profits well ahead of conscience and scruple, were the main ones. There was also the state with its troops and an occasional warship on the Mersey (the Empire's cruisers were not only deployed on the high seas against foreigners). In Liverpool there were major confrontations all through the later history of dockland, including major disputes in 1879, 1890 and 1911. To this list must now be added the 28-month dispute from 1995 to 1998, during which the workforce that was left of the once mighty army of dockers, at Seaforth, fought against their sacking for refusing to cross a picket line that was by then perfectly legal. As so often, the men were at odds with their full-time officials who, at all levels, had been driven into timidity by the Conservative government's anti-union legislation. It had been the same in 1988–89, when the employers finally got rid of the National Dock Labour Scheme. The men of 1995–98, and their women, almost prevailed, as their international campaign blossomed into real support across the world's ports, and container ships were diverted, by their owners, to other harbours.

Earlier industrial battles were more local affairs, though often with support in other ports and always drawing the attention of government given the importance of international trade to Britain's economy. The seamen were also often involved, though for their own reasons and grievances; sometimes the dockers and the seamen struck together with an impressive solidarity. That was most evident in 1911, when almost all Liverpool's port transport workers came out, starting with the dockers in sympathy with the seamen. Others followed as it became a virtual general strike – 'near revolution' as Lord Derby put it to Winston Churchill, then Home Secretary. The city almost came to a standstill as railway workers and even tramwaymen struck. At the height of the dispute 60,000 were on strike, with troops on the streets and warships in the harbour; after two months it ended in victory, except for the tramwaymen.

Sixty years on, after many more strikes, most unofficial, it all seemed to have been worth while. The strikers of 1879, as well as those of the late 1960s and the early 1970s, would all have believed that they had played an historic role in the progress achieved in Liverpool in the years after Devlin, even if those who had been involved in 1967 still had their doubts about that landmark settlement. They were right, but for the wrong reasons. They missed the old casual ways, but still would have conceded that working at the docks was now a good job, with decent pay and conditions *and* security. They also thought that the National Dock Labour Board would hold the line on jobs for registered dockers under the Scheme. That it could not do.

Yet the National Dock Labour Board and the local boards in the ports were a clear advance on the road towards industrial democracy, even though that destination was never reached. The employers were required to share their power with the union, something that would always irk them. But joint control required joint decisions. The union representatives could not have their own way, though they were used to making deals. The scheme required the maintenance of a reasonably stable, properly paid labour force, signalling, therefore, an end to casualism. That objective was not a problem for the unions. For the employers, modernisation and mechanisation were irresistible sirens, making it always difficult for them to sustain employment whilst seeking, as employers,[6] to replace labour by capital.

The container was the most radical innovation, linked to the use of specialised lifting equipment. The scale and nature of the equipment transformed the dockside, and waterfronts soon began to look very different. Huge gantry cranes, mounted across the ships, could unload and unload directly from and onto the open decks of specially constructed container ships, soon known as 'lo-lo' (lift on–lift off) operations. Lorries with containers could also drive onto and off the decks of giant ferries in ports such as Dover, and these came to be known as 'roll-on, roll-off' or 'ro-ro'. Even the humble, ubiquitous pallet greatly increased efficiency via its companion, the fork lift truck, though that had long been a familiar piece of equipment, and not only in the ports.

By the 1970s, just at the time when dockwork was becoming a much sought-after job, in Liverpool as elsewhere, modernisation was well on the way to destroying it. The container in particular was posing a mortal threat to the nature of traditional dockwork and to the numbers employed on the waterfront. A conventional cargo vessel took twenty times longer to load or unload as a container ship of the same tonnage. Container ships were also getting much bigger, with a further fall in labour costs relative to capital. Traditionally the dockers' job had been very labour-intensive (at one time there were around 20,000 dockers in Liverpool), but now the work was being machine driven. To make matters worse for the dockers, the containers were being packed ('stuffed') and unloaded ('stripped') away from ports, with the result that dockers could not insist that such stuffing and stripping be done by registered dockers, even though they tried in the only way they could, by strikes and embargoes against the use of containers. That ultimately failed. The world of the waterfront was once again being turned upside down. Devlin ended casualism, but nothing could be done for the survival of the 'greatest game'.

The dock labour force was also changing in character. In 1978 a third of dockers were over fifty, a proportion that had increased to 40 per cent ten years later. The younger men were opting for redundancy, seeing the writing on the wall and taking what was on offer, the settlements bolstered by a national agreement between employers and the Transport and General Workers' Union (the Aldington-Jones agreement). The older men tended to stay on: it was all they knew. But, overall, technology and redundancy combined almost to destroy waterfront labour. 'Voluntary' redundancies became a flood. They were even endorsed by the union's popular (a rare accolade with dockers!) General Secretary, Jack Jones, who had been a docker himself, at Liverpool's Garston Docks. The Aldington-Jones committees in the ports provided an easy escape route. In 1967 Liverpool had 11,500 registered dockers. Less than a generation later, in 1989, this number had shrunk by nine-tenths, to just 1,100.

Away from the waterfront, a false dawn was also the experience of other Liverpudlians, those who had left the docks and the ships in the 1960s for jobs in the factories. The bright prospects and optimism of the 1960s did not last. In thirteen years, from 1971 to 1984, half of the new jobs disappeared, a total approaching 100,000. As significant as the closure of Tate & Lyle in 1981 was that of British Leyland, at Speke, in 1978. The dole numbers, already the nation's highest, was inflated by the addition of 3,750 former car workers. 'Britain's Detroit' was going the same way as the first 'Motown' in Michigan, though much faster. Their new, and not so new, estates were soon showing signs of blight from the disease of mass, chronic unemployment.

Many people left. Liverpool's population, 867,000 before the war, had fallen to 510,000 in 1981. Some part of this was the increasing failure of Liverpool's economy to provide jobs. It was no consolation that the rest of the country was not much, if any, better off. But it was doubly unfortunate that Liverpool's decline as a port should coincide with the disappearance of job alternatives, for ex-dockers and others, in industry and manufacturing. The old dream of a more balanced job market more like other big cities, such as Manchester, became close to reality in the 1960s. Within ten years it had largely unravelled, and even the docks were struggling to keep up. The Mersey Docks and Harbour Board's optimism of 1965 had long gone, along with the board itself. The people of the old dockland communities had also gone. So had their familiar houses in their familiar streets.

Meanwhile, the employers, nationally and locally, saw their chance and began to mobilise. They challenged the decisions of the local boards in the courts, and continued to lobby the supposedly favourable Conservative government (though initially without much success and even opposition), towards the abolition of the National Dock Labour Board, promising to seek a national agreement in its place. In 1989 Mrs Thatcher, at first surprisingly reluctant, finally obliged. The Board knew that the rank-and-file would respond. But they were ready, and so was the government. It had all worked in 1984–85 with the other champion strikers, the miners. Why not again?

The National Dock Labour Board was abolished exactly a hundred years after the Great Strike in London for the 'dockers' tanner'! Its removal was the next-to-last line of national defence of the dockers' hard-won rights, although wider global developments, as well as technology, were shifting the goalposts. As the Bill was going through Parliament the shop stewards, heirs to the old 'unofficials', were pressing for an early strike. A statute would be more difficult to deal with, although both the TGWU Executive and the stewards both saw no prospect of the Bill being withdrawn. A comprehensive agreement with the employers, at national level with local variations, was more practicable and seemingly possible. Even so, the shop stewards still pressed for quick action. The union, fearful of a legal assault on its funds, opted for the courts. That eventually succeeded in the Lords, but it was a pyrrhic victory. The momentum for a strike stalled and though the dockers in the required ballot, in law, voted two to one for strike action (the first lapsed ballot had the same outcome) the action did not begin until three months after the official announcement of abolition. If speed was of the 'essence', the 'essence' had long evaporated. The government even brought forward the date of the royal assent to the Act, before the official national strike began, the last of its kind in the British port transport industry. The government's new-found enthusiasm was matched by the employers' strategy. It played the Mr 'Nice' and 'Nasty' cards. 'Nice' was immediate voluntary severance at enhanced terms, aided by the government agreeing to pay half for each docker. 'Nasty' was a campaign of dismissal or of new, inferior contracts. Dismissal alone was reserved for the militant, local activists, initially at Tilbury, which was another traditionally militant port, like Liverpool. It worked by weakening both resolve and numbers. In less than a month the TGWU executive called the strike off, still pinning their hopes on a national agreement.

The post-strike phase resembled the aftermath of a bloody battle. The employers took few prisoners and saw the surrender as unconditional. They rejected a national agreement and even abolished their long-established national body, the National Association of Port Employers. Local employers could fire as many union activists as were still standing, as the redundancy lists – no longer dressed up as voluntary – were imposed. The new contracts even included compulsory overtime and casualism: men were required to be on call, near a telephone. Interestingly, the telephone had been introduced to the Liverpool docks by Richard Williams in 1912, in order to facilitate the movement of surplus labour between stands. This had been the first official, though minimal, attempt to limit casualism. Now, ironically, the telephone was being used as the instrument of the system's return.

Sooner or later it was likely that there would be a 'last stand'. It was also just as likely that it would be in Liverpool. It began in September 1995 and ended in January 1998. The dismissed men, well over 400 in number, refused to cross a picket line. Those picketing had been dismissed earlier. The old front-line solidarity had survived Devlin's disapproval by forty years. The other survival, from 1989, was the union's fear for its funds from endorsing unofficial action, even though the men, with the energetic and effective support of the women, argued that they were not on unofficial strike; they had been dismissed. The union still maintained that its funds would be in danger of sequestration in the courts if it endorsed the Liverpool dockers' actions by threats or actions of its own. The rank and file, as ever, were at odds with their officials. The 'oldest game was no more', but in other ways part of the game was still being played.

This book is the long story of the Liverpool waterfront and those who worked on its docks and in its warehouses and lived together in its once densely crowded streets. Its rows of cheap, often jerry-built terraces have now gone[7] although the street names often remain, reminders of a vanished past. Many of its docks have been filled in, a few transformed into leisure attractions with warehouses re-emerging as luxury apartments. The old Liver, Cunard and Dock Board buildings remain, but now have occupants only marginally connected with the seaborne trade, if at all. The centre of dock commerce has moved five miles to the north, to Seaforth.

For some the passing of the old waterfront will stir no regrets. Even in the better days working life on the docks was never easy, and we should not dress it up in too much nostalgia. But many, on the evidence of their own accounts, found much of value in the close communities of the waterfront neighbourhoods, particularly in the frequent periods of hardship.[8] Some nostalgia is, therefore, in order for the lost world of Liverpool's dockland streets. Some is also in order for the brotherhood that dockers found on the docks, including its power to bridge deep, sectarian divides when required, especially during strikes. Even altruism influenced the tough lives of the waterfront. Sympathy strikes against employers in dispute with others, or a refusal to cross another group's picket lines, were commonplace, including that of the 1995–98 'last stand' in Liverpool.

The crowded, clannish solidarity of the old waterfront communities is now in the past.[9] Yet the Port of Liverpool is still there and, in terms of tonnage at least, is thriving again as well as competing, revealed in its improving national rankings. But the active port at Seaforth, is no longer seen by Liverpudlians on a daily basis. Nor is it, strictly speaking, in Liverpool. Nor do many now depend upon it for jobs; it has, in any case, too few to offer. There are also, at the time of writing, dark clouds on the horizon. The global financial crisis is beginning to threaten the 'real' economy, which, as Liverpool knows, hits trade first. There are also concerns about the Irish economy, important, as always, to Liverpool as well as the Irish people. For Liverpool, tourism, leisure and retail developments, including the giant new shopping centre Liverpool One, are the present and the future. Although the jobs there might be tedious, mostly paying little, and often part-time, even these are under threat as bubbles continue to burst. More easily seen is that Liverpool is no longer the 'port city'. The port and the city have gone their separate ways.[10]

Liverpool is a coastal Lancashire town again, tower cranes still piercing the skyline as the criss-crossing searchlights in 1941. The dockside cranes are now mostly gone or little used as developers, with an eye for the main chance, as the old merchants before them, even as the crisis deepens, assess the longer term potential of the remaining warehouses for making a lot of money. Even Toxteth, riotous a generation ago, might yet become a desirable, up-market postcode for some of Liverpool's smooth talking, sharp 'suits'. These new movers and shakers might even be able to tell you, perhaps proudly, that their fathers and grandfathers were dockers.

OVERLEAF

Map 1. Liverpool in 1898. Towards the end of Victoria's reign the docks were close to their maximum extent, except for Gladstone Dock (1927) and the giant Seaforth Dock system to the north (1971). The city's main roads, streets and landmarks were also not very different from today.

WWW.MAPSEEKER.CO.UK

WALTON ON THE HILL

Anfield Park Cemetery

STANLEY PARK

CANADA DOCK

R   I   V   E

SCALE OF HALF A MILE

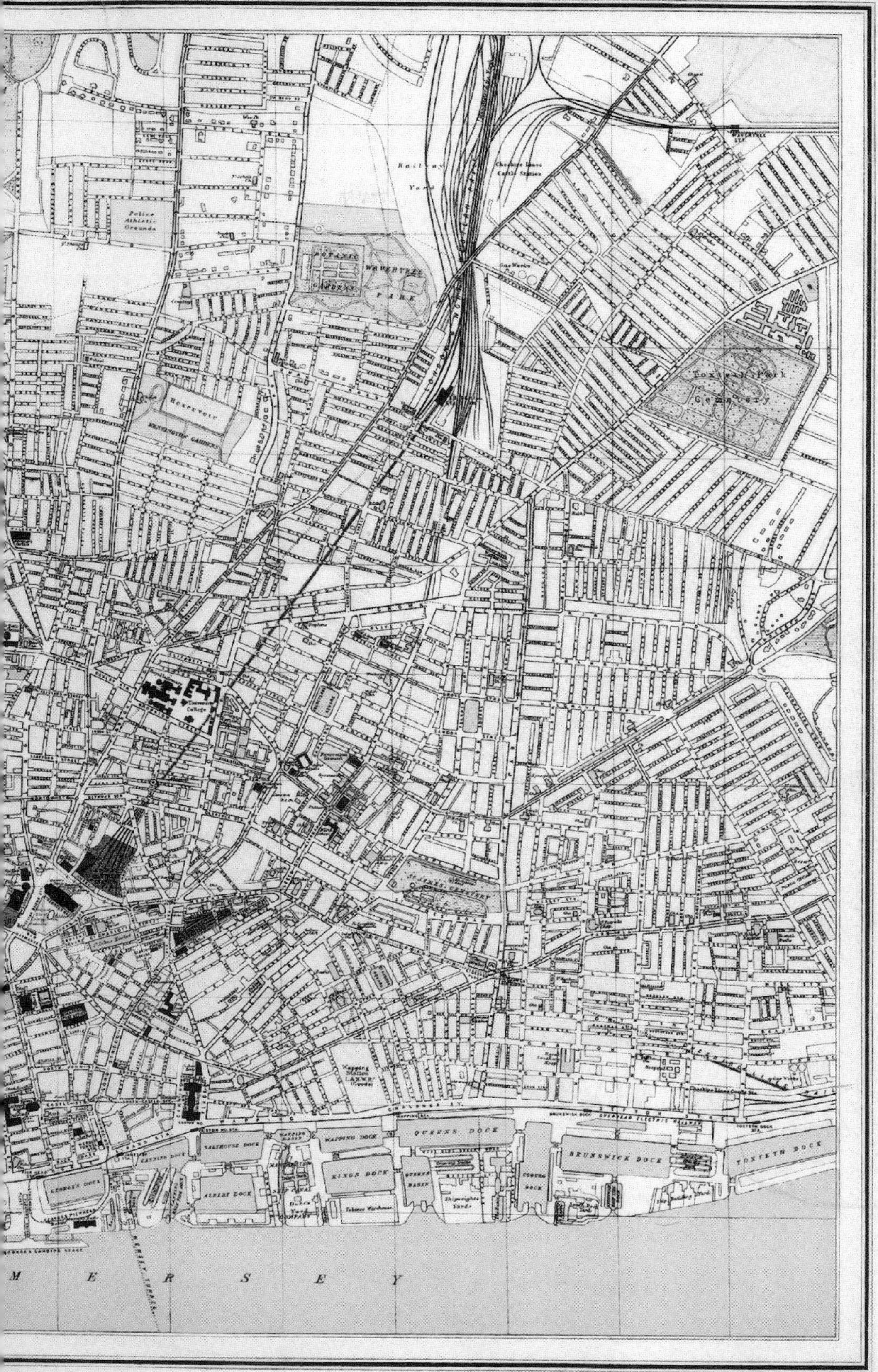
Police Athletic Grounds
Railway Yard
Botanic Gardens
Wavertree Park
Toxteth Park Cemetery
Reservoir
Kensington Gardens
University College
St James's Cemetery
Wapping Station L.&N.W.R. (Goods)
Queens Dock
Wapping Dock
Salthouse Dock
Canning Dock
Georges Dock
Albert Dock
Kings Dock
Queens Basin
Coburg Dock
Brunswick Dock
Toxteth Dock
Tobacco Warehouse
Shipwrights Yards
M E R S E Y

CHAPTER ONE

'Something wonderful':
Liverpool and Empire in 1911

I came to Liverpool, a stranger some six or seven years ago, knowing only that I was about to take up residence in the second city of the greatest Empire the world has ever seen. I admired its vast docks, its stately shipping, its splendid shops, its lovely parks. It seemed to me that this was a city in which one might be proud to be a citizen; a city which must be administered and governed by men of high capacity and generous temper.

(The Reverend Richard Acland Armstrong, 1890)[1]

REVEREND ARMSTRONG was justified in these first impressions. A map of 1898 (*see* pages 12–13)[2] reveals how far Liverpool had come in the near 200 years since the opening of its pioneering first wet dock in 1715. By the time this map was surveyed, the docks stretched along the waterfront for seven miles, and behind them lay a large metropolis.

Nor would Armstrong's first impressions have been seriously challenged, in Liverpool and elsewhere, even by those who shared little in those achievements. Children sitting on their wooden benches in cold Victorian and Edwardian classrooms, perhaps especially in cities such as Liverpool, were very familiar with the large, glossy, cloth wall maps weighted down with wooden poles, showing in bright colours the colonies or 'possessions' of the rival European powers. The British territories, coloured in red, were so vast that they were an 'empire on which the sun never set', as their teachers would proudly remind them. They would also be likely to tell them that the British quarter or even third of the globe, as well as the rest, was patrolled by Royal Navy cruisers by day and night. Britannia – firmly though benignly – ruled the waves to keep difficult foreigners in their places and to allow British merchant ships to go freely about their business, their red ensigns fluttering aloft and making the world safe for trade, if not for democracy.

Reverend Armstrong was an educated man – a Unitarian minister – yet socially would have been some distance below Liverpool's 'men of high capacity and generous temper'. At the same time, he would have been light years above those at the bottom. There were people such as Pat O'Mara, born in the slums

14

of Liverpool's waterfront in the same year that Queen Victoria died. Too young to fight in the Great War, he was to enlist as an American marine in the next: a war that was just as bloody and even more vicious. But as a boy at his desk in St Peter's School, Seel Street, Liverpool, surrounded by Irish Catholic boys, the familiar tales of empire worked their usual magic. He wrote of his schoolboy days, over thirty years later, in Baltimore, in an America that was then hitting rock bottom, earning a precarious living from writing and driving a taxi:

> The Empire and the sacredness of its preservation ran through every textbook like a leitmotif. Our navy and the necessity of keeping Britannia ruling the waves is another indelible mark left in memory – though the reason for this was never satisfactorily explained. Pride in our vast and far-flung colonies and the need for their protection and preservation were emphasized, as was the confidence that in any given crisis the colonies and the motherland stand as one. The British always won wars – not the English but the British – giving the impression that we were all more or less brothers under the skin, the Irish, the English, the Welsh and the Scottish. We were the kingpins; and we were always in the right ...
>
> And then came religion – and ah! that was something else again. Oliver Cromwell might have been a hero in Protestant St Michael's but not in our school ... what I derived from my elementary English-Irish schooling was an intense love for the British Empire and an equally intense hatred for England as opposed to Ireland. Our mothers and fathers, of course, were unequivocal in their attitude – destroy England, no less! But we children at school, despite the intense religious atmosphere of the Catholic school, were rather patronized and Britishized – until we got back to our shacks, where we were sternly Irishized ... The paradox has remained in my make-up for years ...[3]

Similar paradoxes were burgeoning at the same time, in the minds of boys growing up in the 'classic' slums of Salford, less than thirty miles away. Frank Richards' stories in the *Magnet* and the *Gem* with Harry Wharton and his 'chums' set social norms much beyond the public school:

> Fights – ideally at least – took place according to Greyfriars rules: no striking of an opponent when he was down, no kicking, in fact no weapon but the manly fist ... We learning to admire guts, integrity, tradition: we derided the glutton, the American and the French. We looked with contempt upon the sneak and the thief. Greyfriars gave us one moral code, life another, and a fine muddle we made of it.[4]

But if life was hard the mind was free. The sea, in Liverpool, always offered young minds scope for dreams and escape to exotic, far away places. Nor were the poets less than encouraging when writing of the sea. Generations of schoolchildren were required to learn, by heart and the cane, a good deal of patriotic poetry, including the verses of Henry Newbolt and John Masefield. Masefield, born in 1878 and with Liverpool connections, may have even seem to have found some romance in the decidedly unglamorous British coastal trade:

> Dirty British coaster with a salt-caked smoke stack
> Butting through the Channel in the mad March days,
> With a cargo of Tyne coal,
> Road-rail, pig lead,
> Firewood, iron-ware and cheap tin trays.[5]

Romantic or not, it was profitable. By the outbreak of the First World War British vessels carried half of the world's seaborne trade. That also meant record business for British ports. In this trade London and Liverpool were well ahead. In 1913 they together accounted for a third of the total tonnage of ships arriving in British ports and a fifth of the tonnage departing. Liverpool's imports were not far behind those of London and, on some measures, its exports were slightly ahead. Some in Liverpool even saw it outpacing London's commerce, so that while London would remain as '... our historic city – the city of culture, fashion and intellect ...', Liverpool would overtake it as '... the greatest and richest ever known to the world ... the commercial city of the future.'[6] But if Liverpool's prospects seemed almost without limit, the fruits of success would be unlikely to touch the lives of the many thousands who played a part in creating them. The Reverend Armstrong also observed the glaring gulf between wealth and poverty in '... the second city of the greatest Empire the world has ever seen':

> But after the first glance I was appalled by one aspect of things here which pressed upon my mind more and more for several weeks, till the sin of it became at times well nigh unbearable ... The hordes of the ragged and the wretched surged up from their native quarters and covered the noblest streets like a flood ... I had seen wealth. I had seen poverty. But never before had I seen the two so jammed together. Never before had I seen streets, loaded with all that wealth can buy, lined with the haunts of hopeless penury.[7]

How favourably Liverpool's well-placed citizens regarded where they lived and worked was perhaps at its symbolic height with the 1854 inauguration of Harvey Lonsdale Elmes' St George's Hall, which Queen Victoria thought 'worthy of ancient Athens'. Foreigners were equally impressed. Even before St George's Hall was built, Herman Melville, on his first trip as a sailor in 1839, compared the developing docks system to the Great Wall of China and the Pyramids. Liverpool's docks he saw as far ahead of New York's tidal harbour. The Reverend Bell, writing for a New York newspaper in 1880, on arriving in the city compared it, this time, not to New York but Chicago: the 'Chicago of England … essentially modern … its rise and progress is something wonderful'.[8] Local, prominent academics added to the chorus of praise. Writing in 1907 Ramsay Muir, Professor of Modern History at Liverpool University (founded in 1903), found inspiration in the 7¼ miles of the sea wall, enduring and impressive as the pyramids (echoing Melville seventy years earlier) and the docks as a place where '… the citizen of Liverpool can best feel the opulent romance of his city …';[9] and in the year Muir's history was published the first of the 'three graces' – the Mersey Docks and Harbour Board building – was completed, soon to be followed by the other two: the Royal Liver in 1911 and the Cunard in 1913.

At the turn of the twentieth century Liverpool's citizens, even its poorest, were undoubtedly and rightly proud of their famous city and its public buildings; but the public building many of them knew best was the workhouse at Brownlow Hill which, at its peak, held more than 2,000 paupers. They might also have felt their city's 'romance', but even those who succeeded in keeping out of the workhouse shared little of its 'opulence'. Significantly Liverpool was the first to appoint a Medical Officer of Health, the celebrated Doctor Duncan, in 1847; but just as significantly the motion in council to appoint him full-time at £700 per annum (about £50,000 today) was defeated by twenty-five votes to eight: instead he was appointed part-time for £500 (£35,000). Duncan described Liverpool at that time as 'the unhealthiest town in England'. Yet sixty years later – and a year before Ramsay Muir's hyperbole in his *History of Liverpool* – another MOH, Doctor Hope, was telling a later city council that:

> … there was not a city in this country, nay in Europe, which could produce anything like the squalor that his officials found in some of Liverpool's backstreets.[10]

And Liverpool had a lot of competition. Seebohm Rowntree's study of York in 1901 reported that one in four 'lacked the bare necessities of life';[11] and in Roberts' Salford, until well into the century:

> Our village, like so many others that went to make the cities of thriving industrial Britain, was stamped with the same poverty, and this right to the outbreak and beyond of the first world war. In among the respectable rows of 'two up and down' houses we had the same blocks of hovels sharing a single tap, earth closet and open midden: each house with a candle for light, an oil lamp or a bare gas jet. Coal the 'low class' and 'no class' barely bought; they picked or stole it from spoil heap and wharf, or, in bad times, dragged the canals for droppings from barges.[12]

Yet by 1912 there were 285,000 paupers in English workhouses under conditions deliberately intended to be worse than those suffered by the poorest outside.

You were better off in prison. In Liverpool's Kirkdale Gaol in 1840 the average weekly cost of food per prisoner was 5*s*.: the more economical workhouse managed to feed its paupers for 2*s*. Nationally, by the turn of the century, the Prison Commissioners, in their annual report of 1901, were expressing deep concern:

> At several prisons where there has been a remarkable increase in the number of offences against workhouse regulations, it is reported that prisoners openly profess this preference for the prison on the grounds of better treatment, greater kindness, better food and more humane conditions. Any statement to this effect by a prisoner, especially if, as often happens, it gains currency in the local press, is likely to lead to misapprehension as to the principles and methods of prison discipline.

The Commissioners considered that the

> ... remedy for this preference on the part of that class of wastrels and ne'er-do-wells who hover on the borderline between the two, is by the adoption by the workhouse authorities of a uniform scale of dietary and task which should not be less favourable than the standard adopted, after full inquiry, for persons convicted of crime.[13]

Liverpool's workhouses undoubtedly made their own contribution to keeping the prisons full. But those outside the prisons and the workhouses, including those in work, had little to cheer about. Poverty in Liverpool's dockland had a good part of its origins in the insecurity and fluctuations of work. Casual employment blighted lives – and baffled liberal reformers and inquiries to eliminate it – from Edwardian times and for some seventy years after. Poverty also meant squalid, unhealthy, overcrowded houses and the spread of disease – as Doctor Hope was telling the City Council in 1906. Though the provision of clean water and a sewerage system had, by the 1860s, eliminated cholera epidemics, insanitary living conditions, ill-health and disease remained widespread.

Much of this arose from overcrowding as Liverpool continued its klondike growth. Between 1801 and 1851 its population grew from 78,000 to almost 376,000. Then, by 1911, it had doubled to more than 746,000. Many were Irish immigrants. Between 1841 and 1851 the number of Irish-born residents of Liverpool rose from 17.3 per cent to 22.3 per cent. This was about ten times the proportion for England and Wales, as a whole, and some three or four times that for Scotland. And though the Irish-born proportion began to fall after 1851 it was still 12.6 per cent in 1891. Glasgow was the only comparable British city, with 10.6 per cent,[14] figures that go a long way to explain the cities' parallel sectarian problems. Large numbers of Liverpool's earlier Irish immigrants were to die from so-called 'Irish fever' and cholera, soon after arriving from the famine and evictions of their homeland. Some are buried only a short walk from the site of the Brownlow Hill workhouse, now occupied by Liverpool's Roman Catholic Cathedral. There, their descendants worship untroubled by part of their history commemorated by a plaque on the wall of Liverpool University's Music Department, in Mulberry Street, which reads:

> Near this place in 1847, some 2,600 destitute Irish Famine migrants were buried in unmarked pauper graves. They had died in extreme poverty in the parish of Liverpool, so ending their flight from the Great Hunger, 1845–52.

Many of those who did survive lived short, unhealthy lives in squalid, over-crowded 'courts', some of which were still standing and inhabited even into the twentieth century. The courts were in easy walking distance of the classical splendour of St George's Hall, which cost £100,000 (£8 million) in the 1840s, and which was under construction at the same time that the paupers were being consigned to the earth on Brownlow Hill.

But magnificent public buildings did not consume all the city's spare cash. Some *had* to be spent on public health, and any savings could usefully go towards maintaining law and order. As the Corinthian columns were being raised on the plateau in Lime Street there were fears that the more than 80,000 Irish-born 'rootless' immigrants '... would turn into revolutionary Chartists'. One approach to such fears was education and exposure to culture. Money was found to build libraries, museums, and accessible classical music was put on in the Hall itself. Less enlightened was extra policing of the streets, with the recruitment of 20,000 more Special Constables. Two hundred foundry workers refused this call to civic duty, declaring that they disapproved of the Queen, aristocracy and Parliament. At the same time five hundred dockers were 'sacked' (or perhaps more accurately not hired at the stand) for a similar show of disloyalty.[15]

Disloyalty, dissidence, strikes and even riots were not unique to Liverpool workers, or even British workers, but in Liverpool they were mostly related to uncertain pay as the port responded to the cyclical upturns and downturns of trade. Early, disciplined resistance, a form of embryonic trade unionism,[16] by skilled craftsmen was followed, in 1775, by violence and rioting by seamen. The seamen's disputes continued but in a more orderly fashion until in the next century they combined with the dockers in the 'Great Strike' of 1879 to restore pay levels cut by the employers, as well as laying the first foundations for dockers' and seamen's unions on a permanent basis.

But the true spectacular was the Transport Strike of 1911, involving carters, railway workers and tramwaymen as well as dockers and seamen. It was well out of the ordinary even in an era when the number of strikes was increasing rapidly – sevenfold for Britain from 1904 to 1910 – and troops were firing on miners at Tonypandy. The Transport Strike lasted for over two months, was often very violent, including its own 'Bloody Sunday', and at one point involved 60,000 strikers – nearly double the number that had been involved in 1879. But it was also the summer when the Royal Liver Building was completed, on 22 June, and its clock was started. It was 1.40 p.m. (the precise moment when the crown was placed on George V's head in Westminster Abbey), and just three days before the beginning of the Transport Strike. And the clock was big (each dial was 25 feet in diameter, 2½ feet larger than Big Ben) befitting nearly everything in the 'Chicago of England'. Before it was installed its makers, Gent & Company of Leicester,[17] caught the hubris of that time in Liverpool's history by organising a lunch for the Royal Liver's directors and guests, reminiscent of the opening of the Albert Dock sixty-five years earlier when the Prince Consort sat down to a lavish déjeuner with a thousand of the great and the good – and doubtless some of the less than good, even if great – in one of the dock's vast warehouses. It was specially decorated for the ceremonial meal by a Mr Troutbeck of Hanover Square, London:

> The pillars and arched brick ceiling were painted of stone colour, the pillars also being ornamented with gold bands which encircled the capitals. The walls were lined with glazed calico, fluted in alternate colours of pink, blue and white. The hangings to the windows were the same with white drapery and pink rosettes, the division below the arches at the windows being fitted with purple moulding.[18]

One wonders what ever became of the 'glazed calico' wall linings and the window drapery when the warehouse was first used for its intended purpose. And what would the porters have made of this decorated, oriental palace (appropriately, it was used for the India trade) when they first weighed and stacked the discharged cargo?

The Liver Building lunch was a much smaller affair but not so different in its swaggering, self-confident style. The 'table', one of the clock dials, was able to seat 39 in some comfort. The building itself soon became iconic, partly because of its massive size and solidity, but also because of its two '… huge, verdigrised cormorants atop the cupolas … their wings outstretched to the Atlantic winds', and 'standing on the waterfront' the 'threshold to the ends of the earth.'[19] It also had claims to being the first 'skyscraper', and the first to be constructed from reinforced concrete.

In 1911 Liverpool's position as a world port had something to do with geography. Even a limited inspection of the map of Western Europe reveals the advantages in the development of Atlantic and world trade of those countries with Atlantic seaboards and deep, sheltered natural harbours. In fact, Liverpool, like Bristol, was an estuarial, artificially created harbour when compared, say, to Southampton. From the early beginnings of Atlantic trade Portugal and Spain had been heavily involved, closely followed by England, France and the Netherlands. On the western side of the British Isles Bristol and the Welsh ports, along with Liverpool, had clear advantages, as did Chester going back at least to Roman times and, at a later date, Glasgow. Chester had obvious extra claims to the Irish crossing, not least for subduing the always turbulent Irish, and William III was to choose the Dee as the embarkation point for his troops in the successful campaign against the deposed James II at the end of the seventeenth century. Yet Liverpool had been challenging Chester's commercial and political dominance well before the end of the seventeenth century though remaining under the authority of its rival for customs administration until 1699. In truth, Liverpool had had no obvious advantage over Chester until the silting up of the Dee turned Chester effectively into an inland town. And while King John had visited Liverpool in 1207, granted it borough status, and had ordered the construction of his castle, this may simply have been to add an alternative crossing point to Ireland. Certainly Liverpool's closeness to Ireland was, and still is, an important influence on its development. But in 1207, and for centuries after, the town's population remained small, mainly working the land and fishing. As a potential port, even a minor one, it mostly seems to have had geological problems, placing clear limits on its geographical advantages.

A cursory view of Liverpool's history might lead to a superficial conclusion that conditions for growth were generally unfavourable and that it was a matter of accident that a port was created. The river Mersey is like a bottle with a narrow neck; on the north side of the neck stands Liverpool, on the south Birkenhead, Wallasey and New Brighton. The estuary is subject to strong tides and the pressure of water into, and out of, the great pool, which forms the container of the bottle, creates strong currents and a high rise and fall of water. It was precisely at this point in the neck of the estuary that the early sailing ships had to berth and load cargo. Further out to sea the channel of the Mersey was, until cut in 1890, obstructed by a sand bar ...
　　... To the landward, Liverpool's means of access were for many centuries equally unpropitious ... the great marshy pool acted as a confining moat to the south and east. It curved inwards along the line of present-day Paradise Street, Whitechapel and Old Haymarket to the point where one now enters the Mersey Tunnel; it also formed part of the defences for King John's four-towered castle on its site of the Old Castle Street, presently the site of Queen Victoria's monument. To the east and north lay the sandstone ridge of Everton brow and Edgehill interspersed with pockets of peat moss, highly dangerous to the traveller in wet weather. Further east lay marshland and heathland and the all-embracing barrier of Chat Moss. Before 1700, only one major road penetrated outwards as far as Warrington, running along the line of present-day Dale Street while to the north there were trackways though the open fields and brecklands to help the traveller on his way to Preston and Lancaster.[20]

These barriers to development much largely explain why, for centuries, Liverpool's '... only visible sign that it was connected with the sea (apart from the fishery) was on those occasions when it became increasingly necessary for the King to mount an expedition to quell an insurrection in Ireland or Wales',[21] and that the town's economy only began to stir at the beginning of the reign of Elizabeth I. That was largely down to the salt trade, originally brought in from Brittany but soon coming from Cheshire. This became the springboard for a growing inland trade (via the river Weaver) and across the sea to Ireland.

Liverpool's merchants soon owned salt houses in Cheshire, and in 1611 a salt works was established in Chapel Street. Salt was '... a vital turning-point in the growth of Liverpool's trade', and as the century developed its ships were transporting '... coal, iron, copper, hops, Yorkshire cloth, alum soap and other luxuries from abroad ... sheepskins, tallow, linen, flax, frieze and mantles, wool, salt herrings and salt beef in increasing quantities'.[22]

Tudor times had also seen the beginning of the development of Liverpool's trading links with European ports in commodities such as leather goods and 'Manchester cottons' (probably a linen mix) in exchange for spices, fruit, wine and grain. The Civil War, including operations in Ireland, interrupted expansion, but growth resumed in the 1670s. Now the Caribbean became a major destination of its merchants, as the sugar trade grew, leading also to the development of sugar refining in Liverpool itself.

Inevitably the gains from trade began to change the face and extent of the town. By 1697 it had 28 streets with names still mostly recognisable today. But though Liverpool was doing well even then it was becoming known as a place where, 'the majority of the town's citizens lived in varying degrees of evil-smelling discomfort, their lives being made tolerable (and perhaps healthy) only by the keen air and the breezes sweeping across Liverpool Bay'.[23]

But its citizens and merchants, though living less than comfortably, were also honing their business skills and earning a reputation for risk-taking that would become even more apparent in the next century. They had also accumulated substantial capital. So attitude and money came together in a potent mix assisted by two important other developments.

In 1672 Lord Molyneux (lord of the manor and later Earl of Sefton) sold overlord rights to the Corporation on a thousand years' lease. This allowed the town to develop the 'Pool' and for the Corporation to accumulate substantial rents as development proceeded. The other development, as noted earlier, was that from the end of the seventeenth century Liverpool had its own Customs House, independent of Chester. By 1700, therefore, the town had control of its own affairs and the money to take advantage of its new-found position. It was ready to tackle the acute problems of its harbour for shipping and thereby build upon its already considerable commercial success to unlock its much greater potential. For its future as a port, it was imperative to have greatly improved access and facilities for the loading and unloading of ships. It was also necessary to develop much improved water navigation and road links with Liverpool's markets in Cheshire and Lancashire.

The trigger to future growth was the construction of the world's first commercial wet dock, which was opened in 1715 on part of the site of the old Liver Pool, although it was only finally completed in 1721. There was then a big gap to the second, Salthouse Dock, opened in 1753. But by the end of the eighteenth century further docks had increased the total to seven and the overall acreage was 28. By then the first dock, renamed the 'Old Dock', was falling into disuse. A private Act of Parliament of 1811 provided enabling powers for it to be filled in, but sentiment kept it open, and in use, until 1826. The Pool, in which the first dock was built, had also long gone, reclaimed from the water for many of Liverpool's now familiar streets. London and Hull, partly for cost reasons were the only major ports to follow Liverpool's successful example before 1815. Glasgow, Liverpool's later serious rival for the transatlantic trade, did not need to: it had the advantage of tidal quays rather than docks. Liverpool also had seriously inadequate berthing facilities, inhibiting growth, as trade continued to expand at a rapid rate throughout the century. Soon, even the much-admired earlier docks were unable to cope, leading to the planning and construction of new and bigger. The site of the filled-in Old Dock saw the building, between 1828 and 1829, of John Foster's elegant Customs House, the fifth building to serve this purpose in two hundred years. It was also the last to be purpose-built. It was fatally damaged by air attacks in 1941.

But as the docks were being built, responding to and increasing the flow and speed of trade through the port, Liverpool's hinterland in Cheshire and Lancashire was completing the interlocking and symbiotic processes of growth. First salt and, soon after, coal were the unglamorous, key products. John Holt, a prominent member of Liverpool's merchant dynasties, saw salt in the town's early involvement in the seventeenth century as having been the '... Nursing Mother and to have contributed more to the first rise, gradual increase and present flourishing state of the Town of Liverpool than any other article of commerce'.[24] This tribute must rank in hyperbole with Amsterdam being built upon herrings, but largely true nonetheless. Liverpool's other 'nursing mother', coal, was abundant in Lancashire and rapidly exploited by those who had it under their land. Yet a bulk commodity such as coal needed an efficient and cheap means of moving it. The then preferred method of improving roads was through the building of turnpikes financed by tolls. These tolls, though a viable means of financing improvements, added greatly to costs. The alternative, led by Liverpool merchants, was a Parliamentary Bill to make the Sankey Brook navigable, linking the new coalfield, east of Prescot, to Liverpool and complementing the land route to the existing Prescot Hall mine. Then, in 1773, the Duke of Bridgewater (who had learned his trade in Europe), connected his own canal to the Mersey.

The Leeds and Liverpool canal, construction of which began in 1774, added a further conduit for coal, this time from Wigan. But the canals were also available for the moving of salt from Winsford, in Cheshire, where Liverpool merchants were buying into brine production. Salt for export could be brought by barge down the Weaver into Liverpool, while coal was transported up the Mersey and Sankey

Canal. The outcome was that by 1775 Liverpool was meeting its own needs and exporting huge surpluses. Salt was also being produced in large quantities, an essential input in fish preservation, metal-working, glass and pottery production and later in the soda, soap and chemical industries. By 1796, 58,000 tons of rock salt were being exported from Liverpool. For coal, the figure for 1791 was 79,000 tons, 57,000 going abroad, and the rest for destinations served by the UK coastal trade.[25]

By the end of the eighteenth century Liverpool had clocked up an impressive trading performance. In 1709 shipping entering Liverpool totalled 14,600 tons; by 1793 the figure was 188,300 tons. For ships clearing the port, the figures were 12,600 tons and 169,800 tons respectively.[26] Liverpool had initiated a dock construction programme that was the beginning of a *system*, overcoming its substantial problems as a harbour and allowing it to develop its potential as a major port, enhanced by its geographical position on the western seaboard of Europe. Liverpool was also fortunate in its location adjacent to a vibrant, rapidly developing, resource-rich hinterland that was at the heart of the first industrial economy. Liverpool's merchants also had the ability, developed much earlier, to spot the main chance and to exploit it fully.

Their commercial instincts also took them beyond trading. They invested capital in the ownership of ships, which took them into the discounting of bills and, over time, the founding of banks, such as Martin's. Most banks in eighteenth-century Liverpool were founded by merchants. At the same time they were placing orders with shipbuilders. By 1789, the year the French mob stormed the Bastille, Liverpool's merchants owned over 76,000 tons of shipping, a large part of the total trading tonnage entering and leaving the port. Most of these ships had also been built in Liverpool, although ship-building tonnage began to lag behind the expansion of trade following the end of the French wars in 1815. Although vessels grew in size Liverpool only had orders for smaller vessels, with those for larger ships going to the east-coast ports, and even Canada, where costs were more competitive. Liverpool merchants continued to invest in shipping but, as always, their first loyalties were to profits. By 1853 half of the vessels trading on the Mersey had been built elsewhere. Though the decline in ship-building was relative, it was still decline, and it continued. As the docks were extended, ship-building was physically as well as financially squeezed, with the skilled crafts required for the building of ships being pushed out by the rising demand for dock labour. By 1871 only 4 per cent of adult males were employed in ship-building. One by one the old firms disappeared: Royden's, with its origins in the eighteenth century, launched its last ship in 1899. The last warship, on the Liverpool side, was the gunboat HMS *Britonart*, built by W. H. Potter at Queen's Dock and launched in the same year.[27] Ship-building had moved elsewhere, including warships to Birkenhead.

Ship-building was not the only casualty to comparative advantage. In the eighteenth century Liverpool had also been home to other substantial, high-quality, craft industries. Pottery, including china and porcelain, was well established in the middle of the century, and in 1794 the Herculaneum Potteries, powered by windmills, were a going concern. The name Herculaneum suggested classical influences, as had Josiah Wedgwood's Etruria pottery in Stoke-on-Trent. Many of the company's workers did in fact come from Stoke, and Wedgwood bought the firm in 1830, transferring its production, and its workers, to his home town. The discarded site eventually became a dock, built in 1864, taking the same name.

Another craft industry to go was clock- and watch-making, which had been expanded in Liverpool in the 1760s by John Wyke from Prescot (a traditional centre for clock-making expertise), whose work was carried on by Peter Litherland. The high reputation of the Liverpool clock-makers grew with the development of chronometers and other navigational instruments in the eighteenth century. But clock- and watch-making, as pottery manufacture, proved to have limited futures in Liverpool as its merchants, shipowners and businessmen increasingly concentrated on developing its commerce, rather than its industries. Liverpool was playing to its strengths. In 1800 its merchants might be forgiven for not foreseeing that the commercial golden goose would eventually lay fewer eggs, and that at some point in the future there would be an inadequate industrial base to maintain the port's economic viability. Their hindsight was as good as our own, their foresight no worse.

The big money made in the eighteenth century from the importing of sugar and tobacco lasted well into the twentieth century. Sugar and tobacco were also to provide significant processing and manufacturing industries for Liverpool until recent times. The importing of sugar and tobacco was in its turn complemented by a lucrative export trade in salt and coal, as we have seen. Though these sources of wealth originated in Lancashire and Cheshire, they were encouraged by the money and backing of Liverpool's merchants. This interchange has been aptly described as '... the triangular trade between Liverpool, the Sankey and the Weaver ... [and] probably as important as another, rather better-known triangular trade',[28] the infamous trade in human beings.

It has been estimated that by 1792 Liverpool controlled five-eighths of Britain's slave trade, well ahead of Bristol and London, and that the profits from it '... raised Liverpool from a struggling port to one of the richest and most prosperous trading centres in the world.'[29] Although this judgement does not take into account the healthy profits earned from trading in salt and coal, the returns that were made from the 'middle passage' – carrying slaves between West Africa and the West Indies in return for British exports – mostly financed the lucrative cargoes of sugar and tobacco that came back to the Mersey. Furthermore, although the profits from the triangular traffic were always uncertain and not always as large as have been often assumed, its odious importance to Liverpool's development '... was that it formed a way of turning over very large sums of money, the comparatively moderate percentage return on which still represented substantial amounts available for re-investment in the town'.[30]

Another source of profits – often as spectacular as it was morally ambiguous –

was privateering. This dubious activity could, and still can, be seen either as as a patriotic, even dashing activity, or simply as state-licensed piracy.

But there can be no such moral ambivalence about the slave trade. Although those involved could see the writing on the wall in the years up to 1806, and were developing new markets in goods in Africa, rather than in people, they bitterly opposed the Liverpool abolitionists, led notably by William Roscoe and his friends. After 1806 the abolitionists' influence rose, leaving a lasting reputation for humanity as well as a physical mark in Liverpool's celebrated collection of 'Athenian' public buildings, notably St George's Hall, and the names of several of its prominent streets. But the rich and famous (although Roscoe became bankrupt in 1820) were not the only activists, even though their contribution was significant. More famous names overshadow the contemporary importance of a blind, Liverpool poet and agitator, Edward Rushton, who attacked Thomas Paine for neglecting the freedoms of black people and wrote a long letter to George Washington, condemning him for his ownership of slaves. Washington returned the letter without an answer.[31]

Roscoe and his circle's attempts to develop their brand of 'gentlemanly capitalism' and high civic virtues, despite their successes, were always likely to be an uphill struggle in the then prevailing climate of rampant and amoral commercialism. At the outbreak of the American Civil War, in 1861, there remained among Liverpool's merchants those who shared neither the culture nor the education of the older elites, supporting the cotton-growing slave-owning Confederacy for their low prices. They revived some of the strident tones of the anti-abolitionists in the years before 1806, especially when they propagated the view that the slave trade had contributed very little to Liverpool's fortunes.[32] Slaving could be a switchback investment, but it provided capital substantial in total, if not always in each actual voyage, which became available for investment in new, post-abolition, markets. This dirty money also came with trading contacts and know-how which survived abolition and became important in the development of Liverpool's African trade. But a common distaste for the ways of Liverpool's merchants remained, even among some of those who made their names and money in Africa after abolition. John Holt, when he first arrived in Liverpool from rural Lincolnshire, observed that, '... mankind is like a lot of hungry pigs fighting over a trough of milk – everybody seems to be trying to pull the piece of food out of his neighbour's mouth.'[33]

Others were less sensitive – including the shipowners. Money was there to make more money. More docks needed to be built, and soon steam power would enter the Mersey. Main chances – as always in Liverpool's history – were there to be seized.

CHAPTER TWO

Building the 'Pyramids'

Liverpoole is one of the wonders of Britain ... what it may grow to in time
I know not.

(Daniel Defoe, 1722)[1]

For seven miles and a quarter, on the Lancashire side of the river alone, the
monumental granite quarried from the Board's own quarries in Scotland,
fronts the river in a vast sea wall as solid and enduring as the Pyramids ...
huge warehouses of every type ... front the docks and giant-armed cranes
and other appliances make disembarkation swift and easy ...

(Ramsay Muir, 1907)[2]

W RITING a generation before Ramsay Muir, Sir James Allanson Picton
was also impressed by Liverpool's astonishing rise. He saw analogies in
the achievements of the ancient Egyptians in '... the enormous pile of warehouses
which looms so large upon the river and in its vastness surpasses the pyramid of
Cheops ...'[3] Picton, like Muir an historian of the city, is perhaps better known, at
least in Liverpool, for inspiring and giving his name to the Picton Reading Room
in the Central Library, a classical domed structure founded in 1875 and modelled
on its world-famous predecessor in the British Museum in Bloomsbury. Picton's
building is still going strong, though damaged in the destructive bombing raids of
1941 and restored in the 1950s. Sir James probably had his own Reading Room in
mind when, though mightily impressed by the scale and strength of Liverpool's
warehouses, was scathing about their appearance: 'The works for strength and
durability were unsurpassable but it is regrettable that no attention has been paid
whatsoever to beauty as well as to strength.'[4]

Picton was referring mainly to Jesse Hartley's warehouses at Albert Dock.
He could also have contrasted Hartley's 'pyramids' with the also durable and
large scale, but still classically elegant dimensions of St George's Hall and the
cluster of buildings across the way on William Brown Street – which included
his own museum and public library. Perhaps fortunately, he did not live to see

the giant Stanley tobacco warehouse, built in 1900 and at that time the biggest building in the world. But taste has transformed many of these 'hideous pile[s] of naked brickwork' into expensive luxury flats for high-flying and aspiring young professionals who, if they have time for such idle thoughts, would find some aesthetic pleasure in the profitable functionalism favoured by Jesse Hartley and Liverpool's Victorian merchant classes.

As we have seen, Liverpool's potential had been noticed much earlier. The 'small town beside a tidal creek' had some clear advantages over its rivals. Its position on the Irish Sea was a convenient embarkation point for the armies of the English monarchs with ambitions in Ireland: King John's granting of its Charter in 1207 was not just because he admired its fishermen or ate their fish. It was also reasonably safe, through geography, from hostile continental monarchs. Beyond power politics and war it was also well placed for trade; first as Ireland became gradually semi-pacified and then, increasingly, as the vast lucrative territories of the Caribbean and the Americas were colonised and developed. Its close and nearby rival, Chester, once the most important town in of Roman Britain, for long overshadowed Liverpool as a port. But its potential was never realised. By the

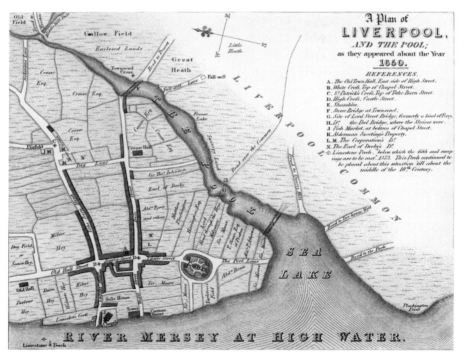

Map 2.   Liverpool and the Pool in 1650. The 'H' pattern and names of the city's principal streets are already in place. The line of the Pool follows present-day Paradise Street.

seventeenth century the ancient port had retained some regional importance and still legally controlled the collection of Liverpool's dues as well as its own. But the silting of the Dee, and successful recourse to the courts, eventually gave Liverpool control of its own revenue collection. By 1688, when the Glorious Revolution was a preoccupation elsewhere, Liverpool was planning its own customs house, had a population of about 7,000 and its growing numbers of ships were trading with most of the known world. War, too, became less of a problem as the British royal succession took on a more peaceful routine, and the nations of Europe settled into a period of relative peace following the comprehensive treaty signed at Utrecht in 1713. Yet, although Liverpool's potential was seen early, observers also saw its problems of nature which needed to be overcome to unlock that potential.

There were two main problems. Liverpool Bay and the Mersey estuary have vast areas of sandbanks that dry out at low tide. The shifting channels need to be kept open and navigable. Constant dredging is needed to maintain and, where possible, increase their depth. Even then, passage through the channels requires effective navigational aids and skilful piloting. The example of the Port of Chester provided an awesome reminder, for Liverpool, of the power of nature, as well as the capacity of engineers to botch the 'improvements' provided for under the 1733 Dee Navigation Act, Chester's potential route to revival.

The Mersey, as the Bay, is also subject to strong winds and currents and a tidal range of thirty feet: the range at New York is, by contrast, only five feet and at Southampton, a later rival, only two. High tide did allow large ships to enter the estuary, but it was difficult to get close to the town given the hazards of the strong currents. The estuary is also at its most narrow at the port's nucleus, which increases the speed of the currents. To minimise these problems the practice was to load and unload cargoes from anchored ships into smaller boats. This was neither safe nor easy. One alternative was the New Quay of 1672 though with similar problems; another was the Pool itself, which helped give the town its name. The Pool was an inlet fed by the tides and a stream flowing from the marshy land to the east. Yet entering the Pool from the river was almost as hazardous as anchoring on the riverbank, and even then the Pool was only available, at low tide, for vessels of limited draught. Ships were also getting bigger. The navigational and berthing problems of seventeenth-century Liverpool are illustrated in Thomas Kaye's conjectural map of the town (Map 2) and the Pool in about 1650,[5] though published many years later, in 1829.

The 'H' shape of the present city's central outline was already in place in 1650 – Chapel, Tithebarn, Water and Dale Streets. Castle Street recalls the site of the thirteenth-century stronghold, its last crumbling remnants demolished in 1725, completing the earlier attentions of the armies of Parliament and Cromwell. The site is now occupied by the monument to Queen Victoria, which survived later violence from war in 1941. Kaye's map also shows a tower at the end of Water Street, on the river, that of the powerful Stanleys, to assist troop movements to and from Ireland. The Customs House, always an important building, is also shown.

Chapel Street, where it meets the waterfront, has its fish market, recalling the importance of fishing to the town's early economy. The stone Townsend Bridge, in the upper left-hand corner, was a vital crossing of the Pool on the road to Lancashire proper. The road to Everton, then an breezy village on the higher ground, is also shown. The main landholdings included those of the Stanley family, and its Earls of Derby, complementing their Tower on the waterfront.

The citizens of the town and the Earl were heavily involved in the Civil War, though on opposite sides. With the peace, more lasting preoccupations took over, notably the now urgent need to improve the port's capacity to handle the rapid expansion of trade and commerce. Population was also now growing. Daniel Defoe, on his second visit in 1690, observed that the town's population had doubled in twenty years. As with most cities at the time, a large proportion of this rise stemmed from migration: growing prosperity was attracting people to live and work in Liverpool, mainly from Lancashire and Cheshire. Some of these would bring wealth, most just their labour. The town was also reported to be attracting 'new' money from further afield as some London-based merchants were believed to have fled from the plague of 1665. Just two years later Sir Edward Moore, a prominent merchant and landowner, with large holdings ('closes') along the Pool (see Map 1) was telling his son that, '… if the Pool be made navigable, the shipping must lie all along the closes, and the trade will be all in them for the whole town … I do not question to see this brought to a head in my time.' [6]

Sir Edward was remarkably prescient, although he was probably reflecting the widespread opinion in the houses and business premises of his friends. He did not live long enough himself to benefit, although his son would. The world's first, enclosed, commercial maritime dock was built in the Pool at the end of Pool Lane, where the closes of the Moore family backed onto the water.

Liverpool's pioneering dock was constructed less than a mile to the south of the old port's nucleus at the end of Water Street, in the Pool itself, on what is now the now largely built-over Canning Place next to the Merseyside Police HQ.[7] It was begun in 1709, opened in 1715, and completed in 1721. Thus began the extraordinary process by which a fishing village, within two hundred years, had become a 'metropolis' and one of the world's major ports. The new dock, later to be called the Old Dock as further docks were added, the beginning of what later came to be known as the South End.

The first dock to be built to the north of Water Street was Prince's Dock, opened in 1821. By then the South End had seven wet docks. The North End system then began to take off, especially after Jesse Hartley was appointed as dock engineer to the port of Liverpool in 1826. Other docks were also being constructed, at regular intervals, in the South End. Thereafter dock-building tended to alternate between the north and south ends of the river. Then, in 1847, Birkenhead began to see its own system develop with Egerton Dock and Morpeth Dock. The last South End dock to be built by the board was Toxteth in 1888, though that bare fact can be misleading. Under an Act of 1898 though planned years earlier, modernisations and improvements to Kings, Queens and Brunswick produced, in effect, virtually 'new' docks. By then, the entire system, on both sides of the river, had long been under the control of the Mersey Docks and Harbour Board, under the 1857 Act of Parliament. On the Liverpool side, at the beginning of the twentieth century, there were over seven miles of docks, a system enclosed by a sea wall '... as solid and enduring as the pyramids' (in Ramsay Muir's graphic phrase) and with a population close on 700,000, ten times that of the census of 1801. Birkenhead was later to add Alfred and Wallasey Docks to its first two and, in 1909, Vittoria Dock. It had also by then become the ship-building port of the Mersey and one of the most important in the country, especially for naval vessels. Though the pace of dock construction inevitably slowed in the later part of the nineteenth century, the successor to Jesse Hartley, George Lyster, had added significantly to the system with new docks, improvements and alterations, including in Birkenhead.

When Lyster took office the age of steam was beginning to put strong pressures on the system of docks, which needed to adapt to the much greater draught, beam and length of ships. Albert Dock, for example, the wonder of the age when opened in 1845, was obsolescent within twenty years as British and imperial trade continued to expand. There was also the need to transport large numbers of passengers, including hundreds of thousands of migrants. Yet for all this Liverpool did manage to adapt as both a port and a city. By the outbreak of war in 1914 its future looked as solid as the monumental buildings along its waterfront. The discerning could, however, even then detect growing cracks in the edifice. The majority of the city's population, too, saw relatively little of the fruits of economic success. Those are stories to which we shall return later. The other story, of the building of the 'pyramids', is still worth the telling.

Thomas Steers and the Old Dock

The first dock project emerged in 1709, although, as we have seen, some merchants had seen it coming some years earlier. Thomas Johnson, one of Liverpool's two Members of Parliament, responding to strong local pressure, invited an experienced, reputable, London dock engineer to draw up a plan for a dock. His name was George Sorocold (1668–1738). His four-acre dock, with berths for a hundred ships, would cost, he estimated, £6,000. Sorocold's plan involved land excavation, using the tried and tested procedures used while digging canals. This would have posed problems, given the terrain, which rose relatively steeply up from the shoreline. This made excavation difficult and more costly than Sorocold's estimate. His scheme lay on the table until, later in the year, the Common Council, Liverpool's local authority, invited Johnson and the other Liverpool MP, Richard Norris, to look for an alternative. The two were hardly disinterested delegate of the public authority. They had their own major interests in the tobacco trade: Johnson's family-owned 'closes' ran down to the Pool; and Norris was to have his own warehouses, alongside the new dock, soon after its construction. But there was early opposition to Sorocold's scheme, which might have influenced the Corporation's search for an alternative. The main protests came from the Cheshire cheese merchants who traded with London by the sea route, anchoring and loading on the other side of the Mersey. Despite being on the other side of the river, they still would have to pay dues even if they did not use the new dock. The cheese merchants later took their objection to Parliament during the passage of the necessary private Act in 1709. They were overruled. By then, Sorocold's scheme had been dropped in favour of the rival design of Thomas Steers (1672–1750).

Steers' approach was preferred partly because its costs would almost certainly be less. Although Steers came up with the same estimate of £6,000 (at present day values about £1 million)[8] Sorocold's calculations were almost certainly too optimistic, while the excavations would have attracted expensive claims from those owning the land. Steers' scheme therefore looked better in terms of cost – an important consideration given that the venture was to be mainly privately financed by Johnson and Norris, although there would have been others putting up some money. Additionally, in using the port's natural feature, the Pool, it had further cost advantages over Sorocold's plan.

The legal procedure of a private Act had long been used in England to enclose arable and common land. This made farming more efficient, through the consolidation of small-scale holdings, allowing economies of scale and the application of new methods. Conveniently it also further enriched the already wealthy at the expense of those who mistakenly thought that working the land for hundreds of years gave them rights, at least to compensation. Liverpool's first dock was a much more acceptable form of progress. Only the Pool was dispossessed, and the cheese merchants would soon share in the rapidly rising profits from trade, even after paying the irksome dues (from which only naval vessels and ships in distress were exempt).

Inevitably, construction of the new dock proved difficult. There were delays, and the costs began to escalate; the £6,000 estimate grew to £15,000. This put back completion, and it was not until 1715 that ships were anchoring in the dock, although its walls were not fully completed until 1721. When finished the dock had 3½ acres of water, but it more than paid for itself (it straight away attracted useful dues of £600 per annum). Nor was the dock itself the only investment. It is estimated that with the associated warehouses the £15,000 became £50,000 and the dock, and the gains from trade, became the catalyst for a 'new town' of many more streets, a church (St Peter's) and the Bluecoat Hospital. Adjacent to the dock itself a vibrant local economy soon began to develop, producing glass, salt, copper and iron. Ships would also be built and repaired, ropes made, metal worked, chandlery sold and sugar refined. Between 1710 and 1750 total investment in the town and its economy has been estimated at £572,000 (£97.5 million).[9]

Liverpool was fortunate in its choice of Thomas Steers, who brought with him a wide range of practical experience. He had earlier built a similar dock at Rotherhithe on the Isle of Dogs on the Thames. Before that he had served in the

Thomas Steers' enclosed or 'wet' dock at Liverpool was a remarkable engineering achievement, the first of its kind in the world. As can be seen from this detail of S. & N. Bucks' contemporary engraving, ships were now able to unload and load in the safety of the enclosed dock, where the water level remained constant, whatever the state of the tide in the river beyond. This became a prototype for docks elsewhere.

army in Flanders, as a quartermaster, and was likely to have absorbed engineering experience from that part of Europe, with its long traditions of water engineering. The Duke of Bridgewater, later active in Liverpool with his own dock, got his knowledge of, and enthusiasm for, canal building from similar 'technological tourism'.[10] Steers' plan was radical in using Liverpool's natural feature: constructing the dock actually in the Pool itself. The construction problems, even so, were difficult. There would be water to contend with from two directions, the Pool fed by its stream from the east and the Mersey's tidal water from the west

Maps 3a and b. Liverpool before and after the construction of the Old Dock. The first 'commercial' dock earning dues (Steers' Rotherhithe project was solely for laying up ships in the winter) was the breakthrough towards rapid development.

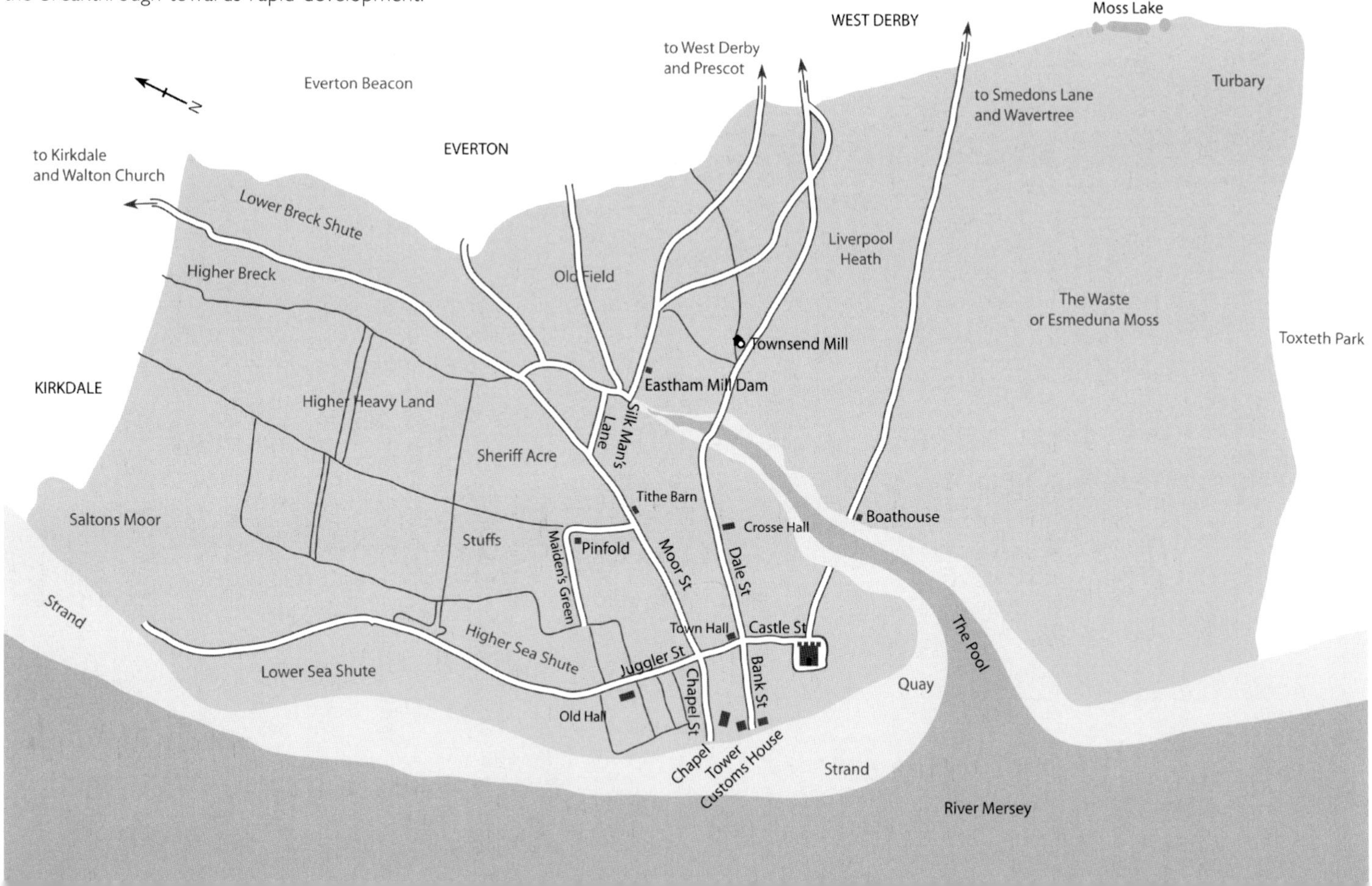

34

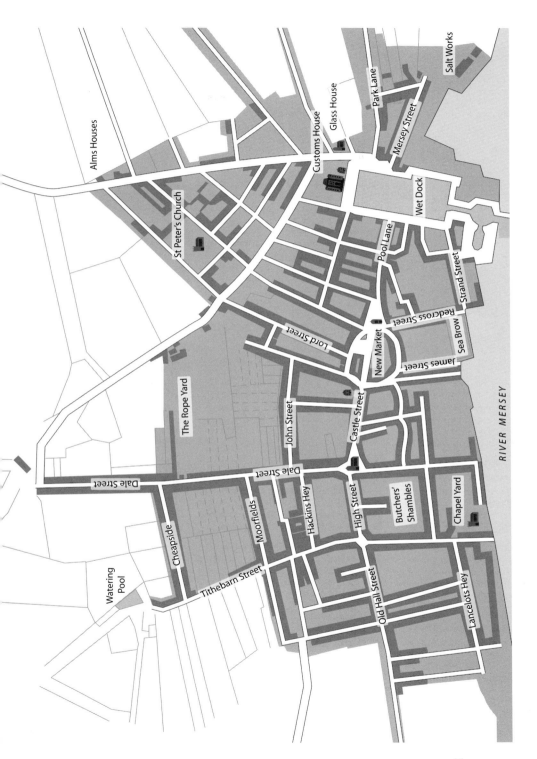

35

with a broad tidal range range. The gate, too, would have had to face the same problems when being fitted. The dock was also sizeable for its time, a rectangle of 200 yards by 100, occupying a substantial area of the Pool, as Map 3,[11] comparing Liverpool before and after the construction of the Old Dock, shows.

In its ambition the dock reflected the burgeoning power and growing optimism of Britain and Liverpool in the early years after its old colonial, maritime and military rival, France, sued for peace in 1713. As a project, in 1715, it was far removed from Ramsay Muir's description as Liverpool's 'first humble dock'. It was certainly the first, but not humble. Its success also made it the prototype for further dock building, even using, until the twentieth century, the dock's depth below the water (the Old Dock Sill) as the datum from which the depths of further docks would be measured.[12]

But it was perhaps the construction method that was most significant. Unlike at London, where all of the docks were excavated from dry land near the river, Liverpool's were created through reclamation from the river itself, in effect extending the shoreline further out into the stream through the creation of what eventually became a 7-mile long artificial and massive sea wall. In Liverpool, only Stanley Dock, which served in part to connect the Leeds and Liverpool Canal to the dock system, was excavated. All the rest were built on land reclaimed from the river. The comparison with the pyramids was not too great an exaggeration, especially since Liverpool's dock construction had to overcome major natural problems. A hundred years later Thomas Telford, the celebrated engineer, even judged that the Liverpool side of the Mersey was a less suitable site for dock-building than the Cheshire side. What Telford could not know was that an assistant of Jesse Hartley, around 1835, had reported 'treacherous quicksand' in Birkenhead's great low-water basin.[13]

Economic development is not of course a wholly technical exercise. There were also other reasons why Liverpool, at the end of the seventeenth century (and Birkenhead 150 years later) were ripe for development. Most importantly for Liverpool, its trade was already growing rapidly and ambitious, wealthy men were in place with significant capital, or access to it. Birkenhead did, of course, get its own share later as well as replacing Liverpool as one of the country's most important ship-building ports, especially for warships, at Laird's Yard, later Cammell Laird's. In Liverpool itself, ship-building was pushed literally to the margins. Following the construction of the Old Dock and, later, Salthouse Dock, the shipbuilders were given notice to relocate on the Strand, between Salthouse Dock and the river. It was an early indication of Liverpool's priorities.

The vanishing Pool

Steers' dock acquired a new customs house, at the north-east end. By the time Steers died the Pool had vanished beneath new streets and buildings, although the line of the stream that fed can still be seen on a map and traced on the ground.

It flowed down the length of what became Haymarket, Whitechapel and Paradise Street, broadening into Hanover Street to Canning Place and towards the old river front, now the Strand. Steers himself remained to live and work in Liverpool. Paradise Street, reclaimed from the Pool and the stream, was named after the street where he once lived, in Rotherhithe. He was deservedly made a freeman of Liverpool and afterwards became a councillor, followed by mayor in 1739. Not surprisingly under a further Act of 1737 he was entrusted with the enlargement of the Old Dock and the design of the second wet dock, originally known as South Dock. It was later renamed Salthouse Dock to distinguish it from other docks being built at the South End. But Steers died in 1750 before its completion, by Henry Berry, his successor as dock engineer, in 1753.

Salthouse Dock was built to serve the needs of the Cheshire salt industry, including John Blackburne's salt works on Salthouse Lane. Following the full opening to navigation of the River Weaver in the 1730s rock salt could more easily be taken to Liverpool for refining. It was also exported in ever-increasing quantities, especially to America, Ireland and Scotland. In Ireland it was used to cure pork; in Scotland for herrings. The second dock was also a welcome relief to the growing congestion in the Old Dock as trade continued to grow.

The Old Dock and Salthouse Dock provided stable berthing for the easy loading and unloading of ships, a spectacular improvement on conditions that had pertained in the Pool. Because of the high tidal range of the Mersey, it was particularly important that ships could berth in a 'wet' dock (i.e. in which water is enclosed at high tide), not least to avoid becoming beached on the shoreline as the tide receded. Facilities were also required for ships to be cleaned, painted, repaired and re-fitted. This was the function of the 'graving' or 'dry'[14] dock. Docks could also change their use. Richard Norris' early graving dock was converted to become Canning ('wet') Dock a century later. In these the Corporation was involved, beginning the dilution of the early, private, venture capital approach. The Corporation also initiated two further graving docks in 1746 and 1756. In addition to graving and wet docks ships, when traffic was heavy, needed to queue to enter a dock or, when cargo had been unloaded, wait for a fair wind to fill their sails and get away — a manoeuvre difficult to achieve in a crowded dock. Such queuing and waiting was the function of the tidal or entrance basin.[15] This further expansion, as new dock building, required Parliamentary approval. The Act of 1737 which authorised the enlargement of the Old Dock and provided for the new second dock also provided for the construction of the Old Dock's basin.

Between 1709 and 1793 (the latter date marking the beginning of war with revolutionary France) the total tonnage of ships entering and leaving Liverpool grew from 27,200 to 358,100. This growth in trade was linked, in both cause and

OVERLEAF

Map 4. Liverpool's dock system in 1795. Many modern street and road names are clearly shown, including Scotland Road, the spine of the old waterfront neighbourhoods.

RIVER MERSEY A

PLAN
of
LIVERPOOL.

SCALE of YARDS

HIGH WATER

effect, to the construction of docks which, by the end of the century numbered seven: the Old Dock (1715); Salthouse Dock (1753); George's Dock (1771); Duke's Dock (a private venture for the Duke of Bridgewater's operations, completed in 1773); Manchester Dock (for barges and river craft using the inland waterways, completed in 1775); King's Dock (1788); and Queen's Dock (1796). The water area of the Old Dock was 3½ acres. When the Queen's Dock was opened, on 17 April 1796, the total water area had grown to 29 acres, or to 10 linear miles of quays for the docking of vessels. To evaluate the full size of the then dock estate, we should also add the sheds and warehouses constructed privately by merchants to accommodate the dockside loading, unloading and storage of goods. There were also the graving docks, near to but separate from dockside loading and unloading operations, specialist timber yards, and the shipyards along the Strand beyond Salthouse Dock. All these, including Queen's Dock opened the following year are shown in Map 4,[16] including the tobacco warehouse adjacent to King's Dock. The map also shows plans for a new dock, adjacent to Bath Street, which would be a major construction, Prince's Dock. But this would have to wait for the end of hostilities with revolutionary and Napoleonic France. The Pool, by 1795, was also no more than a distant memory. The once pioneering Old Dock of Thomas Steers, which had begun the process of dock construction and established the pattern, had become a near relic, virtually marooned in the middle of the rapidly growing town.

By the end of the eighteenth century the town's familiar central old streets were also extending outwards to newer thoroughfares. One of these, Scotland Road in the upper left-hand corner of Map 3 would soon become famous, even infamous, as the heartland of Liverpool's most raucous, riotous, poor and often dissident waterfront neighbourhood – though long a welcome and welcoming haven for sailors from all corners of the world. Long before this, in 1796, however, it still passed through the meadows of the windmill-lined villages of Kirkdale and Everton, where the wealthy could escape the bustle and grime of the inner city and the docks. Within seventy years the meadows and green hills, as the Pool, had vanished.

The wars with France brought severe dislocation of trade. The long pause in capital accumulation postponed new dock construction until the passing of a further enabling Act in 1811. This gave authority for the building of the small Union Dock, some improvements and extensions to existing docks, and the construction of Prince's Dock, which opened in 1821. It was easily the largest built to that date, at eleven acres, entered through two 45-foot locks from its own half-tide basin (i.e. without locks) to the north and that of George's Dock to the south. Construction cost £650,000 (£48.5 million).[17] In 1827 the Old Dock was finally filled in and its dry dock, after the excavation of a further two feet and the addition of gates, was converted to a wet dock (Canning Dock), which opened in 1829. These major developments arose from the pressures of the still rapidly increasing trade and the associated growth in dock revenue as well as the effects of advancing technology. The outcome was that dock water space, in the early years of the nineteenth century, increased as much as for the previous hundred years. By then, from 1824 and for the next thirty-six years, dock construction was firmly in the hands of Jesse Hartley.

Table 1 The growth of Liverpool's dock system, 1715–1821

Principal dock	Year opened	Location	Depth below datum (feet)*	Dock engineer	Original water area (acres)†	Cumulative water area (acres)
1 Old Dock	1715	South	ODS	Thomas Steers	3.50	3.50
2 Salthouse Dock	1753	South	–	Thomas Steers/ Henry Berry	4.75	8.25
3 George's Dock	1771	South	4' 6"	Henry Berry	5.00	13.25
4 Duke's Dock	1773	South	4' 2"	Henry Berry	2.50	15.75
5 Manchester Dock	1775	South	–	James Brindley	0.10	15.85
6 King's Dock	1781	South	5' 0"	Thomas Morris	5.25	21.10
7 Queen's Dock	1796	South	5' 0"	Thomas Morris	7.25	28.35
8 Prince's Dock	1821	North	–	John Foster	11.75	40.10

* The depth of water at the dock entrance ('sill'). This varies according to the tide. For the first dock, the Old Dock, it was 25 feet below high water in ordinary spring tides and 11½ feet at neap tides. This, the Old Dock Sill (ODS) was the datum from which the depth of further docks was measured until the twentieth century. Hence 5 feet below ODS meant depths of 30 feet to 16½ feet. Salthouse Dock's original sill level was not recorded when constructed, but it was deepened, in 1840, to 5 feet below the ODS (see Ritchie-Noakes, *Liverpool's Historic Waterfront*, p. 169).

† Excluding alterations, extensions and reductions.

Source: Hyde, *Liverpool and the Mersey*, appendix IV. p. 247; Ritchie-Noakes, *Liverpool's Historic Waterfront*, appendix 1, pp. 169–70.

Table 2 The growth of Liverpool's dock system, 1829–45

Principal dock	Year opened	Location	Depth below datum (feet)	Dock engineer	Original water area (acres)	Cumulative water area (acres)
9 Canning Dock	1829	South	—	Jesse Hartley	4.00	44.10
10 Clarence Dock	1830	North	3' 2"	Jesse Hartley	6.00	50.10
11 Brunswick Dock	1832	South	5' 6"	Jesse Hartley	12.50	62.60
12 Brunswick Half-Tide Basin	1832	South	6' 1"	Jesse Hartley	1.75	64.35
13 Waterloo Dock	1834	North	7' 8"	Jesse Hartley	6.25	70.60
14 Victoria Dock	1836	North	6' 6"	Jesse Hartley	5.75	76.35
15 Trafalgar Dock	1836	North	6' 4"	Jesse Hartley	6.50	82.85
16 Coburg Dock	1840	South	6' 0"	Jesse Hartley	4.50	87.35
17 Canning Half-Tide Basin	1844	South	6' 2"	Jesse Hartley	2.50	89.85
18 Albert Dock	1845	South	5' 5"	Jesse Hartley	7.75	97.60

Source: Hyde, Liverpool and the Mersey, appendix IV. p. 247; Ritchie-Noakes, Liverpool's Historic Waterfront, appendix 1, pp. 169–70.

Jesse Hartley's Liverpool

Jesse Hartley was born in Pontefract on 21 December 1780. His father, a stonemason and bridge builder, guided his early career in the same profession, and he was to design and construct many masonry bridges across England and Ireland. But he had no experience of dock construction on his appointment as dock surveyor in 1824, at the age of 44. He very soon got it. His first two projects, Clarence Dock and Brunswick Dock, opened in 1830 and 1832, were built for special purposes. Clarence, at 6 acres, was to accommodate steamers, and built away from the other docks since at that time steamers were thought to be a fire hazard at the dockside. Clarence Dock was also later to become well known as the dock where immigrant ships disembarked masses of Irish, especially those seeking refuge from the famine after 1845. Dublin Street, appropriately named, is still there, on the other side of the Dock Road. Brunswick Dock, at twice the acreage of Clarence, was built for the timber trade, although that did not exclude other cargoes, especially when Hartley's last project, Canada Dock, was opened in 1859. Canada Dock was almost 18 acres in extent, with special modern facilities for timber handling, although Brunswick, the original timber handling dock, was not immediately replaced. Up to 1865 ships entering the dock and carrying timber were never less than 40 per cent of the total, rising even as high as 85 per cent. This was because Brunswick Dock, with its specially designed sloping quays, could accommodate the purpose-built, timber cargo vessels. These facilities had been enhanced by a direct railway line, built in 1835. But the dock's specialist construction led to its over-use so that sailing ships had to wait for an average of 30 days before discharging their timber. By 1875 only a quarter of the ships at Brunswick Dock carried timber, and by 1895 it was fewer than one per cent.[18]

The loss of the timber trade to Canada Dock also began the final stage of the demise of ship-building in Liverpool. The yards had for long been the poor relations to dock construction in the competition for land. Those conveniently adjacent to Brunswick Dock's timber were the last to go as the timber trade gradually moved north to Canada Dock. The last saw to be launched on the Liverpool side was in 1899.

Despite the loss of its timber trade, Brunswick Dock continued to be busy in an era when every yard of dock space was needed to keep up with Liverpool's exponential growth. Now it became the main focus of ships trading with West Africa and South America and, later, the Mediterranean and coastal trades. These were vessels suited to ports with shallow draught, a feature of Brunswick Dock even after it was made deeper and wider. Canada Dock, purpose-built rather than adapted, retained its timber-handling role until, in a very different era, the Royal Seaforth Dock was built to handle all the bulk cargoes of the port, including Canada Dock's timber and Brunswick Dock's grain.

Between Clarence Dock in 1830 and Canada Dock in 1858 Jesse Hartley designed and supervised the construction of eighteen docks as well as warehouses, sheds, hydraulic machinery, dock walls along the river front and offices and other buildings for officials and key dockside workers. During his tenure he added a total of 140 acres of wet docks and ten miles of quays. By the time of his death, Hartley had, over just thirty-six years, built half of Liverpool's then dock area. In money terms the total cost of Hartley's innovations and extensions, including land purchase and warehouse construction, exceeded £5 million (£412 million). By 1847, the port's debt in bonds, which required authorisation by successive Acts of Parliament, was just short of this figure.[19] Hartley's works were expensive, but as Table 1 shows, they had a major effect upon the volume of trade. Between 1820 and 1860 (i.e. just before Hartley's appointment and at his death) the tonnage of ships entering the Mersey, and requiring berthing, unloading and loading facilities, rose from less than one million to 4.7 million.

Table 3 Tonnage of ships entering Liverpool, 1810–1910*

1810	734,400
1820	805,100
1830	1,412,000
1840	2,445,700
1850	3,536,300
1860	4,697,200
1870	5,728,500
1880	7,524,500
1890	9,654,000
1900	12,380,900
1910	16,654,100

* Based on dock dues paid. *Source*: Francis E. Hyde (1971)[20]

Ships were also growing in size, requiring increasing dock depths, wider entrances and gates, and longer quays. Steam was also beginning to replace sail. The first steamboats appeared on the river in 1815 though even before that on New York's Hudson and Glasgow's Clyde. In 1819 the first steamship to cross the Atlantic entered the Mersey on its way from New York to St Petersburg. In 1840 the new Cunard Company began its fortnightly service to New York with the *Britannia* and three sister ships. It was soon followed by other new shipping companies (or 'lines'), such as White Star, Inman, Holt, Harrison and Elder Dempster, steaming to wider destinations. These big ships needed special docking facilities. The George's landing stage, built initially in 1847 for the various ferry services, was more than complemented by the Prince's landing stage of 1876, half a mile long, then claiming to be the biggest floating structure of its kind in the world.

Steam had revolutionary implications for the docks, in terms of costs, timetabling, turnaround times, coaling facilities and dockside technology. It would also transform the ancient occupation of the sailor, as well as introduce new occupations with different skills. Yet the age of steam was surprisingly slow in coming. When the first steamboats appeared on the Mersey they seemed more suitable for river traffic, though when steam was applied to tugs, the problems of large sailing ships, when manoeuvring in unpredictable weather and wind conditions, could be minimised. But a large sailing ship also represented a heavy capital investment to its owners not to be lightly replaced by an even more expensive, speculative steam vessel with the associated problems of new manning and occupational challenges. Sailors, too, and their officers, would resist the abandonment or dilution of their lengthily acquired, proudly held, historic skills for the simpler, more routine ways of the steamship. Somewhat paradoxically, however, given the contrast in skills, when steamships and sailing vessels worked the same routes, the steamship sailors were paid higher rates than those on sailing ships.[21] The differential may have been set to encourage sailors to make new careers in steam, which would again reflect the pressures resisting a rapid decline in the sailing ship fleet in Liverpool, as elsewhere. The construction of the Suez Canal, in 1869, would prove to be the turning-point.

By 1869, the major problems of steamship technology had also been resolved, and steam became a serious threat to sail. But even then, in Liverpool, the sailing ship lingered on, even as steam was transforming the waterfront and those who worked there. In numbers, though not in tonnage, they held their own into the early years of the twentieth century, including in Liverpool. Tonnage in 1906 was 98 per cent steam. Fifty years earlier it had been 16 per cent.[22] Sailing ships, though still numerous, were mainly confined to the smaller docks in the South End, including Hartley's Albert Dock. They were, of course, much smaller than steamships and by then mostly coastal and river craft. Significantly, Jesse Hartley's last project, Canada Dock, was in the North End and almost three times the acreage of his first. It was much larger than Albert Dock, opened with fanfares, in 1845. But Hartley's 1845 project remains his most celebrated achievement, surviving into our own time as the focus for Liverpool's new tourist and cultural roles, although it was almost demolished in the 1980s and the site converted to a car park.

When Hartley was designing his masterpiece in the 1840s sailing ships still dominated the oceans and coastal waters. Steam-powered vessels had first entered the Mersey well before the Albert Dock was construction, but it would be forty years after the dock was opened before its inadequacies were fully exposed for the use of ever larger, ocean-going steamships. Hence the main issues of Hartley's day, in relation to dock construction, were the security of cargoes in open docks and the need to reduce fire risk. These pointed to the use of secure, fireproof warehouses on the quays, especially when bonded warehouses (subject to excise duties only when goods left the warehouse) were introduced, in London, after the Act of 1803. A system of publicly owned warehouses did not reach Liverpool until the Albert Dock, when Hartley and his associates looked to the existing example of London's St Katharine's Dock.

Hartley's project, with advice from Philip Hardwick who had designed London's fireproof warehouses, incorporated five, large, multi-storey structures behind the quays. They were constructed of brick and iron following successful tests of their fireproof qualities on large-scale models in Coburg Dock. For security and access the warehouses were enclosed within a wall, with watch huts and an iron gate. They were bonded and owned by the Dock Trustees; they also conformed to an integrated design, avoiding the speculative, often badly located warehouses built

OVERLEAF

Map 5. Liverpool's dock system in 1862. Jesse Hartley's achievement (he died in 1860) is evident from this map. Note, too, the beginning of the Birkenhead system, by then also under the control of the Mersey Docks and Harbour Board.

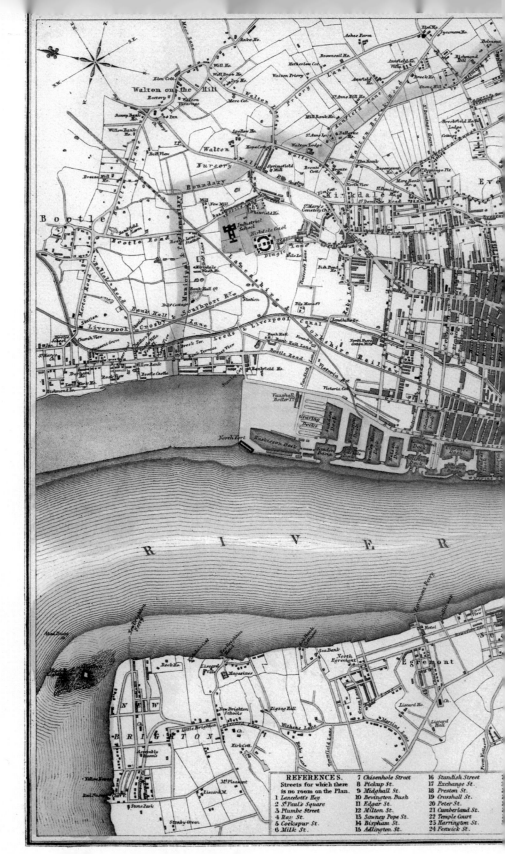

REFERENCES.

Streets for which there
is no room on the Plan.

1 Lancelot's Hey	13 Sawney Pope St.
2 St. Paul's Square	14 Bispham St.
3 Plumbe Street	15 Adlington St.
4 Ray St.	16 Standish Street
5 Cockspur St.	17 Exchange St.
6 Milk St.	18 Preston St.
7 Chisenhole Street	19 Crosshall St.
8 Pickup St.	20 Peter St.
9 Midghall St.	21 Cumberland St.
10 Bevington Bush	22 Temple Court
11 Edgar St.	23 Harrington St.
12 Milton St.	24 Fenwick St.

RIVER

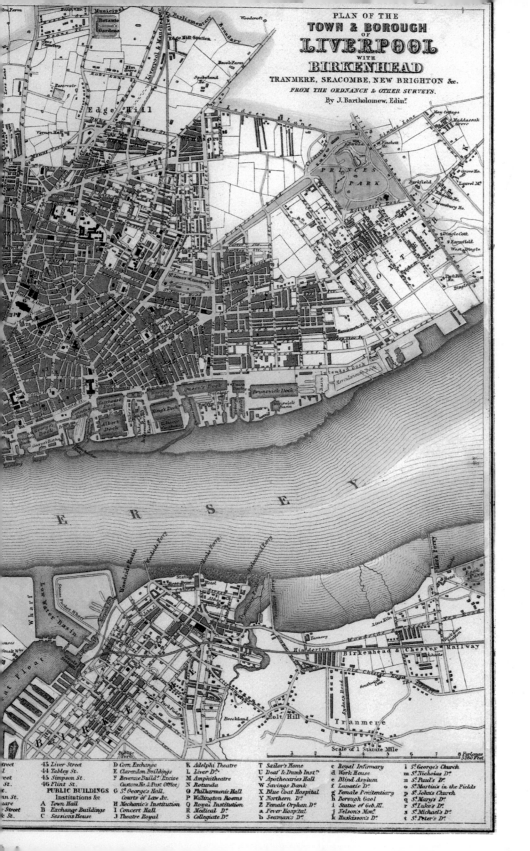

PLAN OF THE
TOWN & BOROUGH
OF
LIVERPOOL
WITH
BIRKENHEAD
TRANMERE, SEACOMBE, NEW BRIGHTON &c.
FROM THE ORDNANCE & OTHER SURVEYS.
By J. Bartholomew, Edinr.

Scale of 1 Statute Mile

43 Liver Street	D Corn Exchange	K Adelphi Theatre	T Sailor's Home	c Royal Infirmary	i St George's Church
44 Tabley St.	E Clarendon Buildings	L Liver Dᵒ	U Deaf & Dumb Instⁿ	d Work House	m St Nicholas Dᵒ
45 Simpson St.	F Revenue Buildgˢ Excise	M Amphitheatre	V Apothecaries Hall	e Blind Asylum	n St Paul's Dᵒ
46 Flint St.	Custom Hoᵉ & Post Office	N Rotunda	W Savings Bank	f Lunatic Dᵒ	o St Martin's in the Fields
PUBLIC BUILDINGS	G St George's Hall,	O Philharmonic Hall	X Blue Coat Hospital	g Female Penitentiary	p St John's Church
Institutions &c	Courts of Law &c.	P Wellington Rooms	Y Northern Dᵒ	h Borough Gaol	q St Mary's Dᵒ
A Town Hall	H Mechanic's Institution	Q Royal Institution	Z Female Orphan Dᵒ	i Statue of Geo. III.	r St Luke's Dᵒ
B Exchange Buildings	I Concert Hall	R Medical Dᵒ	a Fever Hospital	j Nelson's Monᵗ	s St Michael's Dᵒ
C Sessions House	J Theatre Royal	S Collegiate Dᵒ	b Seaman's Dᵒ	k Huskisson's Dᵒ	t St Peter's Dᵒ

by private developers. Hartley also innovated by incorporating hydraulic hoists and cranes into the design. The final bill, of £700,000 (£57.5 million), was a big one, but the project was undoubtedly state-of-the-art when it was opened in 1845. The fireproof quality of the warehouses, including their wrought-iron roofs, was especially innovative at a time when cotton mills were regularly being burned to the ground.

Hartley's long tenure allowed him to conceive of the docks as a system, so that ships could move between docks. Hartley's paymasters, the Dock Trustees, were careful with money, but they also had confidence in him, in part because he was such a strong and determined character. In one year, 1849–50, he spent £315,000,[23] (£28.5 million). But it was all carefully costed and, undoubtedly, value for money. By the time he died, his contribution to Liverpool's rapidly growing wealth had been more than significant. Between 1830 and 1860 dues from tonnage entering the Port had trebled. He did not, of course, design beautiful structures – as Picton pointed out. His designs were strong and functional. Sometimes, though, his enthusiasm for stone (he was trained as a mason) strayed into medieval, castellated ugliness as some of his 'monuments' along the Dock Road still testify. Curiously, despite his contemporaries being impressed with his charisma and self-confidence, he was poor with words and dreaded giving oral evidence at the many parliamentary committees which he was obliged to attend – much like George Stephenson, his contemporary, as Picton again observed.[24] His words were his docks. When Brunel's *Great Britain*, the biggest ship in the world, was launched in 1843, it found an eventual berth big enough in Liverpool, but not in Bristol, for its service to New York.[25] Birkenhead, too, had already seen the beginning of its own system, as Map 5 (*see* pages 46–7) illustrates for 1862.[26]

The port's working population was also expanding at an astonishing rate, as workers from Lancashire, Cheshire and particularly Ireland came looking for work, encouraged by tales of opportunity, growth and good pay. By 1861 the population of the borough had grown to 444,000. It had been 287,000 only a generation earlier, in 1841, and fewer than 100,000 in 1811.[27] By the time that Isaacs drew his impressive 'aerial view' in 1859 (*see* pages 50–1), Liverpool was shown to have grown into a large metropolis.[28] In commerce and trade volumes it was beginning to rival London. Less happily, its rivalry also extended to the poverty, poor health and low well being of its population. In its lack of public health provision, especially, Liverpool broke all records. Not for nothing was it said to be 'the black spot on the Mersey'.

Table 4 The growth of Liverpool's dock system, 1848–58*

Principal docks	Year Opened	Location	Depth below datum (feet)	Dock engineer	Original water area (acres)	Cumulative water area (acres)
19 Salisbury Dock	1848	North	6' 7"	Jesse Hartley	3.50	101.10
20 Collingwood Dock	1848	North	6' 3"	Jesse Hartley	5.00	106.10
21 Stanley Dock	1848	North	5' 6"	Jesse Hartley	7.00	113.10
22 Nelson Dock	1848	North	6' 1"	Jesse Hartley	8.00	121.10
23 Bramley-Moore Dock	1848	North	5' 6"	Jesse Hartley	9.50	130.60
24 Wellington Dock	1850	North	6' 2"	Jesse Hartley	7.75	138.35
25 Wellington Half-Tide Basin	1850	North	6' 9"	Jesse Hartley	3.10	141.45
26 Sandon Dock	1851	North	6' 6"	Jesse Hartley	10.00	151.45
27 Huskisson Dock	1852	North	—	Jesse Hartley	14.75	166.20
28 Wapping Dock	1855	South	5' 4"	Jesse Hartley	5.10	171.30
29 Wapping Basin	1855	South	5' 4"	Jesse Hartley	1.50	172.80
30 Canada Dock	1858	North	6' 6"	Jesse Hartley	17.75	190.55

* Excludes graving docks; Morpeth Dock (3.25 acres) and Egerton Dock (3.75 acres) were the first Birkenhead docks. J. M. Rendell was the engineer. Both opened in 1847.

Source: Hyde, *Liverpool and the Mersey*, appendix IV. p. 247; Ritchie-Noakes, *Liverpool's Historic Waterfront*, appendix 1, pp. 169–70.

OVERLEAF

Isaacs' panorama of Liverpool in 1859. These panoramas were viewed from balloons. This one is very accurate, illustrating the scale of the dock system the year before Jesse Hartley died and the large number of ships at berth in the river. Although steam was no longer a new technology, sail is still clearly important.

LIVERPOOL RECORD OFFICE

CHAPTER THREE

Steam on the Mersey

In the very year of the peace [1815] the first steamboat appeared on the Mersey, the harbinger of a total revolution in the seagoing trade of the port.

(Ramsay Muir, 1907)[1]

... by the end of the 1860s, Liverpool men, by experiment, had successfully put their ideas to the test. Working in the new media of iron and steam they had launched upon the world a series of new shipping companies whose operations, by the end of the century were to embrace the five continents and most of the shipping lanes of the oceans. As a result, Liverpool ships traded in every port and brought back to the docks and warehouses of Liverpool the wealth flowing from a new commercial enterprise.

(Francis E. Hyde, 1971)[2]

I N HIS LATER YEARS Jesse Hartley was assisted by his son, John, replicating the earlier partnership of the Stephensons on the railways. John Hartley's contributions also went beyond the technical. He was more than able to provide eloquent, persuasive evidence to the many inquiries and parliamentary committees that were associated with every major new proposal. In that he greatly outshone his father who was reportedly tongue-tied and impatient on such occasions. Jesse had also disliked going to London, where the evidence was normally taken, something which probably would have endeared him to many of his Liverpool or Yorkshire contemporaries. Yet John, unlike his father, suffered from poor health and only worked directly for the Mersey Docks and Harbour Board for one year and, even then, only half-time at an annual salary of £1,750 (£111,000). His father's pay, for a full-time post, was exactly double, at £3,500 per annum (£222,000).[3] John's poor health forced his resignation though the board retained him, as a consultant, until his death in 1871.

George Lyster and the Age of Steam

John Hartley's able successor as dock engineer was George Fosbery Lyster; like the great Jesse Hartley, Lyster served in the post for a total of thirty-six years. By the time he retired in 1897 (he died two years later), Lyster's contributions to the waterfront were comparable, at least in extent, with those of Hartley. He built docks at both ends of the estate, including the Alexandra Docks' innovative system of branch docks and Hornby Dock in the North End, as well as Herculaneum, Harrington, and Toxteth Docks in the South End. He had also worked as J. M. Rendell's protégé in the construction of Birkenhead's first two docks – Morpeth and Egerton – which opened in 1847. Later he made his own reputation in Birkenhead with the large-scale Alfred and Wallasey Docks, in 1866 and 1878, which eliminated Rendell's engineering errors. Nor did he neglect to pass on his skills, his own son carrying on the dynastic tradition with the construction of the Brunswick Entrance Locks in 1905. Father and son together were also responsible for the original design of the Liverpool Overhead Railway, although its detailed planning and construction were entrusted to different hands.[4]

Lyster's contribution can perhaps even be seen as more significant than that of Hartley, even though he added less to the dock acreage than his even more energetic predecessor: about 100 acres to Hartley's 150.[5] When Hartley was dock engineer the ships entering and leaving the port were still mainly sailing vessels. During Lyster's tenure, from 1861 to 1897, the number of steamships was gradually overtaking those under canvas and greatly exceeding them in total tonnage and size. Even as early as 1870, just a year after the opening of the Suez Canal, 30 per cent of British steam tonnage was in Liverpool ships.[6] Sailing ships were still numerous, but increasingly were confined to the South End docks. The big steamships, including the giant passenger liners, mainly berthing at the North End, required docks with longer quays and wider and deeper entrances. By 1900 the average tonnage of vessels owned in Liverpool had increased fivefold since the first, steam-driven, passenger lines had begun operations sixty years earlier. Steam was transforming Liverpool's (and Britain's) shipping and docks just as it had propelled Britain into the industrial age.[7] That was Lyster's world, and it was a difficult one.

George Lyster can also be credited with making the first, critical step (though, curiously, he was very unwilling) in delivering Liverpool from the ever-present threat of the sandbanks in Liverpool Bay. These banks shift constantly with the strong westerly winds, blocking the approaches and channels to and in the Mersey. In 1876 he had observed centrifugal sand pumps dredging the River Loire for the foundations for a bridge. His first attempt in Liverpool failed until the development of the steam turbine after 1880 which, applied to the centrifugal sand pumps, made possible the first successful dredging of the channels in Liverpool Bay in 1891, even though the board's 10,000 ton dredger, *Leviathan*, had no need for turbines. Yet, Lyster's own 'technological tourism' (as that of Thomas Steers and the Duke of Bridgewater in the previous century) along with his own talents and perseverance, eventually made the breakthrough. In the meantime New York, at the other end of the 'ocean greyhounds' run, had dredged its own sand bar by an extra two feet, allowing vessels, especially the liners, to enter or leave up to a draught of 26 feet, whatever the tide.[8]

As well as having to contend with the new age of steam and the problems out in the Bay, Lyster also had to relate to a different employer and a new organisation, the Mersey Docks and Harbour Board, established by yet another Act of Parliament in 1857. The new Board, though established when he was dock engineer, barely affected Hartley's work. By the time it was getting under way Hartley died, typically in harness, in 1860.[9]

Under new management: the Mersey Docks and Harbour Board

The Mersey Docks and Harbour Board – or Dock Board – was a statutory body that would have control over both sides of the Mersey's docks from 1857; this body took Liverpool and Birkenhead into the modern age. The crisis of the late 1960s and early 1970s led to its abolition and replacement, in 1972, by the Mersey Docks and Harbour Company. Unlike in many other ports, including London, a large part of Liverpool's earlier development had owed its success to the municipal authorities. From 1710 to 1825 the Common Council was alone responsible for dock development, although private financial interests had always played some part, as in the initial funding of the first dock and through the political and other pressures brought to bear by powerful port users looking for profits and social and political advancement. However, Acts of Parliament were always required to authorise new projects and to raise the necessary, secured capital.

The Act of 1811 had formed the 21 strong Trustees of the Dock Estate who were, in fact, also members of the Corporation. The number of trustees was enlarged by a further statute, in 1826, to include representatives of the users – the first time in the port's governance. This did not prevent disputes and may have precipitated some of them. As Liverpool prospered after the wars against France, some of those who gained in return contributed little. Freemen of the town were exempted from paying dues until the Municipal Corporations Act of 1835. The wider Corporation, too, could also veto the decisions of its own trustees and allocate port revenues to Town Dues, for the benefit of the town's development, rather than that of the port. The corporation then poured fuel on the long-smouldering coals. In 1853 it secured the approval of a parliamentary committee to purchase Birkenhead Dock Estate from its municipal authority for £1,143,000 (£98.4 million). The Corporation then promoted a Bill, in 1856, to develop Birkenhead's dock system further, with Jesse Hartley having provocatively rejected the development plans of J. M. Rendell, the engineer of Morpeth and Egerton Docks, as 'unsound'.[10] By then, of course, Hartley knew of the quicksand.

Liverpool Corporation's now growing band of enemies then moved in rapidly.

Table 5 The growth of Liverpool's dock system, 1862–1972*

Principal docks	Year opened	Location	Depth below datum (feet)	Dock engineer	Original water area (acres)	Cumulative water area (acres)
31 Canada Half-Tide Basin (later Brocklebank Dock)	1862	North	–	George Lyster	10.75	201.30
32 Herculaneum Dock	1866	South	8' 0"	George Lyster	3.50	204.80
33 Brunswick Branch Dock	1878	South	1' 0"	George Lyster	1.50	206.30
34 Langton Dock	1879	North	9' 0"	George Lyster	18.00	224.30
35 Alexandra Dock	1880	North	12' 0"	George Lyster	17.75	242.05
36 Alexandra Branch Dock No. 3	1880	North	12' 0"	George Lyster	7.75	249.60
37 Alexandra Branch Dock No. 2	1880	North	12' 0"	George Lyster	9.50	259.30
38 Alexandra Branch Dock No. 1	1880	North	12' 0"	George Lyster	9.00	268.30
39 Harrington Dock	1883	South	11' 3"	George Lyster	9.00	277.30
40 Hornby Dock	1884	North	12' 0"	George Lyster	17.00	294.30
41 Toxteth Dock	1884	South	11' 2"	George Lyster	11.50	305.80
42 Brunswick Entrance Locks	1905	South	19' 0"	Anthony Lyster	1.25	307.05
43 Gladstone Dock	1927	North	25' 0"	Thomas Newall	49.00	356.05 †
44 Royal Seaforth Dock	1972	North	–	Martin Agar	85.00	

* Excludes graving docks; Birkenhead, during this period, added four principal docks to its system: Alfred Dock (1866, 8.5 acres), Wallasey Dock (1878, 12.75 acres), Vittoria Dock (1909, 12.00 acres) and Bidston Dock (1933, 10.5 acres). Alfred and Wallasey were under George Fosbery Lyster with Vittoria under his son Anthony George. Bidston Dock was built under the direction of Thomas Lord Norfolk.

† This figure, as an estimate of the total dock acreage in 1927, as well as excluding earlier alterations, extensions and reductions to existing docks, does not allow for closures. It also precedes the total closure of the South End docks to commercial traffic in 1971.

Source: Hyde, Liverpool and the Mersey, appendix IV. p. 247; Ritchie-Noakes, Liverpool's Historic Waterfront, appendix 1, pp. 169–70.

First among them was the powerful Great Western Railway, whose interests were better served by Rendell's plans. The railway company was joined by Manchester's commercial interests, including the powerful cotton manufacturers. These were led by Manchester Corporation who, representing the Manchester users of Liverpool and Birkenhead docks, sought primarily to abolish Liverpool's power to use dock revenues for the town's purposes. Manchester's also had a not-so-secret agenda. The Corporation and special interests had been formulating their own plans for a ship canal to bypass Liverpool's domination and control of Manchester's trade, although it was as late as 1876 before even modest, limited, proposals actually emerged.

The outcome was a Bill to take control of the docks from Liverpool Corporation and give it to a new statutory, independent body. The Bill was even managed through Parliament by Manchester's town clerk. It was also significant that the new board would have Mersey, not Liverpool, in its title since there was a strong case for all the docks to be controlled by one authority rather than the two then in existence (Birkenhead became a borough in 1877). The Bill reached the statute book in 1857. Liverpool Corporation lost its control of the Birkenhead docks with compensation at the price it had paid in 1853, £1,143,000. It was also compensated for the loss of its Town Dues at £1,500,000. Taking the years 1861 to 1881 together, the new board's total dock revenue amounted to more than £2,500,000.[11] The compensation figure was adequate but certainly not generous, especially in the long run.

Liverpool was also now firmly in the lists against its rival Manchester, and understandably fearful of its ambitions. Manchester had been discussing its own plans earlier in the century to build a canal linking its manufacturers and traders to the Mersey estuary. The Duke of Bridgewater's earlier venture was limited to barge traffic, and the Mersey and Irwell navigation was by then choked with silt. The charges on the railway links to Liverpool were also higher than the canals. The first enabling Bill for the Manchester Ship Canal was put to Parliament in 1884. Not surprisingly, the principal hostile witness was Liverpool's dock engineer, George Lyster. Two further bills were required for the project to pass into law, and the Manchester Ship Canal was eventually opened in 1894.

This unsavoury period in the old rivalry between Liverpool's self-styled merchant 'gentlemen' and their sneering references to Manchester's manufacturing 'men' had outcomes that could not have been confidently predicted. Manchester seemed a very serious rival in 1894, but Liverpool's docks were not ruined or by-passed, although Manchester's competition was far from negligible. Liverpool had problems of its own, of its own making. The canal performed well enough for Manchester, in time, to become the fourth port of the UK after London, Liverpool and Hull. Liverpool's fears had, however, been exaggerated. It cost more than expected to send a large ship, with cargo, along the canal. Birkenhead, the third party, for a long time also saw itself as the forgotten pawn, relatively neglected by the Liverpool-based board, remaining a town of 'unqualified promise'.[12] As for Liverpool and Manchester, their bitter rivalry eventually cooled as both came to see the railway companies, with their monopoly charges, as the common enemy, the real villains of the piece.[13] The Board also had other emerging problems with which to contend. Liverpool maintained its place as the country's leading export port, but growth was beginning to slacken. Though small, the cracks, seen earlier by some, were beginning to widen in Edward VII's reign, hastened by the bitter, violent transport strike of 1911, a 'general' strike in all but name. Three years later Britain was fighting a desperate, destructive war in which Liverpool was a key but vulnerable player.

The Ocean Greyhounds

Liverpool's emerging problems in the early years after 1860, even if they had been clearly self-evident, would not have been widely believed. As late as 1907 in his *History*, Ramsay Muir denied any decline. In the 1860s Liverpool had an enviable dock system that then would have still looked both new and the state of the art, with massive, granite walls all along the riverside and for miles along the Dock Road. Dock offices and officials' houses newly built, stood at dock entrances. The dock gates and cranes and machinery, along the quays, were impressive. The docks themselves would have bristled with hundreds of masts, and played host to an increasing number of steamships. Thousands of porters, horses and carts and railway wagons thronged the always congested quays – there was always a shortage of space – as cargoes were unloaded, checked, weighed and taken by cart and porter's trolley into sheds and warehouses that were stacked almost to their ceilings with the world's merchandise. On the ships in the docks loading and stowing would be in progress, skilfully organised and directed by stevedores with their calls and special hand signals to crane drivers above. When safely loaded, the ships would sail on the next tide into an estuary full of ships and craft of all sizes. On the river ferries criss-crossed with commuting passengers, some going further down the river, and day trippers to the rapidly developing New Brighton which, by 1867, had its own pier and, later, a tower taller than that at Blackpool. Dredgers and hoppers were busy keeping the channels clear for cargo ships and the giant, sleek-lined passenger liners with their brightly painted funnels and symbols proclaiming the companies that owned them. Small, busy tugs were engaged in the seemingly impossible tasks of easing large vessels through dock entrances only barely wide enough or deep enough to take them.

It was all very impressive, even though the town (which became a city in 1880), continued to have acute, shaming problems in areas such as housing, sanitation and public health. Those who lived along the docks suffered particularly badly, despite the worthy efforts of officials and energetic philanthropists. Despite the hardships, Liverpudlians of all classes would still have been proud of their metropolis at the height of its prestige, much as Romans might have done, plebeians as well as patricians, in the time of Marcus Aurelius, unable to imagine their Rome and its Empire even in decline.

The most impressive symbols of Liverpool's seeming permanence were the liners of the powerful steamship companies, the 'ocean greyhounds' as they were known. The liners ran to strict timetables, with thousands of passengers strictly segregated by class: the rich could sail in decadent, pampered opulence, while many of the poor could afford only to travel in 'steerage', obliged to embark at the same time as the cargo and the 'baggage not wanted on voyage'. At the end of voyages there would be time for cleaning, refurbishing, replenishing and polishing,[14] before the liners took on thousands more, travelling to usually distant, sometimes exotic places. The names of the steamship companies still have a resonance to Liverpool and British ears,[15] and a few have even survived into the present day, having adapted to changing times and ways. Cunard is still with us, for instance, although far from what it once was, even placing orders for new cruise ships in French yards rather than the Clyde. Cunard's fine, renaissance palace building still adorns Liverpool's waterfront, but now as offices for a multitude of other enterprises. Cunard's transatlantic service began in 1840. Others, such as the Inman Line (1850) and White Star Line (1869), were founded to compete with Cunard as the New World grew to receive what seemed to be unlimited numbers

An Ocean Greyhound. Cunard's *Mauretania* (affectionately known as the 'Maury'), was launched in 1906. At that time it was the biggest, fastest and most luxurious ship in the world. After service as a troopship in the Great War it returned to the Atlantic run in 1918, serving for a further seventeen years before being broken up, at Rosyth in Scotland, in 1935. Its sister ship was the equally luxurious but ill-fated *Lusitania*, sunk by a German submarine in 1915.

© LIVERPOOL RECORD OFFICE

The White Star Line's *Britannic*, shown here with a small fleet of tugs, was the biggest of the three sister ships built at Harland & Wolff's Belfast yard. The others were the *Titanic* and the *Olympic*. The *Olympic* survived, but the *Britannic* shared a similar fate to the *Titanic*, sinking after being struck by a mine in 1916 while on duty as a hospital ship in the Mediterranean.

© LIVERPOOL MARITIME MUSEUM

of passengers and their families, by sea. The busiest route was into New York from Liverpool. Many more were to follow. Between 1860 and 1900 it is estimated that 5½ million left, as emigrants, from British ports. Of these, 4¼ million went from Liverpool.[16] They came to New York from all corners of old Europe, as the United States sought to fill its vast continent.[17]

Samuel Cunard was to take the early credit for helping to make this possible, though when it proved profitable he soon attracted serious competition. He was Canadian, born in 1787 into a whaling community, and by 1830 owned, with his brothers, a forty-strong fleet of whalers and other vessels. The Cunard family thought big, and a year later their first steamship successfully crossed the Atlantic to Liverpool. In 1839 Samuel, too, arrived to get seriously into steamships, a purpose greatly helped by his securing the contract to carry mail across the Atlantic, just at the time when mail was becoming the cheap and accessible way of communication. Cunard moved quickly. In the same year, with a George Burns, from Glasgow, he founded the North American Royal Mail Steam Packet Company, an Anglo-Canadian operation with four ships. The first was the famous *Britannia* (which by this time also literally 'ruled the waves') inaugurating the company's regular transatlantic service. Charles Dickens was one of the *Britannia*'s most famous passengers for his trip to America in 1858. By 1880, rapid growth and the heavy capital investment required made it necessary to go public, with a joint stock company. The Cunard Steamship Company was the outcome, though its eponymous founder had died two years earlier at the age of 91.[18]

Cunard had two main rivals, the companies of William Inman and Thomas Ismay, although Alfred Holt, the gifted marine engineer, was responsible for the innovations in engines that turned marginal operations into profitable ones. Inman's New York and Philadelphia Steamship Company was founded in 1850. The first White Star ship sailed in 1849, under the ownership of Wilson and Pilkington, until the 'flag and goodwill' were sold to Ismay in 1867. Both these lines, like Cunard, had early problems with wooden ships driven by paddles which were neither sufficiently efficient nor reliable. They also had to carry a great weight in coal, which aggravated the efficiency and running cost problems. Then came the pioneering breakthrough, Alfred Holt's *Cleator*, an iron ship with a screw propeller.[19] Alfred Holt's engine designs were decisive. Their propellers were more efficient and reduced coal consumption greatly, reducing weight, increasing speed and delivering profits. His innovations also made it possible for him to start his own service, though on the Far East run, rather than the North Atlantic, with his Ocean Steam Ship Company known, popularly, from its funnels, as the Blue Funnel Line. Alfred Holt, later to become a member and chair of the Mersey Docks and Harbour Board, had, like his father, principled reservations over the conduct of Liverpool's new men, who John Holt saw as '… hungry pigs fighting over a trough of milk …'[20] Alfred differed, strongly, as chairman, with some members of the board on several important policy issues, as Stuart Mountfield tells us, 'He had, in a very high degree, the interests of Liverpool at heart and could not understand the attitude of his colleagues on matters such as railway rates which acted to the disadvantage of the port.'[21]

Holt's disagreements largely focused around the Manchester Ship Canal scheme which at the end of the 1870s was in its concept stage. His nephew, Richard, later Sir Richard, was also to be chairman of the board until his death in 1941, '… saddened by the sight of his beloved Port already ravaged …'[22]

Alfred Holt's line, operating in the Far East, Africa and South America, made most of their money from trading, although passengers were also part of their business. The North Atlantic route lived and died by passengers. But the run became more and more competitive requiring substantial numbers of passengers to cover operating costs and service the capital debt. Cunard competed and survived better than most including its most celebrated rival, Thomas Ismay's White Star Line. Like Cunard, it had its own fine, distinctive building on James Street on the old waterfront, designed by Norman Shaw (the architect of New Scotland Yard in London) and opened in 1895. It was described in the *Architectural Review* as making '… everything around it look little and mean … and still holds its own among its big neighbours'.[23]

Ismay's buildings, and offices, like his ships, were famous for their style, furnishing and décor. Ismay bought a house on the Wirral that was then only twelve years old and demolished it to build 'Dawpool'; Norman Shaw was again the architect. Dawpool cost £53,000 and took two years to build. It was a reproduction of an Elizabethan manor house, of local red stone. Unlike those under the first Elizabeth '... there was not a single nail in the whole structure, only the finest brass screws'. It was so large it took thirty-two servants to run it.[24] Ismay was only thirty when, in 1864, working as a senior partner with

Dark days for the White Star Line. The *Titanic* memorial with the 'three graces' behind. The news of the sinking of the *Titanic* first came through, by telegraph, to the White Star Line's distinctive head office in James Street.

© LIVERPOOL RECORD OFFICE

William Imrie, he bought the failing White Star Line. Though well educated, he was apprenticed, at sixteen, to his father's ship-broking agents in Liverpool. He also had the advantages of his father's financial support as a timber merchant and shipbuilder as well as a shipbroker. Imrie, Thomas Ismay's partner, also had expensive tastes, owning an equally large house in the Liverpool suburbs, now a convent. The Ismay sons followed their father's example with their own '... semi-stately homes ...'[25] One of them, J. Bruce Ismay, became Chairman and Managing Director of Ismay, Imrie & Co. when his father died in 1899. He always sailed, as a passenger, with new ships on their maiden voyages, including the *Titanic* in 1912. He survived, though he suffered years of vilification for so doing.[26]

The era of the 'ocean greyhounds' was coming to an end even as Thomas Ismay was building his elegant offices on the old waterfront. One reason was the paring down of profits by the capital needs of such large, luxurious ships, with their crippling overheads, as fierce competition kept fares down. It has also been argued that it was Liverpool's emigrant traffic that turned losses into profits. That tap was turned off from 1914 to 1918 and in the 1920s the United States began to impose selective quotas as well as to apply drastic limits to the overall numbers. In 1914 1.2 million entered the country and in 1921 it was still 800,000. The Emergency Quota Act in the same year soon turned the tide of immigrants to a trickle, no more than 100,000 by 1930. The depression years that followed finally brought the era of mass immigration to an end, with only 38,000 arriving even in 1945.[27]

On the other side of the Atlantic the Depression was exacting a heavy toll on Liverpool's trade and employment. It was also in a depression year, 1934, that Cunard absorbed Ismay and Imrie, and the name of the White Star Line disappeared with it. Cunard had also moved its liner operations to Southampton, Liverpool's always dangerous rival. By then it was clear that the era of the passenger liners was drawing to a close. It was also clear that a port such as Southampton was even better placed for trading with the Americas. In the halcyon days of the ocean greyhounds glamour was hiding Liverpool's many growing problems as well as stressing the importance, in the longer term, of maintaining its trade in commodities, carried in its cargo ships.

The ebbing of the tide

Isambard Brunel and Robert Stephenson, the greatest and best known engineers of their day, had close connections with Liverpool. Robert and his father George (a rough though talented character much like Jesse Hartley) were involved at the beginning of the railway age with the spectacular success of their locomotive, 'The Rocket', at the Rainhill Trials, just outside Liverpool, in 1829. The Liverpool to Manchester railway's first terminus was in Crown Street, behind what is now one of the buildings of the University of Liverpool. The terminus was moved to Lime Street in 1838 and there it has remained, famous in war and peace as well as for Maggie May.[28]

The Canadian Pacific Line's 'Empresses' were as well known on the Mersey as those of the Cunard and White Star. One of the latest was the *Empress of Canada*, though there were several of the same name. One, which served as a troopship in World War II caught fire on the Mersey in 1953 and was scrapped in the following year. This photograph, with a crowd of onlookers, shows the salvage operation under way in 1954.

Brunel's big iron ships – the *Great Britain* and the *Great Eastern* – were sometimes on the Mersey, although Liverpool's docks were not large enough to accommodate *Great Eastern*'s paddles. Brunel and Stephenson might well have been personally acquainted with Jesse Hartley within the small circle of engineers who would meet regularly in their institutes and discuss all the latest developments. Less happily, Brunel was a witness at the parliamentary hearings (Hartley was not present) that ended Liverpool's Corporation's attempts to retain its control over the Mersey docks. Samuel Smiles, in his widely read celebrations of the lives of engineers,[29] the heroes of the age, seemed to rate dock engineers lowly: unlike the designers and builders of canals, railways and bridges, they did not even merit inclusion. Smiles' neglect does not detract from the skills, talents and energies of men such as Hartley.

The years after 1860, with Brunel, Hartley and Robert Stephenson all recently dead, marked the beginning of the period when Britain, and Liverpool, began to lose their way. As Eric Hobsbawn put it:

> This sudden transformation of the leading and most dynamic industrial economy into the most sluggish and conservative, in the space of thirty or forty years ... is the crucial question of British economic history ... essentially these are discussions about bringing the horse back into the stable after it has gone. It went between the middle of the century and the 1890s.[30]

In the case of Liverpool, the decline was becoming especially apparent after 1905, '... even to the casual observer ...' some, not easily described as 'casual', did not accept it, even then.[31] Ramsay Muir, while alluding to '... the period of competition ...' does not give it enough weight. Other nations, notably Germany, Japan, then France, and the United States went much beyond catch-up in the later years of the century. The United States, in particular after the Civil War, took great advantage of the economies of scale and new methods applied to mass production industries and, later, such new industries as chemicals and electrical products. Before that Britain had flooded the USA with its cheap, mass-produced manufactures. After that, British exporters found it far more difficult to hold their own against American internal competition. Even at home, Britain, once the dynamic innovator in iron and steel production, began to fall behind in the application of ever newer technologies to raise productivity.

Liverpool clearly thought it was different: cool, objective analysis said otherwise. It was, after 1860, still growing in its tonnage and revenues and 'decline' was still largely a relative concept. But there was a '... slackening in the rate of progress ...', as Hyde carefully puts it (p. 139). He was much less cautious two pages further on: 'By 1914, the high peak of achievement had been reached and passed; the lean years were about to begin.'

What was Hyde's justification in painting such gloomy prospects at the height of Britain's and Liverpool's Edwardian heyday?[32]

After 1850 there was a levelling-off in the growth of Liverpool's major imports and exports, despite heavy investment in the port's infrastructure and the growing capital of the steamship companies. The annual overall rate of growth of tonnage had also slowed. It was 2.8 per cent from 1716 to 1850 and 2.1 per cent from then until 1914. This poorer performance was largely explained by foreign competition for trade and, into the twentieth century, domestic competition from the smaller ports up the river to Manchester as the Ship Canal began to expand its activity. The Dock Boards' receipts fell in every year from 1907 to 1910.

Manchester's ship canal did not prove to be such a danger to Liverpool as was once feared, but it did make a difference. Ships entering the Mersey could also by-pass Liverpool and Birkenhead for their other competitors up-river. Such ships would only have to pay the harbour dues, which were not related to tonnage, and therefore smaller. Hyde calculated that these lower earning harbour rates grew from 18 per cent to 21 per cent of the total dues between 1900 and 1913, so limiting total revenue. There was also the increasingly fierce international competition for the passenger trade, even though Liverpool still led the way, leading to major changes in ownership.

The fierce competition facing Liverpool's shipping companies re-affirmed the case for concentrating on the more reliable, cargo-carrying trades rather than the uncertainties of the prestigious but much less profitable passenger trade. The White Star Line was taken over by the USA's Morgan combine in 1902, forming, in 1934, a defensive merger with its long-time rival, Cunard, and even then running into difficulties. The merger was insisted on by the government in agreeing to help fund the construction of the *Queen Mary*. Even cargo, which twenty years earlier had been Liverpool's bread, butter and jam, was not in robust health. As the First World War broke out its share of UK exports was 36 per cent: in 1860 it had been as high as 45 per cent. Over the same period Liverpool's share of imports fell from a third to a quarter.[33] Nor was the Dock Board living up to its 1857 expected promise:

> By the late 1870s the Mersey Docks and Harbour Board had become a highly ineffective body which combined poor planning and management with a high degree of complacency. In the 1880s the situation deteriorated even further, and it is not until 1890 that the Board showed signs of recognising that it had a problem ... The changes happened in time to save the port from collapse which at times seemed a distinct possibility ...[34]

The Board was also being charged with extravagance, even delusions of grandeur, not least in the construction of its new dock offices in 1907, on the site of the old George's Dock.[35] On its centenary in 1957, even Mountfield, commenting on the same period fifty years earlier, observes a certain hubris:

> ... a buoyancy in the tone of the discussions of the Board ... which was in keeping with the heyday of Empire and the paramount position of the nation as a great power, a great mercantile community and the centre of the world's finance.[36]

The same charge could be levelled at the owners of the '... potently famous ships of British Mercantile power, the liners of Cunard and White Star ... operated from grandiose offices on the Liverpool waterfront.'[37] Of equal grandeur were the new offices of the Dock Board and the iconic Royal Liver building forming, with Cunard's 'renaissance palace', the enduringly famous 'three graces'. The last hurrah of the old Empire was less enduring, threatened by the Great War, after which the cracks in Liverpool's trading edifice widened to become plainly visible.

Edwardian hubris. This 1907 photograph of the river and the Dock Board building also shows the sites of the planned Cunard and Liver buildings (note the advertising billboard), also to be completed in Liverpool's Edwardian heyday. The overhead railway can be seen in the foreground. Just ten years old at that time, it was demolished fifty years later.

Before the war Harrods had been planning to open its first store outside London, in Liverpool. These plans were cancelled in 1920.[38]

Gradual relative decline was plain for later historians such as Hyde to see. In Liverpool at the time it was not so apparent. In part, that was because Edwardian Liverpool's attention was gripped by events elsewhere, where tension was building towards a war in Europe that would prove to be easily the most destructive, bloody and destabilising in history up to that time. Certainly, Liverpool was going through a difficult patch, but the achievements over two centuries of spectacular growth had been immense and must have instilled a considerable reserve of self-confidence and pride. Liverpool was still the second port in the United Kingdom and one of the biggest and most successful in the world. It had accumulated great wealth, prestige and experience, and there was every reason to have faith that it could surmount its difficulties to prevail in the future. It also had the advantage of trading within a vast empire which to an extent would protect it from the blasts of competition and, later, depression, which caused such havoc between the wars. It also still had a heavy concentration of wealthy families and individuals within its boundaries that gave it, as a city, a well above average revenue base. Its major weakness, which would yet come to haunt it, was its excessive reliance on the port and its associated trades, industries and occupations. That could be an asset when trade and commerce were buoyant, but could be disastrous when it turned down, with not enough industry, outside shipping and the docks, to cushion against hard times.

And whenever trade turned bad, it was Liverpool's toilers that bore the brunt. Charitable activity, though often widespread and generous, was never enough to bridge the wide gap, for many, between getting by and being close to starving. Liverpool's workers and citizens took pride in its success, but many thousands, though playing a crucial part in that success, had no access to even its most modest fruits. That applied to those manning its ships, the great majority of those working on its quaysides and in its warehouses, as well as the large numbers of those working in the offices of its docks and shipping lines.

The relative poverty of the many arose largely from the casual nature, irregular pay and the always excess labour supply associated with working on ships and in the docks. For centuries the availability and amount of dock work had varied, literally, with the winds and the tides. For most dock workers, neither work nor wages could be relied upon from one day to the next. And because of the nature of the work, particularly in the era the of sailing ship, this precariousness was largely seen as unavoidable. Nor did the dockers endure alone: their situation was also the lot of their wives and families. Liverpool was also a magnet for those seeking refuge as well as work. They would add greatly to its numbers and, in consequence, to its problems.

Yet, as we shall see in subsequent chapters, at no time did those working and living at the margins passively accept their fate. They organised themselves, combined their efforts, albeit fitfully. They resisted hardship and poverty, and they fought back, provoking often a fierce counter-reaction. Then they had to fight again.

CHAPTER FOUR

The other side of wonderful

The great development of steamships and docks has brought it about that the City's prosperity largely depends upon casual labour, the most degrading as well as the most insecure form of employment; and that Liverpool has to deal with a social problem more acute than that which faces any other city.

(Ramsay Muir, 1907)[1]

This then was Liverpool in the nineteenth century. New wealth was in the pockets of new men. A new poor lived in new hovels.

(Anne Holt, 1936)[2]

T HE DIFFICULTY for many along the waterfront was in finding regular work. The enormous variability in the amount of work on the docks, combined with an ever-present over-supply of labour, helped perpetuate a 'casual system' of employment that harked back to much earlier practices in pre-industrial times. The majority of dockers were unskilled or semi-skilled labourers who were hired by the day or even the half day. If a docker was not selected for work – and the employer's decision was as final as it could be arbitrary – he would be sent home without pay. At the beginning of the twentieth century the Bristol-born docker and trade union leader Ben Tillett described the twice-daily 'call on' on the Thames:

> We are driven into a shed, iron-barred from end to end, outside of which a foreman or contractor walks up and down with the air of a dealer in a cattle-market, picking and choosing from a crowd of men, who, in their eagerness to obtain employment, trample each other under foot, and where like beasts they fight for the chances of a day's work.

For a long time the casual system was a major cause of many of Liverpool's social problems. Interestingly, Ramsay Muir also points to the large dependency of Liverpool on casual labour for its prosperity. Attempts to remove or even limit casualism frustrated the efforts of reformers even beyond 1947 when the prize finally seemed to be within their grasp. But it would be another twenty years[3] before the employers and the union put the final seal on their efforts to give permanent, secure work to those working in dockland. By then, however, it was already too late. Soon technology and geography rather than strikes[4] would begin to pull the carpet away, taking with it most of the jobs as well as the Mersey Docks and Harbour Board itself.

The problems and intractability of casualism were not confined to Liverpool. They featured at other ports and, as a practice, it was long seen as a necessary evil. It had cost advantages for the many small employers. Interestingly, many dockers also preferred it to the limitations they believed would stem from permanent employment; in this attitude they were often opposed strongly by the leaders of their own unions, who campaigned consistently against the system. These leaders included James Sexton and James Larkin, national officials who had worked on the docks in their early days. But if casualism was no more of a problem at Liverpool than elsewhere it was made worse by the port's greater dependence on trade and shipping than other UK ports. Trade depressions, which always hit employment in ports first before spreading out into production and manufacturing industries, affected Liverpool more sharply and deeply because of its relative lack of other industries. Even those industries that were closely associated with Liverpool, such as grain milling, sugar refining, and tobacco processing and, up to 1899, ship-building, arose from cargo trade and were therefore closely linked to its ups and downs. When Liverpool, as other ports and the rest of the economy was suffering under the 'Great' Depression, which lasted from 1873 to 1896,[5] it was by then also seriously at additional risk from the structure of its employment. This was also the case in the even 'greater' depression after 1929 which needed rearmament and a war economy to regain full employment. In the 1930s Liverpool's uniquely vulnerable position left it with an unemployment level well above the national average. Its heavy dependence on trade was revealed by the statistic that only 40 per cent of its workers, when employed, had jobs in production and manufacturing. For the country as a whole it was 60 per cent.

By 1871 fewer than 5,000 adult males worked in Liverpool's shipyards, and in 1899 the last ship went down the slipway from the last yard. The docks' and warehouses' insatiable demands for casual labour had also forced out the once established and familiar skilled craft industries in the town's streets, such as clock-making. It was easier for young men to drift down to the docks for easy money to pay for carefree ways. Towns such as Birmingham and Manchester, with their stronger manufacturing bases, offered much wider and stable prospects. Even when Manchester became a major, internal port its manufacturing sector remained important and helped the city to weather trade declines more easily, unlike Liverpool, even through as late as the 1891 census Liverpool had more metal workers than Manchester, perhaps because of the ship-repairing and boiler-making trades.

By the 1901 Census, 20,000 in Liverpool were classified as 'dock and wharf labourers'. Wage rates were also normally above those of the crafts, which encouraged some men to abandon their hard-earned skills to work on the docks. James Larkin was one of those,[6] although the skills of wheelwrights, farriers and others remained important. Liverpool's pay rates – for those in work – attracted labour from the towns and villages of Liverpool's hinterland, mainly Lancashire, Cheshire and North Wales, but also further afield, including emigrants from Ireland desperate for anything to keep body and soul together. Liverpool gained a reputation for readily available work and good pay with little skill required. It was a false prospectus, as newcomers soon learned. *Rates* were very different to *earnings*, since work was mostly only available on average for three days per week, with little more even in good times. Much of the work, which required strength, agility and stamina, was also often skilled in the sense of having been acquired from experience. Those without such experience or know-how, such as most newcomers, had fewer opportunities for regular work and at lower levels of pay. Newcomers also had to bear the hostility of those who believed that priority should be given to 'Liverpool men', especially if they did not join the union. Sectarianism also played a part. It was a disadvantage to be a Protestant in the North End Docks, which were largely dominated by Irish Catholics workers. In the South End, where Protestants were more numerous, it did not help to be a Catholic. Jack Jones, who worked in the South End Docks, found that it hindered his early political ambitions.[7]

The impact of casualism

Casualism arose out of, and was maintained by, the fluctuations in trade of a large port, over-dependent upon the volume of ships coming into the docks. Fluctuations were both seasonal and cyclical and at all times dependent upon favourable weather and tides. None of these factors was in the control of shipowners and crews, although, as the docks were extended, enclosed quays did offer safer berths. The tides and weather, too, became less disruptive with the introduction of steam-driven tugs to get sailing ships safely to and from their berths.

The outcome for workers was that employers routinely sought to maintain excess supply so that variations in demand could always be met. Labour could then be hired on a casual, day-to-day basis except for a regular core of experienced men who would mostly, though not always, have work. Some companies, such as Cunard and White Star, retained a complement of genuinely permanent employees. But these firms were exceptional. The usual excess of supply over demand, even when the port was very busy, was further augmented by men from outside Liverpool looking for work, as well as those drawn from other occupations. There would also be a few seamen seeking some ready cash between ships. The excess, and the long tail of 'casual casuals' also suited employers perfectly. It helped to keep a cap on wages, and made it difficult for unions on the waterfront to organise and maintain solidarity. Nor did cheap, readily available labour encourage employers to install labour-saving machinery, except, eventually, for bulk cargoes such as grain. Until modern times porters used little more than handcarts and trolleys, complemented by strong arms and strong backs, to move cargo from quayside to shed and shed to quayside.

Photographs and personal accounts from around the country portray vividly the back-breaking work that was involved. They show men loading Welsh slate at Caernarfon's busy little dock, as well as London's 'deal porters' man-handling timber from cargo ships: 'The shoulder of an experienced deal porter is said to develop a callosity which enables it to bear the weight and friction of a load of planks. But even with a hardened shoulder the deal porter has an unenviable task. To carry over a shaking slippery plankway a bundle of shaking slippery planks, when a fall would almost certainly mean serious injury, is work for specialists.' Competition for jobs also encouraged petty jealousies and sectionalism, even violence, among the men, undermining solidarity and unionisation. It also led, inevitably, to bribery and corruption.

Reformers, union activists and a few enlightened employers recognised the manifest evils of casualism, but many were resigned to what they saw as its inevitability because of the natural fluctuations of wind, weather, season and trade. Dockers, too, could see no alternative, and many even claimed to prefer it for the freedom it gave them to decline work, with no questions asked, by the simple expedient of not turning up for the morning or afternoon 'call'. That preference was one of the many factors leading to inertia and to the acceptance of a system that led to such dire consequences for those affected by it. It was, therefore, not until 1912 – in the wake of the serious disruptions and disturbances of the transport workers' strike and the growing strength and influence of the National Union of Dock Labourers then recognised by the port employers[8] – that there was a serious attempt at reform.

Some years before that, in 1899, Eleanor Rathbone, of the old, Liverpool merchant family, known for their liberal values and philanthropy as much as their wealth, had turned her detailed attention to the baleful effects of casualism. Charles Booth had done the same for London a year earlier. He published his first volumes of *Life and Labour in the East End of London* in the same year as the great strike of 1889. These initiatives fully alerted middle-class, liberal consciences to the desperate lives of dockers and their families, although the groundwork had been laid by Henry Mayhew forty years earlier.[9] William Rathbone, Eleanor's father, looking for practical solutions proposed, for Liverpool, a pool of registered dockers seeking work. The employers would not accept such limits on their convenient over-supply, while the dockers feared it could restrict their job opportunities. William died before he could press the case for reform further, but he had already asked his very able daughter for help.[10] The outcome was the publication, in 1904, of a painstaking, ultimately devastating report.[11] She estimated that of the 20,000 seeking work on the docks, on average they only found it for three days in the week. This average also concealed wide variations, with a corresponding impact on earnings. She revealed the case of a porter who, in 1899, over an eight-week span, received a weekly income as follows: 22s. 8d., 40s. 4d., 28s. 0d., 22s. 2d., 9s. 8d., 17s. 0d., 13s. 8d. and 29s. 11d.[12] Since it was customary for a man to keep a fixed sum for himself, his wife and family would bear the full impact of his fluctuating earnings. His own life, too, would suffer, alternating idleness with bouts of often intense, hard work would not encourage regular, sober (in both senses) habits.[13] Eleanor Rathbone was right on both counts. In 1874 in Liverpool 12,000 were arrested for drunkenness, one tenth of the number for the whole country. The town, in the same year, had almost 2,000 public houses, as well as some 750 other premises where alcoholic drink could be purchased.[14] In 1899 in the areas around Scotland Road and Vauxhall Road – the spines of the dockland communities – there was one public house for every 156 people.[15] The pub on every corner was far from a myth, although many were little more than the size of a modern bar, with little in the way of comforts.

Eleanor pursued the case for the reform of casualism, which her father, in 1883, saw as '... not a good system for the employers and a wretched one for the men'. She said similar things to the 1910 Royal Commission on the Poor Law and even argued there that reform was not enough:

> I have been driven to the conclusion that the final remedy lies in the taking over of the whole work of loading and unloading ships in the port by the corporation or the Mersey Docks and Harbour Board or some other public body with a representative element.[16]

That proved too radical for most. Although her work led to meetings between the employers and the union, they could not agree except to keep things as they were. Then, in 1912, local Ministry of Labour officials, spurred on by the Liberal government, proposed the first reforms, drawing upon Eleanor's work. Their efforts were also helped by Liverpool's transport strike in the previous year, the most widespread, violent and bitterly fought in the port's history. By the end of the strike, though, the National Union of Dock Labourers could claim victory: thereafter the union was universally recognised by the employers.

The author of the report,[17] which was the basis of the reforms, was a senior Ministry of Labour official in the North West. His analysis included detailed statistics of excess supply, over time, confirming Eleanor Rathbone's earlier work, but also how demand could be better organised to meet it. This was the origin of the clearing house system, by which excess labour in one dock could be directed to a shortage of labour in another.[18] Yet casualism still reigned. The reforms were a long way from what was needed but were a small step in the right direction.

Meanwhile, life along dockland – too often ruled by poverty and squalor, and too often interrupted by disease and early death – continued to follow most of its old, well-worn paths.

Life along the waterfront

Casualism on the docks was not the sole cause of Liverpool's social problems and the precarious position of its working population. Dockland — the parts of Liverpool intimately connected with the work of the port — was a seven-mile long strip of land, never more than two miles wide, stretching from Garston in the south to Seaforth in the north. On the Mersey side, it followed the line of the old Overhead Railway, fondly known as the 'Dockers' Umbrella'. Up from the Pier Head, in the North End docks, it reached its widest point, stretching east beyond Scotland Road and Great Homer Street into the old 'Orange' areas around Netherfield Road and St Domingo Road. These were perhaps the principal outer limits of dockland,[19] about two miles from the docks. This was a reasonable walking distance to and from work. The 'spines' of old dockland, running from the south, were Park Road and Sefton Street, along Wapping and Strand Street, into New Quay, Bath Street, Waterloo Road and Regent Road (the 'Dock Road') and beyond to Seaforth. Other 'spines' would include the line of Paradise Street and Whitechapel splitting into Vauxhall Road and Scotland Road. Scotland Road itself divides into Kirkdale Road and Stanley Road (originally Gore Street) in its progress towards Bootle.

By the beginning of the nineteenth century Liverpool in its broad outline was already recognisable as the city of today. The Liverpool of 1831, with the adjoining parishes and townships — still then leafy, airy places to live — is illustrated in Map 6, overleaf.[20]

The old docks are now mostly deserted, many semi-derelict, and some long filled in, except for the busy tourist heartland around the Albert Dock and the docks forming the Freeport, dominated by Seaforth, some five miles to the north of the Pier Head. The streets closest to the docks largely survive, but most in name only. The courts, back-to-backs and tenements are long gone, too, and, in some cases, after several demolitions and reincarnations, there are now rows of low rise, well-kept, red-roofed villas. The old warehouses of Jesse Hartley and George Lyster are increasingly finding new, converted uses, often as expensive flats and penthouses. Many of the old pubs have disappeared, or are in an advanced state of dereliction, on the verge of demolition. A few, though, have been restored or converted into restaurants. Overall, there is plenty of space for further development.

When the port was expanding, the opposite was the case, with space close to the docks very much at a premium. With constant pressure for commercial space, there was little room for houses to accommodate those who worked on the docks who would, of necessity, need to live within an easy distance of work and the twice daily call. Besides the dockers, there were many other categories of workers, including clerks in the offices, recording, tabulating, accounting and invoicing. In numbers they were not far short of those working on the quaysides. These had more security and a steady, though small income, although their prospects were

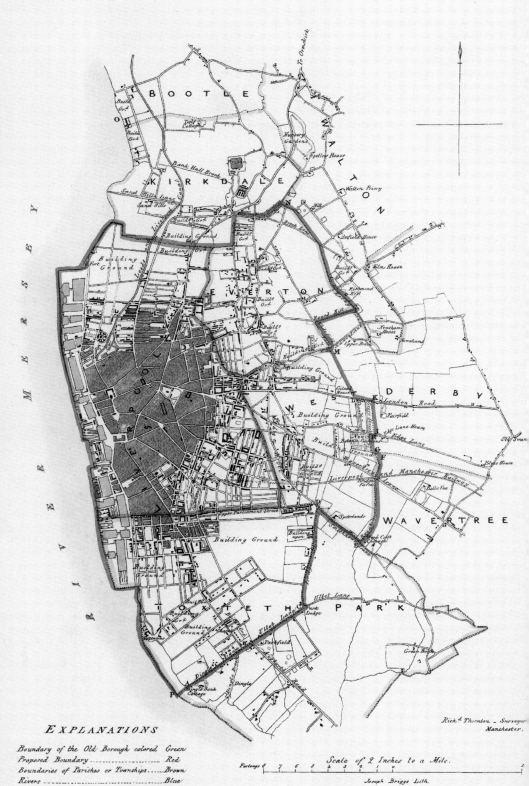

1831.

MERSEY

BOOTLE

WALTON

To Ormskirk

KIRKDALE

EVERTON

DERBY

LIVERPOOL

WEST

London Road

Liverpool and Manchester Railway

WAVERTREE

Upper Parliament Street

Building Ground

TOXTETH PARK

Ullet Lane

Dingle

River Mersey

EXPLANATIONS

Boundary of the Old Borough colored Green
Proposed Boundary -------- Red
Boundaries of Parishes or Townships ..... Brown
Rivers -------- Blue

Rich.ᵈ Thornton - Surveyor
Manchester.

Furlongs 8 7 6 5 4 3 2 1 0   1
Scale of 2 Inches to a Mile.

Joseph Briggs Lith.

Rob.ᵗ K. Dawson

actually little better than those of the dockers, even though they jealously guarded their social distance from those dirtying their hands for a living. Then there were the seamen, fast living and fast spending when on leave, but still needing somewhere to live for their often semi-destitute wives and families. Others, of all social classes, flocked into Liverpool to work and settle, including the talented risk-takers looking to make their fortunes from trade and shipping. Most of the immigrants were unskilled and poor. They came over in ever-growing numbers and mainly from Ireland. Many also came to take ship to America. Some of these stayed in Liverpool because of poor health or because they did not have enough money to pay the fares, or both. Not surprisingly, the population – both working and unemployed – grew at a rapid rate. In 1831 Liverpool's population was 165,000.[21] Between then and 1891 over 350,000 were added to the total.

As we have seen, a good number of Liverpool's immigrants were Irish. In 1851 almost 73,000 of Liverpool's residents were Irish born, that is almost one in four. The Irish settled all along the waterfront. In 1851 they were most heavily concentrated in the North End and in four wards: Scotland, Vauxhall, St Paul's and Exchange. These wards had 42,000 of the total, that is well over half. Of these Scotland Ward housed 18,000 and Vauxhall 12,000.[22]

Scotland and Vauxhall wards are bounded by Scotland Road in the east and Waterloo Road in the west, just up from Clarence Dock and Waterloo Dock. Clarence Dock was the main port of disembarkation for the Irish who fled the great famine there after 1845. Dublin Street is still there, now without residents, though then crowded and leading up from the dock on Waterloo Road into the also crowded streets, back streets, alleys and courts off Scotland Ward. In 1845, and for a hundred years, Scotland ward and its neighbour Vauxhall were bywords for deprivation, squalor, disease and early death. The condition of their lives pricked some of the consciences of the comfortable, the opulent and the wealthy in their large houses in fine streets, but most distanced themselves from the poor, both psychologically and physically. Liverpool was not alone in its long failure to share even a small part of its blessings among all its citizens. But it led the way in its special shame and special appellation as the 'Black Spot on the Mersey'.

The Black Spot on the Mersey

Casualism hung like a brooding, dark cloud over the lives of workers on the waterfront, reaching beyond work and well into their domestic and family lives. The processes of hiring were unfair, inefficient, demoralising and degrading.[23] Even those with easier access to relatively permanent jobs were sometimes

compelled, by the irregular fluctuations in available work, to take their chances on the 'stand' alongside the even less fortunate, less experienced and less favoured, the 'casual casuals' as Eleanor Rathbone and other investigators came to call them. What work was available, day to day, was rarely enough for all those seeking work and, when it was, did not guarantee regular, stable incomes for the men and their families. Young, fit, single men could cope well enough with irregular earnings: the older, married men much less so, even though all would be affected in some degree:

> All the incentives built into casual labour were bad: 'the system offered no inducement to sobriety' [As Eleanor Rathbone told the Royal Commission on the Poor Law], it discouraged enrolment in friendly societies; it aged workers prematurely; and it made boys reluctant to enter apprenticeships.[24]

All these problems would routinely be passed onto their families, especially wives:

> The hard-drinking, free-wheeling culture of the port victimised wives and children in particular, for dockers tended to give only the smallest weekly sum to their wives for household expenses 'all above this sum being spent by the husband on his pleasures' [Eleanor Rathbone again]. Burdened with children and usually unable to earn, wives were powerless to respond. They were the unseen victims of economic downturns and spousal neglect alike.[25]

Many wives did, however, work to supplement their meagre budgets. Mostly, they had no choice. They would clean the houses of the better-off, take in washing or sell cheap fruit and vegetables in the street. They would of necessity be accompanied by their children, the older girls as 'little mothers' supervising the younger children. Selling inexpensive items such as matches was also common, with children, as was straight-forward begging. The families, often large, would 'invade' Liverpool's fine shopping streets, where business and handouts were more likely, constantly being moved on by the police, mindful of the susceptibilities of the more prosperous citizens as much as the dictates of the law. Some enterprising mothers opened 'shops', usually no more than simple displays of a few goods in their front window. These would usually be casual operations, like the work of

LEFT

Map 7.   Liverpool's Dockland in the late nineteenth century. This detail of the 1891 Ordnance Survey map shows the tightly crowded streets of the Vauxhall Road area. Close inspection shows courts behind the street frontages as well as rows of terraced houses and industrial premises intermingled with residential areas. Scotland Road, runs from up the right-hand side of this section, and can be distinguished by the tramlines that ran along it.

their husbands, depending on circumstances. A few would prosper, growing into established corner shops, but always vulnerable to the irregular employment and incomes of their customers.

Credit was usually necessary but had to be carefully controlled to avoid going out of business. That could be a difficult, even heartbreaking, balancing act.[26] If shop credit was not available local money-lenders would offer small loans, even a few shillings at a time, to tide mothers over small gaps, at usurious interest rates. Shame was attached to such borrowing, although pawning, as a practice, was judged as acceptable, even semi-respectable, since it was so widespread.[27] Almost anything could be a 'pledge' for a loan, even clean washing or, most commonly, the husband's suit, pledged every Monday and 'redeemed' on a Friday for the weekend. Pawnshop windows were full of 'unredeemed pledges' for sale, including suits, but mainly jewellery such as watches and wedding rings. If all else failed, charitable relief was usually available, though under the strictest of rules and conditions. At the end of the line was the much-feared workhouse,[28] which could easily be the lot of a blameless family where the father had a disabling accident or had been killed in an accident, common enough in dock work. Some men simply walked out unable to cope. Such misfortune, without help,[29] would normally condemn a deserted wife and her children to the workhouse. Paradoxically, though

Famine and the Irish. This plaque, its inscription in Gaelic and English, is high on the still existing dockside wall of Clarence Dock. The dock was filled in in 1929 and a power station built on the site, a landmark for nearly seventy years until demolition.

PHOTOGRAPH: AUTHOR

The Perils of Immigration. This plaque is on the wall of the University of Liverpool's Music Department. Nearby is the Roman Catholic Cathedral, formerly the site of the workhouse. Poverty, destitution, disease and death were closely related, not least among Irish immigrants.

PHOTOGRAPH: AUTHOR

the workhouse brought shame and undeserved disgrace, it would have at least afforded better shelter and regular, though limited, food.

In 1844 population density in Liverpool reached 140,000 per square mile, more than that of Manchester, London or Leeds. (For purposes of comparison, Mumbai in 2010 is rated as the world's most densely populated city, at 76,793 per square mile, albeit an average over the whole city.)[30] Two years later it was being claimed that 90,000 Irish fleeing the Famine entered Liverpool in the first three months of 1846, and 300,000 in the twelve months from July 1847.[31]

The Irish had for long chosen to settle in Liverpool, since at least the fourteenth century. But the numbers now arriving alarmed the authorities, and a campaign developed to halt Irish immigration. Overcrowding along the waterfront had certainly been a serious problem for some years, but now there was a serious over-reaction. Some 20,000 special constables were sworn in, and 2,000 troops were in camp in Everton.[32] The police were ordered by the Stipendiary Magistrate, Edward Rushton, to count the number of 'poor persons' disembarking at Clarence Dock (i.e. eligible as 'paupers' for poor relief), as distinct from those coming to look for work and those seeking to emigrate. Liverpool was the main British port for emigrants, especially to the United States. The emigrants would have had some luggage, although those coming to find work would have been difficult to distinguish from paupers, who might also have been looking for work. The most careful estimates, despite their subjective source, suggest that between 1847 and 1854, the number of deck passengers, apparently paupers, entering Liverpool reached its peak in the first year (116,000) and its lowest point in 1854 at 6,679.[33] These figures would be swollen by those who were not paupers and would find work, as well as those intending to emigrate but who stayed to find work and homes. Some would perhaps have been daunted by the cost and perils of crossing the Atlantic. Even the much shorter crossing from Dublin to Liverpool, in a paddle- or screw-driven steamer, was uncomfortable, long (usually 13 hours) and potentially dangerous. By the spring of 1847 it was estimated that of those making the crossing since 1846, 105,000 stayed to live in the town,[34] if 'live' was the correct word. Many of the men, too, would be looking for work nearby, that is, at the docks. That would swell the ranks of the 'casual casuals', increasing distress and tension among the workers on the waterfront. In the neighbourhoods near the docks the existing acute problems of what we now call 'multiple deprivation' would become much worse. Before the Famine about 30,000 lived in cellars and 60,000 in 'closed courts'. The 'new citizens', totalling 105,000, would also now need to be found housing which was often even below sub-standard. Many of these would also soon be sick or dying.

A typhus epidemic in Ireland had produced convincing evidence that the disease, by 1847 universally and poignantly known in Britain as 'Irish fever'[35] was strongly associated with poverty, poor diet, damp conditions, lack of clothing and incomes below subsistence levels. These were the conditions of those, mostly Irish, inhabiting Liverpool's cellars and courts. Their unhappy lives were also the lot of many British-born inhabitants of all the other large cities in the country, although the immigrant Irish suffered the most. In June 1847, the 'Irish Fever' was showing fatalities 2,000 per cent above average. By 1849 it was joined by cholera, following a previous outbreak in 1832 as well as an influenza epidemic in 1837. Catholic priests, vulnerable from their duty of administering the sacramental last rites, also died in numbers with their parishioners. Thirteen in all succumbed to typhus, ten of these in 1847. The Reverend John Johns, a Unitarian, was the only Protestant clergyman to die. The Unitarians ran a mission in the slums: the Anglicans did not.

Smallpox, the ancient scourge, was also at large, but the unholy trinity of typhus, dysentery and diarrhoea were the main causes of death from epidemics in the peak year of 1847. These three accounted for almost 8,500, of which about 70 per cent, some 6,000, have been estimated to have been of Irish birth. Perhaps understandably, the Irish got the blame for bringing typhus to Liverpool. *The Liverpool Mercury* had no doubts, advocating their early return to Ireland, pointing to '... the filthy state in which the poor people arrive and the shocking, damp, dirty places in which they herd – as many as thirty to a cellar ...'[36] The *Liverpool Post* joined the *Mercury* in berating the *London Times* for exaggeration. The 'Old

Thunderer' had equated Liverpool's horrors in 1847 to London's Great Plague of 1665. The *Mercury* was right in terms of deaths. Liverpool's total of 8,500 for the year 1847 compares with London's 1665 rate of 7,000 *per week*. But the *Mercury's* view reflected a disturbing complacency for a wealthy mid-Victorian town with access to the considerable technological, scientific and medical advances of its time. Doctor Duncan, no stranger to the collection and deployment of statistics, nevertheless agreed with the 'city of plague' criticism, although he ascribed it, like the *Mercury*, to the immigrant Irish who 'inundated the lower districts'.[37] The *Liverpool Albion*, another local organ, perhaps put the finger on the real pulse of those 'new men' with the 'new wealth' in an era when spectacular rises to great wealth could be followed by equally spectacular falls into bankruptcy, poverty and the workhouse. The *Albion*, in maintaining that Liverpool remained 'exceedingly healthy' continued to 'welcome distant friends ... on business or pleasure'.[38]

There was undoubtedly considerable prejudice against the Irish, but if Liverpool's elite, the moneyed classes and their influential friends, had gone down into the courts, cellar swellings and 'slums' along the waterfront, they would have observed that many of Liverpool's indigenous population were also living in a 'filthy state' in 'shocking, damp, dirty places'. And they had been living like that for a long time,[39] well before the Irish landed in such large numbers. The condition of their lives had for long corroded the boasts of those claiming to have built the 'Second Port of Empire'. Nor did they note the contributions of the generations of those who built and worked the docks and the sailors who crewed the ships. Yet the evidence of how people lived along the waterfront was beginning to accumulate and to be written down and publicised, even before the 1830s when Dr Duncan was active, and almost twenty years before his pioneering appointment. He also made sure that his evidence reached those with power and influence, at first locally, and later nationally to the members of many investigations, commissions and parliamentary committees.

Duncan's Liverpool

William Henry Duncan, though born in Seel Street (Pat O'Mara's slum of a century later), in 1805, was a graduate of Edinburgh University's celebrated School of Medicine. The reputation of that august institution took a temporary nosedive in the late 1820s when it was revealed that its Dr Robert Knox was making his important advances in surgery aided by the regular supply of still-warm corpses of victims murdered by the infamous Irish immigrants William Burke and William Hare. Duncan would have been at Knox's anatomy lessons as a student, a coincidence of time and events that would later be used in Liverpool by angry, mobbing crowds alleging that the doctors had fabricated the extent of disease for gain and imagining a link between Edinburgh University's macabre surgical history and Liverpool's medical practitioners – especially their very own Dr Duncan,[40] who was now practising in the fashionable Rodney Street, on

Liverpool's high ground well away from the slums of the waterfront. They had yet to learn of the mettle of the doctor.

When Duncan returned to Liverpool, in 1829, he combined ministering to the needs of the wealthy with caring for the destitute sick. Liverpool then had just two dispensaries (in the north and south) for the medical needs of the poor, financed by charity and the parish. Their funds always fell well short for even the most basic needs of the people who flocked to their doors, especially during the epidemic years. Duncan was honorary physician to the two dispensaries, serving the northern and southern ends of dockland, although he spent most of his time in Vauxhall, in the north. Vauxhall ward and its neighbour Scotland ward were the two town wards where the Irish immigrants mostly came to live. Vauxhall ward was where Duncan's hands-on education into the lives (and often early deaths) of many of Liverpool's poor began, most tellingly in the first wave of cholera in 1832. In that year a ship tying up at Clarence Dock recorded 83 deaths at sea out of a crew and passenger list of 349. Ashore there were many more.

Duncan recorded his experience, mainly from visiting the homes of the sick, in the *Medical Gazette* of 1833. He personally attended 216 cases of cholera, of which 56 were to die. In analysing the statistics he found a clear difference between those living in houses and those in cellars, courts and lodging-houses. In the houses one seventh of all cases died; in the other 'dwellings' the proportion was a quarter.[41] His local reputation as a caring, energetic physician to the poor and his ability to draw lessons from his experience were quickly established. Within a few years he would go national.

Vauxhall's living conditions were now attracting attention from the influential. One of these was John Finch. Finch, a self-made merchant, had wide interests and active, Owenite views. He founded the Liverpool Cooperative Society and was involved in the formation of an early dockside trade union, the Liverpool Dock Labourers' Society. Though both soon foundered, he remained active working with the Unitarians, who were making a mark in the work of caring for the poor, as well as in the emerging temperance movement. His Christian, Utopian Socialism had little lasting impact in Liverpool except for his survey of Vauxhall, which provides a detailed snapshot of the work and lives of Liverpool's poor in 1842.[42]

The dominant ethnic group in Vauxhall were, unsurprisingly, the Irish, at 45 per cent. A large number of these, though not only the Irish, lived in courts. Overall, Finch judged that 53 per cent of the living conditions of residents were 'tolerable' or 'better'. The rest, therefore approaching half, he considered to range from 'bad' to 'destitute'. Such revealing data confirmed what could readily be seen with the eyes, but when collated, publicised and enumerated would become difficult to ignore. The conditions in Vauxhall Ward were similar to those in Scotland and St Paul's as well as Exchange towards the town centre. These wards had the worst housing conditions, although they were little better than the rest along Liverpool's waterfront. Nor were the Irish always Catholic. They often lived in uneasy proximity to the Protestant Irish, both prone to frequent outbursts of sectarian violence.

Other immigrants, such as the Scots and Welsh, were usually Protestant. The Welsh were especially numerous and commonly seen to be more diligent and community-minded. Former slate quarry workers and miners, for instance, built most of the docks, and many took their skills into house-building, including the ubiquitous terraced cottage, which they built economically, quickly and mostly quite well. It is still noticeable, in Scotland ward, towards the waterfront, that many streets have Welsh place names, such as Denbigh, Cardiff and Bangor. The Welsh were also active as shopkeepers and, when on the docks, often secured the better, more responsible, regular jobs.[43] Yet most of the Liverpool working class, whatever their origins, had very difficult lives and often early deaths. The revelations of how they lived, provided by Duncan, Finch and others, were also being replicated for other towns, notably in nearby Manchester where Friedrich Engels was, in 1844–45, gathering even more explosive information. First published in Germany, Engels' work would lose some of its impact by not being published in Britain until 1892, although it did appear in the United States five years earlier.[44]

Meanwhile, Dr Duncan had delivered another statistical broadside, pointing again to Liverpool's housing deathtraps. His 1840 report to the Select Committee on the Health of Towns revealed that Liverpool had 2,400 'closed' courts, housing 86,000 people, with each court having but one privy, that is, on average, one for the use of thirty-six people. The supply of water to the privies was also limited and, in consequence, they were invariably blocked and a major health hazard in conditions where diarrhoea and dysentery were endemic. He calculated that Liverpool's population excreted 6,000 tons of solid matter per annum with a sanitation system that was totally inadequate and, for large numbers of the population, non-existent: the 38,000 who lived in cellars.

In 1842 he told the Royal Commission on the Poor Law that he doubted if there was a single court in Liverpool with an underground drain so that 'emanations from this pestilential surface'[45] were liable to lead to fever. Life expectancy at birth in Liverpool at that time was fifteen years. He might have added that life expectancy had been much higher in the Liverpool of two hundred years earlier.[46]

Duncan returned to housing, with more alarming details, in 1844 and 1845, with two reports to the Inquiry into the State of Large Towns and Populous Districts. One-third of Liverpool's working class then lived in courts, with a further one-eighth in cellars. Houses were healthier places to live, as John Finch demonstrated, but the 32,000 in them were living in heavily overcrowded homes, with an average of seven in each, with the usual two bedrooms between them. Some would have many more living together, with further consequences for the already high levels of infant mortality. In Liverpool in the 1840s 53 per cent of children failed to reach five years of age. Only four of Liverpool's twenty miles of streets had sewers. Every year 1 in 400 died of fever: in the courts it was as bad as 1 in 30.[47]

Cellar and court living was undoubtedly the greatest hazard to the health and survival of Liverpool's rapidly growing population. Dr Duncan's hair-raising statistics made it plain that, while the ferocious waves of epidemics that hit Liverpool in the 1830s and 1850s arose from the coming together of a deadly, cocktail of factors, housing was at the root of the evil, especially for those condemned to eke out their precarious lives in cellars and courts.

Liverpool did not finally have clean piped water to meet its needs until as late as 1857, two years before Glasgow. Before then people living in cellars, particularly, were routinely using water that had accumulated in pits '... in which have been thrown dead dogs and cats and a great many offensive articles ... for culinary purposes'.[48] That report, for the year 1836, came from the area between Scotland Road and the Mersey, a large part of dockland and where most of the Liverpool Irish lived and worked, and just four years before the first wave of cholera had hit Liverpool.

Those who survived the regular visitation of cholera, dysentery and diarrhoea still had to contend with malnutrition or periods of near-starvation. Even in better times — a relative concept — food would for many be inadequate and of poor quality. That was partly explained by casualism on the waterfront with its inadequate, irregular earnings. Many contemporaries moralised about personal failings among the poor themselves. They blamed the Irish, in particular, for their supposed fecklessness, poor household management and improvidence. Even their own Catholic priests (many of whom were actually English rather than Irish), often supported this view. Others, however, disagreed, including those whose judgements were based on some experience. Although heavy drinking and drunkenness were singled out, one large employer of Irish building workers, over many years, explained that drinking arose from their kindness and hospitality towards each other.[49] Overall, it remains difficult to see how the supposed character traits necessary for survival and progress could survive the severest levels of multiple deprivation visited upon all those living in Liverpool's slums up to comparatively recent times. This was especially the case for those families trying to survive upon the irregular, low take-home pay of the waterfront. The moralising judgements of the middle classes — even those heavily involved in charitable and reforming work for the poor — were formed from the vantage point of comfortable, stable, sober, clean, respectable lives. There was a gap in comprehension here that few could bridge.[50]

Incomprehension through lack of direct experience did not necessarily inhibit action. Voluntary philanthropy had existed in Liverpool in the eighteenth century, and had grown rapidly since then. By the middle of the nineteenth century, spurred on by the rapidly worsening conditions in which most people lived, and their association with epidemics and premature death, philanthropy expressed itself in a 'torrent of charity'. Families such as the Rathbones had been heavily involved in charitable work through several generations, culminating in Eleanor Rathbone developing her concerns and activism in Liverpool and then taking to the national stage as a Liberal Member of Parliament. Earlier, Elizabeth Rathbone had helped the celebrated Kitty Wilkinson, the wife of a porter in the family's warehouse, to found the first public baths and washhouse. Even earlier, in 1788, the fourth William Rathbone had been one of the founding members of the Liverpool Committee of the Society for the Abolition of the Slave Trade, an initiative that earned him the deep hostility of the slaving fraternity.

Such practical, hands-on philanthropy of the eighteenth and early nineteenth centuries began to be supplemented or supplanted by the efforts of those who were as much or even more concerned with the morality and faith of the poor than the mere health of their bodies. Redemption of the soul was seen as the starting point, the *sine qua non*, of salvation. Moral regeneration and encouraging self-help were seen as the best ways to limit or even bring an end to poverty. Others, notably the Unitarians, saw it from the opposite angle. For them the leading light was Reverend John Johns who, as well as charitable efforts in the slums (which caused his early death from cholera), pressed for the closing of the court dwellings and even the provision of universal education by the state.[51] That was much too radical for most. There were even those, as the epidemics of the 1830s and 1840s lost their fearful potency, who looked on charity as a fashionable way of passing the time or the means of penetrating the higher echelons of society.

By the 1860s charitable relief had lost its way, becoming indiscriminate and disorganised. Another William Rathbone (the sixth) used his influence and prestige to press the case for organised charity. But even before he was elected to Parliament in 1868, other preoccupations led him to withdraw from the practicalities of organisation. That was left to others in the form of the founding, in 1863, of the Liverpool Central Relief Society (CRS), bringing together three separate societies. The CRS arrived '... to assist families in times of crisis while also inculcating those habits of thrift that would keep them independent of such aid in the future'.[52] In principle that meant avoiding the situation where assistance itself turned them into paupers. In practice, it meant distinguishing between the 'deserving' and 'undeserving' poor, in effect little different from the principles of the 1834 Poor Law. Organised charity was clearly not everything, and the principles of the CRS and charity as a whole were being seen as wanting well before the end of the century. The problem was that poverty was not responding at all quickly to the ministrations of the dispensers of charity. By 1902 the Toxteth Committee of the CRS was reporting that:

> The drink question, the labour question and the housing question seem to stand in the way of all attempts to deal effectively with distress ... In many cases the relief given serves only to tide the applicant over some temporary distress which may, and probably will recur.[53]

Different problems were tackled by different means. Eleanor Rathbone and her associate Florence Melly (another old Liverpool family) were prominent members of the Toxteth Committee, and the report suggests their stamp, especially that of Eleanor who was already heavily involved in attempts to resolve the 'labour problem' – casualism. The 'drink problem' was just as difficult to tackle, though the temperance movement was more associated with encouraging moderating drinking than eliminating it. The two were also related, although the campaign against excessive drinking had to be left to the temperance societies. Casualism, in contrast, was to receive official attention eventually from the Ministry of Labour, though it would be generations before regular employment became a real feature on the waterfront. Housing, by contrast, became a concern of the municipal authorities and was a major priority between the two world wars and after. By then the central government had become the most important player and from 'the cradle to the grave'. William Beveridge and his contemporaries at Balliol when Eleanor Rathbone was getting into her stride on the labour question, were being encouraged by the College's Master, Edward Caird, 'to go and discover why, with so much wealth in Britain, there continues to be so much poverty and how poverty can be cured.'[54] These questions remain largely unanswered even in our own times.

The curing of poverty was not within the scope or even the will of organised charity. This still had a role, but increasingly no more than gap-filling, for specific purposes, or for the practical expression of a wealthy and energetic individual's particular charitable concerns.[55] Meanwhile, official collective energies and initiatives had been released by the Municipal Corporations Act of 1835. Liverpool was among the first to make its mark in beginning to provide the basic building blocks of civilised life in council housing, sanitation and clean, available water. Later it would add education to its portfolio, but it would have to return to housing again and again during the whole of the next century.

The 'holy trinity': housing, sewers, water

The Municipal Corporations Act of 1835 was the first stage in the founding of genuine, effective local government following the Great Reform Act of three years earlier. It was to prove to be the democratic catalyst towards making Britain's Victorian cities healthier and safer places in which to live. But institutional changes themselves did nothing to alleviate poverty. For that the poor would have to wait much longer and, for some, it would never come at all. For the urban poor, simple survival was the first imperative. And their poverty made a great difference to their health. First, food would mostly be insufficient and of poor quality. Second, they were often unable to pay doctors for their services. And third, above all, they were usually unable to afford the rents for decent houses that were well ventilated, dry, clean places to live, with easy access to adequate sanitation and clean running water. Not that such accommodation was even been available, at affordable rents, at a time when Liverpool was wholly unable to cope with the rapid, natural growth in its population, let alone the large extra numbers crowding into its streets from the surrounding towns and countryside and from Ireland. Land was also scarce, and housing had to compete with other uses. Soon the railway companies would be buying up land and demolishing buildings, and limiting even more the space available for housing.

The Irish suffered the most, many forced to lived in the worst accommodation. Cellar living was the greatest hazard to health and survival. The courts were a close second. In 1789/90 it was estimated that 6,780 were living in cellars. In 1836 that number was at least 31,000. In 1840 it had grown to about 38,000, with another 86,000 in courts. The cellars were built under street houses. They were usually one-room dwellings measuring around ten by twelve feet with headroom of no more than six feet and with one window at street level. A cellar would have no ventilation, an earth floor, and would be infested with rats, mice and other dangerous, often lethal, vermin. There could be as many as four to five beds in a cellar, sleeping up to twenty and without sanitation.

In terms of squalor, the inaptly named 'court' was only barely better than the cellar. It was a grotesque, partial solution to dockland's space problem. A clergyman, preaching in Liverpool in 1845, told his audience:

> It is not that there are more courts in Liverpool than in other towns ... but so freely has human life been sacrificed here, rather than that land be sacrificed ... that the average size of a court in Birmingham is twelve times the average size of a court in Liverpool; whilst in Birmingham no such thing could be discovered as a human being living in a cellar.[56]

The courts were narrow alleys, up to fifteen feet wide, with as many as nine three-storey houses on each side, severely limiting light into their windows. At the end of the court there was commonly a wall forming the backs of more courts or houses, producing what was termed a 'closed' court. Here one or two privies, usually overflowing, and an ashpit would be available for the use of all the court dwellers which would also often be used by those in the street beyond the court opening. The courts would also have one, sometimes two, standpipes for filling buckets and other containers, but rationed by limited turning-on times for short periods in the day or during the night or early morning.[57]

These were the conditions in which many Liverpool people lived. They had no alternative, and the courts even lingered on into the next century. The plans of many can be seen on the large-scale Ordnance Survey maps of the early twentieth century. By then the better off did have an alternative, and were increasingly moving away from dockland into the outer streets and suburbs, a safe distance from the poor and with the benefits of sewers and clean water.

The efforts of Dr Duncan and others eventually began to make their presence felt. They were helped by the national publicity given to Liverpool's catastrophic death rates and its recurring cholera, fever and other epidemics, generally, well ahead of its many rivals in Victorian Britain's own race to the bottom. Ramsay Muir tells us that Dr Duncan '... drew such a picture of squalor, disease, misery and vice as no city could endure to appropriate to itself ...' [58] that it aroused the Town Council to unprecedented action. This came by way of two major steps.

First, it promoted two private Building Acts, in 1842 and 1846 which, among other powers,[59] gave it the authority to construct sewers in all its streets, to inspect and condemn housing as unfit for human habitation, and to appoint an expert as Medical Officer of Health (MOH). Dr Duncan's claims to be the first MOH could not be ignored. Once appointed he moved fast. During 1847, 5,000 cellars were inspected and condemned, although most of the poor unfortunates who were turned out of them had nowhere else to go. A further Act, in 1864,

Twentieth-century poverty. A 'closed' court in George V's Liverpool. This photograph off Edwin Street dates from 1913, but fits the earlier descriptions of Liverpool's courts.

© LIVERPOOL RECORD OFFICE

A closed court off Scotland Road. This court, also photographed in 1913 in Silvester Street, where the author went to school in the 1940s, has similar 'amenities' to Edwin Street, although the residents, in both cases, reveal the same desperate poverty. Cellars are also evident. It was to be as late as the post Second World War clearances before all the courts were finally swept away.

© LIVERPOOL RECORD OFFICE

allowed the Council to alter or demolish the condemned dwellings, purchasing them from their owners. This was important in removing and replacing the very worst of the slums, although the process was not fully completed until after the Second World War.

The second major step was the provision, at last, of abundant, piped, clean water. Up until 1848 two water companies had supplied water from local wells in Bootle and Toxteth Park. But it was far from a constant supply, and was provided publicly only through standpipes. It was therefore totally inadequate for drinking, bathing, washing and cleaning. The Council bought out the two companies and replaced the water supply from the local wells with two reservoirs, constructed north of Bolton. These were piping clean water, in abundance, by 1857. So great was the demand, however, that following a long drought from 1864 to 1865 a further Act of Parliament, in 1870, allowed for the making of a great lake, in North Wales, to meet all of Liverpool's needs. Ramsay Muir, this time matching fact more closely to hyperbole, put it well: 'The making of Lake Vyrnwy is an achievement almost as great as the making of the docks, but in some ways it is a still nobler one.'[60]

The man largely responsible for the foundations of that 'still nobler' achievement was the now unsung James Newlands, Liverpool's first Borough Engineer,[61] doing for water and sanitation what Duncan had done for social medicine. As early as 1857 most houses had water, many had lavatories, and a few even had baths. The streets were increasingly being paved and cleaned, and rubbish was being cleared. New houses were coming under planning regulations as well as lodging-houses and knackers' yards. Public conveniences were being erected. Inevitably, the Liverpool Land and House Owners' Association opposed the new planning regimes and the sanitary and other regulations introduced by Newlands' colleague, Thomas Fresh, Liverpool's aptly named first Inspector of Nuisance. Their partnership was, in the end, irresistible.

By 1872, Eric Midwinter tells us of an observer's admiration for their achievements: '... the victory of the water closet is now assured'.[62] Despite this, much still needed to be done to achieve even tolerable lives for most of those living in dockland. Even thirty years after Liverpool had had the blessings of modern sanitation some were still living and dying in cellars. James Larkin, who had seen it all and lived through it, was still capable of deep shock and disgust, in the twentieth century. His words are just as powerful today.

> We went down into one of those subterranean dwellings they have in Liverpool, down below the earth ... In the corner lay the body of a dead woman and, on its dead breast, on its dead breast is the figure of a child, about two months old, sucking, trying to get the life blood out of the breast of a dead woman. And then there were two little girls, one seven years old and one of nine, and that was in the year 1902 ... in a Christian City, in a street called Christian ...[63]

CHAPTER FIVE

Working on the old waterfront

It was hard work, requiring physical strength, versatility, quickness of mind and an ability to work in concert with your workmates. The idea that dockwork is unskilled is a nonsense, although I would not go as far as Jimmy Sexton's description of a docker ...

(Jack Jones, 1986)[1]

Although he was classified merely as a casual labourer, the all-round docker of those days, knowing his business from keelson below to gantling block aloft ... required the intelligence of a Cabinet Minister – possibly not a very high standard now – the mechanical knowledge and resource of a skilled engineer and, in addition, the agility and quick-wittedness of a ring-tailed monkey.

(James Sexton, 1936)[2]

JAMES SEXTON was writing his autobiography some fifty years after he worked on the Liverpool waterfront, in the 1880s. He was describing himself. Before he was a docker he was a sailor on a square-rigged sailing ship. On the waterfront he would use the skills and experience of a seaman. Sexton had learned the seafaring trade under sail, although even in his day the steamer was already replacing the sailing ship. Jack Jones worked on the docks some fifty years later, in Garston, just beyond Liverpool's South End docks, and owned by the railways. Sail survived longer in the South End, but by the 1930s it had almost disappeared here, too. Though James Sexton became the long-serving General Secretary of the National Union of Dock Labourers, until it was absorbed as part of the Transport and General Workers' Union in 1922, his early experience was very different to that of Jones.[3] Nor was he born in Liverpool. He was from Hull and as a youth worked for Pilkington's glass works at St Helens before going to sea and then into the docks. Jack Jones was born on Merseyside itself, the son of a docker, and like Sexton, rose to the rank of General Secretary, for the much bigger, 'general' union, the TGWU.[4]

Despite their differences in experience, and being separated by half a century, which saw many changes on the waterfront, Sexton and Jones both stressed the levels and nature of the skills involved. They were far from being alone in this, and the dockers themselves resented the widespread view of their work as requiring little more than strong arms and even stronger backs. Better-informed outsiders, who even included the lofty and influential – judges, politicians, civil servants and academics – supported the dockers' view of themselves. As William Beveridge, hardly a son of toil, put it in 1930: the specialised docker was as 'irreplaceable as a patternmaker'.[5]

Dockers were not skilled in the sense of having a specialised expertise built through a long apprenticeship and hands-on experience. But many were specialised – some highly – and with great pride in their jealously guarded 'craft'. That they had to work with, and alongside, many workers without their acquired knowledge and experience led outsiders to lump them all together as 'unskilled labourers'. The stevedore, for example, was often a former seaman, as Sexton, with valuable, relevant experience, and many enjoyed a reasonably secure, comfortable family life. Yet a stevedore, outside the docks, would still have found it difficult to be recognised as a skilled worker. This perspective would have been emphasised when, as the port's trade went into one of the recurring troughs of the trade cycle, the stevedore and other specialists would occasionally have no choice but to take their chances with the less skilled at the early morning hiring stands along the Dock Road. Outside perceptions of the docker were not helped by the fast-drinking, fast-living, feckless style of life along the waterfront; some even drank when working. The pilfering of alcohol was a well-established 'perk' in the sheds and warehouses of dockland.[6] Wages in the early days were also sometimes paid by gang foremen in public houses on Saturday evenings, providing a natural temptation for human celebration at the end of a hard week's work. That not a few men lived industrious, blameless and sober family lives counted for little in the stereotype.[7] Outsiders noted, too, the large number of dockers. At the peak there was a pool of labour of around 20,000 to 25,000 looking for work, and not always finding it, most of whom lived within a two-mile wide strip extending along the river. Seeing them as the 'lumpen proletariat' was always a temptation to those who knew little of their lives.

Dock labourers, therefore, varied greatly in experience, type and skill. And to their number must be added a host of other workers along the waterfront, with many different employers, including the Dock Board. The Mersey Docks and Harbour Board was never a large-scale employer of dockers; it never had more than 700 on its books. But it did have a large complement of key workers, such as engineers, maintenance workers (including their own carters carrying materials), dock gatemen, and the specialists in the graving docks. The many carters employed by the companies[8] were essential to the movement of goods, as were their successors in the cabs of lorries and as late as the 1950s horse-drawn vehicles that could still be seen on dockland streets. Railway workers moving goods' trains in and out of the docks also became an essential and familiar part of dockland, although it was not until 1896 that the board permitted railway company locomotives on its tracks, given the long history of mistrust between the board and the railway companies. Seafarers on leave were also very numerous and always making their presence felt, along with officers, engineers and many others such as firemen, trimmers, greasers and donkeymen. As passenger steamers became numerous, the port would also have to find living space for all of these, as well as ships' cooks, bakers, butchers and stewards. Another prominent occupation, as steam took over, was the coal-heaver, the famed Hercules of the waterfront, labouring to fuel ever-hungry boilers. Others working in the industry included those on the river itself, such as pilots, tug boat captains and their crews, as well as those engaged in the essential task of dredging to keep the shipping lanes open. There was also a large contingent of security employees, guarding ships and installations and discouraging pilfering along a waterfront that brimmed with valuable merchandise and food.

Yet another army, on shore, worked at desks in a wide variety of roles. Clerks were employed to handle the vast and growing volume of commercial paper. One 1870 estimate for Liverpool as a whole, covering all specialisms and grades, was 17,400, not far short of the dockers' labour force. Given the importance of the docks to the town's maritime economy, a substantial number of the clerical labour force would have been employed by the shipping companies, albeit mainly at the lower grades. Nor would their pay have been much more, if at all, than the average docker.[9] Keeping up social appearances would also have added to their living costs so that, in some cases, their lives would have been even more stretched and precarious than those of the dockers who felt they had little social status or pretension to protect.

On the waterfront

On the waterfront itself the number and range of jobs, and the variations within and between them, presented a bewildering picture to observers and outsiders and perhaps even to some insiders. Nor was there much change, through new methods and machinery, until well into the twentieth century. Manual handling was for long the docker's life, as can be seen from photographs that date from Edwardian times and later. Waterfront workers also had a wide range of employers, from the big passenger and cargo steamship companies, operating in the larger North End

docks, and the smaller companies, of sail as well as steam, in the older and smaller docks of the South End. The Garston dockers, of which Jack Jones was one, were different again. Their employer was the London and North Western Railway. The big steamship operators, such as Cunard, Inman, Elder Dempster and T&J Harrison, hired their own labour, at their own stands, as well as employing a core of permanent staff. The smaller operators, many with only one vessel, used the casual hiring stands, usually through the services of independent master stevedores and master porters who acted as agents. It has been calculated that on Liverpool's waterfront in 1914 there were 246 employers.[10]

The total number employed on the docks varied cyclically, seasonally and on a daily basis. Furthermore, over time they were subject to changes (generally slow over time), through developments in technology, notably in grain and coal handling, which affected numbers independently of the normal ups and downs in port traffic. These changes influenced the way jobs were performed, as well as creating new jobs and rendering others obsolete. The most dramatic, however, involved steam ships replacing sail. Ships soon became much bigger, as well as faster, with larger holds and steam winches. Larger ships required wider, deeper dock entrances. Steam created many more jobs on ships, mainly below deck, and the old sailors' skills were no longer required.

Table 6 The conversion from sail to steam: Great Britain, 1878–1915

| | Sailing ships | | Steamships | |
	Number	000 tons	Number	000 tons
1878	21,058	4,239	4,826	2,316
1888	15,025	3,114	6,871	4,350
1889	14,640	3,041	7,139	4,718
1890	14,181	2,936	7,410	5,043
1891	13,823	2,972	7,720	5,307
1892	13,578	3,080	7,950	5,565
1893	13,239	3,038	8,088	5,740
1894	12,943	2,987	8,263	5,969
1895	12,617	2,867	8,386	6,122
1900	10,773	2,096	9,209	7,208
1905	10,059	1,671	10,522	9,065
1910	9,090	1,113	12,000	10,443
1915	8,019	779	12,771	11,650

Source: B. R. Mitchell (1962), *Abstract of British Historical Statistics*, Cambridge: Cambridge University Press, pp. 218–19, cited in Ken Coates and Tony Topham (1994), *The Making of the Labour Movement: The Formation of the Transport and General Workers' Union, 1870–1922*, Nottingham: Spokesman, Table 5.3., p. 130.

Steam and hydraulic applications were also transforming dockside machinery. Cranes were increasing in size and capacity.[11] Dock gates, swing bridges, capstans, pumps and sluices were increasingly using hydraulic power, and small trains were being, used alongside horses and wagons, to move goods right up to the quayside. George Lyster, a well-informed though perhaps partial judge, considered Liverpool, at the end of the nineteenth century, to be ahead of London in the mechanisation of the dock estate,[12] although London was unusual in continuing until remarkably late its use of many privately owned river wharves as well as its enclosed docks, and was overall not considered to be a highly mechanised port. Yet despite these advances, physical handling remained a continuing feature of dock work, in Liverpool and elsewhere, until well into modern times. This was largely because, for employers, labour was readily available, always in surplus and therefore cheap. The men too, resisted mechanisation that destroyed their skills as well as reducing the amount of employment available.[13] Liverpool was of course not alone in all this. Chronic under-employment was a disturbing, destabilising feature of all British ports. Liverpool dockers even had an advantage. They were hired by the half day, unlike the London men who were taken on, and potentially discharged, on an hourly basis.

Liverpool, however, surprisingly differed from Birkenhead in its clear demarcation between 'shipmen' and the porters working on the quays and in the warehouses. Birkenhead, where port activities began later and with a clean slate, did not have that demarcation. Liverpool's distinction between shipmen and porters was also not very common elsewhere.[14] It was, however, not the only distinction. The overall complexity belied the simplistic use of the term 'dock labourer'. The shipman/porter distinction is useful as a first approach. Another helping to explain the complexity is to make a distinction between the individual jobs that the men did and the basis on which they were employed. If 'dock labourer' does not do justice to the variety of jobs and the skills involved, nor is the term 'casual' sufficient to describe the nature of the employment of all dockers, let alone other waterfront workers. It is true that Liverpool dockers had no guarantee of work other than the half day for which they were hired; their jobs were therefore called 'casual', that is impermanent. Though such a condition of employment was widely seen as unacceptable (though not to many of the men themselves) it was not, in practice, universal. There were many variations within the system. Although nearly all men were potentially casual, some were actually more casual than others. Furthermore, some jobs were always better paid, by custom and practice, and more often than not permanent, such as the stevedores, the most senior of the shipmen.

Two stevedores, one on the starboard side, the other on the port, supervised the loading and unloading operations of eight labourers for each hold. The stevedores were highly skilled and often former seafarers, which enhanced their knowledge, status and experience. Their responsibility was to ensure that cargo, loaded in tiers, was stowed safely and securely in order to limit movement in rolling seas

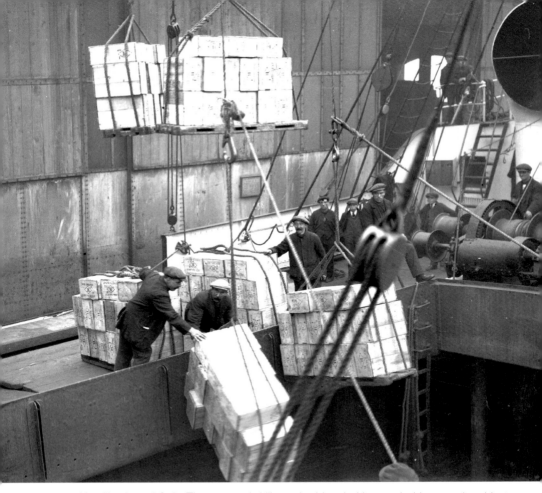

Handling boxed fruit. The care and skill required in winching a valuable cargo is evident, as is the precariousness of some of the packing and loading.

and possible fire. Badly stowed cargo could endanger both the ship and its crew. Cargo had also normally to be loaded in rotation so that different consignments could be unloaded readily at different ports.[15]

The stevedores and their gangs, working in the holds, had the services of a 'man over hatch'. It was his job to control the lowering and raising of cargo in and out of the hold, in tandem with the crane or winch driver, through a series of shouted instructions and hand and finger signals. The winches were steam-driven, another job specialism and for which boys were commonly trained, under supervision. There were also riggers, the old sailing term, who controlled derricks or set up specialist lifting tackle. The docker carrying goods on and off the quay to the side of the hatch would also need to be skilled and nimble of foot. Nor were all these jobs in any sense independent of each other. Flexibility was important, too.

Loading and unloading required the efficient, safe coordination of many roles, as Jack Jones emphasised recalling his working days at the docks. It was also inherently dangerous and, given the economics of shipping, had to be carried out at speed, especially after steamships were introduced. All of the dockers in a 'team' therefore had to look out for each other. Despite their interdependence, however, there was a long-established hierarchy of jobs, which was reflected in entrenched pay differentials. Given their special responsibilities, stevedores enjoyed a daily pay differential of two shillings over the other shipmen. They, in turn, earned 6*d*. per day more than the quay porters. These rates, over a fifty-year period to 1922, are shown in the following table:

Table 7 Basic day rates in the port of Liverpool, 1870–1922

	Stevedores	Other shipmen	Quay porters
1870	7s. 0d.	5s. 0d.	4s. 6d.
1879	6s. 6d.	4s. 6d.	4s. 0d.
1880	7s. 0d.	5s. 0d.	4s. 6d.
1915	8s. 0d.	6s. 0d.	5s. 6d.
1916	9s. 0d.	7s. 0d.	6s. 6d.
1917 (April)	10s. 0d.	8s. 0d.	7s. 6d.
1917 (Sept.)	11s. 0d.	9s. 0d.	8s. 6d.
1918 (May*)	12s. 6d.	10s. 6d.	10s. 0d.
1918 (Oct.*)	13s. 6d.	11s. 6d.	11s. 0d.
1919 (Apr.*)	14s. 2d.	12s. 2d.	11s. 8d.
1920*	Minimum daily wage 16s. 0d. (80p)		
1921*	Minimum daily wage 14s. 0d. (70p)		
1922 Mar*	Minimum daily wage 12s. 0d. (60p)		
Oct*	Minimum daily wage 11s. 0d. (55p)		

* National Wage Agreement. Hours worked were also reduced in the April 1919 national negotiations from 51 to 44 for a normal week.

Note: Prices almost trebled between 1870 and 1920 and then fell by over a fifth from 1920 to 1922 as recession began to impact on wages and prices. These fluctuations affected the purchasing power of the daily rate. For example, the quay porter's daily rate (in post-decimalisation 'new money') was 22.5p in 1870, rising to 55.8p in April 1919 and falling back to a 55p minimum rate at October 1922. The purchasing power of these day rates, in 2007 values, was £18.39, £27.00 and £21.46 respectively. However, by 1922 few men had as much as three days work per week.

Sources: Shaw Report 1920 and First Annual Report of TGWU. Cited in Taplin (1985), op. cit., p. 17.

The day rates shown here do not, of course, reveal how much a man actually earned over a week. This fluctuated, often widely, according to how many days he found work at the stand. That was rarely more than three and, for some, considerably fewer. That was also consistently the case after the post-war boom

Heavy cargoes. Tobacco handling, using an early version of a fork-lift truck, inside the Stanley Tobacco Warehouse.

subsided into depression in 1920, without any upturn into well into the next decade. Even three days at the 1922 rates was far from a living wage, although unemployment benefit between the wars did mitigate some of the consequences of little work and low pay, though its effect was limited. Furthermore, although Liverpool was primarily a day-rate port, those rates could be supplemented by a large number of extra payments for certain kinds of work (for example, weighing by quay porters or 'trimming' by shipmen for certain cargoes such as bulk copra and flour). Overtime could also be available in the evenings, and on weekends or public holidays, at enhanced rates of pay. Piece rates were also paid (usually per ton) for heavy or dirty cargoes such as rock salt or metal ores. The grain bushellers (discussed later) combined both types: a day rate plus a supplement per 100 sacks. However, the common feature of all work was variability, which could sometimes be quite extreme. Heavy traffic in the port would mean long working weeks at a fast pace.[16] That could then be followed by much less work or a period of idleness. This could and did undermine steady wages and steady lives, although for some it had its attractions.

Despite the large number of available premiums, special payments and supplements, the differential between the shipmen and quay porters remained a constant feature of earnings and take-home pay. It should not, however, be assumed that the skills of the shipmen were always of a higher order than those of the quay porters. They were different, however, and it has to be conceded that working around the hatch and in the hold was more hazardous than on the quay or in the warehouse. Yet even those porters who simply trucked the goods and merchandise to and from the quays and into and out of the sheds and warehouses, or onto horse-drawn carts or lorries or railway wagons, needed special qualities. The expert handling, moving and stacking of heavy weights, over long periods, required experience, care and stamina. Others had knowledge of, and experience with, certain cargoes such as timber or bulk salt. Others, such as the coal-heavers, had to have exceptional strength. It was also widely believed that a man would be worn out by the job after five years. Even when coaling became mechanised, some was still done on the river, these men scrambling up nets on the ship's side carrying heavy baskets of bunker coal on their backs from the Mersey 'flats' (barges) moored alongside. 'To be built like a coal-heaver,' was a common expression in Liverpool well beyond the disappearance of such titans of the Dock Road.

The handling of heavy cargoes such as tobacco, timber, grain, sugar and salt required expertise as well as strength. Tobacco had its special, bonded storage arrangements. Timber also had its own special quays and handling equipment at Brunswick Dock and, later, Huskisson and Canada Docks. Grain handling required the skills of 'bushellers', who filled and stitched the sacks. Large-scale technology, the grain elevator or 'devil' (because it destroyed jobs?), eventually despatched those skills,[17] although it took some time before mechanisation of grain handling became universal. Cotton, a big money-spinner for the port over two centuries, employed its own specialised porters along the waterfront, skilled in

Special skills. Loading and unloading a steam locomotive was not work for novices.
© LIVERPOOL MARITIME MUSEUM

handling the giant bales. Other porters worked exclusively for the coastal trade in the smaller docks in the South End, including the Albert Dock, which handled the sailing ships and smaller steamers. Another specialism was fruit. The fruit porter was exceptionally knowledgeable and skilled, working directly for a merchant. He had the responsibility of dealing with highly perishable, valuable and variable cargo. He would sort the fruit, classify and weigh it and then carefully warehouse it for the attentions of the merchant and his representatives. Some fruit arrived already boxed and required special expertise in loading and unloading.

In describing how men were employed it is useful to classify dock labour under four headings. First, there were these who, as indispensable specialists, worked regularly or even permanently for shipping companies and merchants. The bigger companies would have the use of permanently allocated berths and their own warehouses or multi-storey sheds, giving those they employed a settled location as well as permanent employment. The stevedores, among the shipmen, would be at the apex of the specialists and treated as such. On the quaysides, the fruit porter would have been a job of the same order. Though nominally casual, they were *de facto* permanent employees.[18] The greater security of such work, and the usual pride in their skills, often saw them living in better homes, with better lives than those below them in the occupational hierarchy. The foreman, who would hire his gang at the morning or afternoon call would also supervise them at work. He was as important as the stevedore, on the quay or in the warehouse, in getting the work done effectively and at speed. He would also normally be employed by a single company, on a regular wage. James Larkin was one of these, a valued foreman for T. & J. Harrison before becoming a union activist. Harrison's clearly saw his potential and promoted him from the ranks.

Those ranks included the second category who could, in normal times, expect regular work on a daily basis and, in time, might advance to more secure, specialist jobs or gain promotion, as had James Larkin. They would often work together, in the same gangs, well known to their foremen who would give them preference at their regular stand, as experienced, skilled and reliable workers. Nor would youth and strength always be a crucial criterion, except for the heaviest of work such as coal heaving or bulk grain handling. There were many jobs that required no physical strength at all, such as the men who checked, weighed and listed consignments. Their work would require a good level of numeracy and literacy, achievements commonly denied to men (and women) in the harsh, limited period of their childhood schooling in Victorian and Edwardian Britain. As to age, the prime age of a docker and his ability to find work was more likely to be the ten years from forty-five to fifty-five, when experience and 'knack', especially in lifting heavy weights, and the capacity to work steadily for long periods, often came together.[19] That is not to say that the composition of a gang always reflected rational considerations. Foremen would have their favourites, the 'blue eyes' as they were known.[20] Some foremen seemingly liked to work with footballers or boxers. Others, a small minority, were susceptible to bribery and corruption (of which more later). But getting the job done satisfactorily, safely and quickly were the main priorities of most foremen. James Larkin was, however, undoubtedly exceptional in his reputation for temperance, scrupulous honesty, reliability and fairness – as well as being popular with his gang despite pushing them hard. He was even known as 'the Rusher'.[21]

The third category of dock worker would find work more difficult to get and might often be disappointed at the morning stand. The options then were to return home or, more likely, wait to try the afternoon call. They might also be experienced men, but no competition for the 'blue eyes', and would be reluctant to move away to other, less familiar stands to try their luck. It might well also be too far to get to the next stand on time after failing to find work, since the 'call' lasted only for half an hour. Surplus labour at one stand could possibly have met shortages at others, but until the telephone appeared at the docks, there was no easy way of letting this information be known. In Liverpool's case that was not until the reforms of 1912. The reforms also introduced a surplus stand, but that innovation did not work well enough and was soon dropped.[22]

The fourth category was the most disadvantaged, Eleanor Rathbone's 'casual casuals'. They would have difficulty in finding any regular work, except in periods of rapidly increasing trade. With a surplus of labour on the docks, even one or two days per week would have been difficult, even in better times. Those times were rare. The Great Depression lasted some thirty years, to be followed by a second of even greater depth only thirty years later. Minimal work suited some, such as those who were still young and reasonably carefree or those inadequate or scarcely fit for work who drifted down to the docks to earn some money on an occasional basis. These true casuals would not be fit and strong enough to sustain a long, hard day and might well be satisfied with a morning or an afternoon. Their numbers would add to, or maintain, the surplus on any given stand and so would tend to keep wages down. In fact, as we have seen, basic day rates in Liverpool did not increase from 1870 until 1915 when the country was at war and dock labour became scarce.[23] Trade was depressed from 1873 until 1896, but there were strikes in 1879 and 1890 and a much wider conflict involving all transport workers in 1911. Prices

Loading cotton bales onto railway wagons. The porters have large trolleys to take the heavy bales. There is a crane to lift the bales, but the extent of manual work is still evident in photographs such as this.

The foreman and his gang. Note the distinguishing headwear.

mercifully falling, but not as fast as wages, fuelled the discontent. Liverpool was, of course, not alone. In the years prior to 1914 across the country the number of strikes and the total number of those involved reached unprecedented levels as unionisation moved into a major phase of growth.[24]

Wage rates on the Liverpool waterfront were, however, widely considered to be better than in other occupations both in and outside Liverpool. That was one of the reasons which made the port a 'beacon light'[25] for those from elsewhere seeking regular employment. That high daily rates were not translated into good weekly earnings over six days was not apparent until the newcomers had sought work at the stands; but many stayed even though they did not get work on some days. Their numbers swelled the usual surplus of labour. That surplus grew even more during the winter months, when unemployed builders and others came to the docks in large numbers looking for work. Even those employers with their own permanent labour force helped to maintain the surplus.[26] Overall, for whatever number of reasons, it has been estimated that Liverpool's supply of dock labour doubled (from 12,000 to 24,000) between 1861 and 1869. That figure was maintained even when trade was brisk there were no more than 13,000 regularly employed.[27] Nor were basic rates in Liverpool at all a 'beacon light' in 1914, even if they had been fifty years earlier, especially in relation to many other British ports, large and small. The Shaw Enquiry of 1919, using 1914 as its comparison year, revealed that Liverpool's highest basic day rate (for stevedores), at 7s., was below the highest at Port Talbot (8s.), West Hartlepool (7s. 11d.) and London (7s. 6d.). Four ports also equalled that of Liverpool: Plymouth, Bristol, Gloucester and Swansea.[28] But Shaw carried far more weight than the revealing of statistics. It was an early milestone in the reform of the management of labour on the docks, and propelled Ernest Bevin to national fame as the 'Dockers QC'. Sexton also played his part for the NUDL, his early experience as a Liverpool docker complementing that of Bevin, in Bristol, as a carter. The Shaw Report and its influence is discussed below in Chapter 8.

A second inquiry, conducted by the Ministry of Labour, and reporting almost at the same time as that of Shaw, was into boy labour on the Liverpool docks. Boys had always been employed in ship repairing and on the quayside. Their employment increased during the Great War to fill the serious gaps in adult labour but, by the end of hostilities, the terms and conditions of their employment were attracting official concern. For dock work the boys, who were usually the sons of dockers, could be taken on until they were sixteen, although if they looked old enough no further questions were asked — as was the case with recruitment into the armed forces. The inquiry took a strong line against young people, so soon after leaving school, becoming '... subject to the vicious conditions of the Docks ...', although it recognised the need of their families to supplement meagre budgets. It also drew attention to the Ministry of Labour's current attempts, from 1912, to limit casualism among adult dock workers while it was fully retained for boys, who were also subjected to the usual humiliating ritual of selection at the stand. It then pointed to the likelihood that the '... power thus given to the foreman is not always wisely used, and in many cases bribes are extorted from the boys at the end of the week in order to secure an opportunity for work in the following week'.[29]

Inefficient, degrading hiring practices, even for boys — and their potential association with bribery and corruption — had for long been seemingly unavoidable features of dockside employment. The reforms of 1912, and the strictures of the Shaw Inquiry eight years later, did little to eradicate casualism not least because most of the men preferred it. In Liverpool (for several days) and in Birkenhead (for a month) the dockers even walked out when the 1912 scheme came into operation. It took a thousand strike-breakers, brought in by the employers, to defeat the Birkenhead dockers.[30]

The centrality and durability of casualism, and its damaging implications for both the men and their families, as we have seen, had for long been recognised by reformers right across the social spectrum, including some enlightened employers. Yet aside from the economic and social problems directly linked to casualism, the actual process of hiring associated with it was, in itself, both abusive and degrading.

Henry Mayhew was the first to bring it to national attention, at a time when cholera was ravaging the poor in every town and city in bustling, thriving, dirty,

Victorian Britain. In 1849 London's *Morning Chronicle* launched a national survey of the conditions in which Britain's poor lived and worked. Mayhew was the newspaper's metropolitan correspondent. With a small team, he concentrated on Bermondsey, a cholera district of London. Between October 1849 and December 1850 he published 82 letters, some of which he later incorporated into his *London Labour and the London Poor*.[31] His graphic accounts caused a sensation and even influenced the writings of prominent authors such as Charles Dickens, Charles Kingsley and Thackeray. Later, concerned scholars such as Charles Booth and Seebohm Rowntree would systematically detail the extent and impact of abject poverty, laying the first foundations towards redistributive public policy and the welfare state. But Mayhew, importantly, was the first to stir consciences, especially of the well-fed and the influential.

His third letter, on 26 October 1849, was from the docks. He interviewed dockers who had formerly been silk weavers in Spitalfields, descendants of French Huguenot refugees driven out by Louis XIV in 1685, but who had been forced to work on the docks as their trade, skills and livelihoods had been lost to mechanisation. Unemployed silk weavers were joined by many others, from master butchers to 'broken-down gentlemen', all trying their luck at the 'call'. He gives a vivid account of the workings of the hiring system in the London docks of 1849:

As the foreman calls from a book the names, some men jump upon the backs of the others, so as to lift themselves high above the rest, and attract the notice of him who hires them. All are shouting. Some cry aloud his surname, some his Christian name; others call out their own names, to remind him that they are there. Now the appeal is made in Irish blarney, now in broken English. Indeed it is a sight to sadden the most callous, to see *thousands* of men struggling for only one day's hire, the scuffle being made the fiercer by the knowledge that hundreds out of the number assembled must be left to idle the day out in want. To look into the faces of that hungry crowd is to see a sight that must ever be remembered.[32]

Understandably, perhaps, Mayhew failed to see that the hiring process had some form and organisation behind it in the foreman's preference for the men he knew to be reliable, skilled and experienced. But all had to submit to the morale-breaking ritual. At mid-century, too, Mayhew was writing in the more leisurely age of sail. The call became even more chaotic with steam, as the peaks and troughs of trade became more exaggerated and turnaround times were shortened drastically. Ben Tillett, the London dockers' leader in the seismic strike of 1889, described a typical scene of '... struggling men ... elbowing each other, using their last remnants of strength to get work for an hour or half hour for a few pence ... Coats, flesh, even ears were torn off; men were crushed to death in the struggle.'[33]

Tillett had a good way with words, but there was substance in them as well. A much later commentator on casualism and the 'free call' – as it was euphemistically termed – tells us of a saying, that a docker dared not have a name of more than four letters, for fear that the foreman would refuse to write it in his book.[34] What was also remarkable is that despite the manifest evils of the call and casualism, despite the efforts of reformers, governments and a stream of condemnatory inquiries, it survived even up to 1967. Mayhew would probably have been astonished. Writing in his fifth letter of 1849, departing temporarily from his '... vocation ... to point out the evil ... for others to discover the remedy ...', he went to the heart of the matter:

> As I said before, however, where there is irregularity of work or income, we cannot expect habits of industry or moderation to be formed ... But as long as matters are so arranged that it is possible for a confirmance of easterly winds to deprive 20,000 individuals of a living and to abstract, in three weeks, as much as £60,000 from the ordinary earnings of the class, why, just so long must the neighbourhood of the docks swarm with the vice and crime that at present infect them.[35]

The system also encouraged bribery and corruption even in the employment of boy labour, as the 1920 Inquiry in Liverpool pointed out. Union leaders less temperate, but drawing on their direct work experience, railed against it, especially James Larkin and, in his quieter way, James Sexton.

Sexton also noted the effects of the transition stage from sail to steam increasing competition and greater turnaround speed bringing with it 'get-rich-quick' types who only needed the signatures of two householders to get a licence from the Dock Board as a master stevedore or master quay porter. They were reluctant to invest in new plant and machinery since labour was so cheap and abundant. Old equipment, however, led to a higher rate of accidents when legislative protection was as yet non-existent and the union, not recognised until 1911, had few powers to force changes in conditions. Sexton also tells us that many of these employers also became involved in sick and burial societies as well as acting as undertakers, and lending money for funerals. They even extended their interests into owning jerry-built houses, built for the workers they systematically exploited and no doubt despised. One even built a dissenting chapel, buying and using reclaimed bricks from the walls of the execution yard of the demolished Kirkdale gaol. Sexton's wry comment on the extent of the power of these unscrupulous employers was well justified: 'Living or dead we were equally in their power, and what they could not get out of us whilst we breathed they tried to wring out of our corpses.'[36]

Sexton had worked as a docker and had experienced corruption from the inside, especially by foremen. Larkin, a docker to begin with, later becoming a foreman was clearly exceptional in not taking bribes or even drinking. That pointed to how widespread bribes were, handed over to foremen in pubs, accompanied by free drinks, at the end of the working week. There were also frequent disputes over the tonnages that were recorded to determine piecework earnings (the weights were recorded only by the employers). Naturally, little trust developed in these situations, the men rightly often suspecting corruption.[37] Sexton claimed to know men who always carried a bottle of whisky in their pockets to oil the foreman's temper at work and to encourage continuing preference on the stand. He even claimed that a very rare few, a disgrace to their class, who connived '... in the sacrifice of their wives in hope of getting work'.[38]

Added to the moral hazards of working as a casual labourer at the docks were the physical. It was notoriously dangerous work. Holds were deep; footholds and the rungs of ladders were often wet and slippery. Slings, ropes and chains, carrying heavy loads with men beneath, were always liable to break. Men carrying sacks that weighed two hundredweights (that is 256 lbs, or 100.6 kg) would run along swaying, narrow planks to deposit their loads. Sometimes their proudly held skill and agility would desert them. Falls, in such conditions, could be permanently disabling, fatal even. The loss of the family's breadwinner would commonly mean the workhouse for his blameless wife and children.

Mechanical equipment – though with some spectacular innovations such as electric transporter cranes, hydraulic roof cranes on two-storey sheds, grain elevators, and 100-foot floating cranes – remained generally primitive even by the beginning of the twentieth century. Most docksides had little more than the use of cranes and ships' steam winches. Dockside railways were a great advance, but there was always friction over freight charges between the big railway companies and the Dock Board, which inhibited their development. Nor did the lorry suddenly displace the horse and cart, although Liverpool did lead the field in steam and motor lorries. Nor was the coal heavier immediately made redundant by coaling technology. Poor maintenance, as Sexton claimed, also made machinery more dangerous. Out of pride, or resignation, the men rarely complained. Sexton criticised his own members for this: 'Not only do they sacrifice themselves, but the helpless ones depending upon them.'[39]

The first set of national statistics for 'Accidents at Docks, Wharves and Quays' was published by the Factories Inspectorate in 1899. For the previous year, 1898, their report told of the staggering number of 41,070 non-fatal accidents and 89 fatal. Cranes, other lifting tackle and falls accounted for almost two thirds (64) of the fatalities. The provisions of the Factories Act did not extend to vessels, and so these figures exclude accidents on ships: following predictable objections of the shipping companies, the word 'ship', which had appeared in the Bill, was excluded from the final Act. The exclusion even applied to barges and ships in mid-stream. Although that exclusion was later removed, it was as late as 1908 before comprehensive dockside safety regulations were implemented fully. But the numbers of safety inspectors with adequate knowledge of dockwork was always limited. It is an old story, which survives into our own time, both on and beyond the waterfront.

Sexton was the most important figure in achieving the early advances in safety regulations, although his members were not appreciative of his efforts. Speed in completing a job, and pride, often meant cutting corners on safety. Complainers also attracted hostility from foremen and men. Even James Larkin, in his days as foreman, was known as 'The Rusher', which suggests an overriding concern for getting a job done quickly. This might also have reflected employers' objections to go-slow tactics, commonly known as 'ca-canny'. Sexton was prominent in encouraging the reporting of infringements of the safety rules. There was little response. Such 'complaining' would have been unpopular, attracting contempt and derision.[40] Compensation claims were also rare. The men would have been afraid to attend hearings, even in support of their colleagues, for fear of losing their jobs as 'troublemakers'. Sexton, who claimed as a docker always to speak up against injustice, came to be labelled by employers as an 'agitator', which limited his work opportunities. He was even seriously injured himself as a young man working on the docks, causing permanent facial disfigurement. Compensation law was also easily turned against injured workers by clever lawyers who were retained by employers. In 1890 total compensation on the Liverpool docks, under the Employers' Liability Act of 1880, amounted to £8,379. The average payment was £41. The 1897 Workmen's Compensation Act allowed for a maximum payment on death of £300. Achieving the maximum was rare and required prolonged litigation. Union membership and access to its lawyers and funds were essential; but even that did not guarantee success. The complainant was required to prove that neither he, nor his workmates, were negligent.[41] That was far from easy, even with a strong case, for a poorly educated working man in the witness box, facing a clever, articulate lawyer with the employer's money swelling his bank account.

By the beginning of the twentieth century conditions for the thousands living and working in Liverpool's dockland had improved from fifty years earlier. But that was not saying much, given how bad their often short lives were in those dark, well-remembered days. For the men (and boys) going down to the docks, their working lives had scarcely improved at all over those years. By 1890, their union was fairly well organised, but by then the employers had also organised themselves and did not concede much. During the 1879 strike, the newly founded Liverpool Employers' Labour Association went into early action to bring in strike-breakers using the tried and tested technique of billeting them in a ship anchored in the Mersey. It would be thirty-two years, 1911, before the ELA was forced to recognise the National Union of Dock Labourers, the 'Liverpool Union'. Even then recognition was conceded only after the most bitter, and certainly the most widespread and violent, strike in Liverpool's long history. The dockers also needed the help of some 50,000 other workers, from the seamen, who began it, to the tramwaymen, who gained little from it.

That struggle would go down as a hard-earned, literally bloody, victory, at least for the dockers who, eleven years later, would become part of a powerful, national organisation with other transport workers, the Transport and General

Workers' Union, led by Ernest Bevin. But that could not happen on the Liverpool waterfront until the men had put aside their differences. They would have to fight the employers in 1879 and 1890, and then again in 1911, to achieve that preliminary goal.

These are the stories of the next two chapters. The dockers' success, especially after 1911, would help pave the way towards the first steps in improving their working lives. That process began in 1912 (even though they opposed it), just a year after the end of the strike and only two years before the onset of the Great War. That human abomination would, as all wars, also play its part in accelerating change. But few major improvements in working lives come about by chance events. Even good laws are rarely inspired by the altruism of legislators and governments. Real advances are borne out of the determination, and suffering, of the workers themselves, men and women, and their families. That lesson was always present along the waterfront. It was confirmed by the events of 1879, 1890 and 1911.

CHAPTER SIX

'All men being brothers ...' [1]

The general conditions at the docks – the bullying, corrupt foremen, the faulty equipment, the long hours and the overall degradation of dock work, together with the searing experience of his near fatal accident, caused incidentally by an incompetent winchman and dangerous machinery – transformed him into an agitator ... when the NUDL was formed he joined the local branch in Bootle and was involved in the 1890 strike.

(Eric Taplin, 1985) [2]

To put it bluntly, things in the Union were in a most unholy mess, and I and my reforming colleagues quickly discovered that our big fight was to be with the chaotic discipline, the ignorance and petty jealousies within our own ranks, rather than with the employers.

(James Sexton, 1936) [3]

J AMES SEXTON's accident involved a crushed cheekbone, a dislodged eye and fractured skull; he was then left for two hours in a shed before being taken to hospital. He barely survived, and was disfigured for life. He was 36 and just married. When he eventually returned to work he was denied compensation and, though put on light work, he only received boy's pay, which was little more than half of what his pay, as a shipman, had been before his accident. There was also a special 2s. 6d. deduction from his first week's pay: the cost of the taxi that had taken him to hospital. Not surprisingly, he became an 'agitator'.[4] More surprisingly, perhaps, he did not become a 'revolutionary'. Many did, in those times, and for much less. In time, too, his 'agitation' turned to looking for settlements and agreements, with employers, where possible without conflict, which advanced the interests of his members. But his own 'searing experience' and disfigurement kept some of his old militancy alive in one important respect. As General Secretary he worked hard towards making the docks safer and achieving some improvement in the levels of compensation. In that he was bitterly critical of his own members over their fatalistic acceptance of the hazards of their working lives.

Sexton's formative experiences were matched by those of James Larkin a generation later. His attitudes and tactical approach were strongly militant, even to recklessness. Larkin, unlike Sexton, also became a 'boss', a foreman on the docks. But surprisingly that did not inhibit his development, in contrast to the moderate Sexton, into a radical firebrand. For a time they worked well enough together in the NUDL, but their ideologies and temperaments eventually led to a clash. One of them had to go, and it had to be Larkin. He had, in any case, moved on to a wider stage, initially in Ireland. By then the NUDL, though not without continuing difficulty, had become a force to be reckoned with on the old waterfront. Later Sexton also moved on. He always had political ambitions, first as a Liverpool councillor, and then in 1918 as an MP, although he still retained his union post. Four years later the NUDL was absorbed into the new TGWU, led by a former Bristol carter, the charismatic Ernest Bevin.

Despite gains in membership, unionisation was actually quite slow to gain ground among the workers of the waterfront. Its sickly origins and erratic development in Liverpool were largely explained by the baleful effects of casualism, sectionalism and sectarianism. Sexton himself complained of and suffered from sectionalism, his own 'enemy within'. In fact sectionalism never did disappear entirely from the Liverpool docks. Dockers also harboured deep suspicions and doubts as to the loyalty or motives of their own national and local union leadership, including of those who had worked among them on the waterfront in their early days. Even Sexton, who so visibly bore the fearsome scars of his working life on the docks, and who as General Secretary had done much for his members, was often barracked at meetings and, on occasion, even had to make his escape almost as a fugitive, from back entrances.

Seamen and dockers

Although they would perhaps have disagreed indignantly, the seamen were not that very different to the dockers. Their employment could also be irregular. They were accustomed to moving on to another job, another ship. They were also widely dispersed at sea for long periods. That made them difficult, even impossible, to recruit into union membership, let alone to organise collectively. The only opportunities came were when they were on leave or on an extended leave between ships. Unemployment among seamen, which increased as trade fell, could offer extended opportunities for organisers to boost membership. But even that was a limited route since joining the union to help secure pay and conditions was only meaningful when they were in work. Shipowners were also often strongly opposed to unionisation, preferring what they termed 'free labour'.

Like the dockers, seamen also had their grievances and complaints of serious abuses. They were often charged extortionate interest rates on loans from their employers ('advance notes') taken out before a voyage, as well as on money paid to wives ('allotments') against their husbands' pay when at sea – a means for employers to make money out of their employees. At sea it was difficult to raise individual complaints and grievances and, as with the dockers and safety measures, they were reluctant to be singled out as troublemakers for fear of retribution. Jumping ship, a common enough practice, was also, in law, a criminal offence, rather than a civil one. Collective action at sea also put the men at risk given the wide, almost absolute, powers available to captains under mercantile law. When ashore, the seamen could easily fall prey to loan sharks and 'crimps', the owners of cheap, often dirty and unhealthy lodging-houses. Legitimate dissent was therefore difficult and, when drunk (or even sober), they rioted, 'the language of the unheard' as Martin Luther King once put it.

Back in the eighteenth century, at the time of Liverpool's rise to prominence, the sea captain's power meant that any dissent among the seamen broke out on shore. Generally small-scale rioting was common. Many other crafts and occupations took part, including potters, coopers and shipwrights, but it was the seamen who were seemingly most naturally inclined to riot. The rioting ashore became well established until, in 1775,[5] it reached a more serious level, as Britain was preparing for war against revolutionary America and trade went into the doldrums. The 1775 riot was effectively a strike, since it arose over a common employer practice, namely a cut in pay. The demonstrations and collective action became ugly, as strikes can do, when the seamen massed, armed, in front of the Town Hall, and proceeded to stone it. It was Liverpool's own storming of the Bastille, but without that event's destructive and revolutionary consequences. The magistrates, as usual, panicked. The dragoons were called in from Manchester to restore law and order, setting a pattern that would be repeated on several occasions over the next century and a half.[6] The event could also arguably claim to have coined the term 'strike' from 'striking the sails', that is preparing a vessel for a period in harbour. Despite the seriousness with which the authorities viewed the events, few of the strikers were arrested. Seamen were popular and had public sympathy, even support, for their actions. There were also the needs of war, which broke out in 1776. Those that were indicted were discharged on condition that they joined the King's navy to fight the seceding American rebels.

After the 1775 riots, it was over a century until the seamen were involved in another serious dispute. By then, new technology was transforming their working lives. Steam was gradually making ancient skills obsolete just as the new trades were creating occupational divisions. All would, however, be driven by the schedules and more frantic pace of the steamships as the owners sought to offset some of their greatly increased capital and running costs through faster turnaround times. These pressures were especially acute among the famous companies running passenger ships on highly competitive routes such as the North Atlantic. The demise of the *Titanic* in 1912 was at least partly attributable to the desire to maintain speed and arrive in New York on schedule.

When settling ashore displaced seamen would often find themselves working alongside dockers. Their experience and knowledge of ships and rigging stood them in good stead in finding work on the waterfront, often in the better jobs, among the shipmen and stevedores. James Sexton was one such example. Therefore, despite the older occupational divisions between them dockers and seamen began to develop a common cause. But that process would take until the last years of the nineteenth century and the early years of the twentieth, even though dockers, seamen and their families commonly lived alongside each other in the mean streets of the waterfront.

Hanging together or hanging separately

If the seamen had difficulty in finding and maintaining common cause even among themselves, so did the dockers. One reason for that, which they shared with the seamen, is that their hiring arrangements 'balkanised' them in separate, often small-scale, labour markets. With the seamen it was the ship for which he had 'signed on'; with the dockers it was their customary stand, or a particular 'company'. The company in question might actually be a master porter or master shipman, often small in the scale of their operations, sub-contracting with a shipping line. Another factor that tended to keep the dockers apart was that a limited number of them worked directly for the Dock Board, while others were employed by the London and North Western Railway.[7]

Working lives, for many, were also strongly influenced by any specialisms that tied them to the dedicated quays and warehouses of the companies or merchants. Most, naturally, would tend to look for work at the docks that were familiar to them, often near where they lived. There was even less movement between the two halves of the system, partly because of different functions and partly because of sectarianism. For the North End was dominated by the large steamships and passenger liners, while the South End had sail and smaller steamships. Both had different cargoes. It was also geographically difficult to move within and between these two major labour markets, which extended over several miles. Travelling along the dock system could also be expensive, even after the Overhead Railway was completed, although employers often provided pre-paid rail tickets for those moving between berths during the working day. Those walking, or perhaps cycling, would also naturally seek work near to where they lived. Importantly, too, the North End was predominantly Catholic, the South End Protestant. This could matter significantly, and at least one occupation, the carters, was dominated by Protestants. The employers also often encouraged division. For many years Cunard and White Star divided the work available among their loyal, reliable and best workers, who could be virtually guaranteed three or four days per week. That gave the employer the advantage of a permanent, available surplus of labour, but also instituted casualism among the less favoured. This impoverished workers and weakened their potential for collective action or unionisation.

To an extent unionisation was also hampered by the absence of a dominant ideology. The writings of Marx and Engels were only widely available, in Britain, towards the end of the nineteenth century and both of them openly despaired of the absence of radical ideas, let alone revolutionary potential, among British workers, in what was the first, industrialised, capitalist economy. Liverpool's close contacts with the workers of other countries did lead to some influence from ideas and ideologies including, at first, the writings of Henry George, the American writer and activist who advocated the redistribution of wealth, especially land, towards the worker. Edward McHugh and Richard McGhee, the first leaders of the NUDL, knew and worked with George. The NUDL originated in Glasgow, and McHugh organised George's 1884 speaking tour of Scotland and in Liverpool. He also worked with George, in New York, founding the American Longshoremen's Union in 1896, although it was wound up two years later. An example of the reverse process, important for a time, was the arrival of the American Knights of Labor in Bootle, in 1889, where they established a branch and remained active in Liverpool, and elsewhere, for a few years.

The Noble and Holy Order of the Knights of Labor had been founded in Philadelphia in 1869. It grew slowly at first, then very rapidly in the 1880s becoming, for a short time, the dominant labour organisation in the USA, reaching a peak of 700,000 members in 1885. Its aims were to bring together skilled and unskilled workers (excluding bankers, lawyers, stockbrokers and traders in alcoholic liquors!) in one union, end 'wage slavery' and build a 'cooperative commonwealth', through peaceful methods. The vagueness of its principles and its ambivalence over the use of strikes (it favoured boycotting goods) handicapped further growth. Its rival, the American Federation of Labor was much less equivocal over strikes and, more importantly, concentrated on the exclusive recruitment of skilled, craft workers. They had clear interests in common, but not with unskilled, industrial workers. The AF of L's exclusivity might have been a less than glorious ideal, but it worked better at a time when American unions were fighting even to exist against repressive laws and fierce employer opposition.[8] On the Liverpool waterfront the Knights were attractive in the early stages of unionisation, given their appeal to the unskilled, especially on the docks. Though they failed to take root beyond the branch in Bootle, and helped in organising the unionisation of the tramwaymen, their espousal of the unorganised industrial worker fed into the emerging pressure from industrial workers for union representation. This 'new unionism' was to spring into spectacular life, particularly in London and Liverpool, in 1889 and 1890.

The more durable and influential ideology was syndicalism with its origins in France and a United States' variant via immigrants from Europe. As the Knights of Labor, syndicalists stressed the case for solidarity, normally exclusively by industry, in preparation for the seizure of the state through a general strike. Some, though, advocated 'indirect' political action as opposed to the 'direct' route of the strike. In the United States syndicalism was, for a time, a major force, in the form of the Industrial Workers of the World (the 'Wobblies') until it became prone to internal dissension and splits in the period up to America's entry into the Great

War in 1917. Its leadership continued to promote strikes and sabotage, methods which the American public generally saw as unpatriotic, especially in wartime. US law also judged their actions to be seditious. IWW's in-fighting, combined with legislative and judicial repression, finally reduced it to impotence and destroyed its membership base, which in any case had never been large. But it had some presence in Britain, including some 'chapters' (branches). Liverpool was also always likely to be aware, if not necessarily influenced, through its maritime connections with the United States.

The ideas of the Wobblies and the Continental European syndicalists, though present along the Liverpool waterfront, could not be claimed to have had much direct influence among the majority of the rank-and-file or even their leaders. McHugh had been in the United States, and Sexton had visited European countries, but they encouraged solidarity, opposing sectionalism, without being syndicalists. Neither, too, favoured the habitual use of the strike weapon. Tom Mann, a syndicalist, was a leading figure in Liverpool's General Transport Strike of 1911, but the rank-and-file's enthusiasm for that strike, across a range of occupations including dockers, seamen, coal-heavers and tramwaymen, did not need syndicalist ideas to inspire solidarity.[9] Ideas are essential, in the long run, to give coherence and form to labour organisations and their goals. But it was wages that put meals on the table in a city that saw 'more dinner hours than dinners'. As we have seen, The seamen had been first in the field of strike action in the eighteenth century, and the dock labourers only got into their stride with strikes in 1853 and 1866, although there was some organisation and limited action in place before then. The South End Dock Labourers' Association was founded in 1849, though it would have been little more than a friendly society and burial club. There was a similar organisation in the North End, but little is known of it. More is known of the Clarence Dock Club, which organised the coastal trade men. The Steamboat Labourers' Friendly Burial Society was also active, certainly in 1870 when it called a minor strike at Nelson Dock. But that was also exceptional. Calling their members out on strike was not normally a practice of these embryonic unions. The men did that themselves, often spontaneously, whether union members or not. On one remarkable occasion, involving the Steamboat Labourers' Friendly Burial Society, a pay increase was secured by recourse merely to petitioning the employers rather than a strike.[10]

The 1870 successes were in a period of improving trade, which continued until 1873. This gave the dockers the impetus to press for better pay and/or shorter hours (the Nine Hour Day). Other occupations, such as the carters and omnibus workers, followed them. Two leaders became prominent during these actions – William Simpson, a former docker, and James Samuelson, a businessman from Seacombe with liberal views. Simpson, who owned and ran 'cocoa rooms' (dockside cafés) at the Pier Head, was a popular orator and champion of the poor, but was reluctant to call strikes, as was Samuelson, who advocated arbitration to settle disputes. Simpson and Samuelson were also involved in later disputes.

Simpson died in 1883 with Samuelson, a Liberal Party activist, surviving until the end of the Great War.[11]

There were some gains in pay and hours during this period, but these were on a sectional basis, each group of workers acting in isolation, including the seamen. The organisations still active remained weak. The Steamboat Labourers' Friendly Burial Society and the Liverpool Seamen's Union (formed in 1872) were not without influence, but their weakness was emphasised by limited objectives and a reluctance to strike. Faced with a push from the employers, they soon collapsed with little tradition to sustain their survival and growth. Skilled craftsmen in the engineering and manufacturing industries, the nucleus of the early growth of trade unions, did not exist in sufficiently significant numbers in Liverpool, as they did in Manchester and Birmingham and even to an extent in Birkenhead's growing ship-building industry. The Liverpool Trades Council, founded in 1848, was also struggling even to exist. After 1873 the trade cycle turned down again, dampening ambition and any incipient revolt along the ever-divided waterfront. Six years later there was still no sign of any recovery in trade. It was going to be a long haul. Few were employed for more than three days a week, and it appeared that the men would have no choice but to sit it out. Then, in unfavourable conditions for action and contrary to all normal expectations, the entire waterfront burst into flames. The spark was provided by the employers.

The year 1879

Just before Christmas, 1878, the port employers, responding to the harsh realities of the Great Depression, met to consider wages along the waterfront. They agreed that they were too high, and that they needed to be cut. The Liverpool Steamship Owners' Association were persuaded to set the ball rolling, and announced a wage reduction for all its shore workers, to begin on 1 February 1879. Stevedores' wages were cut from 5s. 0d. to 4s. 6d. per day; porters' from 4s. 6d. to 4s. 0d., and with overtime down from 8d. to 7d. per hour. The cuts only applied to the North End. The South End dockers' employers came together in a different association, that of the sailing ship and smaller steamship owners, the Shipowners' Association. Their association had not agreed the cut. Across the river, in Birkenhead, the shipbuilders and boilermakers were, in contrast, being told the same bad news as in Liverpool's North End — a cut in wages and longer hours. Their unions, notably the 'labour aristocrats' of the Amalgamated Society of Engineers, looked for a deal — 50 per cent of the proposed reduction or arbitration. The employers fanned the flames by rejecting both.

The Birkenhead men struck on 31 January 1879. They were followed, the next day, by the Liverpool porters at the North End docks, whose wages had also been cut. Then, only a week later, Liverpool's South End dockers came out in sympathy, even though their wage rates remained intact. Earlier in the week the corn porters had walked out, as well as the coal-heavers. The carters, Protestant-led, were also spoiling for a fight. Within a week estimates of the numbers on strike were approaching 35,000, by then including the seamen, who had their own grievances, which included pay.[12] All logic suggested that it would not last long, and would all end in tears. But it lasted for three weeks, and it would be much longer before the collective anger would abate. The strikes were also spontaneous, familiarly known in our own times as 'wildcats' (a term borrowed from the United States), and without any initial leadership. Daily meetings, at the Pier Head, also became a feature. This allowed a leadership to emerge, carried along by what was widely seen as barefaced exploitation by the employers, acting in combination. The obvious lesson was for the workers themselves to combine and maximise their strength. Although sympathy strikes were then almost unprecedented along the waterfront, traditional sectional and sectarian differences were now put aside, if only temporarily, emphasising their common economic and class interests. The employers did not realise what they had done. The events of February 1879, and the solidarity that emerged, would prove to be the first, most important step towards what the employers had brought on themselves and most feared: the end of 'free labour' and the emergence of permanent trade union organisation along the waterfront.

The strikers had their leaders in the first week: William Simpson and James Samuelson, the popular veterans of 1870–72. Simpson's oratory and 'militant moderation' was complemented by the quieter methods of Samuelson, who sought a better future for dockland through negotiation and arbitration. They were joined by John Fuller and John Maitland, dockers from the North End. All four were prominent at the weekly mass meetings, although their advocacy of arbitration fitted ill with the militancy of the rank-and-file who, quite correctly, suspected arbitrators who were rarely independent, let alone able to appreciate the case for the wage cut to be restored, in full.

The mass meetings were, however, orderly, democratic and enlightening. Liverpool's newspapers (*Daily Courier, Daily Post* and *Mercury*) were impressed by the conduct of the mass meetings, and were generally sympathetic to the strikers' cause, reporting, in detail, the plight of the families along the waterfront as the strikes progressed into their second and third weeks. The meetings also made it clear, for the ears of the better-off, that there was a difference between wage rates and earnings. With often no more than three days work per week, under the casual system, even in better times, a cut in the wage rate was catastrophic. William Rathbone, the local MP, was made aware of the crippling effect of casualism and underemployment at one of the Pier Head meetings to which he was invited; he misjudged the mood, and indeed the case of the strikers, by recommending a return to work, on the reduced wages, pending arbitration. Yet by the end of the first week even the Liverpool Trades Council was urging the men to go to arbitration. By then the seamen were out, demanding an increase in pay, better on-board conditions, the ending of the recruitment of unskilled men, and the reform of the advance note and allotment system to remove abuses and extortionate interest rates. By now the port was virtually paralysed, the *Liverpool Mercury* estimating that 60,000 were out of work, a figure that included those not on strike but whose jobs were affected by the dispute.[13]

In the second week the employers moved towards serious action. Strike-breakers were brought in from Glasgow, Manchester and Hull. They also maintained, in the battle for public opinion, which was normally sympathetic to the cause and sufferings of the dockers and their families, that the dockers' claims at the Pier Head meetings to be earning an average of 15*s.* per week was a gross misrepresentation of the true figure. They put it at up to twice that amount. In fact, even the daily rates for shipmen and porters before the cuts, at 5*s.* 0*d.* and 4*s.* 6*d.* (see table, p. 99) would have required full-time working with overtime, to approach the employers' figure and at a time when depressed trade kept the working week much lower. An average of three days available work was the widely accepted estimate, and that gave credibility to the dockers' claim of 15*s.* Eleanor Rathbone's inquiries were to confirm, some twenty years later, that three days' work was the normal expectation of most men looking for regular work. But truth is the first casualty of strikes as well as of war, and the exaggerated claims of the employers might well have weakened the dockers' cause.

The cause was further weakened in the third week by the arrival of yet more strike-breakers, this time from Bristol, the Midlands and North Wales, as well as more from Glasgow and Hull. There were reports that many, on arrival, claimed not to know they were strike-breakers and refused to work. Hearts and minds were probably less important in encouraging their return than threats of violence laced with money collected to help pay their train fares home.[14] By then the magistrates, urged on by the Mayor, with government support, had called in the 5th Dragoon Guards and the 96th Foot. The Mayor, Thomas Bland Royden – last of the Liverpool shipbuilders, deputy chairman of Cunard, director of the London and North Western Railway, the leaseholder of Garston Dock, later Conservative MP for West Toxteth, created a baronet in 1905 – was also urging arbitration, with himself as referee! The dockers were not impressed. Nor were they impressed by the efforts of Simpson and Samuelson to find a compromise in a wage reduction for those permanently employed, leaving casual, daily rates intact. The employers countered with restoring the cuts in return for an extra hour on the day and a reduction in overtime rates – or arbitration. At a mass meeting of at least 80,000 the employers' proposals were unanimously rejected. A split in the leadership had also emerged. Maitland and Fuller found it difficult to accept the extent of the compromises being sought by Simpson and Samuelson.[15]

As the strike entered its third week there began a major drift back to work as the employers brought in more strike-breakers from Wolverhampton and, again, North Wales. The strike was now largely confined to the North End docks, led by Maitland and Fuller, with daily Pier Head meetings now being held near Huskisson Dock. These had now become angry affairs, as the Chief Constable warned Fuller and Maitland of the consequences of a breach of the peace. The leaders agreed to end the daily mass meetings. The last was on Friday, 21 February.

Across the river, the Birkenhead men continued to hold firm, showing an obduracy which became well established and familiar until well into the next century. But they could not hold out alone. In Liverpool, hunger and the end of the mass meetings had sapped morale. The final straw came on Sunday, 23 February, at Masses in churches all across the North End, where the predominantly Irish Catholic dockers lived and worked. A letter was read out from Dr O'Reilly, the Roman Catholic Archbishop. He showed a proper concern and admiration for the suffering and courage of all those involved, but berated those strikers who took action against those returning to work. His arguments, though cogent and influential among many Irish Catholics along the North End, stopped short of any criticism of the employers' actions and the covert support of the Mayor and the Council for the employers' stand. His intervention, however, finally encouraged the dockers to petition Maitland to call off the strike. As the strike collapsed the Birkenhead dockers had no alternative but to vote to return to work. By 26 February it was all over, The seamen did better, but only marginally. They achieved little of their pay demands – only a few companies settled – and had to accept only promises to improve conditions and remove abuses. The strike gradually petered out, and by 12 March there was peace, of a sort, along the entire waterfront. In reality it was '... no more than an uneasy truce'.[16]

The smouldering coals of bitterness and resentment were fanned into flames by the usual retribution of the foremen and managers, who refused to hire 'agitators',[17] and other 'troublemakers'. The dockers' next step was both early and predictable, and it came from Birkenhead. James Samuelson, who had urged the case for a union during the strike, chaired a meeting on 26 March 1879, which passed the following motion:

> That this meeting of lumpers, quay porters, coal and salt heavers, working in the Birkenhead docks, cordially approves the establishment of the Birkenhead Amalgamated Dock Labourers' Union and Benefit Society and pledges itself to support the same by every legitimate means in its power.[18]

The Liverpool dockers followed the Birkenhead lead in the same year, forming the Liverpool Union of Stevedores, Labourers and Quay Porters. By April 1880 the *Courier* was reporting that '... an agitation has been on foot, principally among the North End labourers, with a view of promoting another strike to obtain their old rate of pay'.[19] The pendulum was by now beginning to swing, just a little, towards the dockers. The local railway porters had secured an increase in pay as the emigrant traffic reached new heights, expanding by 22 per cent in the year to March 1880.[20] A dock strike was now far from the employers' wish list. The men were also now better organised and went even further: the Liverpool and Birkenhead unions decided to combine to press for a restoration of the old wage rates. There was also the news, from London, that their dockers had gone on strike on 22 April.

Samuelson was against a strike and, in response to a conciliatory letter from the unions urging a restoration of the old rates, the Steamship Owners' Association offered arbitration. Samuelson was to represent the dockers, Richard Lowndes the employers, with both sides assisted by Counsel. Lord Derby agreed to 'umpire' the proceedings. Meanwhile, the carpet was beginning to move from under the employers' feet. Some dockers had already gone on strike for a restoration of the old rates, and the employers' association allowed the companies involved to settle separately without prejudice to the reference to arbitration. That should have concentrated the arbitrators' minds. It did, to an extent, but tardily. The arbitrators met on twelve occasions and even widened their enquiries to consulting employers as well as collecting details of wage rates in all the other major ports of the UK. It was therefore not until the 28 May (almost a month after arbitration was agreed) that the award was made public. It restored the old rates, back-dated to 10 May, but only for three months. After that date the arbitrators were prepared to consider the reference again. It needed little perspicacity to judge that this was a permanent award, as it proved, despite the inevitable huffing and puffing by employers and familiar union allegations of evasion and back-sliding by employers. The dockers' success also gave fresh hopes to the seamen.

Like the dockers, the seamen now had unions: the Seamen's and Firemen's Union (Liverpool Branch) of 1879, and the Amalgamated British Seamen's Protection Society. The latter was the Liverpool branch of a London society dating back to 1872, although there were allegations that it was an employers' front for the deployment of strike-breakers. Even so, like the dockers, they buried their differences, if only for a time, and formed a joint committee to press their claims. The outcome was a demand for an across-the-board increase of 10s. per month. The employers' immediate rejection raised the temperature. The committee's chairman recommended arbitration, as in the case of the dockers. That was voted out, and a strike was approved. The seamen were out for ten days, but the Steamship Owners' Association refused to concede. Its members, however, broke ranks and nearly all came to sign separate agreements to end the strike.

The restoration of the pay cuts was a considerable success for the dockers at the time, although with hindsight it was a two cheers victory since the 1880 award set rates that were to remain unchanged until 1915, an outcome used with considerable effect by Ernest Bevin at the 1920 Shaw Enquiry.[21] The *Liverpool Daily Courier*, as we saw earlier, noted that the strike revealed the inadequacy of Liverpool's daily wage rates as an indicator of actual weekly pay. The *Courier* also drew unhappy comparisons with other ports, revealing Liverpool's growing inability to compete explained, it claimed, by the Dock Board's cloying bureaucracy and high dock rates and dues.[22] That, through its effect on traffic and revenue accruing to the shipping companies, would weaken their ability to pay living wages, though they needed little incentive. More ominously, it was becoming clear that the exponential growth experienced by Liverpool up to 1870 was beginning to abate. All was not what it seemed on Liverpool's busy, bustling waterfront. The 'pyramids' were already revealing tell-tale cracks.

The seamen's success was less clear-cut since it was on a piecemeal basis and may not have been universal. But well-publicised strikes always educate far beyond their immediate location. William Rathbone, though bearing the name and reputation of a liberal Liverpool family and a Member of Parliament, was not well informed on the importance of the distinction between the dockers' daily wage rates and actual weekly earnings until he attended one of the early Pier Head mass meetings. The strike also revealed the iniquities of the seamen's working conditions and pay arrangements, and their legitimate grievances over their fragmenting status.

Two bills quickly surfaced in Parliament, eventually becoming one statute – the Merchant Seamen (Payment of Wages etc.) Act, 1880. Primarily the Act targeted abuses: the advance note, wives' allotments, and the practices of the seamen's lodging-house keepers, the 'crimps'. The advance note, which allowed a seaman preparing for a voyage to borrow, for kitting out, from his future earnings (usually at usurious interest rates) was made illegal from 1 August 1881. The allotment note, which provided for a seaman's family, also at extortionate interest rates, was subjected to regulation. The crimps, who were commonly in the pay of employers to supply seamen at short notice, often getting them drunk to do so (an abuse akin to the practices of Royal Navy press gangs that had been abolished in 1809) were forbidden to go on to ships, and their lodging-houses came under the regulatory control of sanitary authorities. Liverpool had had such authorities since 1864.[23] Regulations were also introduced for wages to be paid promptly at a voyage's end. On status, grades of seamen were introduced and four years' service were required for promotion to able-bodied seaman (the 'AB'). The legislation was comprehensive and clearly had been influenced by the events in Liverpool from 1879 to 1880. Viscount Sandon, the Liverpool MP and friend of the brewer, Andrew Walker, presented one of the original bills. There were some doubts as to the Act's effectiveness, but it was a promising start.

Although the gains of 1880 were far from substantial, and were to prove ephemeral,[24] they accompanied some advances in waterfront solidarity, even though the newly founded unions did not survive. Of the four unions that had emerged in 1880 (three if the alliance between the Birkenhead and Liverpool dockers' union is counted as one), all had disappeared within the decade as trade continued on its fitful path.[25] Even at their peak they had few members, probably well below a thousand in each case. Many dockers and seamen, on poor pay, had to be convinced of the value of union membership, which also required dues and sometimes entrance fees. In any case they found it difficult to trust union leaders, even any leader at all, an attitude largely rooted in the casualism of the docks. Yet the seamen and the dockers also did well enough on their own in 1879, coming together in common cause and soon finding their own leaders. They also proved themselves capable of behaving with commendable discipline and responsibility, despite the terrible privations of themselves and their families. Their daily mass meetings at the Pier Head were also models of rank-and-file democratic debate. The meetings also demonstrated how important such regular gatherings are to maintain solidarity and morale, as the 1889 dock strike in London also demonstrated. The authorities in Liverpool were aware of this and were quick to respond to the charges of violence (which was actually surprisingly limited and occasional) as a pretext for a banning order.[26]

The dockers also successfully put aside their often deep, religious differences notable in the predominantly Protestant South End's early sympathetic strike in support of the mostly Catholic, North End. As the strike was losing momentum, religion became important again, seen in the men's response to the Catholic Archbishop's plea, read at the always well-attended Sunday mass, to return to work. He did, of course, touch a nerve in the suffering of the dockers' families. He had personally worked among them during the 1847 epidemics, although religious leaders normally tend to support the political and social status quo. But the Archbishop had been silent for three weeks, a silence which *could* suggest an ambivalence borne out of some recognition of the strong feelings of the dockers.[27]

The seamen, too, had learned from the events of 1879 and 1880. Their working lives had common features with those of the dockers though, if they were to achieve any gains, they would largely have to rely upon themselves. But it would also help for them to forge common alliances with the dockers – even if out of self-interest rather than brotherhood. Those common interests would be tested again, in 1890. Both, too, were to learn that there was no substitute for organisation, for permanent trade unions to turn natural solidarity into effective pressure and success. Nor, unfortunately, was there any alternative to the strike for concentrating the minds of employers who would normally hold the reins of power, especially in times of depressed trade which became alarmingly frequent after 1870, further aggravated by growing competition from other ports. Even in conditions of increasing port traffic, when concessions were possible, the employers conceded not out of weakness or altruism but to maintain trade and profits. In good times strikes add nothing to an employer's revenue stream; working seamen and dockers do.

Then, in 1880, a revival in trade seemed to indicate, at long last, the ending of the Great Depression. Those hopes were disappointed as trade turned down again in 1883, even more so than in previous years. The waterfront then returned to its usual condition of abject poverty, only marginally softened by private charity and Poor Law relief. In such conditions the nascent unions then became little more than charitable organisations raising money to sustain the families of their dwindling members. That was followed by their inevitable collapse. By 1886 the seamen's and dockers' unions had disappeared.

The emergence, fall and re-emergence of seamen's and dockers' organisations, dictated largely by the trade cycle, was almost another 'iron law' of classical economics. In that they shared the experience of all unions in the early days of their existence. Membership, then and now, also largely determined revenue. In the growth years it had to be big enough to provide a level of paid dues sufficient to sustain them during the inevitable downturn. That would also be a time when dockers would have difficulty paying their dues faced with more urgent priorities. Hard times would also allow employers to go on the offensive, refusing to hire 'agitators' and 'troublemakers' and, if they could, cutting wages. Employers also, with very few exceptions, resisted unionisation as well as insisting that union members work alongside non-union labour. They also frequently and effectively resorted to bringing in blackleg workers. Cunard even maintained a permanent complement of 'scab' coal-heavers to deploy during strikes. They would soon be needed. Trade began to revive towards the end of 1888, and with it the waterfront workers' employment, optimism, restlessness and organisation. Again it was the seamen who pulled the trigger. By Christmas they were on strike, remaining out for two months. In the summer of 1889 they were out again, for a further five weeks. Within a month a handful of dockers joined them. Their numbers then grew steadily until, by the spring of 1890, the entire waterfront was again at a standstill.

The 'labour war' of 1890

The seamen's actions of 1888–89 arose primarily from continuing discontent over pay and conditions: they even opposed the 1881 discontinuance of the advance note and its abuses. The strikes were also better organised by the emergence, in Liverpool, of branches of the National Amalgamated Union of Sailors and Firemen. This new union had been founded in Sunderland, in 1887, by J. Havelock Wilson. Ten other ports followed the Teesside lead, including two branches in Liverpool and another in Bootle. The new union survived until 1894 but, by then, had chalked up some victories, including a number of pay increases of up to £1 per week. In 1889, membership was increasing by up to 500 per week, standing at a total of 7,000 in May. Growing membership and confidence soon began to develop into a demand for formal recognition. But the employers, the Steamship Owners', remained obdurate, led by the powerful Cunard. By the summer of 1889 distress among the seamen and their families forced the union to offer arbitration to settle their claim. The employers, seeing their moment, quickly refused, and the strike began to disintegrate, the union unable to prevent a drift back to work.

During the seamen's strikes the dockers offered sympathy, but no more. Their own independent action began slowly, limited to the South End, in the autumn of 1889. By then the waterfront had its own new union, the National Union of Dock Labourers, founded earlier in the year in Glasgow. By 1890 Birkenhead also had an NUDL branch, a £1 entrance fee, and a willingness to explore using boycotts of other ports to inhibit black-legging and strike-breaking by employers. The significance of the new union and its methods were not seen at the time, and was inevitably overshadowed by the startling reports coming in from London. What was to become known as the 'Great Dock Strike' on the Thames broke out on 12 August, accompanied by open air mass meetings and, soon, regular processions of some 20,000 strikers, their families and sympathisers, with flags, banners and marching brass bands. These served the same role in maintaining morale and solidarity as had Liverpool's Pier Head meetings in 1870. The London strike and demonstrations were widely reported in the Liverpool newspapers. Press coverage was also perhaps even greater for the Liverpool tramwaymen's 'agitation' beginning in June 1889 and lasting into early 1890. The *Liverpool Mercury*, in particular, led public opinion in its support for the 1,600 employees, legitimate grievances against the United Tramways Company.[28] But what was soon to take place on the waterfront was even more profound. With little exaggeration it was described, at the time, as a 'labour war'.[29]

Liverpool's new union, the NUDL, by then consisting of three branches, sought to make an early mark by drafting a code of rules that it would seek to apply along the waterfront. The code, a single document focusing all their claims and grievances, included a detailed list of claims for occupational wage rates, overtime and special rates, hours of work, and meal breaks. The code was beyond a wish list. The NUDL's three branches had a combined membership of 10,000, which was approaching half the total potential dock labour force. Mass meetings were held in February 1890 to expand numbers. John Burns and Ben Tillett, the heroes of the successful London dock strike were invited to speak. By then some employers were offering to accept the NUDL's code as trade continued to improve. The men could see that for themselves, finding work at the call became much easier, even for the casual casuals. Their confidence was growing as bargaining power began to tilt in their favour. There were also still scores to settle from the events of 1879 when the employers were firmly in the saddle. But, as became customary along the waterfront, the union organisers, who often had an agenda rather different from that of their members, struggled to maintain solidarity and discipline and avoid unofficial action. At the same time, the separate organisations of coal-heavers, carters and the South End Association, though often actively sympathetic to the NUDL, were always ready to secure separate, favourable deals for themselves, as were the seamen. The Knights of Labor were also still active in Bootle, and aroused interest despite their differences in organisation, aims and methods to the more conventional union. It was to be expected, therefore, that should action originate unofficially with one group, it would spread rapidly along the waterfront, forcing the NUDL's hand. That group was the grain handlers. The issue was the always important and explosive one of mechanisation.[30]

Unloading grain was the job of the 'bushellers' who filled and stitched the four bushel (two hundredweight) sacks for the grain carriers who carried them, at pace, along planks to the quay. They worked fast, each moving some forty-five tons per day, with piecework providing good pay.[31] The introduction of the grain elevator greatly increased the speed of unloading and cut labour costs massively. One comparison was that six men feeding ('trimming'), one elevator could do the work of forty-five bushellers and carriers. The work done was not entirely the same: the elevator took the corn to the top of the warehouse or silo, rather than in bags to the quayside, but it remained clear that the elevator would eliminate a large number of jobs. Furthermore, piecework was replaced by a trimmer's day rate. The union's rules set 6s., which some employers conceded. The trimmers at Huskisson Docks then struck for 7s. and the removal of the elevators. Union delegates from the Bootle branch went to see the strikers, advising a return to work. They were threatened with being thrown into the dock. Other delegates from another branch, supported by a telegram from Glasgow, the NUDL's headquarters, instructed the men to stay out. There was also a widespread refusal, throughout the docks, to work with non-unionists, even though official union policy was for employers to give 'preference' to union members, rather than the closed shop. The union had also issued 'buttons' (badges) [32] which members were required to wear when working, to 'separate the sheep from the goats' and to put pressure on the non-unionists to join. This resulted in the recruitment of 3,000 new members in a fortnight, each paying a 2s. 6d. entrance fee, although some of these were subsequently refused membership at branch level. [33] By then many dockers were calling for a general strike to enforce the union's terms and conditions. The button was also now being widely worn where union members were refusing to work with non-union men.

The growing strength of the strikers, though spontaneous and largely unofficial, brought Edward McHugh, the NUDL's General Secretary, from Glasgow to take control of the situation. By 7 March 20,000 were out. The North End docks were at a standstill except for those employers who accepted the NUDL's rules. The South End dockers remained at work, most being members of the South End Labourers' Association. Some master stevedores in the South (and even a few in the North) agreed to hire only union men, directly via the union office. [34] The majority of employers were not, however, conciliatory. They had also, themselves, combined.

The Employers' Labour Association (ELA), formed in February 1890, brought together thirty steamship owners and twenty master stevedores and porters. [35] The association's members employed 60 per cent of all of the port's seamen and dockers. It had its own offices and officials, a fund to combat strikes, and during the 1890 strike spent £32,000 importing about 10,000 strike-breakers who were billeted in depot ships on the river. [36] Though a powerful, well-resourced organisation, the ELA was not supported by all the major employers, including Alfred Holt. Holt, the civil engineer, who founded the Ocean Steamship Company ('Blue Funnel') chaired the Liverpool Steamship Owners' Association in 1876 and, later, the MDHB. He refused to join the ELA. He also recognised the Seamen's Union and accepted the NUDL's code, a step which branded him, among fellow shipowners, as one of the 'weaker brethren'. [37] He was also a Unitarian with a reputation for humane actions. The shipowners' view reflected the tough line of the majority of ELA members, who aimed to starve the dockers back to work and on their own terms.

Meanwhile, events were beginning to turn ugly. The focus of the men's anger was the employers' use of strike-breakers, or 'knobsticks', and their refusal to restrict hiring to union members. The union was much more accommodating on non-union labour, and were willing to accept the compromise of a preference for union members. That drew hostility to the NUDL from its own members. So the strike became a power struggle between three parties at odds with each other, enlivened by colourful language. McHugh denounced the employers as 'idlers, thieves, robbers and beggars', as others talked of 'revolution', and the docks becoming a 'slaughterhouse'.[38] But alarmist language was a poor substitute for solidarity and food. Privation grew alarmingly in the third week, as the NUDL's allies in the other unions, including the seamen, agreed settlements. The NUDL had no option but to settle, ending the dispute at the end of March 1890.

The union makes us strong

The NUDL's agreement with the ELA gave them some of the rules in their code, such as a maximum night shift of nine hours and a 12 noon to 1 p.m. dinner break. A weekly contract was also offered, but turned down by the men who were still wedded to the illusory freedoms of casualism. Most importantly, they agreed to work cooperatively with non-unionists and not to wear the union button, except at the stands, for identification. There was also an agreement for the union's members not to boycott or 'black' Liverpool's ships in other ports, in disputes in which they were not involved. Overall it was undoubtedly a comprehensive victory for the ELA, especially on the central issue of employers' hiring rights. Nor was there any increase in wage rates, except for a codification of some premium payments. While the short-term balance sheet favoured the employers, however, the NUDL, though less than a powerful presence on the waterfront, had secured *de facto*, though not official, recognition. It would of course lose many members in the early years after the strike, from a 'claimed' membership of 18,000 in 1890 to 8,463 in 1892, with many branches collapsing as unemployment grew, with the employers going on the offensive again. But a partial recovery to a stable membership of 10,000 secured the NUDL's future until it formed part of the TGWU in 1922.

Sectionalism did, however, continue to undermine effective solidarity. The NUDL did not affiliate to the Liverpool Trades Council (LTC) which could only offer sympathy rather than institutional support. There were also too many unions all along the waterfront only too ready, at the sound of gunfire, to retreat into securing their own interests. Nor was the NUDL itself a united, cohesive unit. There were real differences between the leadership and the members over the employment of non-unionists and the reform of the casual system. Nor did the leadership of McHugh and McGhee last much beyond the end of the strike.

Sexton, who became General Secretary in 1893, admired their commitment, but blamed them for not tackling sectionalism and indiscipline. He also saw a weakness in their middle-class origins, in contrast to his own.[39]

Sexton had, of course, served his time at sea and on the waterfront. Edward McHugh, born in Ireland had lived most of his life in Scotland, working as a compositor in Glasgow and heavily involved in radical causes. Richard McGhee had similar origins but had worked in Glasgow as a skilled engineer.[40] Both were firm advocates of the ideas of Henry George and, though they did not found the NUDL in Glasgow, they were there at the beginning. McHugh became General Secretary at the age of 36, and McGhee was President (he was 38), both being formally elected in 1889. The new union soon claimed 3,000 members in Glasgow, and was ready to establish itself in Liverpool. Its rapid expansion owed something to the stirring events along London's waterfront in 1889, and by June 1890 was claiming a total membership in Liverpool of 18,000. Although the true figure was probably nearer 10,000, such rapid growth was a major achievement, for which McHugh and McGhee deserved much of the credit.

Sexton was on strike himself in 1890 but other than that his activism was minimal. Yet within three years, on 1 January 1894, he was elected to succeed McHugh. Michael Connolly, from Birkenhead, became President. Sexton retained the leadership for the next twenty-eight years. Although he was frequently and fiercely criticised by the rank-and-file, and often strongly challenged in office, he survived and, during his tenure, the NUDL also survived and grew. Despite all the criticism that followed him, at all levels, he must have been doing something right. That was also the view of Lloyd George, who knew Sexton well, especially when he was President of the Board of Trade and Minister of Munitions during the Great War. He wrote the foreword to Sexton's 1936 autobiography, concluding that he had '... earned his right to the crown of wild olive, the garland of a faithful life, usefully and honourably spent in the service of his fellows'.[41] Fine words but, despite Sexton's flaws, actually well earned.

CHAPTER SEVEN

'All the King's horses …'

… let Churchill do his utmost, his best or his worst, let him order ten times more military to Liverpool and let every street be paraded by them. Not all the King's horses with all the King's men can take the vessels out of the docks to sea.

(Tom Mann, 1911)[1]

… the transport strikes of 1911 alarmed some even more than the General Strike of 1926 …

(P. J. Waller, 1981)[2]

It seemed that some sort of fever had spread itself through the workers of the country, particularly in transport, and most of all in Liverpool.

(Stuart Mountfield, 1965)[3]

MOUNTFIELD's judgement, quoted above, was written more than half a century after the epic events of 1911; it reflected the fears of many at the time. The strike brought Liverpool and its shipping to almost a complete standstill for over ten weeks, and, as in 1890, it was accompanied by the deployment of mounted troops, infantry, and two warships, one, the *Antrim*,[4] on the Mersey. There were many new and troubling features to this dispute: there was major public disorder; there were rioting and looting; the bringing in of police from outside Liverpool, partly because the local force may have sympathised with the strikers;[5] a furious and provocative baton charging by the police of a peaceful, though large demonstration; the consequent erection of defensive barricades in some streets; and the deaths of two strikers at the hands of armed troops. A local journalist, Philip Gibbs, observing these events, wrote later that Liverpool in 1911 was '… as near to a revolution as anything I had seen in England'.[6] Margaret Postgate, then eighteen, recalled 'what was almost a civil war …'[7]

From his more lofty perspective Lord Derby took an even more definite and alarmist view, telling the then Home Secretary, Winston Churchill, via the Lord

Mayor, that, in his view, '... a revolution was in progress.'[8] Well before Churchill became a national wartime hero, he was infamous among many workers and their families for sending a general at the head of troops into the Rhondda Valley to quell disturbances arising from a miners' strike there. More worrying for the great and the good was that the transport strikes in Liverpool, though serious in themselves, were part of a larger, national 'great unrest'. They feared the influence of the syndicalists, especially on the waterfronts, as well as the equally persuasive oratory of the democratic socialists and Marxists. Europe, too, was preparing for war, and there had been a dress rehearsal for revolution in the abortive Russian uprising of 1905.

The strike was the increasingly used weapon of the British labour movement. Between 1900 and 1907 working days lost through strikes averaged 2.7 million a year. In 1908 that figure rose to exceed 10 million, though in the next year it fell back to fewer than 3 million. From then, until the outbreak of war in 1914, the annual lost days always exceeded 9 million and, in 1912, passed 40 million.[9] Liverpool, however, still looked special in the scale and duration of its strikes, which were seen by Hikins as '... spearheading a national movement'.[10] But although 1911 stood out in Liverpool's long history of industrial disputes and confrontations, its course, conduct and outcomes actually fell short of being truly revolutionary. But it was a significant and historic event for all that. For the seamen it was another landmark in their long struggle for even minimal justice. For the dockers it was partly a settling of old scores from 1890, although, importantly, it consolidated the status of their union, the NUDL.[11] It was also something of a Mersey version of London Dockland's remarkable Great Strike of 1889, though marginally less disciplined than that better known dispute. Yet 1911 was to achieve more for Sexton's NUDL than Tillett's London dockers achieved. That had a lot to do with the charismatic Tom Mann, one of the heroes of 1889, who had honed his energetic, organising skills even further by 1911. He had also learned even more from his involvement in labour disputes during his travels abroad, and his embracing of syndicalism gave more fire to his belly and strength to his arm. He was the most prominent leader of the Liverpool strikers in 1911, along with major contributions from the seamen's Havelock Wilson, and, of course, James Sexton.

Sexton had much less glamour about him than Mann and was no syndicalist; but he was effective. He was more in the traditional British mould of trade union leader, tough but moderate, seeking the best for his members though always ready to find an early settlement through compromise. He was also, like many trade union leaders, anxious to avoid strikes, to minimise disruption to his members' working lives and, wherever possible, to develop a good, constructive rapport with the employers. That style of leadership frequently got him into trouble with the rank-and-file along the waterfront. They had little respect for, or trust in, their employers, a lack of trust that even extended to union leaders, given those leaders alleged closeness to the employers. Furthermore, most union leaders, including

Sexton, favoured the replacement of casualism by permanent employment. They shared that view with liberal reformers and the more enlightened employers. That closeness even to the better employers made the men even more suspicious of Sexton. Even Ernest Bevin had a problem with their defence of casualism, once describing the system, to union officials, as, 'the liberty to go home with nothing'.[12] Yet Sexton was fully alongside Mann during the strike, though always on the look-out for a negotiated outcome. He was also a vain man, and twenty-five years later did reveal some bruising of his ego, resenting '... the wildly extravagant demands and the promises of interlopers'.[13] Coincidentally both he and Mann had been born in the same year, 1856, in difficult family circumstances, and had led equally deprived early lives; they also both lived to good ages, Sexton dying in 1938 when he was 82, and Mann three years later, at 85, of a blood clot on his brain. Mann's old, long-time friend, Ben Tillett, who lasted only a further two years, was at his funeral to deliver his valediction, his power to move with words undiminished.

Though all three were calendar contemporaries, Mann and Tillett rose to prominence a few years before Sexton. At the time of the Great London Strike, in 1889, Sexton was not widely known beyond the waterfront in Liverpool. He had been on strike in 1879 and was among the first to join the NUDL of McGhee and McHugh at the union's first Merseyside branch in Bootle. It superseded the branch of the Knights of Labor of which Sexton had been an equally enthusiastic member. Two further branches of the NUDL soon followed, covering the docks around the Pier Head and Toxteth. A fourth was opened in Birkenhead. The rapidly growing membership had a further boost from speaking visits to mass meetings, including Ben Tillett and John Burns, fresh from the triumph of 1889. Sexton would probably have been at these meetings, proudly wearing his NUDL button and drawing inspiration from their speeches. He was destined to go further and quickly, but in 1889 the heroes and the spotlight were on another waterfront.

The Great Strike of 1889

London's Great Dock Strike of 1889 was a major event in Britain's and the capital's history, with 100,000 on strike, bringing the whole port to a standstill. Yet it remained a disciplined, peaceful affair. It was also closely associated with the rapid development of new unionism, taking organised labour beyond its early, narrow origins in the skilled crafts into the mass organisations of relatively unskilled labour employed in large numbers in the new, large-scale industries of the late nineteenth and early twentieth centuries. Yet, despite the numbers involved, and the widespread contemporary attention that it attracted, its immediate benefits were not sustained. That was unlike the Liverpool strike twenty-two years later, which developed into a bitter, violent fight to the finish, and succeeded in its most important objective, the winning of recognition. Power, authority and order in the London of 1889 were also never seriously challenged. That was far from the case in the Liverpool of 1911, during which, at one point, even control of the local economy seemed to be beginning to shift towards the Strike Committee. In the end there was a drawing back from the brink, and agreements with the unions were reached. But to some well-placed observers, it was a close run thing, 'near to revolution'. Yet London in 1889 was the big dress rehearsal, a metropolitan spectacular that caught the imagination and widespread sympathy of many well beyond those directly involved. It also provided another stage for labour leaders of stature, not least the charismatic Tom Mann who was to play a major, decisive role in the Liverpool of 1911. The Great Strike of 1889 was the first step towards the eventual bringing together of the British waterfront and other transport unions, in which Liverpool and the NUDL were major players, to form the Transport and General Workers' Union in 1922.

The Great Strike was fuelled by a long series of grievances and unresolved, small disputes. The 'spark'[14] was lit by the *Lady Armstrong*, a sailing ship with a cargo of tea being discharged at the West India Docks, on the northern end of the Isle of Dogs. Like for the American colonists of Boston, over a century earlier, tea was to be the inflammatory pretext for history-making, although for the dockers, as for the Americans, trouble had been brewing for a long time. The dispute was over a bonus payment known as the 'plus', which was paid on tonnage. The actual weight was never revealed to the men, and was a long-standing practice under contract and piecework in other ports as well as London, including Liverpool and Dublin. Not surprisingly, it was also a long-standing cause of trouble. Ben Tillett, the young General Secretary of the Tea Operatives and Labourers' Union called the practice, quite accurately, 'systematic robbery'.[15] He was called in by the men to advise them on 12 August 1889. By then they had prepared all of their grievances and demands, soon to be echoed all along the waterfront. These included the complete abolition of contract work and piecework; a basic hourly wage rate of 6d. (which became known, famously, as the 'dockers' tanner'); an hourly overtime rate of 8d.; and two 'call-ons' each day for four hours' hiring, as in Liverpool. Tillett tried to restrain the men until the employers had replied. He failed, and they walked out on 14 August. Tillett immediately sent telegrams to Tom Mann and John Burns. Mann arrived on the same day. Within two days Burns was heading a demonstration of 6,000. The stevedores, lightermen (who unloaded larger vessels in mid-stream into smaller, unpowered lighters), seamen and firemen soon threw in their support, followed by Will Thorne's gasworkers, who had recently won the eight-hour day without a strike. Within just over a week, on 22 August, the entire port was at a standstill. At its height 100,000 were on strike, with 15–16,000 pickets. London had seen nothing like it.

A single strike committee was established early to coordinate and control the strike. Its members had solid organising experience, strong leadership skills and the power to persuade. The support of the stevedores (the Amalgamated Stevedores Labour Protection League) was especially important. Its General Secretary, Tom

McCarthy, was also an influential member of the strike committee. The strength of the committee was that they were all *of* the strikers as well as *for* them, the Wat Tylers, Jack Straws and John Balls of their generation. The committee and the strikers also enjoyed widespread public sympathy, even extending to the middle classes, which scarcely wavered over the three months of the stoppage. The press, too, mostly followed public opinion, especially the *Manchester Guardian* and, for most of the time, *The Times*. Well-to-do London had also long been in sympathy with the plight of the London poor, through the work of novelists such as Dickens, and with Elizabeth Gaskell writing in similar vein drawing on themes in the industrial North. For London, the disturbing reports of Henry Mayhew for the *Morning Chronicle* had, some years earlier, attracted a wide readership. They would be followed, around the time of the strike, by the academic, detailed and revealing research of William Booth and Joseph Rowntree. Another journalist with crusading talents was Annie Besant. In 1888 she had given a platform to the grievances and exploitation of the Bryant & May matchgirls, whose widely reported strike had ignited the consciences of Londoners and paved the way for the dockers the following year.[16] Cardinal Manning was another important ally. His support and direct involvement at all stages raised and maintained the strikers' morale as well as giving an important moral dimension to their case, especially important to the dockers who were mainly both Irish and Catholic. Manning told them that God, as well as justice, was on their side. He believed it, and so did the strikers.

The leading light on the strike committee – Ben Tillett of the Tea Operatives and General Labourers – was soon the leader of the London dockers as a whole. Tom Burns, the Scottish former engineer, a charismatic speaker and natural leader, already well known as an elected member of the London County Council, was also much more than a 'gas and water' socialist. Crowds came to hear their leaders speak, especially Burns, on the daily marches or 'cavalcades' of strikers and their families accompanied by brass bands. The marches were an important influence on public opinion, partly because of their size but also because they were peaceful and orderly, a welcome surprise to the comfortable and well-off who expected misbehaviour and violence from working men, especially the dockers, the stereotypical 'dock rats' of the waterfront.[17] Tillett was himself a docker and Burns had, for a time, worked at the docks. Tom Mann was less in the limelight, but did the crucial job of co-ordinating and deploying up to 15,000 pickets with limited funds, as well as organising the South Side strikers. As Smith and Nash, contemporary chroniclers of the strike put it:

> He was the eyes of the strike, always ready to see where there was necessary work to be done, and to set to work to do it. Strong and wiry, and capable of great physical endurance, and withal cool-headed and quietly energetic, he applied himself to the details of organization, which frequently carry with them the success or failure of the movement, and yet are so often overlooked

by those who are great at beating the big drum. When occasion required, however, he would beat the big drum as well as any, and with all these qualities he combined an unswerving loyalty to his comrades ...[18]

Tillett and Mann came from highly deprived backgrounds, but like many leaders of labour movements, especially then, they were self-taught, widely read intellectuals. Burns had a substantial library in his home, and Mann was an accomplished lecturer. Another prominent member of the strike committee, Will Thorne, the gasworkers' leader, remained poorly educated, even semi-literate. Eleanor Marx, Karl Marx's youngest daughter and unpaid secretary to the strike committee, helped him to improve his reading and writing.

Funding was as critical as picketing. The strikers' families needed continuous support, the scale of which grew with the numbers on strike. At the peak, some 100,000 were on strike, meaning the need to find money to sustain up to 500,000 (including families and dependants), for just over a month. The total money raised amounted to £46,000. Of this an astonishing proportion, £30,000, came from the 'colonies', mainly Australia, including contributions from members of the British Cabinet and Parliamentarians of Queensland. The 'public generally', at well over £10,000, contributed more than twice as much as the trade unions' £4,000. The Australian donations were, however, the key, making it possible for the strikers to hold out and win.[19]

Victory, which came on 14 September 1889, was hard-won and at great cost, but still sweet. The hourly rate was to be 6d. and overtime, at 8d. (6 p.m. to 8 a.m.), was conceded, along with a minimum call-on of four hours at time rates: previously hiring and discharging could be by the hour. Contract work for bulk cargoes was abolished and converted to piecework, the rates negotiated by the company and dockers' representatives, with the 'plus' divided equally between all the gangs doing the work. Tillett's union also grew during the strike, from a few hundred to 18,000. It also re-launched itself as the Dock, Wharf, Riverside and General Labourers' Union (DWRGLU) which, within two months had 30,000 members. Aside from London, the new union had branches in eight other ports (Bristol, Southampton, South Wales, Hull, Ipswich, Harwich, Gloucester and Medway) and two abroad: (Rotterdam and Amsterdam). Ben Tillett remained General Secretary with Harry Orbell, the organiser of the Tilbury strikers, and Tom McCarthy, of the stevedores, as national organisers of the new union. Tom Mann became the President. The DWRGLU (on the waterfront known as the 'Dockers' Union), together with the 'Liverpool Union', the NUDL, which by then also had a new name, the National Union of Dock Labourers and Riverside Workers in Great Britain and Ireland (NUDLRW), came together in 1922 as the nucleus of the new, general union, the Transport and General Workers.

But those days lay well in the future in the years after 1890 when trade depression again returned to weaken the London-centred Dockers' Union. In 1890 it had 56,000 members. By 1892, only three years after its historic success, it was down to 23,000 and still falling, to reach 10,000 in 1896. The NUDL suffered a similar fate. Its 50,000 members in 1890 were 8,500 in 1892 and, though it then began to regain members, it had not reached 14,000 by 1900.

The employers, as always, would now counter-attack. In London they reneged on the 1889 settlement. The old, secretive approach to the 'plus' system returned, the companies refusing access to the dockers' representatives. By 1890 the employers' associations had also begun to flourish, across Britain and in all trades. At the docks the Shipping Federation was formed, and soon began to bring 'free labour' into every British port. In Liverpool the recently founded Employers' Labour Association also began to turn the screws. The NUDL's high point of 1890, when half the membership was in Liverpool, led it to move its headquarters from Glasgow to Liverpool. But that did nothing for membership, which began to fall, with many branches collapsing through lack of funds. In 1893 McHugh and McGhee resigned. James Sexton became the new General Secretary. It was the end of an era, and not only in Liverpool. Had the sacrifices of 1889 and 1890 really all been in vain?

On a simple, short-term calculus of gains and losses the waterfront workers of the first and second ports of Empire had little to show for their epic struggles and privations against the powerful, heavily resourced and resourceful employers, who were now learning to act in local and national combination. But such a calculus is never more than a part of the bigger picture. The struggles of the seamen, of the waterfront workers in London, Liverpool and many other ports, big and small, of the gasworkers in the large provincial cities as well as in London, were the nucleus and beginning of a seismic shift in Britain's labour landscape. New workers in new unions, less skilled but more aggressive, more influenced by radical ideologies as 'labour' became 'Labour', joined the older ranks of the 'trades', the old aristocrats of the factory, the shipyard and the mill. There were some early clashes in aims and means, but both, in due course, mutually prospered from the existence of the other.

On the waterfront, in Liverpool as in London, dockers, carters, stevedores, coal-heavers and all the others learned the hard way the value of solidarity over sectional self-interest. Yet sectionalism, especially in Liverpool, was put aside only temporarily. The binding ideologies of the left, even syndicalism, did not run as deep as those in authority often assumed. Syndicalism was an ideology inspiring leaders more than the led and, even then, their words were not always followed by actions. The strike was also a weapon deployed by all for immediate, tactical gains, often without any very long-term or revolutionary world view.

So if the victory in London in the autumn of 1889 was not permanent, it must still be seen a huge beginning. Tillett stayed at the helm, while Mann began to move freely right across the British labour and political landscapes, until in 1901 he took his family to New Zealand, followed by Australia where his organising energy was given full rein.[20] He was also buffing and polishing his own brand of revolutionary socialism, combining ideology, rhetoric and bargaining. That combination he would get his chance to put into effect in Britain. His opportunity came, after Southampton, in the Liverpool of 1911.

Mann, Sexton and Larkin

Recalling his part in the events of 1889, Will Thorne observed that Mann was '... a streak of human quicksilver', here, there, and everywhere, commanding, pleading, cajoling, enthusing ...' Ben Tillett would later describe him as 'a giant, a power'. The three were, of course, friends as well as comrades, not always the same thing. Tillett and Mann would remain so until the end of their days and, as good friends, were able to quarrel and differ, sometimes profoundly, but always to forgive. Much of that was perhaps due to Mann's generous spirit. Tillett was a man of courage and achievement who never wavered in his championing of the poor and oppressed, but he was '... quick to imagine slights and insults'. He fell out with John Burns and then, in a letter, accused Mann of being '... faithless, cowardly, selfish and mean'. He believed that Mann had opposed his request from the union to pay his lawyers following a failed libel action against a newspaper. Mann's response to Tillett's letter, maintaining that the accusations were groundless, says much more than words:

> You declare all friendship off now, well let it be so but not with my endorsement. I plead no virtue, I lay nothing against you, and I shall only be too glad to meet and fraternise, and whether you will or no, I shall continue to love and admire you.[21]

Sexton and Mann were never so close again, but their association in 1911 was central to the final outcome. Mann's experience, energy and commitment – allied to Sexton's lengthy, hands-on, knowledge of Liverpool's docks, dockers and employers – was a powerful combination. James Larkin, Sexton's former colleague in the NUDL, was not involved. He had been suspended by Larkin in 1908 and, by then, had his own patch in Ireland. It remains intriguing as to what part Larkin would have played in 1911 and how well he would have related to the other big players. Sexton clearly admired his energy and impact on the Liverpool waterfront, but had doubts concerning his sincerity and judgement, especially in his work for the NUDL in Ireland. Their final bitter break was early in 1911, when Larkin gave evidence against Sexton in Sexton's action against the publication of a libellous pamphlet. Sexton won and was awarded damages.[22] Yet, in the final analysis, it was ideology and methods, more than temperament, that made even a limited association impossible. Both made important contributions towards better lives for working people, but Sexton's cautious, pragmatic methods and limited, gradualist aims could never coexist with the '... stormy petrel of Irish trade unionism and the prophet of revolutionary socialism'.[23]

In practice Mann shared some of Sexton's caution and pragmatism, but did not often parade his avowedly syndicalist world view on the stump,[24] as Larkin did in both words and deeds. Sexton also maintained that Larkin's libel action against him undermined his standing in the NUDL and political reputation outside. The union also lost its Irish branches to Larkin's Irish Transport Workers' Union, later followed by the defection of the Glasgow branch which, in 1911, formed the nucleus of the west coast's Scottish Union of Dock Labourers.

Liverpool's long hot summer

Sunny days bring people on to the street in numbers, but as temperatures and tempers climb old grievances can be readily aired and, just as readily shared. Liverpool, in 1911, was not alone among British ports in harbouring feelings of extreme discontent. Elsewhere the suffragettes had also begun to campaign a few years earlier with an effective cocktail of obstruction, civil disobedience and violence. They were rarely out of the headlines, as well as the minds of authority, and were planning to step up their campaigns in 1911, a year that was to prove to be the beginning of a lengthy, spreading wave of strike action. Between 1911 and 1914 there were over 4,000 strikes, losing, in total, more than 70 million working days. Some were very big affairs. Twelve of the strikes each exceeded 500,000 days lost. A few others, though below that figure, were of great significance. They involved railwaymen, and Liverpool's dockers and seamen.[25] The seamen were especially irate, so that in 1911 the Liverpool men were far from alone, as events moved towards the first national seamen's strike. The trigger was pulled at Southampton on 9 June, five days ahead of the national stoppage planned to begin on 14 June.

The Southampton seamen had successfully delayed the sailing of the passenger liner SS *Olympic*. Southampton, by then, had largely taken Liverpool's place as the main focus of the long-distance passenger trade. The *Olympic's* wealthy, mainly first-class passengers were well put out by the delay, as was the Shipping Federation which, for the first time in twenty years, was unable to supply strike-breaking crews to its shipowner members.[26] That had something to do with the presence, at Southampton, of Tom Mann, who in 1910 had been invited by Havelock Wilson to organise his National Sailors' and Firemen's Union members to mount an effective challenge to the power of the seemingly invincible Federation. In that Wilson was probably both encouraged, as well as disappointed, by the emergence in Liverpool, in 1909, of a new seamen's union: the National Union of Ships' Stewards, Cooks, Butchers and Bakers.

For a long time Wilson had sought to organise the stewards, the 'smart young men in buttons', but their carefully maintained social distance from the sailors on deck and the firemen below decks made it difficult for them to see themselves as potential trade union members, let alone members of Wilson's union. But the stewards' emerging leaders were different. The new union's general secretary was Joe Cotter. Cotter had first gone to sea as a cook, but became a steward on

MANN ADDRESSING CROWD.

Tom Mann on the platform on his arrival in Liverpool. James Sexton is not present, but at least two other members of the strike committee (Frank Kilkelly and George Milligan) are there on Mann's right. Kilkelly and Milligan, both devout Catholics, were dockers' (NUDL) delegates. Milligan, an able and popular man, turned down a national appointment in the newly formed TGWU in 1922, to stay in Liverpool as Area Secretary. Note the 'minders' at the base of the platform. The men in straw boaters were probably ships' stewards.

Cunard's famous transatlantic liner, the *Mauretania*. In 1909 he was sacked for agitating against Cunard's employment of foreign workers.[27] It was therefore no coincidence that he founded the new union in the same year. He was also a syndicalist, as was the union's treasurer, Fred Pearce, as well as Liverpool Trades' Council's James Murphy. The syndicalist movement's Merseyside membership was never substantial, especially in 1909,[28] but its members were well placed and influential in the unions and dominated the strike committee that emerged two years later to control and direct the transport strike. The key influence on the strike committee was, however, Tom Mann.

Mann's syndicalism emerged some years after the Great Strike of 1889. He first turned his organising talents (well honed by that strike) to the benefit of the Independent Labour Party (ILP). He was elected National Secretary in 1894, unlike the other prominent leaders of 1889, who soon went into politics. Burns became an MP in 1892 and later a member of the Liberal government. Tillett entered Parliament in the same year, the first docker to do so. Thorne took some

Marching to the St George's Plateau, 31 May 1911. This is the traditional route (Myrtle Street, Hardman Street, Parliament Street) that was still used during the 1995–98 dispute. The tramwaymen, in their caps, are on the right.

© LIVERPOOL RECORD OFFICE

time, joining them in 1906, after several attempts. Mann remained with the ILP until 1898. In 1893, curiously to some, Mann thought seriously of becoming a priest in the Church of England.[29] Then, in 1895, like the other members of the 1889 quartet, he turned his attentions to politics. He was an unsuccessful candidate for Colne Valley in 1895, despite campaigning with his usual energy. It was reported that he spoke at twenty-five meetings the day before the poll. He then almost won Aberdeen North in a by-election the following year, losing by just 430 votes.[30] In 1897 his third attempt – at Halifax – was also a failure, but by then he was becoming disillusioned by his wider failure to bridge the continuing divisions among his fellow socialists in the ILP. This would have been aggravated by the personal attacks on him by the three prominent members of the party's leadership – Keir Hardie, Ramsay MacDonald and Philip Snowden.[31] He was also becoming increasingly internationalist in his outlook and activities. He resigned from the ILP in 1898, and by the time he had decided to leave for Australia, which he did n 1902, he was embarking on an intellectual as well as a physical journey. His experiences, as well as his involvement with the Industrial Workers of the World (The 'Wobblies') in 1905, began to take him away from the parliamentary route to socialism to the direct route of classical syndicalism.[32] By the time he returned to Britain, in 1910, he was the tailor-made leader for Liverpool's 'near revolution'. For company on the strike committee, he would also have the company of Liverpool's syndicalist coterie.

Strike for Liberty!'

When Mann got off the train on 14 June 1911, Liverpool was enjoying a fine summer, just as London had done twenty-two years earlier. He was soon in the thick of the action. With Ben Tillett and others he helped to launch a federation of transport unions, the National Transport Workers' Federation, which soon had seventeen affiliates. Havelock Wilson's seamen were also becoming increasingly restless, especially following the shipping employers' curt rejection of the union's offer to negotiate. A rash of unofficial strikes in several ports was beginning to force Wilson's hand. He declared the intention to call an official stoppage, secretly planned for 14 June 1911, although by then all port workers throughout the country were beginning to act to press their own special grievances and claims. There were also outbreaks of rioting and looting, especially in Hull where some fires were also started. One Hull town councillor who had witnessed the events of the Paris Commune of 1870 saw parallels in the port with the actions of the French female firebrands, *les petroleuses*, of the Humber.[33] The main spotlight was, however, already shifting to the west coast.

On 31 May the National Transport Workers' Federation had organised a mass demonstration at Liverpool's St George's Plateau. Havelock Wilson, Will Thorne, James Sexton and Ben Tillett were on the platform. A resolution was passed urging all transport workers – dockers, carters, coal-heavers, railwaymen and others – to support the two seamen's unions in the coming dispute. The NTWF had secretly planned for the wider strike to begin on 15 June, but rumours spread that it would start on 14 June, encouraged by the Southampton seamen jumping the gun the day before. Tom Mann also arrived, on 14 June, just as 500 firemen refused to join two ships (of the Canadian Pacific and White Star lines) berthed at the North End. Mann, by now appointed chairman of the strike committee, addressed a dockside meeting of the strikers and their supporters. He declared the beginning of the strike, displaying a poster: 'War Declared: Strike for Liberty.'

With these words there was set in motion what was to be called, among other things, a 'convulsion', lasting seventy-two days, involving a national strike of seamen, later to be joined by the railwaymen, striking nationally for the second time, in August. There were also local strikes of dockers, carters, tugmen, bargemen, coal-heavers and tramwaymen. Similar actions were under way in most of the other ports. Although Liverpool was not alone, it was 'spearheading

'Bloody Sunday', 13 August 1911, at St George's Hall Plateau. This has been a popular public space in Liverpool since the time the hall was constructed, not least for demonstrations and protests. It was also used by the dockers for meetings in the 1995–98 dispute. There are a few middle-class onlookers, who would witness the police baton charge. The banner in the middle of the photograph is that of the National Union of Dock Labourers.

© LIVERPOOL RECORD OFFICE

a national movement', and even an international 'upheaval'[34] which was only stopped in its tracks by the outbreak of war in 1914.

The May demonstration was a massive affair, lasting three days, beginning with marches, bands and banners from both ends of the city. But it passed off without serious incident, and the evident widespread solidarity soon bore fruit. The key demand of the seamen was for recognition of their unions. The Shipping Federation and its members had for long been obdurate on this central issue, seeing discipline on board ship in a military light, with seamen's representation as almost mutinous. Several of Liverpool's companies were, however, not in the Federation. This partly explained the NTWF's strategy of using Liverpool, the employers' weaker link, as the national spearhead. Four companies – Alfred Holt, Cunard, Booth and the Canadian Pacific – quickly conceded on the demand for recognition and a wage increase. White Star, another non-member, prevaricated, as other companies, members of the Federation, began to dig in. Then the Federation itself moved into action with its usually effective strategy: strike-breakers were brought in from other ports. The Federation, however, now found itself in the new situation of a national strike. The non-unionists in Liverpool also began to

The NUDL banner on 'Bloody Sunday'. Note the alternative term, 'Red' Sunday.

behave in a surprising manner. They not only supported the strikers, but also began to sign up in unprecedented numbers. Solidarity broke out all along the waterfront as the Federation found itself unable to bring the usual ready supply of strike-breakers into Liverpool to man the idle ships: they were everywhere on strike themselves. The union, the NUDL, had already decided not to handle the cargo of any ships owned by companies that had not settled with the seamen. Even the mostly Protestant carters were now in unison with the largely Roman Catholic dockers. By 27 June the fiercely anti-union Federation was weakening. The Liverpool branch of the Federation was giving its members freedom to settle independently; indeed, many already had. The shipping companies had now broken ranks irretrievably. It was a handsome, even historic victory for the seamen. They had advanced their pay and conditions but, above all, they now had the recognition that the Federation had for so long denied. At a critical time they also had the support of the other unions along the waterfront, especially the dockers. It was a lesson in solidarity.

The next morning, the 28th, over breakfast, the shipowners were reading in their copies of the *Daily Courier* that the strike was over. They were perhaps more relieved than pleased, but felt better about themselves for the *Courier's* praise of their generosity towards the seamen! But their coffee had hardly cooled before news began to come up from the waterfront that 4,000 dockers had walked out.

The Birmingham Police off duty, playing cards. They has a fearsome reputation and could be relied upon to be rigorous with strikers or demonstrators. Note the onlooker to the right.

Even worse, at 9 a.m. the entire crew of Canadian Pacific's *Empress of Britain* (its owners were a company that had settled early in the strike) came out in support of the dockers. More, the seamen were marching triumphantly along the North End docks calling on other seamen from ships on the Atlantic run to join them. By that evening 10,000 men from all sea and land trades were on strike. The entire dock system was at a standstill. The crew of the *Empress of Britain* gave their reasons. In the words of a ship's steward:

> Yes, I admit we have got what we wanted ... we have no grievance with the company, but there is a question of honour at stake. The dock labourers struck purely in sympathy with us, and now we are going to do the same for them.[35]

The union leaders and the strike committee would have been surprised by the spontaneity and size of the mass walkout. As worldly men they would have perhaps been even more surprised by the seamen's explanation. Nor would they privately have favoured the indiscipline of unofficial action. But the committee moved quickly. They went back to the shipowners to demand recognition for the dockers. Within a week they had it, including in some cases the acceptance of the NUDL's own code of rules on wages and conditions which had first surfaced as long ago as

90.[36] Union officials in the branches now found themselves almost overwhelmed with the large numbers seeking to join the newly recognised NUDL. In only two weeks James Sexton had achieved the recognition for which he had fought for years. The employers now had to contend with a mass movement.

Mann, the born-again syndicalist, along with Joe Cotter and Fred Pearce, saw this as an example of how industrial action, given total solidarity, could even overthrow capitalism. The *Courier*, on 29 June, shared some sympathy for the dockers, but was more afraid of the possible outcome of the '... spirit of revolt, combined with a feeling of federal brotherhood'. But the *Courier*, also accurately, judged that this remarkable solidarity might not last. They may even have agreed with Mann, the veteran of many struggles, who valued the key importance of solidarity, but solidarity tempered with discipline and patience, and the need to maintain sufficient popular support. Public opinion was as important then, as now. Employers also had greatly superior resources compared with the unions, and they knew it. A counter-attack was only a matter of time. It was preceded by playing for time. While recognition of the NUDL had been almost universally granted, most shipowners had conceded little on pay and conditions other than an agreement with the strike committee to a conference in a month's time to consider all matters. It was not enough for the North End members of the NUDL, who refused the committee's instructions to return to work pending the conference. Mann, Sexton and Cotter, assisted by George Milligan,[37] the Secretary of No. 12 branch of the NUDL, which held the cards of most of the dockers holding out, had to use all their powers of oratory and persuasion at mass meetings to hold the line. They succeeded, but it was a close-run thing. The return to work was finally achieved on Monday, 3 July.

Meanwhile, other workers were joining unions in large numbers and as the proportion unionised rose, traditional fears and insecurities were put to one side and the tendency to strike spread. Throughout July, when the dockers were working, waiting for their conference to begin, there were strikes of tug boat men, young workers on the passenger ferries, cotton porters, oil mill workers and women shoemakers at the Walton Rubber Works. The tramwaymen were also signing up in large numbers in their new union – the National Union of Enginemen, Firemen, Mechanical and Electrical Workers. Before long they too would be 'out'. Then, as the long hot summer went into August, and the dockers and shipowners were reaching agreement, the railway workers took the dispute into a new and more dangerous phase.

The railwaymen had been restless for some time over the inability of Lloyd George's system of Conciliation Boards[38] to deliver sufficient and reasonably early progress on pay, hours and conditions. They also tended to blame their own officials for their lack of fight, in much the same way as the dockers with the NUDL, especially James Sexton. On 5 August the lid blew off. Not surprisingly it was in Liverpool. On that day an unofficial strike began at the North Docks Depot of the Lancashire and Yorkshire Railway. The company responded in its

An armoured police van. Note their physical stature when men were generally much shorter than they are today.

Mounted police protect a convoy. The horse may have slipped, been taken ill, or even died in harness.

A convoy under escort. This looks less like a convoy, more a show of strength, with mounted police and soldiers with rifles at the slope. The strikers would appear to be marching on the left, by the warehouse. The Overhead Railway is on the right.

usual fashion, blacklisting strikers and bringing in replacements. Over the next three days separate strikes at other companies and sympathy strikes in support of the Lancashire and Yorkshire men spread rapidly. By 8 August all rail traffic at the docks had ground to a halt; 4,000 were on strike. The strike committee immediately declared its support as trains stopped across the North West and soon across the whole country. But, symptomatically it took the four railway unions' national leadership until 17 August to follow the lead of the local men and make what was a *de facto* national strike an official one. By then the government had already played its hand.

Winston Churchill was at the Home Office. He was no stranger to decisive action against strikers, up to and including 1911, earning him lasting opprobrium among many of the working class even beyond the Second World War. Hull was the first target, the authorities frightened by the large numbers in the streets. Extra police and troops were sent in; predictably, the crowds rioted. Liverpool was next. The size of the crowds, though behaving peacefully, led the magistrates to send in increasing numbers of police. Then, responding to minor incidents, they began to lose their nerve. However, the decision to appeal to the Home Office was not made until the strike committee declared its support for the striking railwaymen. By that date, Wednesday 9 August, 15,000 goods' porters were out, with mass pickets at the entrances to Central and Lime Street stations. Lime Street faced

LPOOL STRIKE 1911 No: 5 H.M.S. "ANTRIM" IN READINESS Carbonora Lpool

Guns on the Mersey. The war cruiser would have been a sinister, intimidating sight to the strikers. As the caption says HMS *Antrim* was 'in readiness'.

on to St George's Plateau, the traditional gathering place for labour marches and demonstrations. By the beginning of the following week it would become the scene of Liverpool's own 'Bloody Sunday'.[39]

On the instructions of the strike committee the mass picket at the railway station allowed essential goods, especially milk, to pass. But the railway companies and police were also allowed to take lorries through the pickets carrying more questionable 'essentials' such as beer. One vehicle was overturned and had most of its barrels taken. The beer was gratefully consumed by the crowd in the continuing hot, thirsty weather. Then, early on the next morning – Thursday 10 August – contingents of police, from Leeds and Birmingham, arrived at Lime Street Station. Churchill had responded with his customary speed and generosity to the call for troops, sending cavalry and infantry to bolster further police arrivals in the following days. One estimate was that by the end of the week '... 5,000 troops and 24,000 police were at the disposal of the Head Constable'.[40]

Meanwhile, the shipowners had added their own provocation. Their agreement with the NUDL on new terms and conditions was signed on 3 August. Within a week, on 10 August, as extra police and troops were arriving in Liverpool the shipowners announced a lockout from Monday 14 August unless the unions lifted their 'blacking' of goods transported by rail. Not surprisingly, even in Parliament, some charged Churchill with orchestrating state support, in a labour dispute, for the employers. On the streets of Liverpool no other view made sense. It was even rumoured, with later evidence to support it, that the troops had been issued with live ammunition. More than rumour, and visible for all to see, was the sight of two gunboats, anchored in midstream, close to Birkenhead, their guns pointing at Liverpool.[41]

Tom Mann had recently launched a weekly newspaper, *The Transport Worker*, which, in its 8 August issue, announced a mass demonstration to be held on St George's Plateau on Sunday 13 August. The day, like many before it, began bright and sunny, and by 3 p.m. the crowds, with bands and banners, including families, were sweltering in the heat. They were in festive mood, listening to the speeches. There was a new confidence and solidarity among workers who were usually more at odds with each other and their union officials rather than with the employers. Tom Mann noted that never in his experience '... did so many workers in such varied occupations show such thorough solidarity as on the occasion [i.e. of the strike as a whole] in Liverpool'. He was especially impressed with the putting aside of sectarianism on the strike committee:

The differences arising between these [i.e. the Protestant carters and Catholic dockers] are frequently of a very emphatic character, but I have pleasure in recalling that, when we commenced the strike and began committee work, it was definitely agreed that neither political nor theological opinions were to find advocacy or expression on the committee. We were engaged purely on an industrial subject and that alone should receive attention.[42]

The other requirement was orderly, disciplined and peaceful behaviour. Against all the odds that was almost achieved. But the authorities always feared large, even clearly peaceful gatherings of united, determined workers. The power of the peaceful marches in London, in 1889, offered lessons for the authorities. The use of police and troops in large numbers, especially in industrial disputes which those involved consider to be economic in origin, can quickly become provocative, even if that is not the intention. Subsequent events also need to be seen in the context of the Liverpool of 1911. Liverpool was still one of the most successful, prosperous ports in the world and two years later, in 1913, the MDHB would post yet another record in the revenue on its accounts. Yet such visible wealth and opulence for the few was against a backdrop of recurring insecurity and seemingly endemic poverty for the many. The events of the summer of 1911 merely confirmed the view from the streets that the employers and the state, with their greatly superior resources, were ranged four-square against them. It was difficult for them to see it as other than class war, even though the syndicalists on the strike committee were mostly careful not to portray the dispute in that way – at least in their public statements – for fear of the inevitable reaction. Their concern was well founded, because a reaction was forthcoming in any case.

The demonstration on 'Bloody Sunday' attracted, at its height, an estimated 80,000 people.[43] There were undoubtedly small scuffles with the police, one involving youths sitting on a window sill of the London and North Western Hotel (now a Liverpool John Moores University hall of residence), which looked onto St George's Plateau; the other when a cart was turned over in Lord Nelson Street at the side entrance to Lime Street Station. Whatever the spark, the police, concealed in St George's Hall, were ordered to clear the plateau, which they did with repeated baton charges. Two hundred were injured, some very seriously, needing hospital treatment. Twenty of those were policemen, as the strikers put up some resistance. Tom Mann, fearing military intervention, closed the demonstration, ordering people to leave the scene. Most of the newspapers, including the *Manchester Guardian's* reporters, condemned the 'merciless use of truncheons',[44] although *The Times* pointed to the critical involvement of 'criminals and rioters', and older sectarian conflicts.[45]

Writing in 1991, White saw the brutal police behaviour as standing out for its 'gratuitous pointlessness' given the demonstration's legality (formal permission had been sought and granted in advance), its peaceful nature, and that the violence was not linked to an immediate, important objective such as taking strike-breakers through picket lines. Furthermore, it not only strengthened the strikers' resolve and case; it threatened to transform the dispute from a complex of separate and sympathy strikes into a Liverpool general strike.[46] That was made certain when a crowd, on Tuesday 15 August, held up a prison van with an escort of troops *en route* to Walton Gaol via Vauxhall Road, a main thoroughfare parallel to the Dock Road. The troops opened fire, killing two men, one a Protestant, the other a Catholic. Both denominations were at the funeral, the incident confirming the evidence of the putting aside of sectarianism – if only temporarily.

The same day Mann announced a general strike of all transport workers. On 17 August they were joined by the tramwaymen and other corporation workers. By then the strike total was estimated at 66,000.[47] The entire city was now at an almost complete standstill. Food and other essentials were, however, kept moving under the authority and control of the strike committee. This control of distribution developed from milk and bread permits to permitting supplies to be delivered to hospitals and charitable institutions. There was also some involvement in allowing the mail to go overseas. The strike committee were seemingly not aware of the significance of what, to them, seemed normal, sensible and unavoidable. Some in the government were, by contrast, considerably alarmed at seeing what they saw as the embryonic development of workers' control of Liverpool's economy. The means of distribution might even be followed by production and exchange, the rest of the new Labour Party's famous Clause Four.

The government moved quickly to bring both sides together. The railwaymen went back on 22 August with not more than the promise of a commission, but morale was high and was to spur an amalgamation of the three railway unions into one, the National Union of Railwaymen, in 1912. The dockers had their White

Book Agreement (its origins in the NUDL's code of rules, drawn up in 1890) as the basis for a return. It had been signed on 3 August even though temporarily interrupted by the subsequent employers' lockout. There was a further threat to the return to peace on the last day. The strike committee ordered the return to work under the White Book Agreement, but quickly rescinded the order when it was learned that the Corporation had refused to reinstate 250 striking tramwaymen. The Corporation relented to save the day, but it was a further two days before the return to work, and even during 1912 some of the striking tramwaymen remained without jobs.[48] The dispute finally ended on 24 August, and the strike committee was disbanded. It had lasted seventy-two days.

The White Book Agreement set up a permanent joint committee to consider and agree upon proposed changes in working practices. Of great importance to the employers was the introduction of a disputes procedure to head off the numerous, short, unofficial strikes that greatly disrupted port work. That provision was also favoured by union officials, who were always struggling against the constant challenges to their discipline and control. The employers were also still free to hire non-union labour, although this was a paper provision since, in practice, only union labour was hired at the stands. For the union, however, the greatest gain was recognition, for which it was prepared to pay the price. That, and the undoubted success of the strike, transformed the NUDL's membership base. Over the year 1911 membership of the NUDL more than quadrupled, to 50,000, of which some 31,000 were in Liverpool. Many were members new to unions, but a significant number came from other unions, *en masse*, to be absorbed by the NUDL. Thus, the dock labourers' ranks were swollen by coal-heavers, tugboatmen, crane drivers, cold storage workers and ships' clerks. When the Galway dockers joined the NUDL in 1913, to form a new branch, the NUDL was re-named to become the National Union of Dock Labourers and Riverside Workers in Great Britain and Ireland.

But success and growth were not without their problems. A substantial number of the members, perhaps as many as half, were in arrears with their contributions, although the union's income still continued to grow at a rapid pace, from £7,783 in 1910 to £25,841 in 1912.[49] Nor were those new to union membership easy to control; they could be prone to division and sectionalism, and were often overtly critical of Sexton's leadership, who was still commonly seen as too close to the employers, despite his efforts during the strike. Often he seemed to be too comfortable in the company of employers, and he was often praised by them. Yet, overall, the NUDL was in far better shape after the strike than before. Many old problems would remain, and new ones emerged. But it was 'a new world altogether', in which the employers had to accept that '... the union was everywhere. It had come to stay.'[50]

The 'near revolution'?

Measured by the number of strikers, Liverpool's 1911 confrontation was not the most important dispute in the four years up to the outbreak of the Great War. According to the Ministry of Labour, for August 1911, the combined total of striking dockers and seamen was 48,000, a figure that had little meaning since it excluded other strikers such as the railwaymen, tramwaymen and corporation workers. Yet even with these the total, about 66,000 at the peak, was fewer than the Lancashire cotton weavers later in the year, and dwarfed by the number of coalminers across the UK. Early in 1912, 1 million were out, totalling nearly 31 million days lost. Two years later, Yorkshire coalminers alone, over the three months from February to April, added 150,000 strikers to the Ministry's data.[51] Coalminers, of course, had always had 'revolution' in their hearts, and achieved that in a little measure in 1947 when their industry was nationalised. They also struck fear into governments, of all stripes, given their large numbers and central importance to the economy – as evidenced by Churchill's military interventions in the Rhondda. Yet seamen and dockers were equally strategic in an economy and empire that was largely held together by merchant ships, passenger vessels and gunboats. Britain was also heavily dependent upon imported food and raw materials, which had to be paid for largely with the export of goods and services. Disruptions in shipping and on the waterfront were, therefore, serious matters requiring government intervention if an early resumption of normal traffic were not achieved. That largely explains why the ports, like the coalfields, invariably attracted early military intervention from government, as in Liverpool in both 1890 and 1911. That 1911 attracted more determined intervention than in previous disputes was not because of the numbers involved, at 66,000, but that it was almost all the labour force, including the seamen. It was a 'general' strike. The London strike of 1889 was not 'general', but the same fate would certainly have befallen it if the dispute had not been organised and conducted in such an impressive and peaceful manner. Potentially alarming to the government and the citizens of London was the prospect of 100,000 marching in procession. The strike leaders were well aware that a peaceful dispute was their only option if they were to succeed. Waterfront workers also had a reputation, unjustly earned perhaps, for indiscipline and violence. But they did have public opinion on their side. The writings of Mayhew, Booth and Rowntree revealed the degradation endured by

LEFT

These men and boys are outside the home of one of the strikers killed by troops on Vauxhall Road. Note, too, that only the men and one teenage boy are wearing boots, probably because they were in work. It was still not unknown, up to the 1950s, to see barefoot children on Liverpool's streets.

many dockside families, which not only drew the sympathy of the middle class, but also their apprehension that the dispossessed might seek retribution. It might even have occurred to the more febrile and fertile imaginations that 1889 was the centenary of the French Revolution.

Liverpool attracted similar, fearful attention, and its 'natural' establishment, including Lord Derby, easily detected 'revolution'. As a port, too, it was not far behind London in importance and in exports, and could claim to be the more important. Together the two ports dominated British trade. In 1911 the seamen also emerged as a national movement, and not all Liverpool's shipowners were members of the aggressive Shipping Federation which could normally expect to bring in non-union seamen from other ports to break strikes. That option was closed off in 1911 by the universality of the seamen's strike. The dockers also came out in sympathy, a response soon returned by the seamen bringing the port to a standstill. Mann and his syndicalist friends on the strike committee saw the revolutionary potential, but dampened it. Others, especially Sexton, feared it. But they were all agreed that anything other than a peaceful, disciplined dispute would attract a strong reaction from the local and national authorities, who would use even minor outbreaks of violence as a pretext for force, even the use of armed troops. That proved to be the case. But such was the excitement of the new-found solidarity among the seamen, dockers and many other workers, even melting sectarian divides, that the events of Bloody Sunday and the deaths from troops' firearms merely strengthened their solidarity and resolve. When the railwaymen joined in, dragging their reluctant local and national union officials with them, the game was up and almost nothing moved without the permission of the strike committee. Nor could ships sail without crews, as Mann pointed out in his 'All the King's horses …' speech. To that extent a 'revolution' was in place, although the strike committee was simply reacting to events.

The unofficial extension of the strike by the dockers following the seamen took Mann and his committee by surprise. The same was the case with the seamen, in sympathy with the dockers and, later, the railwaymen. The committee was always looking for a favourable settlement, and the strikers themselves for recognition and the outlawing of non-union labour, although a wage increase was always welcome. The syndicalists on the committee were very pragmatic revolutionaries, and it is doubtful if syndicalist platform rhetoric influenced the rank-and-file much beyond getting them fired up to continue the struggle. As Taplin puts it, following Holton: 'The most that can be claimed is that workers adopted 'proto-syndicalist' behaviour, that is forms of social action which lie between vague revolt and clear cut revolutionary action.'[52]

Even more prosaically, for the men and their families, as the weeks passed deprivation and minimal strike pay made a settlement more and more imperative. The river was full of ships with cargoes waiting to be unloaded by dockers. The seamen had a choice of ships, with good prospects for work and wages. Nor did the railwaymen, or their leaders, have a tradition of militancy. Waller, in his account, lists improvements in wages and conditions and the general recognition of unions as the strike's objectives,[53] pure 'business unionism' and anathema to syndicalists. All the members of the strike committee would also have welcomed the emergence and maintenance of widespread solidarity as the means of winning these objectives. Solidarity was therefore never the sole property of the syndicalists. Mann, too, in practice less than a revolutionary, saw permanent solidarity 'as a first step towards fuller industrial unionism'.[54] The strike did achieve solidarity, although on Merseyside it would always be difficult to make it permanent. But it was enough to achieve permanent, recognised industrial unions for the dockers and seamen. In that Mann's role was significant, despite Waller's dismissal of Mann (with Havelock Wilson) as '... an ill-assorted pair with lengthy, but blemished records of labour activism ...', although he concedes that Mann was a '... magnetic figure on a platform addressing rough and discontented men, with his black hair, his flashing eyes and his tumultuous speech peppered with expletives ...'[55] He was clearly an extraordinary man who attracted admiration and scorn as he attracted friends and enemies. Yet the workers of the waterfront gained much that was lasting from the summer of 1911. Mann's role in that was decisive, and White's assessment should be seen as the most balanced: 'All in all Mann's leadership in Liverpool must be regarded as one of his great achievements.'[56]

If there was any revolutionary potential in Britain in the early years of the twentieth century, it was not alone, but in seriousness it was well behind the situation in the European mainland, where it was moving at a furious pace, especially in Russia and Germany, and where it would heighten to a crescendo during the Great War. Even in the USA the labour movement was as strongly influenced by socialist and syndicalist ideology as much as the political caution of the American Federation of Labor and, in many ways, its development was the mirror image of that in Britain. Yet in Britain war fever was to slow down and moderate radical ideas; in the USA it largely eliminated them. Blood-letting on an industrial scale became the preoccupation of all but a few, for four long years. Liverpool, too, was caught up in the fever as even dockers enthusiastically put on uniforms to load and discharge cargoes as well as go to war itself. Yet again was the world truly turned upside down.

CHAPTER EIGHT

War, peace and the union

The casual system freed the docker from the necessity to work a continuous six-day week, at the same time offering him the opportunity of relatively high earnings for irregular spells of employment. To many men these arrangements had a strong appeal ... This does not mean, of course, that the dockers placed no value on a secure income, only that they did not value it above all else.[1]

(Gordon Phillips and Noel Whiteside, 1985)

On His Majesty's Service
I wish to appeal for the immediate help of every man, woman and child in my effort to reduce the consumption of bread. We must eat less food; especially we must eat less bread and none of it must be wasted. The enemy is trying to take away our daily bread. He is sinking our wheat ships. If he succeeds in starving us, our soldiers will have died in vain ...[2]

(Ministry of Food, 1917)

Undoubtedly the sense of common purpose was at that particular moment stimulated by the collapse of the economy in 1921 ... Such events concentrate the mind. There was a sharp sense that 'if we don't hang together, we shall all hang separately'.[3]

(Ken Coates and Tony Topham, 1994)

T HE COLLAPSE of the economy in 1921 concentrated minds just as the 'near to revolution' events had ten years earlier. A period of peace and stability along the waterfront was needed to fill pockets and stomachs, to calm tempers and to mend broken heads. Even the employers were beginning to see the light, although their 'road to Damascus' conversion was far from complete on the waterfront. They realised that their traditional ability to break strikes with ease had passed. They now had to learn to negotiate and to compromise in good faith. But, above all, they had to accept that the union was there to stay.

In Edwardian Liverpool peace along the docks and at sea had been crucial as tension and war fever mounted. The Kaiser's Germany was flexing its military muscle as it prepared and planned for likely war with France, Russia and Britain. The war party in Germany welcomed it; in Britain, too, there were those who looked forward to a showdown on land, sea and in the colonies, especially Africa, where German ambitions were growing. In any conflict British strategists were well aware of the vulnerability of the country's supply lines and the consequent need for efficient working ports and a strong navy to protect mercantile trade. In that respect Liverpool was especially important because of its large volume and the direction of its trade with North America and the Empire. Its dockers and seafarers needed to be kept sweet and at work. More widely, the industrial unrest of Edward VII's reign also needed the close attention of policy-makers. The need to put a lid on strikes and lockouts in the ports was also directly linked to the readiness of the navy for war, not least through its dependence on coal.

Labour unrest and coal had in fact come together a good eleven years before the national stoppages on the ships and in the ports, in the Wales of 1900. The Taff Vale railway, along with two other small lines – the Barry and the Rhymney – linked the Welsh steamcoal collieries to the ports of the Bristol Channel. The fleet and the foreign coaling stations of the Empire were dependent on this coal, as were the ships of the mercantile marine. It also fired the furnaces of the South Wales ironworks, making the plates for the Navy's new Dreadnoughts. The Taff Vale railway 'servants' (the union) were just as aware as the coalowners and the government of the strategic importance of their jobs in the movement of coal. Of more immediate concern to them was the sacking of a signalman for leading a strike to improve their pay. With the support of their Union, the Amalgamated Society of Railway Servants, they walked out. They were soon picketing the station at Cardiff to persuade the brought-in strike-breakers to get back on their trains. Although support and sympathy for unionisation was widespread and far from confined to the workers, the directors of the Taff Vale took a hard line. They were strongly backed by the coal, iron and shipping interests as well, as the Cardiff Chamber of Commerce, who feared sympathy strikes by the dockers at the ports. The company had already denied the ASRS's demand for recognition, now increasingly common elsewhere, including on other railways. After the failure to break the strike they went to the courts for an injunction and damages. Though the Court of Appeal overturned the High Court's support for the company, in July 1901 the House of Lords finally imposed a fine, damages and costs on the union, totalling £30,000. That was a vast sum in those days. At 2007 prices it is still a penal figure, around £2.5 million, especially in relation to the limited funds of an early trade union.

The early effect of this blow to the legitimacy, even existence, of all trade unions was to give a powerful boost to the emerging, embryonic Labour Party in the form of the Labour Representation Committee, which had been founded only a year earlier. After Taff Vale the LRC did not have to persuade unions to affiliate. Up to February 1901 41 unions with a total membership of 353,000 had affiliated. That amounted to only 29 per cent of the TUC's affiliated membership. By February 1902, seven months after the Law Lords' decision, membership was 455,000, and by the next year (February 1903) the number of unions was 127, covering 847,000 members and 56 per cent of the TUC. Growth inevitably levelled out but by the time the LRC had transformed itself into the Labour Party, in February 1906, the union count was 158, with over 904,000 members, representing 58 per cent of TUC membership.[4] The Labour Party, the political 'wing' of the labour movement, had become a political force, both in the country and Parliament, with funding derived from rising membership and, mainly, union affiliation. A measure of the sea-change is that in the 1900 election the total expenditure of the LRC had been £33,[5] yet within a generation it was forming a minority government.

The trade unions and the nascent Labour Party were not alone in being alarmed by Taff Vale. So was the Liberal Party, the standard bearer of radical, though pragmatic, reform which, in 1901, had seen the 'labour question' as settled. It was not surprising, therefore, that the newly elected Liberal government of 1906 would soon pass into law the Trade Disputes Act, reversing the troublesome Taff Vale judgement. The Act confirmed official support for the legitimacy of trade unionism, which had been carefully nurtured in Parliament through the recommendations of a series of royal commissions beginning in 1867 to resolve the 'labour question'. Bringing the unions in from the cold recognised their vulnerability against the power, organisation and resources of employers. But this owed little to altruism and any ideas of social justice. It was a pragmatic response to growing numbers (though these were always far from sustained) and increasing public sympathy, notably during the spectacular, peaceful processions that had marked the 1889 Great Dock Strike in the capital. There was also the belief, among the establishment, that recognition of the 'fifth estate' would underpin the status quo and, in particular, discourage disruptive strikes. That also implied concessions by employers, especially a willingness to negotiate with them following recognition. But legally protecting trade unions against employers' natural instincts was not easy, given the peculiarities of English common law. The chosen legislative device was to give trade unions 'immunity' against actions for damages, whether through official or unofficial action, by its officers or members. The approach was perhaps the only one available, although, surprisingly, it was seen by Sydney and Beatrice Webb as going too far. The Act of 1906, however, was never seriously threatened until the election of the government of Margaret Thatcher in 1979.[6]

The reforming Liberal government of 1906 complemented its legislation with the expansion of the role of the Labour Department at the Board of Trade. The Board had been founded twenty years earlier, though its politicians showed little interest in the problems of unemployment and underemployment until Winston Churchill took office in 1908. His strong instincts for social reform – belying his later reputation for readily using troops to support the employer interest – led to the passing of the 1909 Labour Exchange Act, to limit the level of unemployment.

Casualism in the ports was attracting particular official interest after the work of influential political activists, such as Eleanor Rathbone, and reform-minded academics and public servants, such as William Beveridge. Beveridge was also, for a time, associated with the Webbs. While not a socialist, he did favour appropriate government intervention. As an economist he also had a distaste for waste and inefficiency, and, inevitably, took a dim view of casualism. Beveridge was perhaps the leading light of the '… progressively minded intelligentsia of that period, and shared its characteristic belief in the marriage of social science and government'.[7]

Richard Williams, who would make his mark on Merseyside, was one of that circle, although he had earlier experience as a company secretary with a mining company in South Wales. That experience with Welsh coalminers might well have stood him in good stead in his involvement with a no-less intractable but very different group of working men, the Liverpool dockers. In 1909 he was appointed to the North West Division of labour exchanges as divisional officer and, during 1911 and 1912, conceived and implemented the first attempt at a registration scheme to limit the casualisation of the dock labour force. The Board of Trade actively encouraged the development of the scheme, with ambitions to extend it, if successful, to other ports. It was also active in decasualisation schemes for other workers in other industries, including building workers, corporation labourers and ship repairers.[8] Williams, who was in Liverpool as employment for peace turned into employment for war, turned his attentions to converting the dockers into quasi-military units, Lord Derby's Dockers' Battalion.[9] Both of his schemes were ambitious. Though essentially unsuccessful, the 1912 scheme did provide important lessons for later attempts at reform, right up to 1967.

Williams was careful to consult his friends, especially Beveridge, as well as local employers such as Alfred Booth and Lawrence Holt, who sensibly favoured union involvement, now recognised across the port and which without which any scheme would inevitably founder. They were also members of the employers' side of the joint negotiating committee, a product of the 1911 strike, which shared equal membership with the NUDL. The initial idea, though not the detail of the scheme, came from Lawrence Holt and James Sexton.[10] That would have done nothing for Sexton's reputation with his members who, despite all his efforts over the years, including 1911, was not popular on the waterfront. Now in his attempts to remove or limit casualism, a system that still had a strong following along the waterfront, he was seen as in league with a shipowner (albeit a 'good' one), a class enemy to the dockers. The removal of the casual system actually had wide support among most employers, liberal reformers and government, albeit with different motives. Williams presented the details of the scheme, with supporting data, to a meeting of the employers' and unions' Joint Negotiating Committee. This was followed, some months later, in April 1912, by a paper read to the Liverpool Economic and Statistical Society.[11] It was a bold approach to cracking the hardest of nuts in dock employment.

Changing the leopard's spots: the 1912 Scheme

Although it was always going to be difficult to persuade dockers of the merits of radical reform, even any reform, of their working arrangements and preferences, the timing of the first serious attempt at decasualisation was especially unfortunate. The dockers, aided by the solidarity of other workers along the waterfront, had only recently, in 1911, won a hard-fought but famous victory. The strike was also against the fiercest of opposition from the majority of shipowners, other employers, and the Corporation and government, supported by heavy-handed police tactics and armed troops. Resentment and bitterness were running as high as the euphoria of victory. There was also no shortage of work along the waterfront, as normal activity was resumed, augmenting the huge backlog of work that had built up during the prolonged strike. The employers were also stepping up the work effort to contain costs and, wherever possible, avoiding the need for costly overtime rates. 'Speed-up', a practice long known wherever men work, had always been feared and resisted along the waterfront, as foremen drove the men to load and discharge ships as fast as possible. Even the firebrand James Larkin had been known as 'The Rusher' when working as a foreman on the docks.[12]

The lack of trust towards employers was well founded from direct experience over many years, and now they were supporting a new scheme to change the way they were hired. It inevitably looked like an attempt by the employers to snatch victory from defeat. Nor, paradoxically, did it help that the NUDL was now firmly established. It was recognised by the employers along the entire waterfront, including Birkenhead, and was signatory to the White Book Agreement, which finally secured peace and work on terms which were significant gains compared to those from earlier struggles. The union was still seen by many as complicit, refusing to acknowledge the ordinary dockers' views. Such antipathy stretched up as far as their general secretary. Sexton was an old-fashioned wheeler-dealer who could claim that his methods had done a great deal for his members, but his successes could do little to dent the deeply ingrained hostility of the rank-and-file to authority, including that of the union. Sexton, perhaps, *was* the Union, and he suffered for it.

The years before the First World War were also a time of great social unrest and industrial turbulence. It was an era when syndicalism, the archetypal ideology of the mass movement, could flourish. Though the Liverpool dockers were far from card-carrying syndicalists, they behaved as though they were, and the real syndicalists in their ranks had a well of discontent on which they could readily draw.

Paradoxically, the 1912 Scheme itself seemed to offer the docker a good deal. Its aim was to limit casualism and some of its most baleful influences, giving reasonable security of employment and earnings. It also sought to limit the numbers of the 'casual casuals', who drifted in and out of the labour pool, undermining the work opportunities for the regular men, a long-held grievance along the waterfront. There was also the inefficiency of the hiring system itself. Dockers failing to secure work on their regular stands were prevented by time and distance and lack of information of the chance to present themselves at another stand. There was no labour market for dockers as a whole, so that the demand for port labour, and the supply of those seeking work, was rarely, and only accidentally, in balance. Estimates showed that in the port's busiest month – usually January – the maximum daily labour requirement was 19,500, as against 27,200 looking for work on the stands as a whole.[13] Eleanor Rathbone had pressed the same point on an earlier occasion, with similar estimates of labour demand and supply.[14] The liberal reformers, including Rathbone and Williams, were unanimous in their view that a virtually permanent excess supply institutionalised casualism, with its unfortunate consequences for steady work and steady lives. Casualism had to come to an end.

Resistance, however, was widespread, strong and occasionally violently. This usually took the form of unofficial strikes, on both sides of the Mersey. Birkenhead showed the stronger resistance, which led to the shipowners threatening to tear up the White Book Agreement and bring in 3,000 strike-breakers, just like old times. These were actions seemingly designed to confirm, to the men, that the employers were intent on greater control to limit their freedom to work when and where they wished.[15]

The Scheme was planned to be introduced on 15 July 1912, on the same day as Lloyd George's National Insurance Act, with which it was linked. The new dockers' insurance card would record the employee's and employer's weekly contributions. The Scheme itself aimed to reduce the estimated labour surplus of some 7,000 and to increase labour mobility across the port as a whole, as Williams clearly stated.[16]

The main features of the Scheme were closely linked to the clearing houses.[17] These, six in all, were to be set up, two at the North End, two at the South End, and one each in the Central Area and in Birkenhead. Dockers were required to register at one of the clearing houses between 1 and 13 July 1912. These would normally be an already existing preference, near to where the men lived and linked to the shipping firm or firms for which the docker usually worked. Each registered docker would have a metal tally, with a number, which he would show at the stand when being hired. The clearing house at which he was registered would also be responsible for paying his weekly earnings, regardless of how many firms he had worked for. This was to eliminate the former practice of a docker having to travel, at the end of the week, from firm to firm to collect his wages. The clearing house also kept and maintained his insurance card.

Each clearing house had a committee of ten, with equal representation from the union and the employers, and with its policies and decisions subject to the final authority of the Joint Committee established in the White Book Agreement. The clearing houses, through the issue of tallies, were intended to control labour supply as demand rose and fell. They also controlled thirteen surplus stands, with the use of telephones for the first time to allow men not hired at their regular stands to find work at other stands. These measures were planned to reduce casual labour usage.

A central office was also set up at the Pier Head to coordinate the operations of the clearing houses. The government's involvement in the hoped-for success of the Scheme was seen in the Board of Trade's underwriting of the costs, via a levy on employers, of 0.5 per cent of the wage bill. The tally system was intended to limit the labour force to those men who worked habitually at the docks, producing a registered labour force largely devoid of casual labour.

Despite not offering permanent employment (such as in the case of the small core of dockers who worked directly for some companies, such as Cunard), the Scheme was warmly welcomed by most employers, the NUDL and the local press. But it was opposed by the dockers. That was not its only major problem.[18] For one thing, not all employers supported the Scheme. More than twenty firms, mainly in warehousing and porterage, continued to hire unregistered dockers. That suited those dockers who were especially unhappy with the reforms, as well as those employers seeing some return to 'free' labour, even though the NUDL was now a strong presence among all dockers. There was still opposition to the NUDL's leadership, fed by scares and wild, uninformed rumours, some of which were deliberately fed, such as that the Scheme would put 10,000 dockers out of work,and that they might be denied the opportunity to find work beyond the port. Williams himself even complained to Beveridge that '… you have no idea of the underhand methods that have been used to smash the scheme'.[19] It was also caught up in the national failure of the new labour exchanges to gain the confidence of those looking for work,[20] a problem that persisted well into the century. Those looking for and offering work at the exchanges and, later the job centres, were always a minority.

There needed to be a '… continued community of interest …' between the employers and the employed if the Scheme was to prosper. The large employers offered that, but it was not returned. That was the Scheme's undoing. Most of the NUDL therefore decided to strike in opposition, with the Birkenhead men out the longest. That was followed by 'passive resistance',[21] against strong union advice. Most dockers did not apply for registration, so that the joint negotiating committee left distribution of the tallies to the NUDL, which was inevitably generous. That led to the loosening of the aim to limit tallies to committed dockers. By March 1912, four months before the official launch, over 30,000 tallies had been issued, '… at least 8,000 more than the maximum number employed on one day, and probably some 1,500 more than the total population normally dependent on the docks for their livelihood'.[22] The total register had rapidly swung from a serious lack of recruits to over-recruiting and to including those it was intended to discourage. These, along with the twenty firms already hiring unregistered men seriously damaged the Scheme. Nor did it, from its inception in July 1912, do anything to encourage regular work habits. There was also little enthusiasm for foremen and dockers to use the surplus stands. Three days' working remained the norm: casualism remained alive and well all along the waterfront. Nor, as Williams had hoped, was it a first step towards regular work, regular pay and regular habits. Even though such ambitious goals were at least planted in men's minds because of the initiatives of Williams, Sexton and their colleagues, the Scheme '... blended, almost imperceptibly, into the landscape of casualism'.[23] By then, as peace gave way to war, the Board of Trade was considering two further options in order to secure regular, uninterrupted working. Both of these ideas were similarly difficult.

The first involved a level of coercion and the spending of money. The second was to offer inducements, such as higher and guaranteed wages, to discourage the commitment to casualism. War kept both options on the table. Nor did Richard Williams, soon to be in uniform, throw in the towel. He saw, as did many others, that permanent employment was ultimately the only way to resolve the dock labour problem. However, he had to concede that this was deeply unpopular. As he put it, '... the doctrine of permanent men stinks in the nostrils of the docker ...' His reasons for this were three. They believed that permanent work meant a loss of wages; there would not be enough work for all dockers; and they were accustomed to a casual regime. For many it was a case of better the devil they knew. If they were to be persuaded to abandon casualism, then that reserve workers would need to be paid '... a weekly *minimum* wage *work or play* ...' (author's italics).[24] Official thinking was clearly moving fast, but it would soon be overtaken by the exigencies of war. The concept of a guaranteed minimum would return in 1920, under the Shaw Inquiry.[25] As an idea it was before its time, and it required another world war to recognise fully the importance of the dockers to national survival. That came in 1941, an especially dark year in British history, not least in Liverpool. It was in the same year that Ernest Bevin (who had made his name at the 1920 Shaw Inquiry) as Minister of Labour, established maintenance for all British dockers.

The Khaki Dockers

The years immediately before the First World War have been characterised as ones of relative social stability and growing prosperity before the destruction and upheaval of 1914 to 1918 would bid it all goodbye and usher in a more dangerous, less secure world. Yet along Liverpool's waterfront these years were very different. In terms of industrial disputes Liverpool has seen little, before or since, to approach the scale and violence of the hot summer of 1911. The dockers could well claim to have won a famous victory in 1911, but bitterness and hostility would remain for some time. They and their families felt harshly judged and treated in face of their just demands. Nor did the employers seem to have changed much, even though they had to come to terms with a recognised union. Meanwhile, the attempt to introduce the 1912 Scheme left the dockers with widespread suspicion of, and deep resentment towards, the combined pressure that was applied by most employers, the Board of Trade and even their own union to accept the scheme. In 1914, at the outbreak of war, therefore, all was not well or settled on the Liverpool waterfront. Despite Richard Williams' optimism, the old casual ways of working were still very much in place, while the docker still saw himself as the free spirit of the waterfront, working when he chose, and distrustful of all in authority – even his own union officials, such as James Sexton.

Yet when war was declared the dockers rallied to the flag in large numbers: perhaps a quarter of the entire workforce volunteered. Even more surprising, astonishing even, was the enlisting in March 1915 of 350 men in three quasi-military formations ('companies'), all NUDL members, into the First Dock Battalion, Liverpool Regiment. The battalion, whose 'soldiers' were enlisted into military-style units and continued to work on the docks, was the idea of Lord Derby, the latest in the long line of aristocratic Stanleys, who had greatly prospered after their ancestor changed sides at the Battle of Bosworth. His successors naturally assumed command in times of crisis. Lord Derby was the commanding officer. Sexton was privately enthusiastic, although in public it felt it prudent to express reservations. George Milligan, the Merseyside District Secretary of the NUDL, was also supportive, as were his officials. Three were, just as naturally, enlisted as sergeants. Richard Williams, with his knowledge of dock labour, became the adjutant, commissioned as a captain. James Kessack, the NUDL's charismatic national organiser, enlisted into the army itself, in November 1914. He was 34 and almost two years to the day after enlisting he was killed in action. Many others followed him. In the first few months of the war 800 dockers would enlist. Most were NUDL members.[26] A second Docks Battalion was formed in 1916, bringing the then total dock labourers' 'force' to 1,750.

The loss of large numbers of the dock labour force was a serious matter made even worse by congestion in the port. Since the ports of the south and east of the UK were more vulnerable to enemy seaborne attacks, most traffic was diverted to the west-coast ports, primarily Liverpool and Glasgow. Liverpool's export trade was seriously curtailed, but became was the principal port for the import of food and raw materials from the Empire and North America, and, after 1917, for the disembarkation of American troops. Plans had been laid to deal with the congestion even before the hostilities began. As early as 1912 a committee was in existence for just such a purpose. In 1916, two years into war, a second committee was set up, to oversee and coordinate port labour. It had to deal with acute shortages, especially of the more experienced dockers who had joined the forces in large numbers. Replacements were found but, inevitably, they were not of the same calibre. As James Sexton often said, the skills and judgement needed to handle cargo in and out of holds were acquired from experience and 'knack', not brute strength. Hence the loading and discharging of vessels was done less efficiently, in more time, thus aggravating the problems.

The problems were also partly relieved, from 1917 by the exemption of dock labour from conscription. This, of course, required controls and in that respect the clearing houses hat had been set up as part of the 1912 Scheme, were useful.[27]

They helped in the registration of men who were willing to work on a regular basis or were not simply avoiding conscription. But their value was limited by the fact that the labour shortages were so acute that it was difficult for officials to refuse registration and the issuing of tallies.[28] It was also easy to blame the dockers for being idle, work shy and lacking patriotism. The NUDL mostly opposed this line, although some took to exhorting their members to work hard for the country, as Lord Kitchener did during a visit in 1915. There was also a limited attempt to bring women into the docks, but they were strongly opposed by the NUDL on the grounds of unsuitability, endangering men's lives and the lack of suitable toilet facilities.[29]

Support for the war among the wider labour leadership was far from universal, and this was the case, too, on Merseyside. The Liverpool Dock Battalion provoked fears of martial law in industries beyond the docks and the 'khaki dockers', in uniform, with their guaranteed full-time jobs attracted resentment and hostility from those not enlisted, the vast majority of the labour force. The NUDL was also anxious to retain its popularity among a sometimes hysterical public. It discouraged strikes or sought early resolution or truces until the war was over. But the policy was always difficult to enforce in that unofficial strikes were the norm. One unofficial stoppage covering both sides of the Mersey, over overtime rates, 'subbing' (advance payment of wages) and the timing of the weekend wage payments, began two weeks before the formation of the First Dock Battalion. It lasted over three weekends and greatly exacerbated the congestion problem. The stoppage, and its 'indiscipline', might also have encouraged Lord Derby to go ahead with his plans to form a second battalion, although he denied this.[30]

The initial success of, and enthusiasm for, the Dock Battalions were not sustained. The idea that such military-style labour, pioneered on Merseyside, could be extended to other ports and to other industries was attracting hostility, especially as Lloyd George and Lord Derby seemed to support just such a development. In particular it was feared that the battalion could be used to break strikes or (which amounted to the same thing) keep essential industries working – a widely supported view in times of crisis, especially war. The government, which was underpinning it, also began to worry about costs. This was especially so when the fluctuations of port traffic meant the battalion sometimes had little work to do. This also caused resentment from those 'civilian' dockers, who also had little work, but did not have guaranteed pay. It was also never more than 2 per cent of the dock labour force and, as such, made little if any impact on congestion in the port. At the War Office Lord Derby also became less directly involved as the battalion ceased to grow to a significant force. He was also concerned at the latent hostility to the experiment on all levels of the labour movement and among many dockers. Any plans to extend it to other ports would have added dangerously to that hostility. Then in January 1917 James Sexton criticised the increasingly independent use of the battalion, although by then it was playing a relatively insignificant role in the deployment of port labour. In May 1917 new regulations required dockers between 26 and 41 to register for military service. Exemptions were available for those working a minimum of 51 hours per week, for which a guaranteed minimum of 44s. od. was paid. Those not exempted would help to make up for the manpower losses on the Western Front.[31]

The Liverpool Dockers' Battalion therefore remained a local initiative that was only locally important for a short time, but it did attract widespread interest beyond Liverpool. Despite this, it never became a model for other ports, and the government drew back from proposing to extend it to other industries, for fear of an industrial and trade union backlash. But it serves as an example of the attractiveness of compulsion and the control of resources, including labour, to those directing a war, especially a conflict which can be portrayed as one of survival. The portrayal was also accurate enough, whatever the feats of the British army in Flanders or the navy at sea or even the dockers on Liverpool's waterfront, the country's Achilles heel was its heavy dependence on imports, especially food, that had to be carried in slow-moving, minimally armed merchant ships. In 1912 the Germans resorted to unrestricted submarine warfare which aimed at starving the British into defeat. The threat of the U-boat was demonstrated, spectacularly, on 7 May 1915.

The *Lusitania* (The 'Lusy') steaming past Kinsale Head in 1915. The circumstances surrounding her sinking have never been fully explained. Many of the crew were Liverpool men. The *Lusitania* was the sister ship of the *Mauretania*.

© LIVERPOOL MARITIME MUSEUM

'Demented Barbarians' [32]

The RMS *Lusitania* sank with the loss of 1,198 lives, including 128 Americans, in just eighteen minutes. It was a passenger liner, not a merchant ship, but its speed and status offered no protection. It was also a Liverpool-registered ship, and its captain was a Liverpool man, as were most of its crew. The sinking followed just two weeks after the Germans first used poison gas on the Western Front. Within hours of the *Lusitania* going down a large crowd, in dangerous mood, began to gather near the Liverpool docks. As it began to move along the streets, rioting and looting began, especially of food shops, not always with German sounding names. One small boy witnessed the smashing of the plate glass window of a pork butcher's shop in Smithdown Road, just beyond the city centre. After ransacking the shop, and taking the food on display, the mob ran upstairs to the owner's comfortable living quarters to do the same. The supposed German and his family had already fled. A grand piano was thrown through a third-floor window to crash noisily onto the street, drowning even the cheers of the onlookers. [33]

This episode was reported in the *Liverpool Echo*, with added colour:

> ... women hurling sausages at one another and one woman scrubbing the pavement with a joint of pork. Other women went home with their aprons full of pork and bacon ... A man came to the gaping hole where the front window had been [and where the piano had been thrown out] waving a handsome mirror over his head, smashing it to fragments against the stone sill amid cheers from the crowd below. [34]

In his autobiography Pat O'Mara recalls vividly the extent to which the loss of the *Lusitania* hit the dockland communities.

> It took about two days for the names among the drowned to be published. They were appalling ... We walked around Scotland Road listening to the cries of the women whose husbands and sons had gone down in the 'Lusy', and we heard the bitter threats made against Germany and anything with a German name. We walked down Bostock Street, where practically every blind was drawn in token of a death. All these little houses were occupied by Irish coal-trimmers and firemen and sailormen on the *Lusitania*; now these men who, barely two weeks ago had carried their bags jokingly down the street were gone, never to return ... Freddie, usually a light-hearted boy turned to me with whitened face and said: 'Listen to all them women crying!' On the corner of Scotland Road ominous gangs were gathering – men and women, very drunk and very angry. [35]

During three days of frenzied rioting 200 shops were wrecked and looted, some burned to the ground. [36] Not all of them were German. Enemy aliens 'were interned for their own safety', as German submarines penetrated to within five miles of the Mersey.[37] The Germans drew back soon after the *Lusitania*'s sinking, fearing that further losses of American lives would bring the United States, with its vast resources, into the war. Almost two years later, unrestricted submarine warfare was resumed. Between February and April 1917 nearly 2,000,000 tons of Allied shipping were sunk, against the loss of only 9 German U-boats.[38] That rate, averaging nearly 700,000 tons per month, easily exceeded the German Admiralty's estimate that losses of 600,000 per month would starve Britain into suing for a humiliating peace,[39] even should America enter the war, which it did in April 1917. The U-boats were also mostly sinking ships without warning, increasing the loss of lives. Lost tonnage peaked in April 1917, at 866,000. That amounted to 8 per cent of the total for the entire war. In 1917 alone 3,000 British merchant seamen lost their lives.[40] Given Liverpool's importance as a source of recruitment, a good proportion of these would have been from Merseyside. Fortunately, however, the tide turned just in time, mainly because of the introduction of escorted convoys in May of that year. Up to then convoys were believed to offer bigger targets for submarines and therefore even greater losses. The Royal Navy was also historically wedded to an aggressive, not defensive, war at sea, the so-called 'Nelson touch'. The Navy did, even so, begin to sink an increasing number of submarines, helped by the entry of the United States fleet into the war and its joint operations in Atlantic waters.

The staggering losses of ships and lives also meant the loss of vast quantities of raw materials and food. In the first six months of 1917 85,000 tons of sugar and 46,000 tons of meat went to the bottom of the sea, while current stocks of wheat and flour were estimated to be sufficient to last no more than two months.[41] Wheat and flour were the most critical since at that time 80 per cent of British wheat was imported, and bread was the staple (with potatoes) of those who manned the armaments factories, filled the troopships and kept the home fires burning. Most of all, people needed bread.

The diet of working-class families in the early years of the twentieth century, and for many years after, was insufficient and restricted, without regular fresh vegetables and meat. In that diet, inadequate though it was, bread was very important, and a major rise in the price of the standard loaf was viewed as a national crisis. Bread and margarine was a familiar meal at most tables, even with lard or dripping. Butter was well known as more nutritious but, especially in wartime, scarce and expensive. When available meat was either a treat or often denied children for the needs of the head of the household, the breadwinner. That was often justified given the predominance of often heavy manual labour for working men. The 'tea' of bread and margarine was usually accompanied by large quantities of liquid tea, laced liberally with sugar. So important was tea, as the national drink, that the government in both wars had plans to stockpile it, albeit for morale rather than nutrition.

By 1917, flour for bread-making was so scarce that it had to be 'doctored' with other grains or even potatoes crushed into the dough. The government had to introduce these ersatz products as 'war loaves'. They were actually more nutritious than the normal white bread of pre-war days, but nutrition was not as yet widely appreciated or even understood. In Liverpool, Sydney Bond recalls how his father, running a small bakery, coped. The potatoes were the main problem.

> You can imagine how awful it was to handle the dough or even to get this potato stuff to mix evenly. So it was a very common experience when cutting a loaf for a piece of potato to shoot out, and that's what the housewives had to put up with. A black loaf full of bits of potato. Oh, I won't say it was horrible, but it had an unpleasant spongy taste and smell.[42]

At times, the people were bordering on starvation, especially in the big cities, where there were limited natural food resources. Food riots were regular events in London and elsewhere. In Liverpool, the windows of food and other shops were frequently smashed for the contents in the window. Even in the better supplied country districts, with their access to local produce, there were problems. The picture of rural plenty and rural contentment was never more than an idyll; even in times of peace.[43] Voluntarism and *laissez faire* were also well-entrenched features of the attitudes of British governments, limiting intervention. Domestic food production had also been far from buoyant. Agriculture had for long been overshadowed by an emphasis on industry and commerce, with their greater returns; besides, food could normally be imported at low cost from the Empire. Almost to the end of the war the government had relied on voluntary rationing by the shops themselves. In February 1918 the government finally saw the light, and general food rationing was implemented, accompanied by price controls and the fines. By then, escorted convoys and the more effective hunting down of submarines had already saved the nation from being starved into submission. Lessons had, however, also been learned.

Such lessons would need to be remembered in Hitler's War, only a generation later. But that was unimaginable in November 1918 as the 'war to end all wars' came to an end, and the soldiers in Europe and the sailors on their ships waited impatiently, even mutinously, to be demobilised. Lloyd George had promised to make Britain a fit country for heroes to live in, and the heroes were anxious for an early part of it. For a time, too, it all seemed to be possible as rationing controls were largely dismantled, and a post-war boom led many to think that the better times would last. At the same time there was some talk of revolution coming to Britain, as Russia continued to implode, and workers' councils took to the streets in Berlin. In 1919 Glasgow also seemed to be involved in near-revolution, as a nationwide explosion of strikes in the same year led to fears of sabotage and syndicalist-inspired class war. As hysteria mounted, recalling the time when Burke had warned the House of Commons of Jacobin daggers being made in Birmingham, the Cabinet were informed of 700 rifles concealed in Liverpool.[44] All Europe was in ferment in the aftermath of war, as ancient monarchies collapsed in violence, and men and women with revolutionary ideologies and intentions took control. There was no reason to assume that Britain would not follow suit. And then, as if to confirm it, the police went on strike.

The Liverpool Police Strike of 1919

The National Union of Police and Prison Officers, to which the Liverpool policemen were affiliated, was formed in the year before the war. The union was not recognised, and on 30 August 1918, at a time of great unrest and rapid union growth in a war-weary country, it called out the 12,000-strong Metropolitan Police as well as the much smaller force of the City of London. The main issue was the demand for the reinstatement of a sacked union activist. To that was added recognition and a pay rise to compensate for falling living standards during the war. Most of the men struck and picketed effectively, using flying pickets. When troops deployed on the streets refused to intervene, Lloyd George had to negotiate or capitulate. He chose to talk, eventually conceding most of their demands, including the reinstatement. He refused to recognise the union, although it was hard to see his negotiations with them as anything other than as a *de facto* recognition.[45] The national union membership soon grew to pass 55,000 as the government prepared its expected counter-attack. The right to strike was denied under penalty of summary dismissal and loss of pension rights. Not surprisingly, limited numbers responded to the second call for a strike in both the Metropolitan and City of London forces. The Liverpool force then led the way. By 4 August a half — 932 out of a strength of 1,860 — were on strike.[46] It began to look like 1911 all over again, but this time with the police behaving like dockers, striking for money and union rights. The difference was that most of the dockers had had a good war, at least those who were covered, from 1915, by reserved occupation status. The Dockers' Battalion had also done well in terms of job security and steady, rising earnings. Many of the striking policemen had survived Flanders to return to jobs whose wages had lagged well behind wartime inflation. The Liverpool Trades Council were sympathetic to their case for the right to combine and withdraw their labour, and even considered calling sympathetic action. But memories of the events of 1911, especially on St George's Plateau, were still strong. The authorities were uniformly hostile. The Council swore in 730 Specials as the government sent in 2,500 troops, with warships again on the Mersey.[47] Tanks, armoured cars and soldiers with fixed bayonets marched down Scotland Road in a show of strength. Liverpool was occupied yet again.

The absence of police on the streets was a godsend to some. When the police were on the beat they were intimidating: a Liverpool policeman had to be over six feet tall, and they always patrolled in pairs, for obvious reasons. Their absence could not be immediately covered by the Specials, and the troops were not trained to quell civil disturbance. So the rioting and looting began and on a scale well exceeding that following the sinking of the *Lusitania*. The policemen, in civilian clothes, standing on street corners, just watched as jewellery, furniture and pawnshops were ransacked. Fish and chip shops were spared destruction. Their food was simply taken without payment. Pat O'Mara and his friend Jackie Sanchez were fully engaged, along with '... respectable looking men and women'. The two friends took two fur muffs from a wrecked pawnshop with the intention of pawning them later. His mother was outraged, although her son thought that she secretly wished to be able to keep the muffs and her Catholic conscience intact. The next day Pat sold the muffs to a 'fence' in Scotland Road. By then the newly sworn-in Specials were on the streets.[48] The rain and later the arrival of the troops helped to restore order, although the Riot Act was read again, and one man was shot dead. Eventually 370 were tried for looting, with 50 in Birkenhead.[49]

The tramwaymen, still with lingering grievances from 1911, took advantage of the mayhem to strike themselves, along with some 2,000 painters and bakers. The dockers and railwaymen made supportive statements, but voted against any action. An official committee, chaired by Lord Desborough, recommended improvements in policemen's pay and conditions. That left the strikers isolated as reinstatement was also refused. By November, 3,000 former policemen were unemployed, their pensions lost. Nationally, the authorities focused the blame on Liverpool, given its strong links with the Irish, '... a class of men who are always apt to be carried away by any wave of enthusiasm', as Sir Nevil Macready, the Commissioner of the Metropolitan Police, told the nation. For that reason, he explained, he always refused to employ them. Lloyd George, in his usual style, proclaimed the breaking of the police strike as delivering the trade union movement from Bolshevism and Syndicalism.[50] Such a stance was not widely applauded, even outside Liverpool. Events in Russia towards the end of the war and in its early aftermath had attracted widespread interest as well as sympathy for their long-suffering people,[51] even if revolutionary ideologies had little support among the British people and within the trade unions. Nor did it go down well among the dissident dockers on Merseyside, for the unions to be perceived, by government, as accommodating. The accusation of collaboration by Sexton and his colleagues came easy to the lips of the docker. However the authorities, not least in Liverpool, remained nervous.

Towards the end of 1920, as the Irish 'troubles' continued, there was a scare that Sinn Fein was plotting to blow up, or set on fire, part of Liverpool's dock system. The Mersey Docks and Harbour Board took the scare seriously enough to enrol large numbers of staff as special constables, by now a familiar strategy on the waterfront. It was a credible scare given the large numbers of Irish sympathisers in Liverpool, but few, on the ground, took it very seriously. Far more prosaic but important for the future of dockland and its workers was the announcement in January, by the Ministry of Labour, of the appointment of Lord Shaw of Dunfermline to chair an inquiry. It had nine members, three from the National Transport Workers' Federation, three employers, and three independents. Shaw was one of the independents. It met for twenty days in February and March 1920. Tillett was one of the union representatives. Ernest Bevin, national organiser of the Dock, Wharf, Riverside and General Workers' Union, presented the dockers' case. He was assisted by James Sexton of the National Union of Dock Labourers.

The Dockers' KC

Throughout 1919 and into 1920 the post-war boom and low unemployment strongly favoured trade union growth; membership rose from 6.5 million in 1918 to 8.3 million in 1920. The proportion of workers who were members of a union – union 'density' – then stood at 45.2 per cent. As boom turned to slump in the summer of 1920 all the numbers began to fall. In 1922 membership stood at 5.6 million, and density 32.0 per cent.[52]

The waterfront unions shared this wider growth, the NUDL's membership rising between 1918 and 1920 from 45,000 to 70,000 as men returned from war and new members were signed up. There were also extra members from the absorption of smaller groups along the waterfront. Revenue from subscriptions also grew faster than expenditure, and in 1919 the NUDL changed its name to reflect its new status to the National Union of Dock, Riverside and General Workers in Great Britain and Ireland. With such a long and cumbersome name, it remained popularly known as the 'Liverpool Union'.[53] Its London and South of England counterpart also experienced growth. The Dock, Wharf, Riverside and General Workers' Union ('the 'Dockers' Union') peaked in 1919 at 98,000 members. The Dockers' Union, which recruited mainly in London, Southampton and Bristol, also fell back as boom turned to slump. But up to the middle of 1920 both unions' morale was high, and conditions were favourable for further advances. The National Transport Workers' Federation (NTWF), strengthened by its growing number of affiliations (by then twenty-six although with its usual difficulties in holding them all together), was pressing for national rates and conditions for all port workers. A strong tide of optimism and idealism was also running though the country, and the dockers were part of the vanguard. Things had to be different. Overall, therefore, throughout 1919 and into the early months of 1920 the NTWF had a window of opportunity to improve the dockers' position in the ports.

In October 1919 the Federation forwarded to the employers a national claim, with ten principal clauses, of which the major demand was 16s. per day minimum (£24 at 2007 prices) for day and piecework under the previously agreed 44-hour week.[54] The employers, disorganised and on the defensive, had difficulty responding to the collective national strength of the NTWF.[55] The negotiations soon broke down, the employers arguing that they were unable to meet a claim that would greatly increase labour costs. They countered with an offer to present their case to an inquiry under the new Industrial Court Act of 1919.[56] Though the Federation had a strong hand, it hesitated, although many dockers were ready to strike. That encouraged the NTWF to agree to the inquiry.

The NTWF was now at the peak of its influence, but it would disappear within two years to make way for the new big union, the Transport and General Workers (TGWU). The TGWU would also absorb the two main dockers' unions in the southern ports as well as in Liverpool.[57] These developments would be associated strongly with the dynamic young national organiser of the Federation, Ernest Bevin. In 1920 he also had his first, national stage, although Sexton's contribution was also both shrewd and constructive. Bevin was an ex-carter, rather than a docker, and his experience was largely confined to ports in the south of England. Nor did his views of casualism – 'the liberty to go home with nothing' – do him any favours, perhaps especially in Liverpool. Sexton had suffered long for his attempts to minimise the more baleful effects of casualism. Interestingly, by the time of the Shaw Inquiry, he seemed to have modified his opposition to casualism, though remaining cautious, or, at least, to understand the dockers' collective concern to protect work opportunities, especially for older men, as well as retaining the 'free and easy Bohemian spirit' of the waterfront.[58] There were several difficulties between Bevin and Sexton, including at heart, Bevin's view that the NUDL, that is Sexton, had consistently failed to advance wage rates in Liverpool, except under the exigencies of the Great War. In 1911 the southern ports, notably London and Bristol, had secured increases. Liverpool, in the same year, its 'near revolution', had gained recognition for the NUDL and consolidated its position on the waterfront, but rates had remained at the 1885 level. Such a reproach might have been unfair, even insulting, to Sexton, but was statistically accurate.[59] At the same time, it would not be surprising if there were a collision between a dynamic, ruthless young official and an older, pragmatic, experienced seeker of deals and alliances, even though Bevin himself also preferred to bargain. At the time of the Shaw Inquiry, Bevin was 38, Sexton 64. Nine years earlier, Mann and Sexton had had their difficulties, but had surmounted them. Mann, however, despite his fiery rhetoric had much of the pragmatic opportunist in his make-up. He was sufficiently different to Bevin to find common ground with Sexton. And 1920 was not 1911.

Yet, despite their differences, Bevin and Sexton were a good team in the context of the Shaw Inquiry. Sexton's cool, measured, accommodating approach and his deep knowledge of the law and working practices of port work, complemented Bevin's oratory and self-confidence – especially on the big occasion. The Federation had chosen well.[60] Bevin was the star turn, a performance that would materially assist the formation in 1922 of the TGWU. He would be its first general secretary and, in the Second World War, the critically important Minister of Labour.

Although the Shaw Inquiry's terms of reference were technically confined to pay, the Ministry of Labour officials remained strongly committed to doing something about casualism. In practice the inquiry did widen its terms of reference to include this in its final recommendations. Pay, however, remained central, and the focus of Bevin's case. His opening address took eleven hours, spread over three days. His oratory was masterful, his evidence compelling and detailed. The employers hired a top-class lawyer, Sir Lyndon Macassey, as well as a number of star witnesses, notably A. L. Bowley, the distinguished academic statistician.[61] Bevin argued that £6 a week was required to support a family of five: Bowley's figure was little more than half of that. Bevin, using Bowley's estimate, sent his able secretary, Mae Forcey, to buy the equivalent in food at Canning Town market. He presented the food in court on five plates. The small size of the amounts met a sensational response in the court and the press, especially when Bevin asked Professor Bowley, rhetorically, whether he had ever carried five hundredweight bags for eight continuous hours with the meagre meal, presented to the court, when he got home?[62] He then followed the now strong case for the 16s. national minimum with evidence showing the wide differentials between ports, with Liverpool men near the bottom. A national minimum of 16s. would guarantee a big increase for Liverpool (from 11s. 8d.), but a reduction for Hull, given its high earnings from piecework of £1 per day. Yet their district secretary, in court, claimed to be confident that the Hull dockers would accept a cut in their pay, reflecting their solidarity and support for the principle of a national minimum for all dockers.[63]

It was a major courtroom triumph for Bevin and the dockers' case. He also persuaded Lord Shaw of the evils of casualism and the case for registration and maintenance financed by the employer. Liberal minds, and even some employers, could see no alternative. Many dockers, at the hard end, had their usual doubts. Bevin was skating on thin ice, especially in Liverpool. But when he went to Liverpool following the Shaw Report's recommendations, he was still given a standing ovation.

The Industrial Court's findings gave Bevin and his team all they had asked for. Bevin had won the argument, but much would depend on the employers' response. They tardily conceded the 16s. per day for the 43 major ports, with 15s. per day in the 38 smaller ports. Special rates were agreed for the rest, the 9 of intermediate size. Bevin also pressed for a registration scheme for all ports, with a £4 weekly guarantee for registered dockers turning up each day at the stand. That was a step too far for most dockers faced with the loss of their 'liberty'. Agreement could not be reached at the July 1920 meeting of the NTWF. By then, boom was turning to slump, and work was receding, a time when the fall-back weekly guarantee would have served the dockers well. Instead the employers responded by cutting wages by 4s. per day, in two stages, in August 1920 and January 1921.[64]

The Federation managed to hold the line in its anxiety to act 'responsibly' after the Shaw Report, heading off discontent in the context of maintaining the principle of national rates, even when falling. Then, in March 1921, the Miners' Federation of Great Britain called a strike. The issue was a pay cut. There was widespread public sympathy over their action, and strong support from the NTWF. It prepared an embargo on imported coal. Sexton prevaricated as other unions, including the railwaymen and carters, continued to bring coal to the docks. He drew bitter criticism from other NTWF affiliates upon the NUDL and from within the NUDL itself, its members always frustrated by Sexton's conservative tactics. At all levels of the trade union movement his reputation continued to plunge, although he had a point in stressing the case for either a strong Federation with delegated powers, or one single union for all transport workers. As he put it, '... the Federation might as well be disbanded tomorrow ... the only alternative to that is one of amalgamation.'[65]

Bevin had been working on the idea of an amalgamated union for some years before Shaw had gone to press, and the idea itself had been around since the 1880s. After Shaw Bevin moved at break-neck speed. Within two years he had achieved what to some had appeared unlikely, if not impossible.

The One Big Union

The 'OBU', as a dream if not nearly a reality, was perhaps strongest in the USA. Its principal advocates were the 'Wobblies', the Industrial Workers of the World (IWW), whose ideas and programmes came via socialist-inspired immigrants from Europe. Its revolutionary sentiments clashed with conservative American political ideas (including those within the trade union movement). Following the war hysteria of 1917–18, many of its leaders were branded as traitors, and by the early 1920s many were still in prison, and its influence rapidly waned. In its heyday, the years before the Great War, its special brand of syndicalist philosophy influenced European workers, its ideas in competition with mainland European versions. Wobbly ideas were also important along the eastern waterfront ports of the USA. Tom Mann himself had come under the spell of Daniel de Leon, perhaps the best-known American in the IWW.[66] Others who shared de Leon's ideas, and who once had close associations with Liverpool, were James Larkin and James Connolly.

The international aims on the IWW's masthead were seen as hopelessly ambitious by other socialists with more practicable goals. One union for each industry seemed more achievable, though still fraught with the pitfalls of localism, sectionalism and inevitable clashes of personality and ambition. These had all been present in sharp relief within and between the unions and workers of the British transport industry for some time. Even the Liverpool of 1911, though it established the NUDL as a permanent presence on the waterfront, still left the union as an uneasy coalition of many trades, many approaches to politics, sectarianism and an almost genetic distrust of the rank-and-file towards their leaders, any leaders, and not just Sexton. That distrust even extended to seamen, despite their coming together in 1911, and their common economic interests with dockers and close community relationships in waterfront neighbourhoods. Sexton himself had long, formative experience as both a seaman and a docker, but neither seemed to give him any advantages.

One union for both seamen and dockers was never a starter in Liverpool. Nor was amalgamation much easier elsewhere, let alone for the other prominent transport workers, the railwaymen, whose cautious union leaderships were often forced to endorse the actions of their more radical members. Yet, to an extent, a common strategy was developing with the formation, in 1914, of the Triple Industrial Alliance of the railwaymen, the NTWF and the miners' federation. But the Triple Alliance soon failed to live up to its promise, and notably failed to act when its third arm, the miners, were locked out in April 1921, to be forced back in June. By then there had been significant progress towards the formation of the Transport and General Workers' Union. It also had a fair wind, nationally, with almost 'full' employment at the end of 1920, though that was soon to change.[67] It was a time for haste. Bevin was the man in a hurry and for the occasion.

Bevin drew up his initial proposals in the spring, and in July the London and Liverpool dockers' unions formed a joint sub-committee of thirteen. Tillett and Bevin (for London) and Sexton and Milligan (for Liverpool) were the leading members, with Bevin elected as secretary and Harry Gosling, President of the NTWF, as chairman. The sub-committee called an August conference of fourteen unions. Thirteen sent delegates who approved Bevin's proposals, including extending the scope of the proposed new union to include road transport. A drafting committee was appointed to present the amended proposal to a delegate conference. Nineteen unions met on 1 December 1920. There was some debate, with amendments moved by Bevin and seconded by Sexton, but the motion to amalgamate was adopted unanimously. By Christmas 550,000 ballot paper had been sent out. The Trade Union Amalgamation Act required at least half the total membership to vote, with a majority of at least 20 per cent. By May 1921 fourteen unions had voted in favour, though not the Liverpool men, the Scots and the London Stevedores. Rules were established and officers provisionally appointed. The new union coming into existence on New Year's Day, 1922.[68]

This was breakneck speed, especially for fractious, divisive workers such as those along the waterfront. Much was down to Bevin's energy, ability and enviable national reputation earned recently at the Shaw Inquiry. Weakness was also a driving force. While the amalgamation process had begun in the boom immediately following the war, it came to completion during a period when TUC membership was falling like a stone, and the TGWU had already lost half by the end of its first year of operation.[69] But the new union's unlikely birth had taken place. Its members included workers from the waterfront, road transport, the metal trades, the chemicals industry, and even ships' clerks. At the beginning it had about 250,000, although key unions were still outside. The Liverpool and Glasgow men had not completed their ballots to the same timetable as the first fourteen. Both did later come in, though not happily in the case of the Scottish Union of Dock Labourers. The London Stevedores, whose old elite status was already under threat on the waterfront, decided to stay out, later to re-emerge as the 'Blue' Union, the National Association of Stevedores and Dockers, which would pose significant problems for trade union unity on the waterfront for almost fifty years.

Liverpool and Glasgow's long history as fully paid-up members of the awkward squad did not allow them to respond as quickly or as readily to Bevin's tough powers of persuasion. Sexton might well have shared the Liverpudlians' natural reservations about southerners, especially such a powerful, ambitious one as Bevin, but he strongly supported the amalgamation. He worked hard to bring his members along with '… hard slogging before we succeeded in getting the majority required'.[70] He was helped by Harry Gosling and Bevin at a major public meeting in the Liverpool Stadium. The resolution was passed unanimously, but it still took two ballots to get the required 50 per cent turnout (even 20 per cent was high on Merseyside) and a positive vote. Taplin even notes, cryptically, that '… it is best not to enquire too closely into the means by which a 50 per cent poll was finally achieved …'[71] The Scottish Union of Dock Labourers did eventually come in, but it took one more ballot than at Liverpool, the final affirmative one in 1922. The SUDL had for long been hostile to the NUDL, which had been founded in Glasgow. Nor did it easily see itself as a mere part of a distant 'English' union run from London. In 1931 the Glasgow dockers pulled out to form the Scottish Transport and General Workers' Union, although it returned to the TGWU fold eleven years later.

Liverpool's tardy endorsement and its continuing reputation for dissidence helped it to be given its own, separate area, No. 12. To be fair, the union did have enough members, with relative stability and unchallenged employer recognition, to deserve it. Its area secretary was to be George Milligan, the obvious choice. His popularity and ability and the special position of Liverpool had actually led to Bevin suggesting a national post for him, which would have balanced the union's two most senior elected officials, Milligan for Liverpool and Gosling with his close associations with London. Characteristically Milligan turned down a national post to stay in Liverpool. His wife supported him. The National Trade Group Committee did, however, have three representatives from Merseyside. There were five Trade Groups (Docks; Waterways; Clerical, Administrative and Supervisory; Road Transport; and General Workers) who came together in a national lay executive for the whole union.[72]

Sexton now stepped out of the action. He was sixty-six and an MP, although he kept his salary with open access to the TGWU's head offices at Transport House, near the Commons, in his role as National Supervisor to the Docks Group. It was 'a bobby's job', he conceded.[73] For all his failings, his legacy was sound: he had many strengths, and left the new union having brought in 70,000 members, funds of almost £50,000 and sizeable capital assets. The Mersey waterfront also remained the best organised in the TGWU. He had the respect and affection of most of the local officials who had worked with him, even though the rank-and-file did not take to him, seeing him as aloof, bossy and patronising, and too close to the employers, though that was the way of the Liverpool men. Writing towards the end of his life, he contemplated his role in the emergence of one union for waterfront workers, going back to 1894, and his great satisfaction in helping to get twenty small unions to '... sink their differences and lose their identities ...' to become (in 1936) '... a compact body of 400,000 men with district offices all over the country and headquarters directly opposite the House of Lords'.[74] Bevin, by then, had been general secretary (elected overwhelmingly) for fourteen years.

The founding of the TGWU in 1922 was, on any reckoning, a major achievement for Bevin and his associates and was to lead to exceptional power and influence for the union in both political and industrial affairs at the highest levels. But its members did not live and work at those levels. They were more directly and immediately concerned with short-term matters, such as having a job and putting the dinner on the table. As the 1920s wore on Liverpool seemed to have gone back to darker days:

> Walk along the line of Liverpool's great docks; look at the silent quays ... think as you go along one of our great streets how few carts and lorries are passing along in comparison to the mighty stream of traffic which flows through the city in ordinary occasions; and then, if you can, if you are privileged, enter the houses of the poor and hear the story of their sufferings.[75]

CHAPTER NINE

'Send it down, J.C.': life and labour between the wars

Liverpool undoubtedly seems to be the last city in Great Britain to catch the hand of prosperity and the first to relinquish its grasp.

(Liverpool Trades Council, 1909)[1]

More than 2,000 dockers stampeded for work yesterday when the White Star liner *Baltic* was due to berth from New York with a miscellaneous cargo of 7,000 tons ... The men began to form up before the vessel reached the landing stage and by one o'clock about 2,000 dockers waited to be picked up for duty. Only about 500 were required.

(*Liverpool Daily Post*, 1931)[2]

One thing my father used to look forward to in the wintertime was the snow to come down. Because you could go to get employed by the Corporation snow shifting and it was a big asset, you know ... He'd be looking through the window and he'd say 'send it down J.C.'. And he used to go down to Vine Street on the stand, and they'd pick so many hundred men on.

(Billy Regan, 1992)[3]

Poverty was permanent, but destitution was intermittent; we all knew the difference.

(Johnnie Woods, 1989)[4]

O N 12 SEPTEMBER 1921 there was a major disturbance outside the Walker Art Gallery, a fine building in the classical style that had been built to house a world-class collection of paintings and sculptures for the enlightenment and pleasure of Liverpool's citizens, including its very poorest. That was as it should be, since the poor and poorest had helped to pay for the famous gallery by their generous and sustained contributions to the coffers and profits of the Liverpool brewer, Andrew Barclay Walker, a rightly celebrated hero of the nineteenth-century's self-made 'beerage'. Knighted in 1877, he was described by Viscount Sandon, 3rd Earl of Harrowby and a Conservative Member of Parliament for Liverpool as 'a very wealthy respectable and unpretending man, and a staunch Conservative'. He died in 1893, leaving £3 million to his fortunate heirs, and his name and paintings to the gallery. Since he was long dead on the day of the disturbance, we do not know whether or not he would have approved of the firm and decisive action of the police, acting in a manner similar to that ten years earlier on St George's Plateau, itself only yards away from the gallery. The demonstrators, a group of the unemployed, were trying to occupy the building to gain some publicity for their plight. Some had lately returned from the battlefields of the Great War to what had been promised as a land fit for heroes. But, by 1921, there were few jobs, especially for heroes. When they subsequently stood in the dock, 'the heads of a number swathed in bandages', the Recorder censured the police for their 'unnecessary violence', and further remarked that he hoped the incident was not generally characteristic of police behaviour on such occasions.[5] He suffered for these remarks, a blatant betrayal of his class. As late as 1934 he was claiming, with apparent evidence, of a '… carefully calculated ceremonial and professional boycott at the hands of the Corporation'.[6] By then even more heroes were unemployed.

Just two years earlier the Merseyside police had themselves been involved in their own 'disturbance'. Some of their number were also returning heroes demanding, with public and trade union support, a living wage and the extension of trade union rights to their own, recently formed organisation. The strike call had been answered by half of the force, but they were soon defeated, the strikers losing their jobs, future prospects and, most importantly, their pension rights. If they had been reinstated some might have been present at the Walker Art Gallery in 1921 and might even have remembered the support of Liverpool people in 1919. Their replacements showed no sympathy at all. The peace had returned to Liverpool.

Liverpool on the dole

Normality had returned in other ways. Those early post-war years had opened with the usual post-war boom. That was soon followed by the usual post-war slump. By October 1920 the total of registered unemployed on Merseyside touched 15,000. Within four months it had doubled to almost 30,000, a threshold that was crossed in the summer. Liverpool's rate was then 13 per cent, with 19 per cent in Bootle and 26 per cent in Birkenhead. The Birkenhead figure was clearly also influenced by its heavy dependence on ship-building, an industry subject to even wider fluctuations than trade. By 1932, the lowest point of the slump, the total out of work in Liverpool was 108,000, or 28 per cent. For ship-building and repair the proportion passed 50 per cent, easily exceeding even railways (39 per cent) and river and dock services (33 per cent).[7] That percentage for Liverpool's dock and river workers compared with a much lower, though still dire, national figure of

22.5 per cent. Even as late as 1939, as the 'recovery' was well under way stimulated further by war preparations, one in four of Liverpool's dockers were still out of work. The national average was half that.[8]

According to Napoleon, Britain was a nation of shopkeepers, but it was also a major power in manufacturing industry, including in most of its major ports. Liverpool had, or would establish, some manufacturing, including vehicles, and there were also the older processing industries arising from trade, such as milling tobacco and sugar. It would even have a presence in the 'new' industries such as chemicals and oil refining along the upper reaches of the Mersey. But it also remained relatively over-dependent, compared with other ports, on trade and its associated industries. Liverpool's trading eggs, once golden, were still the major presence in its basket. But its former strength was now a weakness. Its trade was over-specialised, too reliant on exports. As exports collapsed, most spectacularly cotton textiles, a large number of the port's jobs went with them. Between 1929 and 1933 the volume of trade passing through British ports fell by 26 per cent. At 20 per cent London lost less than the national average; at 32 per cent Liverpool easily exceeded it. By value, a more important indicator, over the seven years from 1924 to 1931, the six major ports experienced very different levels of disaster. Liverpool, easily the worst, hit 42 per cent of its 1924 level, followed by Manchester with 48 per cent. Glasgow and Hull were at 58 and 59 per cent respectively. Southampton weathered the storm much better, at 72 per cent, with London at 73 per cent.[9]

Liverpool's passenger trade with North America had also been in free-fall, with the switch to Southampton virtually complete by the 1930s. This prestigious trade was actually not all that valuable to Liverpool. The cargo liners, owned by the same companies, were far more important in financial terms. But passengers were symbolically important, and any loss dented Liverpool's pride and self-confidence. The old rival, Southampton, also held the better cards. It had better harbours with a minimal tidal range, and geography had given it a better location for all destinations of importance, including North America. The relocation of the passenger trade also reduced the work opportunities for Liverpool's seamen, already severely limited by the contraction of trade. Others, such as clerks, were also badly affected. Between 1918 and 1932 the once large, black-coated army lost 6,000 jobs, with 5,000 standing idle. They were mostly men, and their jobs were also increasingly under threat from women. Women were cheaper (usually 'accepting' half the men's wage) and were widely considered by employers to be more adept with the new, labour-saving machine – the typewriter.[10]

None of this favoured the forward march of labour, although the NUDL had sufficient residual strength to form a significant part of the TGWU in 1922. The new union in its turn was a part of the survival, even some growth, of the wider labour movement. The other 'wing' of the labour movement, the Labour Party, also began to win seats on Liverpool Council from the Liberals, and the first Labour MP was elected in a by-election, in Edge Hill, in 1923.[11] Nor did unemployment and depression necessarily limit the use of the strike weapon.

Liverpool men remained fractious and difficult to organise, but much less than before the Great War. Sectionalism would remain as well as unofficial action, but, with the new union greatly helping to hold the line, this was less of a problem than in earlier days. Sectarianism, too, began to lose its general potency as a disruptive force. The Liverpool labour movement maintained an impressive solidarity before, during and after the General Strike of 1926. That solidarity would largely hold along the waterfront (though with some major challenges) until shifting trade patterns, revolutionary technology and employer power, buttressed by government and punitive labour laws, rapidly reduced the dock labour force to just a few hundred by 1995. Even then, during the long dispute from 1995 to 1998, the old solidarity remained impressively intact, helped by innovative new tactics that almost won the day.[12] But it was also clear that the day of the traditional docker, even more than the coal miner, was almost over.

The General Strike, 1926

Ernest Bevin had always preferred oratory, discussion, negotiation and persuasion, often robust, to picket lines. He was also good at these things, as his union and the nation were to witness at the Shaw Inquiry, its proceedings widely publicised in the press. His officials naturally took the same line as Bevin. They were also moving with the grain of change. Encouraged by government, employers had been accepting, even welcoming, the paths of orderly, agreed procedures, negotiation and compromise. Those processes had been consolidating for some years, with official landmarks in the Conciliation Act of 1896 and the emergence of 'Whitleyism' in 1919.[13] Another milestone came in 1920, when the International Transport Federation and Bevin opted for public scrutiny in a court of inquiry rather than confrontation, to win their case for a national minimum of 16s. per day.

Unemployment and under-employment continued to haunt the waterfront, undermining numbers, resolve and union strength. Yet there would still be times when collective bargaining, conciliation and arbitration would try the patience of impatient men, with frequent bouts of disenchantment with their own leaders aggravating the entrenched, justified distrust of their employers. These attitudes were endemic along the Mersey, but they were less evident after the General Strike, which was itself, though short, on the whole an impressive demonstration of disciplined solidarity, including in Liverpool. The presence of that solidarity, which usually ensured victory or, at least, a favourable settlement, largely explained the disappointment of those involved on the front line at what seemed the TUC's loss of nerve.

Only two years earlier, the emergence of the first Labour government in January 1924 was clearly a cause for celebration and optimism within the labour movement, even though it was a minority administration requiring the support of the Liberals under Asquith. Yet Ramsay MacDonald's administration was hardly the stuff of radical dreams, even preparing troops to move essential supplies during a three-day national dock strike that involved 110,000. Ernest Bevin had demanded an increase of 10*d*. in two, 5*d*. stages. The Liverpool employers, who had left the National Association of Port Employers two years earlier, accepted, though with bad grace.[14] Bevin was also less than impressed with the Labour government's approach to intervention: 'I only wish it had been a Tory government in office. We would not have been frightened by *their* threats. But we were put in the position of having to listen to the appeal of our own people.'[15]

Bevin's wish came true, but much sooner than he thought. Within nine months the government was out of office. The Conservatives were back with an overall majority, led by Stanley Baldwin, 'the peacemaker'. Things would then get even worse, with the miners as the trigger. The miners were, as usual, burning with old grievances against both the employers and government, especially Conservative. The coal employers had long earned themselves the unenviable reputation – not unchallenged – as the most callous and profit-obsessed in the country. But they could also always count upon state support,[16] given the importance of coal to the economy, the Empire and the Navy. The Welsh miners, especially, along with the usual privations, had several times suffered the pain and indignity of British troops armed and actively deployed in the coalfields, fingers on triggers. Churchill, the miners' well-remembered villain of the valleys, was also back in office, now as Chancellor of the Exchequer (despite pleading ignorance of economics). In May 1925 he restored sterling to the gold standard, thus raising export prices and cutting exports, notably coal,[17] at a stroke. The coal owners demanded a cut in wages and a return to the eight-hour day from the seven that had been conceded in 1920. The miners argued that the positive, available remedy was for the employers to improve the efficiency of their 'production, distribution and administration'.[18] The answer was probably somewhere in between, but there was no time for such objective calculations, and in the meantime concern and apprehension regarding the likely actions of the miners was building.

The government moved in with a subsidy in July 1925, to maintain miners' wages and hours until a royal commission, under Sir Herbert Samuel, reported. His report, in January 1926, recommended wage cuts. The Miners' Federation, led by Arthur Cook, the South Wales syndicalist, reacted obdurately with the famous slogan (with echoes of the 'dockers' tanner' of 1889): 'Not a penny off the pay, not a second on the day.' Symbolically, Baldwin's subsidy was to run out on May Day, 1926. Meanwhile the Trades Union Congress, which had formed a General Council in 1921, was beginning to exert the authority given to it by its affiliates to act on their behalf.[19] It took up negotiations with the government towards a settlement of the coal dispute. It also pledged full support for a national strike in support of the miners should negotiations fail. When the government broke off negotiations on 3 May, the TUC '... was left with no alternative but to declare a strike that it did not want and for which it was not prepared'.[20]

The General Strike began on 4 May 1926. The government had been preparing for such an outcome since July of the previous year. By November a plan was in place to secure essential supplies through the deployment of troops to assist the police and a greatly expanded force of special constables. There was also a focus on keeping transport moving, on the buses, trams, trains and lorries, by recruiting volunteers through the newly formed Organisation for the Maintenance of Supplies. Volunteers would also be used at the docks and in power stations, assisted by senior staff. The Emergency Powers Act of 1920 was also available to the government, with wide powers to make arrests and search premises. The government's planning also included using the BBC's facilities for bulletins and announcements.[21]

The government's comprehensive preparation put the General Council of the TUC at a serious disadvantage: it had only begun to prepare a week earlier. But its organisation and the response to the strike call were undoubtedly effective. A million miners were already out, and the TUC added one and a half million other workers. The transport workers were the most numerous, under the banner of Ernest Bevin's TGWU. Their numbers were swollen by power workers as well as workers in the heavy industries of chemicals and iron and steel. Engineering and ship-building were called out after a week. The TUC coordinated the strike at its Transport House headquarters in Eccleston Square, while a strike organising committee encouraged local towns and cities to replicate the central organisation. These were called Councils of Action. In Liverpool a Provisional Council of Action, with a perhaps intended revolutionary name, was already in place, set up by the Trades Council in July 1925.

The success of the strike call was apparent on the first day. Much of London had stopped work, with little public transport running as, '... the docks, the furnaces and the power stations all became as silent as the pits [and] ... in all the large centres of population it was a strange and eery experience'.[22] Nor did the government's willing volunteers make much of an impression, especially on the trains. The railway network was a complex system requiring special operating skills and individual and collective experience, rather than mere enthusiasm. There were hardly any goods' services and, at best, no main-line company was able to operate above 20 per cent of its passenger trains.[23] However, a serious error by the TUC occurred when it called out the newspaper and print unions, depriving it of any media influence. It did produce its own daily, the *British Worker*, printed by the *Daily Herald*, the first issue on 5 May. The government's *British Gazette* was got out by Churchill on the same day. Yet by the end of the strike the *British Worker*'s distribution problems, and the government's requisitioning of newsprint, kept its circulation down to 700,000: the pro-government *Gazette*, by then, exceeded two million.[24]

The government was still able to move essential supplies, and the TUC was granting permits for food and medical supplies and the postal services, but even so, by the third day, the strike was having some success. Not surprisingly, too there was evidence that some in the middle classes would have preferred an early a settlement rather than a disruption of their orderly lives. Lloyd George favoured negotiations, as did the Archbishop of Canterbury, who advised a return to the bargaining table on the basis of the miners' subsidy, cancellation of the strike, and the reinstatement of dismissed strikers.[25] The government was also showing some signs of losing its nerve in turning to the law. It argued that the strike was illegal since it was politically motivated. If that charge could be made to stick, it would have left the trade union leaders open to claims for damages and the sequestration of their unions' assets.[26]

As expected the level of support for the strike varied widely throughout the country. Merseyside's response was expected to be strong given its traditions, strike experience and strong union organisation. The government clearly concurred, remembering 1911, and even before the strike two battalions of troops were on their way under sealed orders, along with a small fleet of three destroyers, two battleships and a troopship from Plymouth.[27] Furthermore, though the strike was not 'general', and the TUC only sought an industrial, negotiated outcome, the term 'general strike' raised alarm bells in Whitehall, especially given Liverpool's significance as a port and the continuing resonance of syndicalist ideas along the waterfront. In the event, the hopes of the TUC and the fears of the government were largely realised. The Trades Council described the response as 'magnificent'. Raymond Postgate provided detail. Liverpool and Birkenhead had a response rate of between 90 and 100 per cent, with Bootle not far behind. The railways workers effected an almost total stoppage, helped by the railway clerks, not usually known for their militancy, who responded with a 95 per cent turnout. The distribution workers showed an 'unprecedented response'.[28] Overall, nearly one third of the employed population came out on strike, with the dockers in their usual place – at the front. Their solidarity did not, however, embrace the tramway men, bus drivers and electricity workers, where the volunteers were especially active. Nor, given problems within their own ranks, did the seamen find it easy to respond, as they did in 1911.

The tramway men, as we have seen, did not come out of the 1911 strike with any satisfaction despite their solidarity with other strikers. Even the demands for their reinstatement received a hostile and then limited response.[29] The fears of loss of a pensionable job were also still very much alive in 1926, so that, although Birkenhead and Wallasey trams stopped, Liverpool's response fell far short of being effective. Volunteers kept at least some services running, while the extra complication of two rival unions limited any chance of solidarity. Bus and coach companies were also commonly non-union, and these services offered alternatives to any trains not running. The ferries, too, continued to run. Their officers were non-union and, in any case, the Council of Action, no longer 'Provisional', considered the ferries to be 'essential to the movement of food'.[30]

On the waterfront the dockers ceased work. But ships continued to move on the river, and in surprising numbers. The explanation lay with Havelock Wilson's National Sailors and Firemen's Union. The seamen's national executive had not voted its support for the General Strike. The Liverpool Branch took a different view. The national union refused to support the local stoppage, and backed this with the securing of a temporary injunction from the High Court, which allowed it to dismiss eighteen Liverpool officials for 'unconstitutional action'.[31] This did not end the local stoppage, but most seamen in the port were from other branches so that ships could find crews. The situation was also eased for the shipowners by the local union's ending of the involvement of the dock gatemen in the strike, given their key role in preventing serious damage to the port's operations.[32]

Overall Liverpool's solidarity was impressive, ut it could not be described as 'general'; nor was it in the rest of the country. The authorities, locally as nationally, were well prepared. Liverpool was part of a North West Division with emergency powers to ration gas, electricity and food, commandeer vehicles and organise volunteers. The Division's volunteers totalled 20,000 (three times the national average). Shipping clerks were also deployed, as volunteers, at the docks, billeted in warehouses to avoid the hazards of the pickets at the dock gates. What is also evident is that many volunteers came from the ranks of the unemployed, including at the docks. Interestingly, their work was officially calculated as much less productive than the regular men (reportedly only one fifteenth of shifted tonnage[33]). This might be exaggerated, but it does suggest, once again, the importance of stamina, skill and experience in waterfront work. Surprisingly, the large numbers of volunteers at the dock did not lead to major disturbances. The unions on the whole succeeded in maintaining discipline and avoiding violence. The relative peace was also helped by the police, who, unlike 1911, behaved 'with remarkable restraint'. There were, however, some harsh sentences, of up to three months' hard labour, imposed under the Emergency Powers Act of 1920.[34]

The general picture of restraint and order should not, however, be exaggerated. The police did draw their batons from time to time, and there were outbursts of disorder and violence on picket lines. Nor was class war absent. The strike was generally welcomed with enthusiasm by moderate opinion among the unions and their members, but some saw the dispute in a wider context as another episode in the struggle to overthrow capitalism. These class warriors included some local political leaders of stature and influence.[35] On the other side of the line the Lord Mayor declared the General Strike to be an attack on the laws and liberties of the land. The press, too, was almost unanimous in its attacks upon the unions, with lurid language, such as the General Strike was 'a pistol placed ruthlessly at the head of the Government and the People'.[36] The TUC General Council was, in fact, made up of essentially moderate, even confused, men who by experience and even nature preferred negotiation to conflict. That was also largely the case within Liverpool's labour movement, although the opportunity to negotiate a settlement was not in their hands. For its part the government was not really interested in a settlement. The prevailing view was to hold out for unconditional surrender. That was achieved, after just nine days, at midday on 12 May 1926.

The strike was actually holding remarkably well, but the TUC was afraid that a drift back to work would undermine the action. Not surprisingly, the government's control of the BBC and the wide circulation of the *British Gazette* made it easy to exaggerate the numbers returning to work. The TUC was afraid that it could not win, faced with such a determined and well-prepared government seeking total surrender. It also feared the revolutionary elements throughout the country as the dynamics of the strike, as all strikes, took the action down unforeseen paths. The miners, too, many with revolutionary dreams and intransigent over their failure to restore their pay and the seven-hour day, refused to accept the terms of the TUC's last attempt to broker a deal via the good offices of Sir Herbert Samuel, the chairman of the 1925 Royal Commission. The miners' refusal to compromise – they held out for a further six months – was a major problem since their cause was the basis for the strike. However, might not the TUC's apparently suddenly loss of nerve be best explained by the fear of victory rather than loss, producing a situation in which an essentially oppositional movement defeats a democratically elected government? [37]

Back in Liverpool there was consternation, mixed with disbelief. This, along with the constitutional need for unions to await instructions for the return from their own executives, delayed the return to work. Then, when work was resumed the familiar problems arose of reinstatement; this was far from universally conceded, despite being urged by both the government and moderate opinion. For their jobs, many were ready to strike again. Certainly it was better than surrender. But what further complicated the demands for reinstatement was that those jobs and services kept going during the strike did so by mainly employing the unemployed. If strikers were to be reinstated, unless extra jobs were available, then the formerly unemployed would lose their jobs. It was a difficult situation when feelings and tempers were running high. In many cases it prolonged the strike through the workers directly involved or through sympathetic action.

The railwaymen held out for a time against the TUC's announcement as the tramway operators, notably at Wallasey, used the defeat as an opportunity to 'weed out the malcontents'. [38] Stanley Baldwin, the Prime Minister, urged employers to be 'magnanimous', but his advice and writ carried little weight with local employers who were so often ready to seize opportunities to push back the frontier of control. Some employers even rewarded those who had worked through the strike, notably Lewis's the department store, who offered to hold wage levels, that is not to cut them, for three years. Cunard's reward was the offer, to its staff, of return trips to Canada. The tramway volunteers were given an extra week's pay. There was strong opposition from Labour members on the Council, but it was no more than words. It was hard to disagree with G. D. H. Cole that the General Strike, was, from start to finish, 'a sorry business'. Those involved deserved a better outcome, not least along the waterfront in Liverpool, where solidarity prevailed in the face of hardship and challenge. The dockers and their families had also long been in the throes of chronic mass unemployment, a condition that was to remain, and deepen, almost to the outbreak of war.

Scraping a Living

In December 1931, the union had to accept a reduction in minimum time rates. Workers on piece rates had more scope to maintain their earnings, but most Liverpool dockers were paid by time. That, and the growing difficulty of finding work at the stands as unemployment climbed steeply after 1929, hit family incomes hard. Unemployment benefit was available as a supplement, but even with that the proportion of dockers' families below the poverty line in the early 1930s was 28 per cent.[39] Added to unemployment and poverty were squalor and overcrowding. Most waterfront workers had little choice but to live near their work, travelling to the daily stands, usually on foot. Housing, particularly good housing, was always in short supply, and the result was constant overcrowding. Nor was the solution to be always found in rehousing in the outer suburbs since (leaving aside the social and familial losses involved), the higher rents and the inevitable fares aggravated the problems of making ends meet.

Caradog Jones reported, for the early 1930s, that 26 per cent of dockers' families, in inner Liverpool, lived in overcrowded conditions, with the figure for all families in inner Liverpool at 15 per cent. Clearly the dockers and their families were in danger of being for ever condemned to the ranks of the poorest of the poor. It also passed across the generations, with almost 20 per cent of boys following their fathers into the docks. The daughters of dockers could not do likewise, but 40 per cent went into factories, or other manual work. Nearly 20 per cent became clerks or shop assistants or dressmakers, with 9 per cent going into domestic service. Some 24 per cent stayed at home to help with housekeeping,[40] normally until they got married, although in the wake of the Great War potential husbands were in short supply.

Caradog Jones' graphic statistics confirmed the harshness of everyday life. It was bad enough when there was plenty of work, but catastrophe when work failed. For many years Beveridge's image of the 'five giants' – want, disease, ignorance, squalor and idleness – fitted dockland very well.[41] He would have seen Liverpool's infamous five at first hand on his visits before the Great War, to discuss Richard Williams' initiatives at the Ministry of Labour to limit the incidence of problems of casualism at the docks. He would also have been very familiar with the strong case for permanent jobs as the principal route out of poverty and blighted lives. That case had long been argued even before Eleanor Rathbone's time, and it had many influential adherents beyond the liberal, humane, intelligentsia, including such as Lord Shaw, the civil servants at the Ministry of Labour, and almost all the Union officials. But the usual protagonists along the Dock Road – the employers and shipowners and the rank-and-file dockers – were locked in mutual mistrust and fear of change, clinging on to the old ways. That Pauline conversion would eventually come, though it would still not be enough. Liverpool's historic reliance on the port for its livelihood would continue to expose its citizens to the whims and recurring cycles of the world's economy and the world's trade.

Grafton Street in 1934. Grafton Street is just up from, and parallel to, the Toxteth waterfront. The housing, though much better than the still existing numbers of courts and cellars would be of poor quality with large families and often multi-occupancy. The Building just visible on the right is possibly a school, adjoining much better houses of an earlier time, with gardens, gates and railings.

Life was better along the waterfront of 1932 than in 1882, but not by much. The pawnshops had not been put out of business, and some children were still without shoes. The diseases of malnutrition, such as rickets, continued to blight lives. A study published in 1992 by a team of Liverpool academics, analysing the levels of poverty thirty years earlier, observed: 'There is no greater indictment of a capitalist system in crisis than its tendency to let people suffer and die because they have too little to eat, too few warm clothes and only cold and insanitary houses to live in.' [42]

In the same study the authors cite a nutritionist, naturally concerned as much with the beneficial effects of the quality of food as much as its quantity. He was writing in 1934:

Many of the common physical ailments and defects could be remedied or even eliminated by proper feeding. Indeed it is probably no exaggeration to say that proper feeding of the population of this country would be as revolutionary in its effects on public health and physique as was the revolution of cleanliness and drainage in the last century.[43]

The reports of those in direct, daily contact with poor families, such as health visitors, read like those of Dr Duncan, several generations earlier. One reports on a widow with four children under eight and total weekly housekeeping of £1 17s. 0d., of which 10s. 6d. was rent.

Her own diet is extremely poor, consisting of bread and margarine, stew sometimes at dinner, no supper and never eggs, fish or vegetables. She suffers from anaemia, and she says it is due to worry and undernourishment.

The health visitor herself commented that she was probably starving herself for the children, who '... look well fed'.[44] It is, however, hard to see how her sacrifices could have done much for the children given the meagre sum available after the rent was paid. Even when a married woman had her husband alive, and at home, it was common for him, the 'breadwinner', to have the lion's share of the meat in the house. The children's needs were seen as less important,[45] especially when incomes were stretched and there was not enough money to spend on food.

At this time the idea of the 'square meal', or a balanced diet, was popular. Another report, from the Minister of Health in 1932, stressed the need for women to have a good diet, especially when pregnant. 'She should become accustomed to a diet which includes ample milk – two pints a day – cheese, butter, eggs, fish, liver, fruit and fresh vegetables, which will supply her body with the essential elements, salts and vitamins.'[46] How could one doubt that this diet, if common throughout the population, would provide a nation of robust, healthy mothers and robust, healthy babies? But it was as far away from most people's lives as the moon. Dockers' family incomes between the wars were too low and uncertain to sustain even a modest diet, as Ernest Bevin famously demonstrated in the 1920 Shaw Inquiry and, in Liverpool, as we have seen, 28 per cent of dockers' families had incomes below the poverty line.[47]

Family incomes, from 1911, could of course be supplemented by unemployment benefit. But this was designed to cover those who were normally in permanent, full time employment. Casually employed and part-time workers – such as dockers – therefore, saw the scheme as discriminatory. The system was not designed for the peculiarities of casual work. The dockers certainly had a good case to be included. They could also be unemployed, and were. But the rules included a requirement to be unemployed for at least three consecutive days or two separate spells within the week. James Sexton, debating the 1920 Bill, in Parliament, which extended the National Insurance Act of 1911 put it well:

... consecutive periods ... can never apply to the man who is idle on the first two days of the week but gets employment on the first or second half of the third day, which employment disqualifies men from receiving benefit.[48]

If Sexton was articulating the views of his members, which seems highly likely, the scheme needed to be changed to accommodate casual workers. Dockers also had little trust in the supposed beneficence of state intervention and its consequent 'red tape'. Sexton had similar views, as did Ben Tillett, leader of the Dockers' Union.[49] The rules had, therefore, to be relaxed, especially since from 1920, mass unemployment became a permanent feature of many workers' lives. Part-time working also had to be brought in, not least because of the social unrest leading from the demoralising effects of long periods without work. Any work was to be encouraged. Benefit not covered by previous employment and contributions could be available on a 'discretionary' basis. Entitlement was made even more relaxed, in stages, throughout the 1920s. For the dockers the key rule was that 'any three days of unemployment, whether consecutive or not, occurring within a period of six consecutive days shall be treated as a continuous period of unemployment'.[50]

According to Phillips and Whiteside, the restrictive rules had to be relaxed in the case of dockers, with their irregular employment, lives and earnings, if benefit was to be reasonably assured. That, though, they argued, led to a seeming abuse, with 'three days on the hook and three days on the book' becoming 'a common working rhythm' on the waterfront.[51] A more colourful account of the way the dockers allegedly 'worked' the scheme is provided by Pat O'Mara:

One could work three days at the dock for thirty shillings and draw three days dole at three shillings per day to boot, making a grand total of forty-five shillings for the week of three days actual work! If one worked four days at the dock, there would be no dole, so the trick was to see to it that only three days were worked. And if no work were forthcoming, there would be eighteen shillings anyway. This beneficence was amazing when my mother compared it with former years.[52]

Pat O'Mara's plausible account complements the authority of Phillips and Whiteside's findings and observations. Yet the latters' conclusion, that 'in all instances dockers received a *significant* income from *two* sources' (which was not just for Liverpool), i.e. the 'hook' and the 'book', has been challenged by Sam Davies. His data reveal that for 1929, over a range of ports, benefit as a proportion of total income averaged 11 per cent, ranging from 2 per cent (Middlesbrough) to Liverpool, the highest, at 15 per cent.[53] Furthermore, the studies and investigations of Eleanor Rathbone and others make it clear that for a docker to find work at the docks for three days every week was the upper end of what was possible, even in good times; and the period between the wars was the longest period of mass unemployment in British history, especially in Liverpool with its over reliance on work at the docks. Even fighting for work at the stands was, as we have seen, not unknown. Unemployment benefit was, of course, a considerable advance in terms of how workers were treated when unemployed, usually through no fault of their own. The dockers eventually welcomed it – when they overcame their suspicions and the rules were relaxed – but it was rarely more than a small, though useful supplement in very difficult times.

It also has to be noted that a mother with dependent children and without a husband's income – through illness, injury at work or death, as the widow mentioned earlier – would have recourse only to the parish or the workhouse. A mother with a husband, even if he was on the dole, would have a better life then a widow, though 'better' is a relative word, not least between the wars. Wives would commonly try to add to the family income by traditional work such as cleaning other people's houses or taking in their washing or ironing. Skilled or experienced women could take work at home mending clothes or even making them.[54] Outside the home casual work was possible cleaning offices and shops or ships newly docked in the harbour. It was a common site to see regiments of women in shawls ('Mary Ellens') converging on a newly arrived passenger liner looking for work and, just like their husbands, some would be disappointed. Another sight was women carrying their own and other people's washing in large bundles on their heads to the public washhouses, like the traditional practice in parts of Africa. Street hawking in the city centre, selling flowers, was also common, often in the company of their children with the eldest (the 'little mother') instructed to keep an eye on her younger siblings. If all else failed, the least timid, especially the children, would beg.

Full-time, even part-time work, outside the home was difficult for women to find and, if married with children, usually ruled out. Women were still largely seen, by society, as housewives and mothers, and Liverpool's employment opportunities were predominantly for men. There was also little assembly line work deemed appropriate for women. Light-scale manufacturing was limited, although industries such as cigarette and cigar manufacture and sweets and biscuit production would eventually come to employ many women. Women were also gradually replacing men in shipping clerk work, but the Depression limited even those opportunities. Domestic service in private homes was one possibility. In the bigger houses in the suburbs this usually meant living in. That could be humiliating and often lonely, as one woman recalls:

> ... first of all one is half a slave ... One is never free. Factory girls have certain working hours and then they are free. We have to work all day and there is never an end to it ... You can't bring a friend in even for a cup of tea ... Do you think it is pleasant to spend one's life with people who make one feel inferior to them? The loneliness is another factor, for sometimes it is days before you can speak to somebody who understands you.[55]

One wonders what happened to such a proud, spirited, perceptive woman having to bite her lip on a daily basis, having no option but to take on domestic work as unemployment for men and women rose to unprecedented levels.[56] Nor was such work covered by the National Insurance Scheme, excluding women from benefit if unemployed. Being married was also as big a problem for women seeking work in the Depression. The 'marriage bar', widespread in many industries, compelled women to leave their jobs at marriage. Overall, the outcome was that in 1932 just 10 per cent of married women on Merseyside were able to find insurable, waged work.[57]

Nor were their children readily able to bring money into the home. For those under sixteen, poorly paid casual work, though often available because the pay was so low, did bring some income to the dinner table. At sixteen, when they became 'adults' in work terms, they would often lose their jobs to younger, cheaper, replacements. One railway worker commented that this practice meant that the railway companies '... were virtually running the railways on junior porters'.[58] By the age of sixteen apprenticeships, in any case extremely rare, were not available.

In general, what employment opportunities there were favoured older, experienced workers, including the dockers. Men in their twenties were especially disadvantaged.[59] By the end of October 1934 the number of young people unemployed in Liverpool was 13,000. As one official put it, 'The best years of their lives have thus, in more cases than it is possible to enumerate, been wasted altogether ...'[60] Fifty years later it was the same story, almost the same words.[61]

Behind the Bread Line

The uncompromising material harshness of many lives, and the bleak realities of earning a living, did not always mean that life could not be enjoyed; it could even be happy. There was also a strong sense of community in dockland areas, with common bonds at work that were aided by the proximity of large numbers living near each other in small, mostly identical houses. Community did, of course, have its downside, with little privacy and pressures towards conformity. There were also the divisions of religion, although Catholics and Protestants tended to segregate themselves by place of residence and even by occupation. The best-known examples were those of the dockers and carters. Regionally, the dockers in the North End were mainly Irish Catholics, dominating the stands. In the South End the opposite held for Protestants. It was also difficult to get a job as a carter if you were Catholic. Another example, perhaps apocryphal, was the alleged 'No Irish [i.e. Catholics] need apply' notice when the Anglican Cathedral was under construction, in spite of the fact that its architect, Giles Gilbert Scott was a Roman Catholic.

Yet in times of industrial conflict, religious differences were, remarkably to some, put aside. At other times, such as when rioting and looting took place during strikes, especially in 1911, old scores, often quite unconnected to the strike, were often settled. Looting, too, was often selective according to religious persuasion. 'Community' would often be identified by a particular street, or by the top end as opposed to the bottom end of one long street, usually when another street running across created a natural divide. Main roads, canals or railway lines would make natural boundaries, acting like state frontiers.[62] This form of geographical sectionalism could lead to some seeing themselves as 'insiders', i.e. long-term residents, as opposed to incomers. These socially created territories would often be within an entire area totally defined by one religion, usually Catholic in dockland.

Religion was not always divisive, especially along the Catholic waterfront, where it helped to hold communities together. The priest was the linchpin, although faith was collectively strengthened on a daily basis in the schools and on Sunday a 'compulsory' mass. Schools could also contribute, in other ways, through individual teachers. Those who taught for many years in the same school and lived in the neighbourhood could inspire children from successive generations and deprived backgrounds to realise their potential. Even if that was often an uphill task, many recalled such teachers with affection, such as Johnny Woods who remembers Miss Atkinson, who lived in Sylvester Street, opposite his own street, and brought out his talent for painting. Passing the 'scholarship' was not, however, universally admired among the children of the waterfront. Being a 'clever dick', a 'college pudd'n' and going to a grammar school in uniform and, especially, wearing a cap, had its own dangers among the class-conscious children of the waterfront. Being good at football was a better route to fame, if not fortune, in those days. Nor were parents always encouraging. Most were poorly educated themselves, and a son doing well at school and passing exams could be unsettling, with additional fears of losing him to the middle class. Girls were even more disadvantaged, being almost always destined to be housewives and mothers. Anything else was usually out of the question. The most pious girls could become nuns, a route that offered some education and, for many, personal satisfaction. A family with a nun among its members wore its distinction with pride. This was even more keenly felt if it had a son who was a priest.

Priests had a huge influence along the waterfront, including the higher clergy. Their teaching and views permeated daily life, including work and strikes, when their Sunday sermons could tilt the balance towards a return to work. Statements from the Archbishop could also be read out at such times. During the 1890 strike, for example, he emphasised the plight of the dockers' families in urging an end to the dispute. In the parishes priests would often publicly rail against poverty and poor housing, and in times of crisis offered sometimes remarkable support. During the epidemics of the 1840s, for instance, the death rate among Catholic priests was at least as high as their parishioners. In the Second World War they were also strongly influential along the waterfront in persuading parents to volunteer their children for evacuation, though souls were always more important than bodies.

Of course, priests were not always popular. Some were feared, and their influence could sometimes seem oppressive. Joan Boyce tells of the priests who took time to visit the evacuees to check on their record of attendance at Mass!

One profession attracting little admiration was the politician, with a few notable exceptions. David Logan, the MP for Scotland Ward was one such. He was in Parliament for thirty-five years until his death in 1964. He lived for years above a newsagent's on Scotland Road, surrounded by his constituents. Another prominent name, a trade union official, card-carrying communist and political activist, was Leo McGree. He became an official in the Amalgamated Engineering Union, but in his youth in the 1930s he was an activist for the unemployed, often on the run from the police and even serving two years in jail. He helped to organise Ford's Halewood plant, and he was involved in all of the significant trade union and political actions along the waterfront throughout his adult life. He was a legendary negotiator, using humour to great effect, as the late Eric Heffer, the Labour MP recalls in his autobiography.[63] When he died, in 1967, thousands followed his funeral procession, many dockers spontaneously leaving their ships to line the streets. Despite this, that evening's edition of the *Liverpool Echo* made no mention of the funeral.

Leo McGree's funeral was an impressive display of unity, but it could cloak a bewildering patchwork of small-scale community loyalties. Parishes, too, had their own solidarities, even those of the same religion. Marriages crossing parish boundaries were often seen, disapprovingly, as 'mixed', despite the same bonds of faith, especially Catholicism. There could even be bitter rivalries *within* parishes, based on family conflicts or even school football teams, despite they and their parents having the same religion and living in the same streets. On one occasion, at least, school football even led to physical violence, as one woman recalled, when she was a girl:

> I'd been to Anfield to watch St Sylvester's school team play against St Anthony's. St Syllies won and so we all came along Scotland Road singing 'Syllies won the cup!' At the corner of Hopwood Street a gang of women from St Anthony's were waiting for us. They laid into us, and it was a helluva fight. The police came to put a stop to it. But, as a young girl, I was amazed to watch grown women fighting each other over the result of a kids' football match.[64]

The unambiguously positive side of community (which all the evidence and personal accounts support[65]) was that it was sorely missed when the old dockland neighbourhoods were demolished, a process beginning on a large scale in the 1920s and 1930s and continuing until the 1980s. The nearness of friends and relatives, across all generations, was in itself a comfort to many. This manifested itself most when collective hardship, such as unemployment and poverty between the wars, or collective catastrophe during the air raids of the Second World War, required collective action and support. It was also evident during personal crisis or hardship, especially common in poor communities. Chronic disease, the sudden death of a husband and wage earner, an accident at work, a desperate mother with too many mouths to feed – all tended to attract direct intervention, help and support, from neighbours, sometimes even over long periods.

'Community' is therefore difficult to define with clarity, but it can be clearly identified in action. Each community could be very diverse. In modern usage each community had within it '... a huge diversity of experience across time and according to age, status, class, religion, race and gender'.[66] Simple stereotypes of places as 'poor, but close knit', 'warm and happy', 'slumland', or 'suffering multiple deprivation', do not do justice to the diversity of life in dockland communities. They were all of these stereotypes, but also much more. People, for the most

Map 8.   Scotland Road. These were the normal limits of the neighbourhood in which must of my childhood life was lived, up to the age of eleven at 45 Doncaster Street. It was much like the life of Robert Roberts in Salford, before the great war with their '... self-contained communities. Our own consisted of some thirty streets and alleys locked along the north and south by two railway systems a furlong apart.' (Roberts, *The Classic Slum.*) See also the detailed map of the Scotland Road area on page 76.

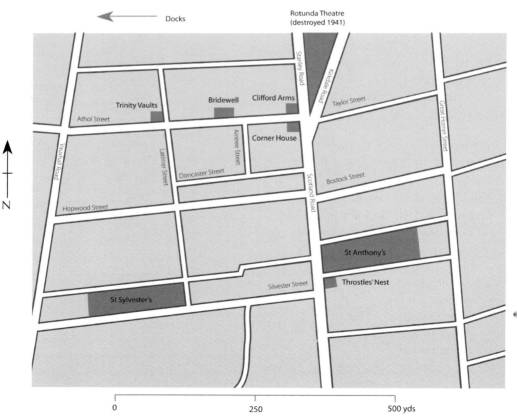

part do still remember these communities with fondness and, particularly, regret at their passing. That might be dismissed as one unavoidable aspect of growing old; but it must also reflect some reality.

Adult memories of happy childhoods, even in what were clearly conditions of extreme hardship, are often strongly held and defended. Johnnie Woods, for example, was brought up on the St Anthony's side of Scotland Road, in Bostock Street. The street is still there, but now with warehouses, grass and trees where his house, one of the terraces, once stood. He recalls head lice and the 'nit' nurse's remedies,[67] bed bugs filled with blood which they burned with candles, and lengths of sticky flycatchers caked black with dead flies, the plague of keeping meat without refrigerators. He also witnessed the humiliation of children wearing pauper clothes, known as 'police clothes', possibly bought through police donations for the poor. Those just up from bare feet often wore clogs with steel, horseshoe rims – 'normal' kids wore the ubiquitous, cheap plimsoll.[68] The clog kids' hair was also closely cropped, presumably to save money on haircuts and to ward off nits, although it only served to mark them out even more.[69]

Johnnie Woods also had a vivid recall of a street with up to 200 children living in it ('one did not go short of mates'). They played improvised cricket and football in the street as the girls played 'hop scotch', 'jacks and ollies' (known as 'snobs' in other regions), skipped and played 'shop'. He paints a picture much like a Breughel painting, busy with childish activity, but now aware, as an adult, of the harshness of the times for their parents:

> For the most part we were happy and ignorant, most especially of our parents' struggle against poverty and unemployment. Most houses were overcrowded, with several generations of family members, and it was one's accepted lot to provide for the aged and infirm.[70]

On the other side of Scotland Road from Johnnie Woods' Bostock Street, but further north, directly opposite the Rotunda Theatre (a popular music hall burned down by incendiary bombs in 1941), was Athol Street. That street ran straight downhill, for about two miles, to the docks. It was crossed by the Leeds and Liverpool Canal and the London and Yorkshire Railway. There were houses along most of its length, on both sides, right down to the docks on the Dock Road. It was a large, living slice of Docklands' life where people lived and worked, not only on the docks, but in local stables, blacksmiths, foundries, abattoirs, sawmills and grainmills, even a large unsavoury, gas works, and served in grocers, greengrocers, bakers, general stores and sweetshops. The schools were all local, and nearly all Catholic. The children walked to them and, when they came home, they played in the street, especially during the long summer evenings after the clocks went forward.[71]

When there was plenty of work in the port, Athol Street would be full of vehicles going up and down to the docks, though even in the 1930s the traffic would still be noticeable. At this date some of the vehicles were still horse-drawn: it would be some twenty years before they finally disappeared. It was also the norm for those working at the docks to walk to work. Pubs were numerous, a constant temptation, although they could also act as networks for tip-offs about possible jobs, and were an important part of community life.

Athol Street was almost wholly Catholic, on that side of Scotland Road, the docks' side. On the other side, Johnnie Woods' side, it was still Catholic, but it soon became Orange Protestant territory beyond Great Homer Street, parallel with Scotland Road. Athol Street was also famous for its police station, or 'Bridewell', the Irish term. It was a sizeable, grim-looking, brick-built, two-storey building that dominated the upper end of Athol Street, only a few minutes' walk from Scotland Road. In a city of many strikes, demonstrations and occasional rioting and looting, the police were well known for head-splitting baton charges, of which Bloody Sunday, 1911, was only the worst. Yet, surprisingly, public and trade union sympathy tilted their way when they formed their own union and went on strike in 1919, to be defeated with most losing their jobs and pensions.[72] But fear, mingled with respect, remained. They were tough, often violent with arrested men, especially when the men were drunk. Appearing in pubs or at closing time to enforce the law was standard procedure, as was checking the padlocks and locked gates of commercial premises at dusk.

Children from the 1930s remember the police for their frequent, petty instructions to 'move on' when playing games such as football or cricket, and their ability to impose summary punishment, such as a sharp smack on the head. They always patrolled on foot, and children and adults took notice as one approached in the distance. Most policemen seemed to behave reasonably enough, although they were often accused, by adults as well as children, of unwarranted restrictions. One, hated by adults and children alike, would allegedly burst the ball if he caught boys playing football in the street. Not surprisingly, he earned the name Hitler for his behaviour (or it might have been his moustache, not dissimilar to that of the German dictator). Germany's 'Führer' was a well-known, mostly ridiculed figure before the war, encouraged by the popular Charlie Chaplin's *The Great Dictator*.[73]

The public would commonly close ranks to protect alleged criminals against the police or often against officialdom more generally. In Athol Street, in the early 1930s, two policemen were badly beaten up. In another incident another two policemen went to stop a fight in a tenement with 'landings' (i.e. walkways). Red hot ashes were poured down on them. One of the policemen was severely burned.[74] Such incidents were exceptional, but the police were no more than tolerated largely because of their 'interference' with what were seen as legitimate pastimes, including popular forms of gambling. 'Pitch and toss' was one of the more popular, played on street corners with two coins, betting on the likelihood of the coins coming down two heads or two tails. If two heads the tosser won, if two tails those betting won. Tossing would continue if neither occurred until there was a 'result'.[75] To the players and the public the game seemed harmless enough, and big money was rarely involved. Yet the police broke up the 'toss schools' on a regular basis.

Money also changed hands, though again rarely in a big way, with street betting on horses. This was also illegal, so complex arrangements had to be in place for collecting bets and paying out, both in the street. Bets were placed using a 'nom de plume' from a recognised list (my grandmother, a hardened gambler of small sums was known as 'Oxo') and 'runners', known to everyone, acted as look-outs for police activity, which was constant. The runners and bookmakers were rarely caught, mainly because they had an efficient look-out system and when on the run were commonly shielded in the houses of a generally sympathetic public.[76]

The other illegal activity, almost close to a sport, or sometimes a necessity, in dockland, was pilfering from the docks. Dockers and their families did not see pilfering of foodstuffs or other goods for personal or family consumption as a crime. It was closer to a right and, in hard times, could help with survival.[77] Dockers also often worked with valuable and desirable cargoes, which brought into sharp contrast their own lives of low pay and deprivation. Pilfering could then easily be seen as redressing, just a little, the injustices of life. Corruption was also an intrinsic part of life on dockland. Some, perhaps most, employers cheated over the weight of goods that were used in the setting of piece rates and, therefore, dockers' earnings and take home pay. It would have been remarkable if dockers did not see it as legitimate to redress the balance a little through pilfering, although the quantities would be moderate. Large-scale operations would have been seen as theft, unless distributed freely among those in need in their community; selective moral positions and Robin Hood co-existed quite happily. A line was usually drawn against large scale operations or stealing from friends and relatives. There was also some element of social protest in pilfering;[78] Robin Hood again.

Such self-applied moral codes regulating pilfering is not confined to one port or one country. It is a universal phenomenon, as Johnson's research makes clear.[79] Along Athol Street it was justified in terms of social justice: 'filling the gap between what people had earned and what they had been paid'.[80] The rationale of moral code or social justice spread beyond the docks, provided again that you did not take from friends and relatives. That also explained why it was a matter of trust and honour not to lock your front door.[81]

Sometimes, though, a big job, if clever and daring, earned acclaim for its own sake. One legendary San Francisco longshoreman achieved his folk-hero status by stealing an entire car – a Model-T Ford – one piece at a time. Another coup was the disappearance of an entire cargo of grand pianos![82] Similar epic tales are talked about in London and in Glasgow. There are stories of luxury carpets for the giant passenger liners, under construction in Glasgow, accounted for at twice the original estimated area. Luxurious, deep-pile carpeting, it was said, graced numerous tenement homes along Clydebank. Even if apocryphal, such stories reveal the moral code sanctioning certain, though usually limited forms of pilfering, not for major personal gain, and growing out of the exploitation and daily humiliations and injustices of working at the docks. Yet in the 1930s even the small satisfaction and revenges of pilfering were mostly ruled out, at least at the docks. That usually required employment, and there was little to be had. Breaking into warehouses was an alternative, but it was risky, and could cross the moral boundary. So hanging around the neighbourhood, grumbling and gambling, helped to stem boredom and slow down the atrophy of self-respect. That was all there was, except for the pubs. The alehouses and vaults could be basic, but they were more comfortable than most dockers' houses. They were where friends met, and told stories and sang the old songs. Even singing was against the law, although no law could prevent it. Dockland was a singing culture, owed largely to its Irish origins. A pub in full voice would fall silent when a policeman came in, but start up again when he left. It was also always difficult for the landlord to get them to go home. 'Time' would need to be reinforced by strong language, even threats.

With great effort by the women, many dockland houses were made nice. But they were often cold and damp and unhealthy. Disease thrived in such conditions. Liverpool was never immune from the old scourges, even though their intensity and death toll was much less than in Doctor Duncan's times. But the new scourge, the 'typhus' of the years between the wars and for a decade afterwards was the dreaded TB ('the consumption') which struck down young and mature people in seeming good health, without discrimination. With minimal medical attention (although the local GPs did their best, sometimes heroically), people were obsessed with 'keeping regular' and other euphemisms. The fortunes of the Beecham's Company were built upon such anxiety, their famous pills passing into everyday language as well as everyday stomachs. In the home, although clean water was universally on tap, hot piped water was almost unknown. If hot water was needed for washing, then a coal or (much less likely) a gas-fired copper might be in the scullery, or there was always the kettle or large pan. Few houses had bathrooms. Sanitation was basic at best: households often accommodated large numbers of people and had to manage with a single, water-flushed lavatory, usually in a small back-yard outhouse; these could harbour fearsome germs and diseases. Public washhouses helped people to keep reasonably clean, but they were far from adequate for everyday needs. So, even for the most fastidious – and there were some – a certain minimum of dirt and grime had to be accepted as unavoidable. Those lives could of course have been dramatically improved with better homes. So their inadequate, unhealthy houses had to go in favour of bright, clean new ones. Many families, especially the young, welcomed their salvation. Some, perhaps not surprisingly and usually the older residents, had their doubts and fears. But progress, they would say, had to come. They thought it would be good for the young.

Building the New Jerusalem

The Conservative-controlled councils between the wars were up for 'progress'. That, to many, was surprising. They were also doing something obvious and practical; they were building council houses, lots of them. Herbert Morrison, a leading light in the Labour Party, was astonished on a visit to Liverpool, to note Tory achievements. Between 1919 and 1939 Liverpool Corporation built 39,000 houses and flats and '... by 1939 about one fifth of Liverpool families lived in council dwellings built in the previous twenty years'.[83] These provided homes for the poor as well as work for armies of builders and suppliers of building materials. The economics of Keynes was at work near the waterfront. The old families, the professionals and the middle class had of course moved away long ago. Why not the working class? The Labour government provided the initial stimulus by the 1930 Greenwood Act. This gave councils the power to demolish houses that were deemed unfit for habitation, along with an obligation to rehouse, a major spur towards council house building. The policy was changed three years later by the concentration of the government subsidy solely on projects that rehoused slum dwellers. By then Ramsay MacDonald's National Government was in power as the jobless figures soared. It responded with hand-wringing and belt-tightening as it cut the pay of civil servants. Metaphors from life at sea were also popular, such as 'battening down the hatches', appropriate to a seafaring nation and Liverpool. Paradoxically to some, Franklin Roosevelt had a different recipe for the leading capitalist nation. He talked of jobs, of rejuvenation, of hope without fear, as he enlisted the goodwill of American workers. That was in 1932. It took a long time to get America back to work and, in the end, Roosevelt had probably less to do with it than the next big turn of the trade cycle's wheel followed by preparations for war, just as it did in Britain.

The economic policies of the MacDonald Coalition government, though intuitively persuasive, were actually in the wrong direction, as Keynes and others were tireless in pointing out. But in housing, and housing legislation, they did better, putting the emphasis on slum clearance. That was what the Liverpool waterfront wanted, although some argued that it was all propaganda and, despite the efforts of the Council '... by 1939 the shortage of homes in Liverpool was as severe as it had been twenty years beforehand'.[84] The schemes were, of course, about rehousing rather than providing additional housing, since the abandoned slum dwellings were 'condemned' even though in some cases it was some time, even years, before final demolition. They were also commonly condemned while families were still living in them, waiting for their turn on the rehousing list. Some refused to move until the bulldozers arrived. Others returned to their condemned terraces after failing to settle into their modern houses.[85] Pat O'Mara, living and working in Depression America, hearing the news from back home, tells of the startled reaction of his mother to how some of the 'slummy crowd' reacted:

And there were new houses being built by the Corporation, with all the new American gadgets such as gas and electricity in them! Several of the slummy crowd, particularly those who had salted away a little during the war, were taking social chances and moving into them. Several, however, finding life unbearable without the oil lamp and the bedroom bucket, were moving back.[86]

Did those moving back really prefer wholly inadequate amenities? Change, even for the better, is always difficult, but if their slum dwellings were no longer slums, with electricity, inside toilets, bathrooms and hot running water, but in the same location and at rents and utility costs which were affordable, would they still prefer 'the oil lamp and the bedroom bucket'? Professor Caradog Jones perhaps got to the nub of the problem:

> So long as the docker is under-employed and casually engaged, it seems fairly clear that the pressure on houses near the line of the docks will never be relieved by the building of new houses, at the present level of Corporation rents, several miles away.[87]

There was even a rent problem in the first phase of council house building in the 1920s. An average council house rent was 14s. per week, compared with that in the private sector of around 10s., a significant difference at a time of high general economic hardship. The high quality of the houses ('Addison' houses) in the first phase (though standards fell later) deepened the problems. They were spacious and healthy with, as Pat O'Mara's mother pointed out, all the latest (i.e. expensive) amenities and American gadgets. They even had hedges to trim and lawns to cut, requiring hedge shears and lawnmowers. One man, whose family were among the first to move into the 'garden suburb' at Springwood, near Allerton, in the 1920s, measured the contrast with precision:

> Springwood wasn't a big estate. A very nice estate, a very select estate. We were lucky, I suppose ... But for us this was a steep increase from 7 shillings a week in a house [their former one] which had only four rooms, one cold tap, no hot water or bathroom, no electric light but one gas light in the kitchen and everywhere else was illuminated by candles. So fuel bills were very low indeed. As well as this was the cost of transport, because my sisters and the other members of the family had to use the trains, so this was a stiff increase in expenditure. But of course that's balanced against the fact that my father (a boilermaker) was in full employment and my sisters were also working.[88]

What would happen to the Mottrams' seemingly balanced family budget should Jim Mottram's father lose his well-paid job and his sisters could not find work?

That might well have been the case in the 1930s, but Jim Mottram's story ends here before that. Eleanor Rathbone, as persistent as ever, was even reporting severe malnutrition in 1929 as a consequence of high rents and other costs in Norris Green, another 'garden suburb'. She was arguing the case for a family allowance system, payable directly to the mother.[89] Throughout the hungry 1930s tenants campaigned for rent reductions. Although some token cuts were achieved, by August 1939 a full-scale rent strike was being organised. The refugees from the waterfront might have been poor, but they had much practice in running a good strike, though ominous events on the Polish border made the action less urgent. But not all action to relieve the pressure of pressing poverty was collective. One well-established tradition was to target the electric meter in the corner with its ability to take washers instead of shillings![90]

Even in the slum houses rents could be unaffordable, particularly when private landlords took advantage of the large demand for housing accommodation that was being exacerbated by slum clearance and the continuing need to live near the docks. Rent were forced up, and in some cases conditions were little improved from those that had prevailed in the glory days of Empire before the Great War. One Catholic priest railed against the privations of his parishioners, in the diction and angry ringing tones of Ireland, fighting for class, not religion: 'It is free houses they should have!'[91] The dockers were even blamed for living near the docks. Yet poor and irregular wages, potentially high living costs in the suburbs, and the need to be at the stands twice a day gave them literally no option.

For all of the Corporation's efforts, their successes and self-congratulation, Liverpool's housing problem seemed intractable. As in our own times, delegations of councillors, Labour and Tory, went abroad for inspiration. Hamburg and 'Red Vienna', with their working-class model tenements, were the new way. They could also house large numbers of families, in decent conditions, in the same neighbourhood. Liverpool's would be ten storeys high, with a playground in the middle and a crèche on the roof. Gerard Gardens was one such tenement-style development, consisting of grand art-deco style blocks that were built in the mid-1930s. But it was all too costly and when completed the playground and crèche had left the design.[92] Even the central heating was no more. Kirkdale and the Dingle also had their tenements. They would all become the slums of the future and were demolished after the war, except for two: St Andrew's Gardens and the former Myrtle Gardens.

The Corporation's slum-clearance programme seemed continually to be chasing their tails. Even in 1933 the infamous courts of Victorian times were still housing 30,000 people; in defiance of the law, even 700 cellars were occupied. Some 24,000 people were on the council house waiting list, and slum-clearance alone required new houses for 15,000 families.[93] Soon, the Luftwaffe bomb aimers, though not specifically targeting waterfront homes and people, would eliminate, in months, some of the worst of the courts, cellars and back-to-backs. Homelessness would now be added to a desperate shortage of houses, any houses. By the end of the war a deep crisis was developing. Successive generations of politicians and activists, local and national, would over the years put their stamp on policies of demolition, construction, rehabilitation and dispersal, but with limited success.

CHAPTER TEN

Dockland under siege: the Second World War

There were around 4,200 fatal casualties resulting from air attacks on Merseyside ... The City Engineer's minutes recorded the provision of a 'special vehicle' with bins to deal with dismembered bodies.[1]

(John Hughes, 1993)

Naturally, we targeted the biggest ships first. That was obvious, the big two funnel ship — we later learned was the *Benares*.

(Rolfe Hilse, U-boat 48, September 1940)[2]

T H E Ellerman Lines SS *City of Benares* had been launched in 1936, its fine lines initially gracing the Indian run. Its first time on the Atlantic run, to Canada, was on 13 September 1940. The 486 ft, 11,000-ton *Benares* had a top speed of 15 knots, and was carrying a total of 406 passengers and crew. The fatal torpedo hit at one minute past midnight, and the *City of Benares* took just half an hour to sink below the waves. The passenger list counted 90 'seavacuees', children aged from four to fifteen who had been escaping the bombs over British cities. Some of the children were from Liverpool. Of the 148 survivors only thirteen were children, 77 losing their lives.[3] This was what was meant by 'total war'. Such attacks were not unexpected, but were always deeply shocking.

The aerial war would be just as devastating as the maritime one. What the British feared most was the so-called 'carpet' bombing. On the Pathe newsreels a few years earlier the world had already watched what seemed to be a dress rehearsal, at the small undefended town of Guernica in Spain, in which several hundred civilians had been killed in a devastating aerial bombardment by German planes and their Italian allies. By 1940, previously unimaginable atrocities were commonplace all over the world, not least in China as the Japanese armies, after 1937, bombed and slaughtered all before them. Even Britain's natural, island defence was no longer such a clear advantage. After the German conquest of Crete in May 1941 there was widespread fear of an airborne invasion, even after

205

The *City of Benares*. The children were welcomed on board by '... magnificent Indian men [the 'Lascar' crew] wearing huge turbans and beautiful clothes with shoes that turned up at the ends. They looked like something out of the Arabian nights.' When the *Benares* was sunk by torpedo on 13 September 1940, 77 of the children out of 90 lost their lives. The commander and first officer of the U-boat were later acquitted of war crimes.

the Luftwaffe's defeat in the Battle of Britain in the autumn of 1940. Nor did that defeat prevent the succession of massed bomber raids over Liverpool, which reached their ferocious peak in the first week of May 1941.

The aerial bombardment of Liverpool was severe, especially during that week in May. Liverpool and Glasgow were high-priority targets for the Germans as sea traffic was diverted to them from the more geographically vulnerable London, Southampton and the east-coast ports. Liverpool and Glasgow were also the principal ports for the strategically vital traffic with North America. This explains the 1,285 convoys that entered the Mersey over the course of the war. One cohort, of several convoys arriving at the same time, totalled 60 ships.[4] But the convoys, even after crossing the Atlantic, had to run the perilous gauntlet of U-boats operating as close as five miles from the estuary. Losses often easily reached 50 per cent of vessels per convoy, but even with such losses there was major congestion in the port as the number of berths destroyed or put out of action by mass bombing raids increased. For one 'brief period' only twelve berths were available out of a pre-war figure approaching 150.[5] The port was even closed, over several periods, for a total of 1,310 hours, with a large number of ships either being sunk when moored in the docks or seriously damaged at anchor on the river: excluding naval vessels, the total was 91.[6]

The most spectacular of these in terms of damage, though miraculously without loss of life, was the ammunition ship *Malakand*. This ship had been berthed in Huskisson dock, when she caught fire and blew up on 4 May 1941. But that was only part of it, as Mountfield put it:

> Only those who saw the Port under these conditions can know what it was like; with ships sunk at odd angles in all sorts of places, long sheds burnt to the ground, great smouldering heaps of debris and roadways blocked with unexploded land mines.[7]

The day the *Malakand* blew up was also one of the eight nights, beginning on May Day, which took Liverpool's fatalities and serious injuries to new heights. The 'May Blitz', as it was soon called, and by which name it has been known ever since, saw 1,453 lose their lives in Liverpool and 257 in Bootle. The losses on those eight nights represented, for the city and the borough respectively, 53 per cent and 61 per cent, of all deaths from bombing over the entire course of the war.[8]

After May 1941 air raids were blessedly few and much more limited in their impact as the Luftwaffe was increasingly diverted to the Eastern Front to support the Wehrmacht's assault upon the Soviet Union which began in June 1941. If bombing on the scale of May had continued for several more months, the loss of life and destruction of homes would almost certainly have ended Liverpool's involvement in the war for at least months, if not years, as the U-boats continued to wreak havoc and even threaten British submission by starvation. Churchill's assessment at the end of 1940 had been ominous: '… the entrances and estuaries of the Mersey and the Clyde far surpassed in mortal significance all other factors in the war'.[9]

The 'mortal significance' of the destruction of docks, warehouses and the losses at sea were not lost upon the population, even without Churchill's warnings. But within the naturally narrower perspectives of most people it is the personal human dimension that hits the hardest. Nor do the actual deaths take account of the large numbers wounded or maimed as well as the traumas and psychological scars – what we now call 'post traumatic stress disorder' – of survivors and their families which defy facile statistical measurement. Those stress factors would include the impact of destroyed homes and the mass evacuation of children to strange towns and villages, some even losing their parents and homes in their absence. Nicholas Monsarrat, in his celebrated novel, *The Cruel Sea*, which was rooted in his own experiences, reports what it was like for those other absentees – sailors returning home on leave from convoys or naval vessels – to find scenes of utter devastation and irreparable loss:

South Huskisson Branch Dock after the enormous explosion of the ammunition ship the *Malakand*. The scale of the devastation is obvious, although some of the damage will also be attributable to bomb damage during the May Blitz, which caused widespread destruction of ships and docks, taking nearly 1,900 lives, across Merseyside as a whole, with 450 seriously injured, 66,000 houses destroyed, and 70,000 made homeless.

A bomb crater in Cazneau Street, Scotland Road, May 1941. This large crater was probably the result of a land mine, sometimes dropped by parachute. It has clearly caused major damage and probably loss of life. The rows of vulnerable terraces, with their densely packed populations, can be seen further down the street. Complete shelter or fast evacuation were not always available.

© LIVERPOOL RECORD OFFICE

... each street we traversed, by a dozen diversions, bumping over hoses, scuttering through broken glass and ruined woodwork, passing groups of intent rescue workers or silent onlookers, showed a more appalling destruction. Tall houses lay in the street, flames showed through empty windows and gaping rents, shops and buildings sprawled over the roadways.[10]

Loss of life, physical destruction and homelessness were, for the most part, the special lot of the people along the waterfront, those living in the crowded dockland streets, from Bootle in the north to Garston in the south. The deaths in Liverpool's dockland were 3,160 out of a total for Merseyside of 4,200.[11] As well as the civilian deaths, Liverpool families suffered heavily from the losses at sea. A port of such size and importance, swollen by its extra strategic significance in the war, was bound to suffer more than most. It has been estimated that the chance of survival if sunk at sea, usually by torpedo in the Atlantic, was less than one in two. As a ship went down, usually very quickly, an early drowning in icy cold waters was the first threat. Nor were the prospects much better when exposed in an open lifeboat over long periods with little food and water. The chances of being picked up were also not high.[12] One authority estimates that 35,000 British merchant seamen lost their lives in the war, but considers even that estimate is probably too low.[13] It also excludes the foreign sailors who traditionally complemented British crews. The *City of Benares* crew, for example, was mainly lascars (Indian or Asian seamen who had been crewing European ships for centuries).[14] Yet many of those who did not come back were Liverpool men,[15] and their families back home were often those most affected by the attacks from the air.

Evacuation offered a route to survival for many, though with its own fears and deprivations, especially for children. Sending them to North America was available for the better-off families. As a child Shirley Williams, the prominent Labour and Social Democrat politician, along with her brother, John, was one of these. Her mother, Vera Brittain the pacifist campaigner and writer, sought to keep her children safe overseas in 'new territories unhampered by the evil nationalistic traditions of the Old World'. It cost £15 for a sea crossing to America, a month's wages for most working men in 1939.[16] Escape was rationed by price, so a subsidy had to be available for the poorest. Many were, however, anxious to pay up.[17] In Southampton 5,000 left for America in two days.[18]

After Dunkirk, the selfish behaviour of some of those with money started to stir consciences, even as far as the government. More important were the offers of homes from Commonwealth countries for children at risk. Canada was the first, followed quickly by Australia, New Zealand and South Africa. The USA was even more generous. The President and his influential, activist wife, Eleanor, offered safety and hospitality for as many as arrived at their shores. The British government responded by quickly putting together a scheme, with preference given to those least well off and most endangered from bombing. For these it was free, but some contributions were required for maintenance from the better-off. The parents of private school children had to pay both the £15 cost of travel and £1 per week maintenance. Yet there were not enough ships suitable to meet anywhere near all the applications, although the rich seemed to have fewer problems for their children, their nannies and even themselves. The ships that did sail had, however, mixed their passenger lists of paying and subsidised passengers as well as adults and children. The *Benares* passenger list included all social classes, although the better cabins were reserved for those able to pay. The disaster did, however, put paid to official support, the government ending its subsidised scheme on 4 October, just seventeen days after the *Benares* was sunk.[19]

The far safer and more accessible alternative, though again it initially required ample private funds, was to escape to the seaside. Two million took this route to destinations of Scotland, Devon and Wales. One luxury hotel in North Wales, in 1940, was a popular refuge for women 'whose sole occupation seemed to be backgammon, a lot of drinking and a little knitting "for the troops"'.[20] The poor of Liverpool, and especially their children, found themselves evacuated in large numbers to North Wales, though not strictly voluntarily. The 'choice' was a simple one: stay and be bombed, or get on the train for Wales. Some found that a difficult choice!

Exodus

The government's plans for mass evacuation in 1938 from the cities to safer areas were borne out of predictions of mass slaughter from aerial bombing followed by the likelihood of rioting, looting and the collapse of social order. The newspapers took a similar line on the loss of lives, the *Liverpool Daily Post* for the whole country predicted 300,000 per week.[21] Liverpool had also had its own history of rioting and looting to confirm the views of those who feared social breakdown amid the chaos of bombing. In the first week of September 1939, 130,000 were evacuated from Merseyside's central areas, primarily dockland, to safer refuges in the country. For the country as a whole, in the same week, the number evacuated was 1.5 million, less than half the planned 3.5 million.[22] Families could, and did, make their own private arrangements, but it was the official scheme that covered the majority of the population. Children were the main priority, since they were seen as the most vulnerable. In any case many of their parents were required to work long hours keeping the cities and factories running as part of the war effort. 'Get the children away' was the call through loudspeakers on vans in the streets following the widespread distribution of leaflets and information. In Liverpool's Catholic areas, the priests were active in encouraging parents to register their children under the 'voluntary' scheme. Joan Boyce, an evacuee, recalls the case of a thirteen-year-old girl:

> The evacuation scheme was supposed to be voluntary, yet people were pressurised from all sides: in school, in church, even in the streets. Father Reilly, the parish priest, warned that it would be the parents' responsibility if children were killed during the bombing. Vans with loudspeakers patrolled up and down the streets shouting: 'Today is your last chance to register. Go to your nearest centre now, before time runs out!' My parents were under great stress and in the end decided it would be best to send us on the evacuation.[23]

The persuasion did not always work. Some saw separation as a much greater loss than the threat from air raids. It was widely believed that bombers would appear over Liverpool right from the first week of the war. That they did not was reflected in the low numbers actually evacuated in the first wave. In Liverpool about a quarter of those children registered to go did not take their places on the scheduled trains. In other cities the proportion of those not going was much higher, such as 78 per cent in Nottingham and 85 per cent in Sheffield. Some of the older children even returned home when they saw the strange, unfamiliar, even unfriendly houses in which they had been billeted. Children brought up in the terrace communities of Merseyside, without experience, social graces or acquaintance with the social norms of rural England, naturally preferred what they had left behind.

Some children did, however, welcome evacuation. It was an adventure for some. Almost all had barely moved away from their own street, let alone their neighbourhood or Liverpool itself – apart from days out to New Brighton or, occasionally Rhyl or Llandudno in North Wales. For others it was 'a mixture of sadness and excitement',[24] with the more sensitive and perceptive children trying to spare their parents' anxieties as the parents, in their turn, kept their worries and anguish to themselves. But whatever the motives and feelings of parents and children the 'first wave' was far from a success in terms of numbers. By the end of 1939 28 per cent of evacuees had returned. This had turned into an exodus in the wrong direction.

The absence of bombing in the first nine months – the so-called 'phoney war' – destroyed the credibility of the evacuation scheme. It began to return at the beginning of August 1940 when the first bombs were dropped, albeit on the other side of the Mersey. Liverpool's first bombs, on dock targets, fell on the night of 17/18 August. Night raids then slowly, though erratically, grew in scale and severity, reflected by the numbers of deaths and injuries. The high-water mark was the first week of May 1941. By then there was a 'second wave' of evacuation.[25] The bombing had also created a homelessness problem and, with nowhere else to go, whole families often threw themselves on the hospitality of those who had given a welcome to their children. But the most important aspect of mass evacuation was not about numbers, whether or not it was misconceived, or proved an eventual success or a failure. The most important aspect, and largely unexpected, was the exposure of the harsh realities of inequality and differences in social class. Britain's 'two nations' had not changed much since the time of Disraeli. Now the two had the opportunity to view each other at very close quarters over a long period. For the most part neither liked what they saw, but significant lessons were absorbed. Government ministers and senior civil servants were shocked by evidence of how most British families lived, as revealed during the evacuation. That salutary shock was to have a major influence on post-war policy.

Plimsolls in the villages

The plimsoll was an enduring symbol of poverty, These cheap, canvas, non-waterproof shoes with thin, rubber toecaps were widely worn by Liverpool's children throughout the inter-war period and beyond.[26] The shoe or boot with a complete sole and wear left in the uppers could be seen even along the waterfront. But these were not common, and the country dwellers' view of Liverpool as 'Plimsoll City' was well judged.[27]

As a matter of policy Liverpool's evacuees were widely dispersed, though within relatively easy travelling distance by train from Merseyside. North Wales was an obvious destination, to the seaside towns such as Pwllheli and Aberystwyth and inland to the small towns, villages and hamlets. Anglesey was also prominent, as well as St Asaph, in Denbighshire. Outside Wales Chester, with good train connections, was a major destination, with the rest of Cheshire, Lancashire and Shropshire also taking substantial numbers.[28]

Some of the children saw the evacuation as a great adventure, even pleading with their reluctant parents to let them go, especially if their friends were going. An added bonus was getting away from school for those who did not value the often harsh, classroom experience. In any case the schools were disrupted or closed and, later, some even destroyed by bombs. Teachers, however, often went with them as escorts. Some priests went, too. Many children, however, were apprehensive and fearful. The older children, often in charge of their younger siblings, would be expected to hide their own fears for the sake of the younger ones. Most Liverpool children were unused to long, uncomfortable train journeys. In crowded trains, without corridors, some would consume large quantities of lemonade, and the inevitable often happened: one teacher travelling to Shrewsbury on a twelve-hour journey, recorded a train which, on arrival, understandably, 'stank'.[29] It was also understandable if by the end of the journey many of those who had been looking forward to travel, adventure or freedom had lost their enthusiasm.

Nor was their arrival always welcomed. When their trains reached their destinations the evacuees would be taken, *en masse*, to reception centres, often village or school halls. Locally appointed billeting officers had the unforgiving, difficult task of finding homes, of an adequate standard, for the children. Householders were often resentful, even hostile, especially in the officially designated 'safety areas' where billeting could be exercised compulsorily. It was not work on which to build a satisfactory career of public service, and resignations were frequent. But homes for the evacuees were eventually found, although not always suitable or even adequate.

The difficulty Liverpool children had, above others from British cities, was a reputation for the usual consequences of poverty of being unclean, vermin-ridden and unruly. This reputation had some basis in truth, and it even extended to their parents. One Liverpool school teacher, travelling with her charges, observed:

I felt sorry for the receiving area or district – the mothers and children are a mixed crowd – black, white and yellow in various degrees, dirty, immoral and quarrelsome and drinking. Pity the poor billeting officer.[30]

Not all evacuees were like this and this school teacher might well have been unfortunate with her group, but the evacuees' reputation, true or not, went ahead of them. The outcome was that on arrival they were medically inspected at the reception centres, the boys' heads shaved and the girls hair cut very short. That was alarming enough for already frightened children. In some cases it got even worse on arrival at their homes. Two sisters were not even allowed into the house until their foster mother had cleaned their hair with paraffin and vinegar in the garden shed. Once in the house they were given a hot bath and their hair was washed again.[31] Others were treated as welcome domestics, in effect paying for being looked after:

I did a lot of ironing at weekends ... The housework was heavy. I had to clean and polish a big mahogany sideboard ... it was just like the TV series 'Upstairs-Downstairs'. I was the maid. I also had to go to school as well as look after my younger sister, Josie.'[32]

Religion could be an additional difficulty. Zealous Catholic priests, as we have seen, were keen to look after the evacuees' souls. But even their zeal floundered faced with the experience of finding the children billeted in Church of England areas. Nor was North Wales' Methodism an appropriate haven for Catholic children, less than pious but guiltily mindful of the requirement to attend Mass.[33] Cleanliness also lived very close by to Godliness in Welsh Methodist households, which could cause problems for even the cleanest, most respectable children. One consequence of loss, loneliness and separation, which was as yet barely recognised or understood by psychologists let alone the wider public, was bed-wetting. A common 'cure' for such an 'abomination' was a round of sustained beatings and humiliating punishment. The unscrupulous, as usual, found an opportunity, even in this, to make some money. Allowances were available for extra laundry costs. In Llantrisant, in North Wales, these rose from a total of £43 in 1940–41 to £350 in 1941–42. Following an inquiry the number of reported cases declined rapidly.[34]

The evacuation was undoubtedly a collision of cultures which even led to complaints from the receiving local authorities against the Merseyside public authorities for sending children in such a poor state of health. Wrexham was one of these, its Medical Officer of Health reporting, on 11 September 1939, that of 800 Liverpool children arriving to be billeted, 35 per cent of the girls and 11 per cent of the boys had head lice, with over 10 per cent of the whole party having potentially serious diseases including bronchitis, impetigo, scarlet fever, chickenpox and tonsil and adenoid problems. Five were suffering from malnutrition. A Wrexham alderman, Cyril Jones, drew a wider lesson:

One result of the evacuation had been to make them realise that were two Englands. One was a civilised country and the other was far below the civilisation that existed in the Wrexham area for many years. These children will be going back to Liverpool when the emergency is over and I only hope that by that time the authorities there will have wakened up.[35]

This 'two Englands' analysis was too simplistic. The countryside was no rural idyll, even though country poverty was claimed to be less of a burden than town poverty. Nor have such attitudes entirely disappeared even in our own times. But there were useful lessons from the widespread experience of the evacuation. One, from observation of actual behaviour, was that the comfortable and better-off were commonly less generous than those less blessed with money, possessions, servants and fine houses. Some continued to report, as Britain struggled for survival, of their difficulties with 'servant problems' or 'disgruntled butlers' and resigning maids. The less well-off were more accepting, without any illusions. Those receiving evacuees also often needed the money. The wife of an agricultural labourer who earned perhaps 30s. a week found the full board for one child of 10s. 6d. (8s. 6d. each if more than one), a welcome boost to her housekeeping. The cost was reclaimed, according to ability to pay, from the parents in the cities.[36] Revealingly, a quarter of families were unable to pay anything. It also has to be noted that many of the adverse reactions and experiences were more closely associated with the first phase of the evacuation. There was also resentment over the strong advocacy for the scheme by the government and local officials during the 'phoney war'. The seeming unnecessary disruption of schooling was also criticised by parents and teachers. These problems undermined the scheme, and large numbers were brought back by their parents, with some even coming home by themselves. That disenchantment was to change as the bombs began to fall in earnest, especially from the beginning of May 1941.

Blitzkrieg!

In 1940 the Ministry of Information issued two short films under the titles *London Can Take It!* and *Britain Can Take It!*, both designed to demonstrate that German bombing would not undermine civilian morale, as well as to influence American opinion towards joining the war. The images of London civilians quickly getting back to life and work after an air raid had some substance in truth, and the German strategy of bombing cities in order to destroy civilian morale was ultimately unsuccessful. But almost none of those living in the towns and cities subject to aerial attack had any real choice in the matter. Leaving where they lived was rarely an option. It was severely limited by the need to work and earn a living. The war effort required them to work to produce munitions and other materials of war, which normally meant them remaining in urban areas under potential attack both at work and at home. The dockers were especially vulnerable, working in or

Rescue! This photograph is held in the Liverpool Record Office, but is from the Imperial War Museum. It shows how effective an Anderson Shelter could be, even after the complete collapse of houses and buildings onto it. However, such shelters were only available to those with gardens or convenient space by their houses, advantages not available to most people in British cities such as Liverpool. The standard shelter was of brick, with a twin concrete roof in the middle of the street and only able to withstand minor blasts.

alongside ships, which were always key targets for attack, even though raids were usually at night. In their account of the attitudes of Bootle's citizens Marsh and Almond saw no evidence that they saw themselves part of a national struggle for 'democracy'. Such abstractions meant less to them than the immediate experience of survival. On the contrary, Marsh and Almond continue:

> Like most British people they rarely articulated what they were fighting for. When the bombs fell, the people of Bootle fought with varying degrees of heroism, and occasional cowardice, for their families, their relatives, friends or neighbours and for their particular part of the world or because it was

their job to fight. They fought for remarkably ordinary things and the fight
was against chaos and 'physical destruction'.[37]

Even the word 'fighting' did not always reflect people's attitudes. In the dark
days of the 1941 May Blitz terms such as 'courage', 'defiance' and 'resolution' were
used frequently in the propaganda war, but on the whole people were trying just to
survive as best they could, hoping to keep their families and homes intact, and to
see their men and women coming home again in one piece. Some just despaired,
or went out of their minds. Tony Lane tells of similar unheroic attitudes among
merchant seamen, much like the soldiers in North Africa where the every-day
needs of ample rations and cigarettes counted for more than distant war aims: 'Hot
tea was more important than the Beveridge Report or the distant future.' Even
more understandably, the same attitudes were widespread in occupied France,
where 'People did not think of their own conduct in the terms – resistance,
collaboration, Petainism – that have been used by historians.'[38]

Nor was the country quite as solidly behind Churchill and the war Cabinet as
was conventionally assumed then, and since. The normally wide social, economic
and political gulf between the government and the governed – even in old,
politically stable democracies such as Britain – may have narrowed in wartime
conditions, but it was still there. Within Britain's peculiar class system were
wide inequalities in income, wealth and opportunity. Even Churchill, for all his
popularity, political skills and democratic instincts, was a member of one of the
old, privileged, aristocratic families. That, given the 1945 longing for a better,
fairer Britain, must have largely explained his rejection by the British electorate
– to his own surprise but not that of the millions of voters still in uniform. Nor
in war was normal business entirely given up. That extended to the growth in
trade union membership and in strikes, despite the 1940 Order 1305, which banned
strikes and lockouts where collective bargaining existed, allowing appeals to a
newly established National Arbitration Tribunal. The boost it gave to collective
bargaining rang bells for Ernest Bevin, by then Minister of Labour. It also suited
Churchill with his seemingly genetic belligerence against strikers, still well
remembered in South Wales and Liverpool.

Belligerence and the law were not enough. Between 1940 and 1944 the number
of working days lost, from stoppages across the economy as a whole, quadrupled.
The miners, with perhaps the longest memories of Churchill and 1926, led the
way. Over the four years their proportion of days lost was over a half of the
total. One stoppage in Lanarkshire, in January 1941, involved 26,000 coming out
on a one-day sympathy strike in support of miners at a single colliery. Another,
in Yorkshire at the end of the following month and into March, saw 20,000 on
strike with the loss of 130,000 working days. The Yorkshire dispute, like many
others in the industry, was over their pay relative to other industries, which had
not sufficiently recovered from the depressed conditions of the inter-war years.[39]
Then, in the same year, in a spectacular dispute at Betteshanger Colliery in Kent,

1,050 miners were summonsed, tried and fined for striking in breach of Order 1305. Only nine paid the fines. Commitment to prison of over a thousand was explained as not enforceable on the grounds that the county gaol was not big enough.[40] Another vital wartime industry, engineering, saw several major disputes, notably the Scottish apprentices who struck in 1943 over their pay relative to skilled rates. The dispute spread to Lancashire and Belfast and, at its peak, involved 25,000. The year before, also in Belfast, 9,000 had come out for the reinstatement of two dismissed shop stewards,[41] a common cause of strikes at the time and for many years afterwards.

By 1943 the end of the war looked as if it might be in sight, and it was perhaps thought that peacetime industrial relations would soon be resumed; this was a critical year for strikes. Sir Stafford Cripps, speaking in Bristol, berated striking workers in aircraft production for sabotaging the war effort. In Liverpool, in July, 1,800 tobacco factory workers struck over the interpretation of an arbitration award setting minimum rates. In the same month city council workers walked out over the delay of an arbitration award on sick pay. On the docks there was a major dispute in August when thirty-four dockers were suspended, at Bramley Moore dock, for refusing to work after 9 p.m. The port was then brought to a standstill when 'several thousands' struck in sympathy. The dispute arose from the men's claim that the guaranteed weekly minimum applied to all shifts ('turns') and not just the first ten, in addition to overtime rates. This major stoppage lasted for eight days and was only resolved by the reinstatement of the thirty-four and an investigation of grievances.[42]

If the old class interests had far from been put aside, even for 'the duration', dockland also had to endure a terrifying aerial onslaught, culminating in the first week in May with the loss, across Merseyside as a whole, of nearly 1,900 lives. A further 450 were seriously injured; 66,000 houses were destroyed, and 70,000 made homeless. The death and devastation stretched all along the waterfront. Liverpool suffered most, followed by Bootle. Bootle, for its smaller size, suffered more, in proportion, than Liverpool. Of the borough's population of 50,000, 20,000 were suddenly homeless. Many of Bootle's famous landmarks were hit in the May Blitz, including the well-known Knowsley Arms on Derby Road. Soon after it was bombed the wreckage was invaded by a large crowd who either consumed, or took away, the pub's entire stock of liquor. In Liverpool, the famous old music hall, the Rotunda, which had stood on the junction of Stanley and Scotland Roads since 1863, was gutted by incendiaries on the night of 3/4 May. It was later demolished. The site, now a bus stop, is still known as the Rotunda. Scotland Road also lost St Sylvester's School.

Judging from their reminiscences, not all children regarded the physical destruction in the same way as their parents. It could provide a vast, changing, adventurous landscape, with the prospect of finds among the rubble, especially when shops were bombed. The stern warnings of parents counted for little to young, adventurous spirits. Some even swam, or drowned, in the emergency water

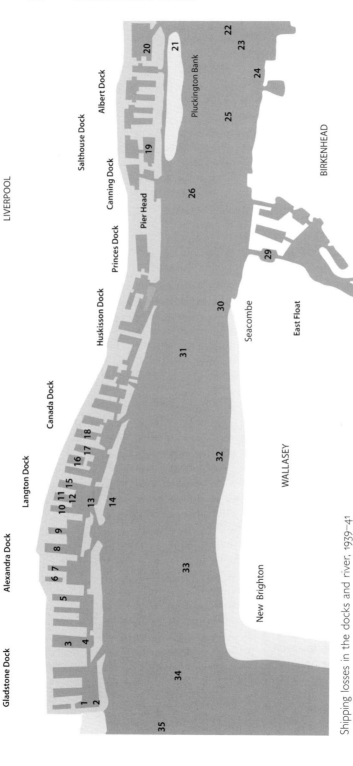

Shipping losses in the docks and river, 1939–41

1. John Wise; 2. Robert E. Peary; 3. Jamaica; 4. Roxburgh Castle; 5. Silvio; 6. Trentino; 7. Marton; 8. Bra Kar; 9. Europa 10. Domino; 11. Baron Inchcape; 12. Stomboli; 13. Tacoma Star; 14. Poolgarth; 15. Europa; 16. Malakand; 17. Elstree Grange; 18. Tai Shan; 19. Sirius Lightship; 20. Lyster; 21. Merton; 22. Tacoma City; 23. Margot; 24. Kerry Coast; 25. City of Keelung; 26. Ullapool; 27. Myrmidon; 28. Mammoth; 29. Bifrost; 30. Royal Daffodil; 31. Silver Sandal; 32. Lucita; 33. Innisfallen; 34. Duke of Rothesay; 35. Elax.

REDRAWN BY CARNEGIE FROM PERRETT; LIVERPOOL: A CITY AT WAR (BURSCOUGH: HUGO PRESS; 2005).

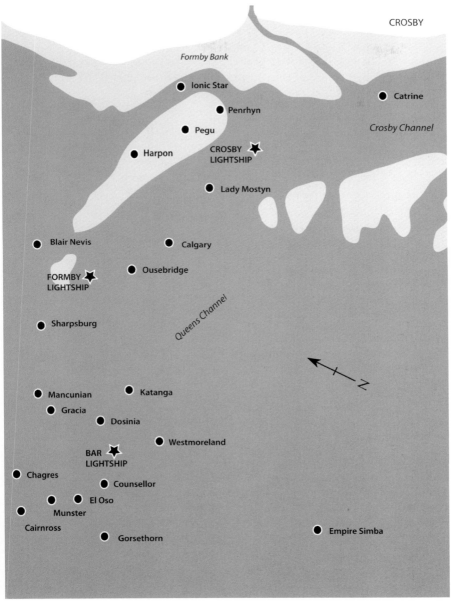

Shipping and lightship losses in the approaches to the Mersey, 1939–41. Submarines could penetrate close to the approaches to target vessels and convoys. The lightships were also a key target.

supplies, the many temporary structures hastily formed from the still-standing walls of large buildings, adorned with three large white letters: EWS. Bombed sites were levelled as quickly as possible and covered with shale. They were soon in use. A gap in a terraced row with two exposed gable ends would quickly become a football pitch with the names of Everton and Liverpool identifying the chalked, full-size goalposts on each gable. It was better than the cobbled street and almost, to the young footballers, tailor-made.

Meanwhile, the dock system – critical even to the country's very survival – was almost on the point of collapse. Bryan Perrett describes it in similar language to Stuart Mountfield: '... a shambles of gutted sheds, rubble-strewn quays and smashed hydraulic machines, choked with sunken and severely damaged shipping.'[43] The scale of the damage to the dock system is revealed by Perrett's graphic bird's-eye illustrations of the losses in the docks, river and approaches to the Mersey between 1939 and 1941. For May alone Hughes lists 36 ships sunk at their berths or on the river, as well as five major pieces of dock machinery, including two grain elevators. Eighty-six other vessels and four pieces of dock machinery received slight to severe damage, and others were burned out. The most spectacular loss, described by Hughes, was the ammunition ship the *Malakand* which destroyed Huskisson Dock as well as wrecking the nearby Overhead Railway Station and track. The famous 'dockers' umbrella' was a special target in itself, as were the lightships at Formby, Crosby and the Bar Lightship in the approaches to the Mersey.

The loss of shipping was the equivalent of a medium-sized convoy. A total 1,285 convoys entered the Mersey from 1939 to 1945, but the losses raised alarm bells in the Royal Navy and the Ministry of War Transport. The remarkable fact, however, was that the port was not put out of action for long; sunken vessels were cleared, and damaged vessels and equipment salvaged remarkably quickly. Large work gangs were recruited for these urgent tasks, including from the armed forces and the unemployed. At the peak of the operation 1,300 men and 162 tipping lorries worked solely on clearing rubble. The effort was such that tonnage landed at the end of April at 181,600, though down to 35,000 on 10 May, by 17 May had reached 85,700, rising steadily to 126,900 on 14 June, a remarkable feat of recovery and reconstruction.

Amid the chaos, destruction and reconstruction, dockers still had to unload the ships. They also had to work faster and more productively, since by early May only half of the normal berths were available for shipping. On 15 March 1941 Churchill had himself demanded greater effort to reduce turn-round times in British ports.[44] To this end, the dockers were brought under the direct control of the Ministry of War Transport. In the First World War dockers had only tardily been exempted from military service, but right from the outset of the Second World War their contribution was recognised officially as vital to the war effort, and they were provided with exemption from military service as a 'reserved' occupation. Then, from March 1942, the dockers were allowed to work on a weekly basis, for any dock employer, in any area of the docks. A regular weekly wage for all along the waterfront, provided stability of employment and earnings for dock work for the first time, . It worked well during the war, although when peace was restored employers and men were free to go back to their old ways.

The actual conditions of work, especially during the May Blitz, were novel and dangerous, regularly interrupted by sirens and explosions and the need to take shelter. But it did not seem necessary for the dockers to abandon their usual 'privileges', even in war. There were regular prosecutions for stealing from the docks, magistrates berating those convicted in patriotic tones. For the most part, the dockers cooperated under the weekly 'forced labour' régime. The regular work and regular pay were inducements more powerful than patriotism.

The physical dangers could, however, be acute, even though bombing raids took place after dark. A dock gateman recalled watching from the roof of a building as the docks burned in all directions. A special, additional hazard was the blackout, a foot wrong leading to a fall into the dock. Sailors, the worse for wear, were especially at risk leaving their clubs and pubs. In 1944, a Bootle emergency ambulance, in the darkness, suffered the same fate.[45]

The port's survival in May had been a close run thing. General Pile, of the Royal Artillery, in charge of Merseyside's anti-aircraft batteries, was not given to exaggeration or alarmism. Yet by the end of the intensive bombing of the May Blitz, with more of the same feared and expected, he was anxious for the citizens' morale:

No one, however old or however young, is out of the firing line, and, while the soldiers and airmen may destroy enemy raiders, it is the citizens themselves who are the last line of defence. It they give way, if they do not restore immediately what has been destroyed, if they fail to get the wounded away to hospital. If they do not get the normal services of the city working again, then a blockade will, sooner or later, be successful.[46]

General Pile saw 'morale' as more than a psychological condition. If it broke it would led to inaction and chaos. It also led to flight. From Sunday 4 May people began to stream out of dockland to sleep in barns, church halls, cinemas and camp in fields in the country and market towns well away from the Luftwaffe's bomb aimers. The authorities soon supported this voluntary exodus with trains and army lorries. On the night of 7/8 May 1941, 50,000 were in this other exodus, although most only stayed the night, with those who had to work reporting for duty the next morning with as much good cheer as they could muster. Many had lost at least one member of their family to the bombs. It is certainly plausible to conclude that had the bombing continued for just a further week on the scale of the first that 'morale', on General Pile's definition, would have collapsed. The rumour mill was also hard at work grinding out stories of unimaginable catastrophes made plausible by the visible evidence of death and destruction. One rumour was that

The Women's Voluntary Service tea van. Cups of hot tea, copiously dispensed, were available at bombing crises and emergencies. This event looks like the morning after an air raid, though not in May 1941 judging by the winter clothes. It took far more than tea to restore morale in the bombed areas, but its presence was symbolic enough for Churchill to stockpile it in both wars.

©LIVERPOOL RECORD OFFICE.

feeding arrangements for those in the bombed areas had broken down, leading to widespread food riots. That, in turn, created a second rumour: that the city was under martial law. The 'Irish', that is Catholics, were also widely blamed for causing panic, including white flags of surrender hung from windows. David Logan, the veteran MP for Scotland Ward, put the white flag rumour down to curtains fluttering from broken windows in his constituency.[47]

General Pile's fears for the collapse of social cohesion did not materialise, but its survival was greatly helped by Göring's strategic errors and the tactical ones of Hugo Sperlle, whose Lufwaffe 3, stationed in Northern France, was responsible for eliminating Liverpool from the war. Hitler, too, played his part, his Operation Barbarossa diverting attention, in troops, aeroplanes and focus, away from Liverpool.

The good news, which could not be predicted at the time on Merseyside, was that the night of 7/8 May was the last major bombing raid of the war. It was also a much lighter affair than the catastrophe of 3/4 May. For the entire month of May 1941, Merseyside's total killed, in all areas, had been 1,453. From June 1941 to the end of the war the total was 78. The last raid was on 10 January 1942, when 15 lost their lives. Yet even at the height of the Luftwaffe's assault, the port continued to function and ships' cargoes were discharged and loaded. On Sunday 4 May five ships entered the Mersey, from Canada, Buenos Aires, Hong Kong, Nigeria, Belfast and the Gold Coast. One vessel left, the *Pardo*, 5,400 tons heading for the Rio Grande.[48] The work of the port continued even as the Kriegsmarine fought a relentless, ruthless campaign in the Atlantic to cut off the country's lifeblood.[49]

After the German invasion of Russia most of the Luftwaffe's attention could no longer be given to the ports on the west coast. It could not fight, for long, on two fronts. The much-vaunted occupation of Crete, also in May, had exposed the limitations of a massed paratrooper attack. That was also a close-run thing, with German losses exceeding 4,000 troops. Thus, the summer of 1941 could be seen as a 'turning point'[50] in Liverpool and Britain's fortunes.

Meanwhile, however, a continuing, desperate life and death struggle was still being fought out on the Atlantic, where the vital turning point did not come until 1943. Again Liverpool was fully engaged in the struggle, the focal point for the development, implementation and monitoring of the battle plans, strategies and tactics of the struggle in what were known as the Western Approaches. Derby House, behind the Town Hall, was the nerve centre (in both senses) of Britain's battle for survival as a fighting combatant. The Battle of the Atlantic was to prove yet another close-run thing.

The 'acme of villainy'[51]

Churchill's characteristically vivid condemnation of Admiral Karl Dönitz's way of waging submarine warfare reflected the current mood. Unrestricted submarine warfare, first introduced by Germany in 1916–18, was continued in the Second World War to universal condemnation. Yet Dönitz and Hitler recognised the capacity of effective submarine warfare to break Britain's lifeline, in food and raw materials, particularly to North America, and especially from 1942 when the USA entered the war.

Dönitz was well equipped by experience and temperament to mastermind the U-boat campaign. He had been a U-boat captain in the Great War, and drew important lessons from that experience. One was a statistical exercise. In 1916–18 a German submarine sank, on average, three ships per month. That strike rate meant that a fleet of fifty operational submarines (a reasonable expectation in wartime conditions) if properly deployed and well commanded, would be able to sink over half of the British merchant marine in one year. The size of the British merchant fleet was estimated as 3,000 vessels.[52] By the summer of 1942 Dönitz was well above his operational requirement. The total fleet of U-boats was almost 400, of which 50 per cent were operational.[53] By the end of that year Dönitz was on course: 1,664 British merchant ships had been sunk, about three-quarters of them (1,160) by submarines, and British imports were running at just a third of their pre-war level. On 4 November Churchill set up a new cabinet committee, the Anti U-Boat Warfare Committee. He chaired it himself, and instructed that figures for losses at sea be no longer released.[54] Nor was there better news in 1943. Using tonnage instead of ships, the average monthly losses to U-boats, in 1942, was 520,000 tons. In January 1943 the tonnage lost was 203,000. In February it was 359,000, peaking at 627,000 in March. Then, suddenly, the situation improved. The losses fell dramatically as those for U-boats rose and, by June, convoy losses were negligible. The Battle of the Atlantic had gone the Allies' way, although at the time, German U-boats were still a threatening presence and would remain so until the end of the war. But the tide had turned in the spring of 1943. The main explanation for this was a change in escort tactics. Admiral Sir Max Horton, appointed Commander-in-Chief Western Approaches on 19 November 1942 was the principal architect.

Horton's predecessor, Admiral Sir Percy Noble, began, and Horton completed, the process of transforming the defensive, negative tactics of the convoys' escort ships into aggressive, counter-attack. Though American entry into the war was a major bonus to operations in the North Atlantic, the decisive factor was the increase in escort vessels, with adequate air cover operating aggressively. Hunter-killer support operations were now put into effect. In the first five months of 1943, 114 U-boats were sunk, and the size of Dönitz's fleet began to decline sharply.

It was at this time that 'Johnnie' Walker, a latter day Drake, entered Liverpool's story. In spring 1943 he was appointed commander of the Second Support Group following successful anti-submarine actions in Gibraltar and the Arctic. On 29 January 1944 his five modified sloops[55] all with birds' names – *Starling* (Walker's ship), *Wild Goose*, *Woodpecker*, *Kite* and *Magpie* – set out as escorts to a westward-bound convoy. The convoy was one of eight, sailing in both directions. A fleet of twenty-two U-boats lay in thir path. Horton had three other escort groups in his command (as well as Walker's) three aircraft carriers, and aircraft flying from Northern Ireland. The battle, lasting twenty days, was fought to the west of Ireland. Eleven U-boats were sunk. Walker's group sank six of them. The Germans sank one merchant ship that had become separated from the convoy.[56]

It was a victory to rank with those of Drake and Hawkins and the sailors of 1588. But like that famous victory over the Spanish Armada, all was far from what it seemed. Horton had vastly superior forces as well as the tactical acumen and ruthlessness of Walker against a submarine force which had known since the previous summer that its time had gone and it was outmatched. But Liverpool, and Britain, had its hero returning alive from a famous victory. To sink six U-boats in one operation was unprecedented; four per month was a good record and, overall, the Second Support Group sank twenty-one. Like all authentic heroes Walker was self-effacing and modest, stressing that his achievements were those of his team of one thousand men. Yet, before the war he had been passed over for promotion, and was officially described as a poor leader. He was the stuff of hero worship with the stories to match. It was also said he could drink a pint of beer standing on his head![57]

On 25 February 1944, *Starling*, *Wild Goose* and *Magpie*[58] sailed into Gladstone Dock to a rapturous welcome from naval and merchant crews lining their ships' rails, as well as the WRNS (the 'Wrens'), with wives and families crowding the quays. All the vessels in the port sounded their foghorns, as was also the custom at New Year, to the accompaniment of cheers and hats thrown into the air. Feted everywhere, and promoted (though not beyond Captain), Walker led more patrols, destroying another three U-boats. He returned to Liverpool on 7 July 1944. Two days later he was dead of a stroke, although it was popularly believed that he had 'worked himself to death'. Like many heroes, he died young, at just forty-eight. At his public funeral at Liverpool Cathedral Horton paid a poignant tribute: 'Nor dust, nor the light weight of a stone, but all the sea of the Western Approaches shall be his tomb.'[59] Appropriately, echoing Horton's words, he was later buried at sea.

The price of victory

Starling, *Wild Goose* and *Magpie* berthed at Gladstone Dock just four months before the Allied D-Day landings in Normandy. It had been a long time coming. But it also meant that, by Captain Walker's death, the Atlantic became a much safer place than it had been for nearly six years. As the Allies overran France along the Atlantic Coast Admiral Dönitz lost the submarine bases from which he had wreaked such havoc. This loss effectively ended serious German resistance at sea, even though it would be a year before the final surrender. The capture of the bases came not a moment too soon. Dönitz was already developing a fleet of more advanced submarines to renew the struggle. These, which never put to sea, were among the 231 submarines scuttled by their crews rather than being allowed to fall into Allied hands.

The Allies had paid a huge price for victory: the Germans a high price for defeat. Their Battle of the Atlantic was, in the end, a disaster. Of 863 operational U-boats 754 had been sunk or fatally damaged. To these would be added the 231 scuttled, in an operation bizarrely named Operation Regenbogen ('Rainbow'), taking the total to almost a thousand. But the loss of life was a much bigger price: 27,491 officers and men had died in action, from their wounds, or drowning. Only 7,000 survived. They also took many British and Allied seamen down with them. Over the course of the war they sank 2,800 British merchant ships and 148 warships.[60] The hazards faced by a slow-moving merchant vessel, even when moderately armed, were much greater than those facing fast, manoeuvrable, powerful warships. This explains why the loss of life in the merchant marine was proportionately higher than in the 'fighting' services. The same was true of the US merchant marine who shared, with the British and Canadians,[61] the perils of the Atlantic and Murmansk runs. Yet their vital role in the convoys received much less praise and recognition than that of their navies. In Britain, this bred resentment.

Resentment was also fuelled by the arrogance and social distance effected by some Royal Navy officers. From within their own number, one officer promoted from the rank of rating, ironically observed that '... making dates with waitresses in Brighton was dangerous and taking a light from another person's cigarette was fatal.'[62]

On land, before peace finally came, such social niceties had to be put aside. There were still reverses, at Arnhem and in the desperate rearguard action in the Battle of the Bulge, as German troops threatened to reach the Channel ports for the second time. There was also a final, vicious, terrifying flurry as Hitler's rockets rained on London, only ending when Allied troops overran the rocket bases. Meanwhile Allied armies were advancing on Germany from all points of the compass, including the decisive Russian steamroller from the East, wreaking havoc and terrible revenge. It seemed that celebration would soon be at hand through it still proved to be long delayed until well into 1945 and, even then, the Japanese were fighting on and only surrendered after the second atomic bomb had vaporised Nagasaki and most of its inhabitants. Japan's price of defeat dwarfed all others.

So for many there was little or even nothing to celebrate, even among the victors. Only the United States had been spared the attentions of the Luftwaffe – the blessing of geography – although total American losses were the highest in its history, after the Civil War, at 420,000 military and civilian. The UK lost 450,000. Such losses, had as they were, were tiny in comparison with those of the USSR, in which estimated military and civilian losses were a staggering 23.2 million.[63] Nor did the news that the war in Europe was over bring any cheer to Americans still in desperate battle against the Japanese in Okinawa in May 1945. For the British, in the jungles of Burma, not everyone even heard the news that the war in Europe was over. Those who did hoped that it would now divert desperately need equipment to the Far East so that it could all end soon and they could also go home. Nor was 'going home' an early prospect, even for those fighting in Europe. Demobilisation, given the numbers involved and their worldwide dispersal, could never be early for everyone, and some releases stretched even into 1947.[64] One Liverpool boy, Cameron Hazlehurst, only four when the war ended, was later to write:

> I'm afraid VE Day was not a big day for me. Much more important was the day I met my father on Lime Street Station in September or October 1946. He had been in India for four years, having left when I was five months old.

The *Empress of Asia*. This fine ship, a Canadian Pacific veteran of the Far East run, was set on fire by Japanese dive bombers of Singapore on 12 November 1941. Most of its over 2,000 troops and 400 plus crew were taken prisoner to work on the infamous Thailand–Burma railway.

© LIVERPOOL RECORD OFFICE.

I can still see him walking down the platform to me in his khaki great coat, carrying a parcel under his arm which turned out to be a present for me![65]

'Victory' meant even less for those who had lost husbands, sons and brothers. Nor did they even think in terms of victory. It was all about survival, about 'making it'. Homecomings, too, were often to children who did not recognise their father, or saw him as a stranger in their mother's bed. Some wives had also found comfort with other men in their absence, the homecomings in such cases marked by bitterness and anger. The stresses of a long war also changed men's lives. Many left as boys and returned as mature, worldly wise, cynical men, to the consternation of their wives.

Wives too had changed. Bringing up children on their own under bombing and rationing as well as often working full-time in factories, offices or on munitions' assembly lines, transformed them into self-confident, even liberated, women. Returning husbands found it difficult to accept how their wives had changed, as much as their wives found it difficult to adjust to the 'stranger' in the house.

Nor did wives always appreciate the stresses and traumas their husbands had experienced. Dorothy Bullock, from Liverpool, recalls her father's return from The North African campaign, after six years. He was a week later than his wife had expected, given the discharge procedure. This made her angry, accusing him of having a disease, explaining the delay. She burned all his photographs of his days in uniform '... as if she didn't want to be reminded of him in the Army. It was not a happy time for us when he returned. He loved us but my mother's bitterness and unhappiness all the time made home life difficult.'[66]

Another shock to servicemen on returning to Liverpool (including Joan Peacock's father), was the physical destruction of the city and dockland and the heightened problems of everyday life:

> All I could see was devastation ... Homes still bombed-out shells. Huge air-raid shelters in what were beautiful parts. Ships burned out in Seaforth Docks. Large concrete blocks along the shore ... Walking miles looking for a house to rent. Still on rations.[67]

Rationing did not finally end until 1953, eight years after the war. Liverpool's housing problems had also been made much worse by the war and remained, almost permanently, in a state of crisis. In 1939 the Corporation was building 3,500 houses per year. The war destroyed, or made uninhabitable, 13,000 of the stock with serious damage to another 19,000. That, in 1941, meant that 32,000 houses were needed immediately without any provision for those who needed to be re-housed from slum dwellings, or who lived in over-crowded, insanitary conditions. Overall, it was estimated that 40,000 new houses for 200,000 people, needed to be built as a matter of urgency.[68] Such problems were universal across Merseyside, but it was Liverpool's waterfront that had suffered most. In the central areas, especially near the docks, whole communities had been dispersed as their streets and houses were destroyed. This process had been going on, though peaceably through slum-clearance since the 1920s, but the war accelerated the process.

Down at the docks recovery proceed uninterrupted after the end of major bombing in May 1941. At first the task of recovery seemed insurmountable given the scale of the damage and the mountains of rubble over cavernous craters, as well as, here and there, still unexploded ordnance. However, despite the often acute shortages of materials and specialist manpower (trained for example to use the limited supplies of oxy-acetylene equipment) it still only just twenty days to clear a wrecked berth of enough rubble to allow cargo to be moved. A further sixty days was required to clear a thousand-foot berth properly, and '... at one time thirty-three were being cleared at once'. Even at Huskisson Dock, where the *Malakand* blew up on 4 May, within a fortnight some of the ground floors of the wrecked sheds were being used again.[69]

Working as a docker under these conditions was arduous and sometimes terrifying,[70] and probably for the first time in the port's history labour was in short supply. But Ernest Bevin was now at the Ministry of Labour. Someone who knew dockers well was in charge and, given the needs of war, he could be sure of their support. If not, Bevin, a decisive and determined man, would use coercion. He appointed Regional Port Directors on the Clyde and Mersey in order, wisely, to keep control away from the employers. In each port he ended casualism for a permanent, registered labour force with a guaranteed minimum wage of £4 2s. 6d. for a 44-hour week, recalling the process begun at the Shaw Inquiry in 1920. Dockers would now be paid (though they had to be registered and on stand-by) even if ships failed to arrive on time, arrived damaged, or did not appear at all because they had been lost at sea. The dockers were organised within specific zones, to which employers were allocated, at specific control points – all under the authority of the Regional Port Director. The new scheme was to be introduced in March 1941. Bevin's bleak alternative to acceptance by the dockers was their call-up and the running of the docks by mobile dockers' battalions, drawing upon the limited example of the Khaki Battalions in the Great War.[71]

The scheme was implemented, through stick, carrot, or Bevin's influence. Generally, it all worked. The turnround time improved greatly, as Churchill had insisted, and the normally confrontational industrial relations were, to an extent, put on hold. The removal of casualism, at least until the war ended, also contributed towards the scheme's success. The port was still a long way from being fully physically restored at the end of the war. It would be the 1960s before the dock system had finally removed the scars and necessary reconstruction and improvements had been made. Even so, despite the destruction and dislocation of the early war years, by 1945 the port at Liverpool was handling the same amount of tonnage as it had in 1939. That did not mean, however, a post-war return to profits. Rising traffic after 1944 was not enough, in revenue terms, to make up for earlier falls.[72]

For Bevin, the suspension of casualism under the scheme was in line with his strong advocacy of its permanent removal, as Sexton and many other before him. Even in war that was not going to endear him to opinion along the Liverpool and Birkenhead waterfronts. But it was an important stage along the long, rocky road towards the end of casualism. Reform would be tried again, in 1947, though it would take another twenty years to end it finally. Even then, as always, the removal of casualism would be fought all the way, not by the union as such, but certainly by most of its members.

CHAPTER ELEVEN

Peace, politics and giant-killing

And then it was the month of May
A thousand-year Reich had passed away.

(Bertolt Brecht, 1945) [1]

... she'd got her prescription from the doctor. She went and got tested for new glasses. Then she went further down the road ... for the chiropodist. She had her feet done. Then she went back to the doctor's because she'd been having trouble with her ears and the doctor said ... he would fix her up with a hearing aid.

(Alice Law, July 1948) [2]

It was really only the wallpaper that was holding up the walls.

(A resident of Athol Street, 1987) [3]

A DOLF HITLER's 'thousand-year Reich' lasted barely twelve years, and for half of that period it was at war. During that six years it brought devastation, suffering and death on an unprecedented scale. [4] When Germany's total defeat and unconditional surrender finally came at Lüneburg Heath, the Allied celebrations were deeply tinged with the gnawing pains of great loss, national and personal, and the daunting task of restoring the mountains of rubble, stretching from the Atlantic to the Urals, back to some semblance of the cities, towns and villages they had once been. Liverpool had seen its share of devastation. Aside from the loss of lives and homes, the docks had been close to being put out of action for a long period, and it would be some years before recovery along the docks could be seen as complete. There were also the problems arising from the great loss of shipping with a looming awareness of a different world less favourable to Liverpool's merchants and shipowners than in the days when the 'second port of Empire' was more than a proud boast. That pride was always shared by the people of the waterfront, though they had seen precious little of its fruits for the hundred years since Jesse Hartley's heyday. As Graeme Milne has put it recently:

232

Knowing how dockers, sailors and their families had to live their lives, it is hard to find much sympathy for bankrupted merchants, or shipowners whose vessels ran aground too often, but perhaps we ought to try, if only in recognition that they all shared an uncertain world, and that the harshness of their political, social and economic relationships was sometimes as much rooted in fear as in greed or arrogance.[5]

When the war ended it was a time of optimism and celebration in Britain. There was a widespread longing for lives and homes well removed from what they had been, for most, between the two wars. It was the claimed and expected reward for victory. Celebration was also in order as hostilities finally ended in Europe and families waited for their men to come home. As the church bells rang in May there was a widespread and deep unease at the continuing scale of operations and blood-letting in the Far East. That apart, the end of the war in Europe was still the best news for a long time.

As with all wars there was confusion.[6] Even Churchill, Roosevelt and Stalin had difficulty agreeing the day that hostilities were finally over and celebrations could begin. That was eventually announced as three o'clock on the afternoon of 8 May 1945. But good news leaks out as well as bad. All over Europe, the day before, the people's bush telegraph was busy letting it be known that the horror was now finally behind them, a message quickly confirmed by radio and newspaper. The banner headlines in the *Liverpool Echo* of 7 May simply announced that the 'War in Europe is Over' and, critically important to Liverpool, 'U-Boats Cease Fire in Last Hours of War'. The paper also reminded its readers, although they would be well aware of it, that 'The War Goes on in the Far East'.

The ending of the war in Europe brought many people out onto the streets. It was a time for celebrating together, and when the official announcement was made the numbers on the streets became a flood.[7] People did as they always do. Total strangers were kissed and hugged as though they were close relatives, even lovers.[8] The beer flowed; the dancing began; bonfires were lit. And they were big bonfires. Liverpool had ample supplies of heavy timber, beams and doors as bombed sites remained uncleared or with timber stacked for removal. The cleared sites were the obvious venues for a big blaze. All neighbourhoods, even streets, had their bonfires, flames reaching up to and beyond rooftop height, frequently replenished with fresh timber. Long cheers greeted the collapse of effigies of Hitler, Goebbels and Göring from the tops of the bonfires into the engulfing flames.[9]

Earlier the church bells had sounded throughout the city, albeit rung with more enthusiasm than skill. The bells had been silent for six years, and the bellringers were either out of practice or substitutes for the skilled regulars, still in uniform in those first days before demobilisation got into its stride. Nobody cared or even noticed the sometimes strange sounds from the belfries. In the harbour the liners, naval vessels, cargo ships, lighters, ferries and tug boats sounded their foghorns, from the deep booms of the big ships to the shrill noises of the small boats and the loud, alarming klaxon sounds of the destroyers. The city's festivities included floodlights on the Town Hall and upswept searchlights, no longer on their war footing, slowly sweeping the sky above St George's Plateau, like the opening of a 20th Century-Fox film. In May 1945 it was all joy and beer as the dancing and mayhem continued until daylight and, for some, beyond. Then, as peace became a continuing reality, and days moved into weeks, normal fun could be resumed. New Brighton, which lay a short ferry journey along the river on the Wirral side, welcomed large crowds once again, especially as Whit Monday fell on 21 May, just two weeks after VE Day. It was the obvious place to go to indulge in further, occasional rowdy celebrations. Some good, local news was also coming in, even unexpected praise. The Liverpool newspapers were carrying the story of a penicillin[10] factory, under construction near Liverpool, occupying eleven acres and bringing jobs for 300. The jobs helped to lessen the still widespread fear of a return to the unemployment levels of 1919–20. Maybe 1945 would be better than 1918? David Logan, soon to be returned once again as the Member of Parliament for the Scotland Division put it simply, but well: 'Do the people want their future way of life to be the deadening, monotonous, hopeless experience of the pre-war years?'[11]

These were days in which goodwill and euphoria were in plentiful supply. There was unaccustomed praise for the dockers. Fulsome official statements were being reported in the first week after VE Day. Despite all the bombing, destruction and dislocation, since September 1939 the docks had moved 70,000,000 tons of cargo, while the number of aeroplanes being unloaded on the quays passed 10,000.[12] Good news was a welcome relief from the stream of reports coming in that the war in the Far East was going badly. Eventual victory was not in doubt, although the Allies were continuing to suffer mounting and unacceptable losses of life as they advanced their slow advance towards mainland Japan. For the Japanese, defeat and surrender were seen as matters of personal and national disgrace, although this view has been subject to some recent revision by historians.[13] Even when the war came to its terrible conclusion, at Hiroshima and Nagasaki, the Japanese military played for time to save face by delaying agreeing to and signing the terms of surrender. It was also perhaps understandable that there was little publicly expressed sympathy for the devastating impact of atomic warfare upon the Japanese people. The strategists in the White House were not alone in calculating that the two bombs had saved many thousands of Allied lives. Widespread regret for the plight of the Japanese and German cities, and criticism of Allied actions, was to come later.[14]

Peace brought paradoxes. For example, not everyone welcomed peace, although none would admit this openly. For some the peace and celebrations were hollow affairs while they awaited or hoped for the return of their men, and there were others who actually regretted the ending of hostilities. The war could be a time of intense excitement: living for now, for the moment, with the fear of death, had become the everyday. Such feelings could be heightened by difficult problems of post-war adjustment to a civilian life of rationing, food shortages and fuel crises, and families (even wives) who regarded them as strangers. Civilians living under the daily fear of air attack, especially in London right to the end, and in other big cities for the first two or three years, would clearly welcome the end of it all; but even then not everybody. For children the excitement might outweigh the fear: at an early age it is had to envisage an early, violent death; the youngest might not even understand the meaning of dying. For children did not always see bombing as the occasion for terror that was for their parents, although that could suddenly change when they experienced its consequences. The wail of the sirens, and the searchlights criss-crossing the night sky, followed by the monotonous drone of the massed bombers and the noise of anti-aircraft shells, made everyday life a secret thrill for some children, especially boys. A common game was to wheel about the street, arms outstretched, swooping and diving as Spitfires downing Messerschmitt Bf 109s. Another was the army game. Boys could be seen drilling in soldierly style, 'rifles' across shoulders, to orders barked by young sergeant majors.[15] War, unfortunately, also has its allures and excitements to many men and some women, even sometimes when they experience its terrible price. But for most, 1945 had something special.

Even in desperate times at the height of the war, there was a growing feeling that when it was over, things should never be the same again. Life should be better, and not just for the few as it had been in the past. One of the good experiences of the war itself was that full employment could be a reality and not just a dream. The other was that a powerful, intervening government could do much to achieve full employment, as well as deliver a society that was fairer, and more secure, while maintaining the old freedoms. It was therefore no surprise that as early as 1942, when the war was far from won, that the Beveridge Plan,[16] as it soon became known, should attract long, overnight queues at the government's bookshops. Change, radical change, was in the air. Three years later its implementation was irresistible.

The 'New Men'

The 'New Men'[17] were actually not so new. Attlee, Bevin, Bevan, Morrison, Dalton, Shinwell, Cripps, Beveridge (the lofty mandarin), and the others, had all cut their political and policy teeth long before 1945. Attlee and Bevin, in particular, had experience of the highest reaches of government over six years of acute stress and crisis.

Beveridge, too, was no longer a young man. He had long been at the heart of things, a formative influence at the Board of Trade as early as 1912 when Richard Williams was putting his registration scheme into action on the Liverpool waterfront. Beveridge was an academic civil servant of the old school. But he was brimful of ideas, many of them closer to the liberal values of Eleanor Rathbone and her friends than to socialism. But he also struck chords in Labour Party circles and, with colourful imagery, he caught the mood and imagination of a war-weary nation. He identified in cartoon form 'five giant' problems – want, disease, ignorance, squalor and idleness, – that he intended to slay. These problems, he said, were roaming freely in all of Britain's great cities, large towns and small towns and even in the villages of the countryside. The war, stressing equal sacrifice, had to an extent limited the worst injustices and indignities suffered by the British working class and the poor, but it had also exposed their lives to view, notably in the experience of evacuation. Some of Labour's leaders, such as Bevin and Bevan, had also experienced personal privation and struggle in their own lives, while Attlee, though born to relative privilege, sought to learn directly from the experience of working people during his time in Stepney, as Mayor, after leaving the army.[18] Some of the Labour leadership had backgrounds similar to that of Attlee, but most Labour MPs did not. David Logan, the long-serving MP, who lived in Scotland Road for most of his life, had seen poverty and the effects of unemployment at first hand, and was not untypical. Not surprisingly, in the 1945 election campaign he pressed the case for full employment. The Braddocks (Bessie and her husband John) also saw the world through Liverpool eyes. Bessie Braddock, elected for the impoverished Exchange Division saw housing and health as the highest priorities. Exchange, another dockside constituency, had suffered heavily from bombing, taking its existing over-crowding to intolerable levels. She spoke of six, seven, eight and sometimes more, sleeping in one room. The darkest days of Victorian living lived on. David Logan, who was also an alderman, was returned unopposed for the Scotland Division, although Leo McGree, the Communist with the vast popular following on Merseyside, did not stand. Bessie Braddock was equally popular but uncompromising in championing her poorest constituents. She was branded a Communist, which she once had been, and she only scraped in by 639 votes, although she increased her vote in every election after that, her last coming in 1966; she remained an MP until standing down in 1970, shortly before her death. Her husband John, never an MP but who remained a major force in Liverpool's local government and politics, was even more uncompromising. During the election campaign, speaking in support of his wife at Picton Hall, he tore into the *Liverpool Echo's* reporting and analysis:

> … starting from the very day of the election, every bit of space that they have got is used to vilify the working-class and Labour movement in every column they print.[19]

Nationally, Labour's landslide of 1945 drew comparisons with the 1832 and 1906 results which also rode on a radical, reforming mood.[20] The party polled nearly 12 million votes, the Conservatives 8.7 and Liberals 2.2 million. This was a remarkable popular victory that was in fact magnified by the peculiarities of the British first past the post electoral system: Labour had 394 seats, the Conservatives 189 and the Liberals just 12.

In Liverpool, fewer turned out to vote than nationally (68 per cent to 73 per cent), with the swing to Labour of 6.5 per cent falling well below the national average. This can probably be explained by Liverpool's Labour vote in 1935, the last election, being unusually large even compared to 1945.[21] The party's share of the vote in 1945 was, therefore, not that far ahead of the Conservatives, who took 41.9 per cent with Labour at 45.8 and the Liberals at 8.2 per cent. But whatever the figures, the campaign in Liverpool had generated a great deal of excitement. The issues were openly discussed and argued over in the streets and on the trams and buses. In the waterfront constituencies, where Labour was strong, the party's loudspeaker vans were cheered as they drove slowly through the streets with Labour's message. Labour posters seemed to be in almost every window.

One family showed their allegiance to the cause by daubing large, white letters on the front wall of their house with the message: 'This is Clem's House.' The paint was virtually impossible to remove from the rough, unpointed bricks, so that when the election was over and the excitement had died down, it remained as a painted political memory, only to be extinguished finally by a bulldozer under the slum-clearance programmes. Outdoor political gatherings, organised or informal, were also common in those days. The cleared bombed sites of Liverpool were ideal for speech-making to large, raucous crowds. Bessie Braddock was a popular draw. Leo McGree, the Communist, also attracted large numbers, although these were often more intent on shouting him down than on listening. Despite his popularity as a trade union official, and his oratory, his avowed Communism was a political handicap in Catholic dockland.[22] Overall, Labour was flying high in Liverpool, and for the first time. Dockland could now add political clout to its industrial muscle. The dockers even had their own Election Day. They were given the day off to vote, and went solidly for Labour all along the waterfront constituencies.

Meanwhile, the dirty, bloody war was still being fought out in the Pacific, plumbing ever deeper depths of barbarity. The *Liverpool Echo*, on 9 August, reported on the atomic bomb attack on Japan and carried the following banner headline: 'All living things seared to death.' The official festivities for the final end of the Second World War began with VJ Day, and continued well into September. Bonfires were lit again, while children's parties returned to the streets brightened up with the usual flags and bunting. Large lettered messages also began to appear, draped across the streets from upper windows, welcoming home countless Jimmies, Pats, Billies and Tommies as demobilisation began to gather pace. What the returning heroes made of the banners is not recorded, but they would have come back very different men from those who went away. Now matured by the harshest lessons in life, some embittered, all once boys and now men. They also came home to a very different looking Liverpool, with bombed sites where there had once been houses, shops, libraries, theatres, cinemas, schools, churches and pubs. Down at the docks familiar, old landmarks had gone. One was the Customs House in Canning Place, that had been built on the site of Thomas Steers' Old

Dock, in 1826. It was demolished after being severely damaged by bombs in May 1941. If there had still been sailors in the now abandoned old Sailors' Home (itself demolished in 1976) on the other side of Canning Place they would have had new views of the docks and river not seen since the days of the wars against Bonaparte. For the waterfront total war had been a new and devastating experience. The Great War had left the waterfront intact: the Second World War had almost destroyed it. Restoring the port's docks and infrastructure was urgent and crucial for trade, employment and morale. Though as always in Liverpool, trade and employment were joined twins, the needs of employment had raised it to an ever higher priority in the task of reconstruction. Full employment was now on the agenda of practical politics. Beveridge had been working on it, and the new Labour government would soon declare it to be its responsibility: another world turned upside down, and it was a truly brave one.

Housing was another major priority. This did not mean just providing habitation, but decent, healthy homes. Liverpool Corporation had done well enough for its citizens in the inter-war years. Between 1926 and 1930 it had built over 20,000 houses, nearly thirty times the rate of demolition. That rate was still sixteen times from 1931 to 1935. In the five years to the war four houses were being built for every one being lost, as 16,000 new houses were built at a time when demolition had quadrupled, to 4,500.[23] During the war the Luftwaffe had made things much worse, increasing over-crowding and squalor, especially along the waterfront where the old poor-quality housing stock had been most vulnerable to high explosives and incendiaries. Even if the better houses were still standing they were often seriously damaged. Homelessness and inadequate, unhealthy, overcrowded housing were major causes of personal and family destabilisation. A nation celebrating a great historic victory needed to demolish and build record numbers of houses in record time. Such was the scale of the problem, that these ambitious aims were still being chased for the next thirty years.

The women bore the brunt of squalid housing and homelessness. Many had been no more than girls in 1939 and six years later had grown into confident, working women who wanted better for themselves as well as their children, those children sometimes profoundly disturbed by the perils of evacuation rather than bombing. They also had to accommodate men returning scarred, often in both senses, by their experiences. But the welfare state had not forgotten women. Even before the general election the first pillar of the welfare state came to the rescue of beleaguered mothers in beleaguered families. On 11 June 1945 the Family Allowances Act was passed. That achievement has to be put down to Eleanor Rathbone. The allowances were first paid on August Bank Holiday, 1946. The take-up was 2.5 million families. Eleanor, the life-long champion of the rights of mothers, did not, however, get her way on the payment of the allowance direct to the mother; it went to the father.[24] But in other ways her parliamentary colleagues had been wholly converted. Leslie Hore-Belisha (famous earlier as Transport

Minister for his 'Belisha Beacons') as the first Minister of National Insurance, piloted the Family Allowances Bill through the Commons. After the election, his successor Jim Griffiths had to go with cap in hand, and low expectations, to the Chancellor of the Exchequer for the money to pay for the new Act. Hugh Dalton, the Chancellor, was later to reveal at the party conference that he gave the money 'with a song in his heart!'[25] The thirties had not entirely gone away in 1945 but, where they had, all were determined they should never return. Deprivation in all its forms was to be comprehensively challenged, with the state for the first time taking a pivotal role.

Sir William: the 'giant' killer

William Beveridge, of Marlborough College and Oxford, was a don and a toff of the superior kind. He was by inclination, dress and precision of speech more at home in the more regulated, deferential world of Edwardian England, from whence he came, rather than the turbulent times of the post-war years. But he had spent a good deal of his time away from country houses and dreaming spires. For a time he was a Liberal MP, though best known in his own circle, as an influential figure in Whitehall. He also had a practical turn of mind, a flair for what could be done by those who practise the 'art of the possible'. He first came to minor note in his early days at the Board of Trade when he was behind Richard Williams' Dock Labour Scheme, in Liverpool, in 1912.[26] But he was far from being a behind-the-scenes public official. That he had revealed in his political phase as an MP. He was also good on the radio, an important attribute in those days of 'fireside chats' and 'radio doctors'. He was also a regular on the BBC's popular 'Brains Trust'. He was thus reasonably well known to the general public, but it would still have been difficult to see him as a national hero. But that is what he became in 1942–43 when the war still hung in the balance.

The Beveridge Report carried a title – 'Social Insurance and Allied Services' – that was not designed to catch the eye of the reader. Yet it attracted overnight queues (as a Selfridge's sale) at HMSO's Kingsway bookshop in London when it was first published on 1 December 1942. On the same morning the BBC broadcast an outline in twenty-two languages. It was even used as a weapon of war. Copies were dropped over occupied Europe and, after the war, detailed commentaries marked 'secret' were found in Hitler's bunker.[27] By the end of 1944 some 200,000 copies of the full report had been sold alongside separate summaries and a pamphlet-size, popular version. Overall, in that year, sales stood at 600,000 copies of all kinds.[28] This extraordinary reception for what was, on the face of it, another dry-as-dust official report, at a time when the nation's independent survival could still not be guaranteed, is only partly explained by Beveridge's celebrity status. The main reasons for the report's reception were its Utopianism, its style, and its timing.

By the end of 1942 Britain had endured three years of desperate conflict, but there was a glimmer of light at the end of the tunnel, as the significance of victory in North Africa and the defeat of the Wehrmacht at Stalingrad were beginning to make apparent. The universal yearning for a better, more secure world was being translated into the practical politics for a post-war world. A land truly fit for returning heroes, for those who had suffered loss, destruction, hardship and bombardment, could now be realistically demanded. Nor was this feeling confined to socialists. Winston Churchill, in a 1943 radio broadcast, spoke of '... national compulsory insurance for all classes from the cradle to the grave', the origin of the famous phrase.[29]

The report's style was unusual, revealing Beveridge's talent for simple, eye-catching explanations of a comprehensive, complex set of interlocking policies. He also made it clear that the policies could and should be implemented. This was well demonstrated by the early passing, even before the end of the war, by the 1944 Education Act, followed soon afterwards, in 1945, by the Family Allowances Act. The welfare state had many authors, but it was Beveridge who provided the inspiration and blueprint, although he did not name it as such and, in fact, disliked the term. 'Welfare' to him would have suggested dependence, and he would probably have had reservations, as a nineteenth-century liberal, of the too free use of the word 'state'. But he did coin the phrase the 'five giants'. These appeared in the report itself, in cartoon form, cowering before a little be-suited man brandishing a sword, possibly Beveridge himself. The infamous five were want, ignorance, disease, squalor and idleness, and it was the eventual banishment of these that was the report's aim.

Beveridge's attack upon Giant Want, or poverty, was the plan's keystone. For this he proposed 'social security', that is a guaranteed minimum income for the family, as a right, without any means test. This guarantee would partly be made up of the soon to be introduced family allowances, Eleanor Rathbone's brainchild. There would also be regular pay through a government commitment to achieving and maintaining full employment. But social security, though the main ingredient, was not enough. There were four other giants to be slaughtered:

> ... social security is one part only of an attack upon five giant evils: upon the physical Want with which it is directly concerned, upon Disease which often causes that Want and brings many other troubles in its train, upon Ignorance which no democracy can afford among its citizens, upon Squalor ... and upon the Idleness which destroys wealth and corrupts men.[30]

Beveridge's comprehensive plan with its interlocking objectives became the blueprint for the post-war Labour government. It was translated into detailed public policy and passed into law between 1945 and 1951. To a large extent, despite changes in government and swings in ideology since then, it remains largely intact. It is also possible to detect the moral perspectives of Beveridge and his circle, at the Board of Trade before the Great War, when they were attempting to remove casualism from dock employment. Insecurity of work and income were the source not only of poverty; they argued that they also 'corrupt men'.

Beveridge's Five Giants had long been familiar figures on the streets of Liverpool before 1945, despite all the important improvements in the conditions of the people over a century of reform.

All British cities did, of course, share the continuing problems of Liverpool; but Liverpool was consistently the worst. Children are always most at risk when living conditions are poor. Liverpool's infant mortality rate more than halved between 1900 and 1940, from 186 per 1,000 live births to 84. But in England and Wales as a whole it had fallen by almost two-thirds, from 154 to 57, and in 1931 Liverpool's age-standardised rate was only exceeded by that in Bootle, Oldham, Salford and Wigan. Even over sixty years later (2004) Liverpool was still at the top of the ten of the most deprived local authorities. Knowsley was third.[31]

Within Liverpool itself the waterfront and adjacent areas remained the most deprived. Even with slum demolition and rehousing in superior accommodation, such as in the Corporation tenements of the 1930s, adult and infant mortality still remained well above that of those living in houses in the well-to-do streets of Abercromby ward (where Dr Duncan had once lived) and above the average for Liverpool as a whole. Better housing alone was clearly not the answer: poverty and overcrowding also played their parts. Even in 2003 Liverpool's mortality rate remained higher than in comparable cities, such as Manchester and Birmingham, and was 27 per cent above the rates for England and Wales.[32] For the living, all the features of multiple deprivation were present, despite determined efforts at local level. Most people were poor, even if not starving, and housing was mostly inadequate. Even 'court' living still existed, and bathrooms and inside toilets still remained rare facilities in parts of the city. Poverty was also associated with inadequate diets, as insanitary housing was a primary source of ill health and serious medical conditions and diseases, such as rickets and tuberculosis.[33]

Children's growth was commonly stunted. Limited dental care, and the normal absence of simple dental hygiene, led to the widespread incidence of decayed teeth. Local doctors, hospitals and dentists did their best under very difficult conditions, but even modest fees and charges were prohibitive for poor people. Some doctors waived their fees for the very poorest,[34] but such altruism was no substitute for a free, national health service. Education, too, had a low priority in the streets of dockland. Most boys left school to become dockers or general labourers, or went to sea like their fathers had done. Girls would mostly find jobs in factories, shops or offices.[35] The Liverpool waterfront had little of the rich cultural and educational aspirations of other working-class communities such as those of the Jews of London's East End or of the coal-mining villages of South Wales.[36] These were, however, rare levels of aspiration and achievement in unlikely settings. Liverpool's waterfront was, perhaps, more typical.

Educating Giant Ignorance

The 1870 Education Act had extended opportunities for children, but few were at school beyond the age of ten, and many worked part-time. In 1902 the school leaving age was set at twelve, rising to fourteen at the end of the Great War. The Attlee government, in 1947, took it to fifteen, and Wilson's Labour administration to sixteen in 1971. This was the national context within which any advances in Liverpool's educational provision took place, especially after the comprehensive 'Butler Act' of 1944. Liverpool did, however, have some special characteristics of its own, including the low numbers staying on beyond the school leaving age. In the 1930s that proportion was only two per cent, and school attainment levels were below the national average. Religion was also a special factor in Liverpool's educational provision. More than half of all Liverpool's elementary schools were either Roman Catholic or Protestant, split evenly. This reflected the importance of Irish origins and lingering sectarianism, albeit this began to weaken in the post-war period. Religion might, of course, have been an advantage given the reputation of such schools for social discipline, especially in the robust Catholic communities of the waterfront. Many Liverpool memoirs attest to the positive influence of religious schools. In Athol Street, between the wars, schools were commonly kept open for two and a half hours after school ended at four o'clock. Teachers ran clubs, games, pastimes, hobbies and play centres to, '... keep the children off the streets until the parents had the evening meal [ready] ... They did things like painting and games, country dancing, ballroom dancing and indoor games like ludo and chess.'[37]

Others point to the special dedication and encouragement of individual teachers. Johnnie Woods remembers a Miss Atkinson, who encouraged his talent for drawing and painting. She lived opposite his school (St Anthony's), at the top of Silvester Street, in one of a neat row of houses, all more substantial and better kept than other houses in the area. He, and other children, called frequently at her house where she would show them the techniques of paint mixing, painting and drawing.[38] With this kind of encouragement, a few thrived against the odds. But the majority still remained educationally deprived, under-achievers, like their parents and grandparents before them. The war made matters much worse, with lengthy interruptions to the education of those who were evacuated. School buildings and equipment also suffered from limited maintenance and bomb damage, even destruction, as at St Sylvester's off Scotland Road in 1941. Training, too, was a matter for concern as servicemen with limited skills returned from the war to a country that had serious shortages in skilled manpower. Some of the more privileged were able to resume their university studies after demobilisation, but this did not enter much into the lives of the children of the waterfront, even though there was a major national expansion in the number of university students, from 50,246 in 1939 to 76,764 in 1948.[39]

Measures to transform Britain's educational system were launched before the war ended by the Coalition Government under the Conservative Education Minister, R. A. Butler, affectionately know as 'Rab' from his initials. He was a one-nation Tory from an impeccable, privileged background, including education at Winchester and Cambridge. But he was a reformer of substance, with his 'tripartite' system of grammar, secondary modern and technical schools. The concept of the comprehensive school was also seriously debated, at the highest levels of policy, in the period up to the introduction of the Education Bill, though more often called a 'multilateral' school at the time. Though such schools were eventually not provided for in the Act, local authorities were given discretion to introduce them, subject to the approval of the Minister. By the time Labour left office in 1951 a few authorities had done so with a total, for England and Wales, of twenty 'genuine' schools.[40] Liverpool, however, can claim the first *purpose-built* comprehensive school, opened in Gateacre. The 1950s witnessed a surge in the popularity of comprehensive schools, although it would take a future Labour Minister of Education, Anthony Crossland, to put government firmly behind their virtual universality.[41]

Butler's 1944 Education Act was, and remained, controversial. The socialists regretted a lost opportunity to abolish public schools once and for all, while many others, including officials at the Ministry of Education, soon saw the tripartite system, underpinned by the especially controversial 'eleven plus' examination, as too rigid. One senior official had described the system, with some distaste, as dividing children into 'golden children, silver children and iron children'.[42] The criticisms of the Bill led many to believe that the incoming Labour Minister, Ellen Wilkinson – known as 'Red Ellen' in her younger days – would press for a different approach. She was far from alone, with strong support at senior civil servant level. Wilkinson, a working-class girl from Manchester, did take a strong line against the educational segregation: 'Can't Shakespeare mean more than a scrubbing brush ... I learned French verbs ... saying them as I scrubbed floors at home.' But her increasing ill-health, and powerful political pressures, meant that the Butler reforms remained intact. Ellen Wilkinson died, prematurely, in February 1947, at the age of fifty-five.[43]

In Liverpool, on the evidence of the eleven plus, most children turned out to be 'iron',[44] so that the numbers staying on at school beyond the compulsory age remained well below the national average, as did the standards reached on leaving school. Liverpool, persevered with the tripartite system until the comprehensive concept began to take root in the 1950s. Development was slow, however, and the final changeover to comprehensive schools with purpose-built or adapted buildings was not complete until 1976.

Treating Giant Disease

The stormy passage of Labour's education reforms through Parliament, post Butler, was as a calm sea compared to the reception given to the National Health

Service Bill, both inside and outside Parliament. Opposition came mainly from the doctors in the powerful forms of the royal colleges and the British Medical Association. The royal colleges were bought off by Aneurin Bevan by retaining a private sector and pay beds,[45] a concession described by Bevan as 'stuffing their mouths with gold'.[46] The concessions even put the royal colleges on his side by the abandonment of a fully salaried service in the hospitals, but did nothing to appease the BMA or the GPs. In February 1948, just five months before the National Health Service Act[47] became law, a BMA poll, reported in the *Liverpool Daily Post*, found that 90 per cent disapproved of the Act and 88 per cent said that they would not work under it.[48] The Act was law, but the doctors were under individual contracts, so that the threat to boycott its implementation seriously alarmed the government. The BMA's vociferous opposition also seemed to be influencing the public, who might be thought to be strongly in favour of a service that was designed to be free at the point of delivery and financed out of a taxation system that was far more progressive than it is today. Yet on the historic day the NHS was inaugurated on 5 July 1948 the involvement of patients was low. In Liverpool, 532,000 were entitled to free medical care under the service, yet on 5 July only 50 per cent had even selected a doctor.[49] The *Liverpool Daily Post* explained some of this by complaints from the better-off that the NHS did not replicate their previous private arrangements in that doctors' visits to their homes were commonly replaced by requests to attend surgeries.[50] The GPs' threats were, however, not followed through. The influence of the royal colleges and the consultants working in the hospitals was, perhaps, decisive. The *Post* reported that on 5 July, on Merseyside, almost 100 per cent of GPs had signed up.

But the complaints and opposition did not go away. Two years later the BMA held its annual, national conference in Liverpool, the third time it had done so in its history. The major complaint then was that the abuse of the service by patients was seemingly endemic.[51] Even the consultants and specialists, who had done well out of the NHS, were edgy. On the first anniversary a report of their grievances found that:

A number of Liverpool specialists ... Many men of high standing, have been placed in grades below those in which they and their colleagues consider they should have been put, with consequent loss of prestige and money.[52]

Doctors at all levels, however, were at pains to stress that they fully welcomed the NHS, and were opposed only to the detail of the Act, which they sought to amend. That was perhaps just as well. The public soon became dedicated converts. For all its faults it was always forgiven. It was seen as the most significant reform in Labour's programme. Even the *Liverpool Daily Post*, among the earliest sceptics, was in 1968 declaring to be '... perhaps the greatest, single social experiment in British history'.[53]

Actual experience, especially for the poor, was what really mattered, and people could always compare the NHS with what had gone before. In Liverpool, in fact, there had been more accessible private and voluntary provision than in most other areas, in part a legacy of the city's alarming problems in the previous century which had led to major efforts to improve the health and welfare of its citizens. By the end of the nineteenth century Liverpool had three general hospitals, twenty others for specialist conditions, and four dispensaries. Some employers provided for their skilled workers through subscription schemes, though their families were not included. Others could get money for treatment through friendly society or trade union schemes, though most had to borrow, look for charity, or help from relatives, friends and neighbours – or go without.[54] The waterfront workers and their families suffered the most, dependent upon low, irregular incomes with little, if anything, left over for medical provision. Doctor Duncan did, however, have his dispensary in Vauxhall Ward, and local doctors did their best to keep fees low, or to waive them, as in Boundary Street.

By the 1930s direct payment or health insurance remained the prevailing system and, though limited, access to treatment was improving. Some large companies, such as Lever Brothers and the railway companies, had their own insurance schemes. For those on low wages and the poorest, other Liverpool companies pioneered a scheme to include all manual and non-manual workers earning less then a specific threshold. This was the 'Penny in the Pound' scheme, in which the voluntary hospitals sought to recruit a steady flow of funds from all firms in the area without their own scheme for their own employees. It provided free in-patient care for employees and their dependants living with them. It did not cover general practice, or the treatment of tuberculosis (then still widespread), which the Council provided for. By the beginning of the 1930s the Penny in the Pound scheme had 275,000 contributors in 6,607 firms.[55] That was a success in any terms, but those out of work were not included. In the 1930s there were therefore record numbers of dockers, with families dependent upon them, without adequate, consistent, medical provision. Many of Liverpool's employers (except those at the docks) were taking part in health schemes for their employees, but the National Health Service, in clear contrast, was free, applied to everybody, whether working or not, men and women, young and old.

The poor had seen nothing like it.[56] It was bad enough being sick, but much worse if treatment could not be afforded or your employer was not in an insurance scheme. After 5 July 1948 none of that mattered. The GPs complained of 'abuses' and, in some cases, that was true. But there was a lot of catching up to be done, and drugs, such as penicillin[57] or insulin for thyroid problems, were now available that would make a significant, almost immediate difference to people's lives. The NHS could also be later credited with the virtual elimination of poliomyelitis and tuberculosis. By the 1960s the TB clinics, attached to hospitals, were being closed down for lack of patients as the early treatment of the disease by drugs and better approaches to living had become widespread. These advances led to great savings on sanatoria, special equipment and units, and the fleets of mobile X-ray vans.[58]

Attacking Giant Squalor

Beveridge's Giant Squalor remained dangerously at large. Between the wars Liverpool Corporation had been among the most energetic in the country in slum-clearance, along the waterfront, and in the building of council houses in the outlying areas to take those displaced, even though the journey to work costs, higher rents and other living expenses encouraged a drift back to dockland which, in turn, worsened overcrowding and squalor.[59] If social housing was not affordable, nor was home ownership via building societies, which was growing but still insignificant.[60] In any case mortgages were the preserve of the salaried and secure, not dock-workers with their high levels of unemployment and variable, erratic earnings. The better houses to rent in the suburbs and access to home ownership were only available to manual workers if conventionally 'skilled' and in guaranteed full-time employment. That good fortune was hard to find along the waterfront.

The Second World War made Liverpool's housing problems even worse:

> … in spite of all the changes in the first half of the twentieth century, the main preoccupation of housing policy in post-war Liverpool was much the same as it had been in the 1880s: the problem of dealing with a large number of slum properties in which a significant proportion of the population still lived.[61]

The housing problem was largely that of the inner city. Outside those areas the problems were less acute, as Map 9 illustrates. This was little consolation to those in need. A Liverpool Corporation survey, by the Medical Officer of Health, for 1 January 1955, listed 204,486 dwellings. Of these 26,959 were candidates for demolition, and 61,274 required urgent repairs if not demolition. Thus, 88,233, or some 44 per cent of the housing stock, was either unfit to live in or close to being so.[62] A decade later, in 1965, it was reported that 78,000 of these properties, that is almost all of them, were still standing.[63] The districts of Everton, Toxteth and Abercromby alone had 33,000 dwellings as candidates for demolition and Blitz redevelopment, mainly in dockland, adding a further need for even new homes as well as outstanding, urgent repairs.[64] Dockland did, however, have the benefit of large tracts of vacant land from the cleared, bombed sites ready for development.

The MOH's 1955 Report had a similarly profound effect to that of Dr Henry Duncan. It led to early action by the Corporation, which began to accelerate its housing programme in the 1960s. Between 1967 and 1978 33,000 houses in the three central wards were demolished at an annual rate that rose to 4,000 by the end of the programme. Only Manchester, with similar problems, could more than match this programme, with 44,000 demolished over the same period.[65] The emphasis was mainly upon high-rise tower blocks interspersed with low-rise

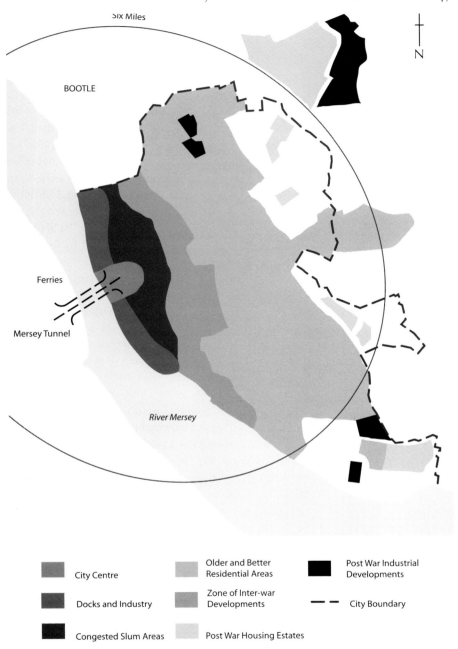

Six Miles

BOOTLE

N

Ferries

Mersey Tunnel

River Mersey

	City Centre		Older and Better Residential Areas		Post War Industrial Developments
	Docks and Industry		Zone of Inter-war Developments	– – –	City Boundary
	Congested Slum Areas		Post War Housing Estates		

Map 9.   Liverpool's housing crisis of the 1950s. See also the statistics of the 1955 survey of the Medical Officer of Health (page 246). Some 44 per cent of all houses were unfit or almost unfit to live in, mostly in the 'congested slum areas' of Everton, Toxteth and Abercromby, where 33,000 houses were still awaiting Blitz redevelopment and demolition.

housing. Large areas of the waterfront, in Scotland Road, Kirkdale and Toxteth, as well as Abercromby and Everton, witnessed the disappearance of miles of old terraces. The new blocks, houses and flats, went up in the same neighbourhoods to help maintain social cohesion and maximise the use of available land. Athol Street was blessed with the well-named, 22-storey Logan Towers. The new buildings were largely prefabricated, and the standard of construction and finish was often poor. The initial allure of brand-new flats with spectacular views soon faded as the realities of high-rise living in sub-standard flats, became apparent. Generally unpopular, most of the tower blocks were eventually demolished, including Logan Towers. The more human scale, three-storey constructions also suffered the same fate, demolished to make way for semi-detached and maisonette houses with small gardens, such as in the Athol Street area, which presently has a good number of these houses with well-tended gardens and retaining nearly all of the old street names.

Liverpool's large-scale, energetic approach to its long-standing housing problems in the post-war years had much to commend it, except its insensitivity. The rapid physical destruction of even slum dwellings ignored the fact that these were also 'homes', however inadequate, stored with experiences and memories. Many had sheltered their residents through a traumatic and violent war. Even actually watching the process of demolition was a disturbing experience, as memoirs and anecdotes reveal. They also reveal the value which people place upon tight-knit communities, as the Athol Street study illustrates.[66] An inside toilet and warm bathroom have to be set against social loss and, sometimes, isolation. Writing in 1957 Peter Townsend, the famous academic sociologist, put it simply: 'The social group is more important than the physical surroundings and every effort should be made to preserve it. This is important for young as for old.'[67]

The more recent developments in Athol Street show that lessons can be learned by municipal planners and architects. A more immediately successful approach was the co-operative such as the Eldon Gardens Cooperative in Vauxhall, a district notorious in Victorian times for its desperate poverty and the keen attentions of Dr Duncan, who had one of his dispensaries in its streets.[68] This cooperative was founded in 1978 to improve housing conditions while maintaining communities intact. It renovates, improves and builds houses at prices and rents attractive to people on low incomes, and who might be denied access to the regular housing market. Run by a board of residents and a staff of 14, in 2005 it had 457 houses on its books, 75 per cent rented.[69] Such was the scale of Liverpool's slums problems that cooperatives, though built on wise, practical foundations, could never have provided the sole solution. With the recent decline of municipal provision, current approaches are now dominated by housing associations and easier home ownership. Yet intractable problems remain. Liverpool still has one of the largest homeless populations in Britain.[70]

Patterns of employment at the docks were also changing rapidly. Actual dock work had always been complemented by a galaxy of local jobs in premises such as foundries, stables, abattoirs, tanneries, breweries, mills and warehouses, and railways – work mostly arising from trade and port activity, which went under the hammers of progress and urban renewal. There was a period, lasting no longer than ten years after 1965, when the old docks, even without the closed South End, were providing decent, stable pay, better working conditions and more fulfilled lives. The number of jobs was, however, shrinking at a rapid rate. Modernisation was another important factor thing; the total transformation, even disappearance of traditional dockwork was another.

In such a time of profound change, despite reform and better times for the economy, the old problems of industrial relations remained. To be sure the employers could work well enough with the officials of the TGWU, but the T & G still had problems with the rival claimants for portside loyalties, the National Association of Stevedores and Dockers, the unofficial organisations both local and national and, later, even its own shop stewards. By the middle of the 1960s most agreed that something had to be done. At such times Britain – it is almost an addiction – tends to turn to eminent, senior, learned judges.[71] Lord Devlin was all of these. He even had experience of previous dock inquiries to his credit. He began work with incisive analysis, persuasive powers and not a little old-world charm. His conclusion was clear: the system of casualism finally had to be ended. To the surprise of many, perhaps even Lord Devlin himself, it did not take conflict with it. It even got worse. The next chapter looks at Devlin's reforms and how they affected life, work and industrial relations on Liverpool's waterfront.

CHAPTER TWELVE

High hopes, false dawns
... old ways, and Devlin

On 28 September 1967 the port transport industry paid its debt to the early union leaders, to Beatrice Webb, Booth, Rathbone, Lord Shaw and Devlin. Casualism no longer existed and it remained to be seen if it could be torn up by the roots.

(David F. Wilson, 1972)[1]

Don't Devlinise – Nationalise

(Jack Dash, 1969)[2]

Affluence and militancy transformed the public image of the docker ... Attention was now fixed not upon his social deprivation ... but on the alarming and widespread consequences of industrial disruption in port transport.

(Gordon Phillips and Noel Whiteside, 1985)[3]

T HE immediate excitement of the hustings in the summer of 1945 followed by Labour's famous victory soon evaporated among the waterfront communities, but there remained a continuing sense of optimism, as people looked forward to the promise of Labour's programme, especially on health. But austerity under Chancellor Stafford Cripps was more than a word, and rationing was still very much in place. Then it got very much worse. This time it was the weather.

At the end of January, 1947 a penetrating easterly began to blow from Siberia as an area of high pressure moved across Scandinavia towards the British Isles. The sun did not shine for twenty days in February as the temperature stayed below freezing. Industry was paralysed. Millions were unemployed. Domestic electricity was restricted, with heavy fines if the controls were broken. Even the wartime blackout was reintroduced. Coal was too frozen to move from the depots or along the snowbound roads, and at a time when coal was often the only source of heating in the home, this brought morale down with the thermometer. When coal was needed most, the people did not have any. Even the imperturbable, almost inscrutable Clement Attlee was showing signs of worry. As the King noted in his diary entry for 30 January: 'I have asked Mr Attlee three times now if he is not worried over the domestic situation in this country. But he won't tell me he is when I feel he is. I know I am worried.'[4] The worrying continued into the spring as flooding followed the great thaw, producing a shortage of uncontaminated drinking water. Liverpool's waterfront was not alone in the appearance of long queues at standpipes. Hennessy summed up the years 1947–48 well as a '... mind-concentrating backcloth of ice, water, dole queues and silent factories ...'[5]

The New Dealers: The National Dock Labour Scheme

Against the grim backdrop of a cold winter, minds had again been turning to the reform of hiring and employment practices along the waterfronts of Britain. Now the mantle of leadership moved towards government and the TGWU. Eleanor Rathbone, who arguably had begun the attack on casualism over fifty years before, had died in January 1946. William Beveridge, who had been heavily involved in reform when at the Board of Trade and Ministry of Labour, now had other things on his mind. Ernest Bevin had been translated to the Foreign Office, but as a member of the Cabinet retained a close interest in the docks. His successor at the Ministry of Labour, George Isaacs, continued Bevin's initiatives, aided and abetted by Arthur Deakin at the TGWU.

The Ministry of Labour, which was established as a ministry in its own right in 1916, had long sought to at least control, if not remove, casualism. Many a union official had found his reputation and influence reduced to tatters by the dockers' strong, sometimes violent, resistance to its removal. Richard Williams' 1912 scheme, in Liverpool, was no more than a small, first step in loosening the grip of casualism. But the Ministry was sufficiently encouraged to press for its extension to other ports. The needs of war provided a catalyst. During the Great War, the government was determined to make port transport more disciplined and productive. Some success in Liverpool, perhaps the hardest nut to crack, would encourage the others. By 1918 most British ports had their own schemes of registration, with the major exceptions of London, Glasgow and Newcastle. Compulsion from the centre was not then fashionable in Whitehall, and local registration schemes remained a matter for agreement between employers and trade unions.

Leaving registration to employers and trade unions, by agreement, made it difficult to control the size of the register. It was especially hard for union officials to refuse the required tallies, even for those who only occasionally attended the stands. London, where voluntary registration was introduced in 1920, found that the size of the register exceeded the daily labour requirement by two to one.[6] Registration could not regulate the supply of labour. The number available and seeking work regularly exceeded the demand from employers. Surplus and underemployed labour remained as important features of the waterfront. Surpluses would only disappear at times of acute labour scarcity – as in the Great War when, initially, dockers were volunteering for the Front and could be conscripted after 1916. As waterfront unemployment rose to unprecedented levels between the wars, it began to threaten social cohesion. Fighting, close to rioting, would occasionally break out at the stands when a rare ship came into the harbour.

Registration was little more than cosmetic, then, but it persisted, and dockworkers did become accustomed to it. To become the foundation for the establishment of a permanent labour force, the system required fallback pay, that is maintenance payments when work was unavailable. Ernest Bevin had such maintenance – in the form of a minimum guaranteed wage – in his sights as part of an effective system of registration as early as the Shaw Inquiry. Lord Shaw was persuaded of Bevin's case as the means of eliminating casualism. His chance came twenty years later as Minister of Labour and National Service. He had real authority and intended to use it.

During the Second World War the effective functioning of the dock system, including the way in which labour was hired, deployed and used, was at least as important in the successful long-term prosecution of the war as the roles of the armed forces and the merchant navy. Should the big west coast ports of Liverpool and, to a lesser extent, Glasgow have been put out of action then the country would have been unable to function. The economy's reliance on imported food in itself made the country vulnerable to actual starvation. Those crude facts made a compelling case for compulsion, rather than the voluntarism of 1914–18.[7] For Bevin, it was also a golden opportunity to realise an important part of his life's work along the waterfront. He was also determined that the necessary innovations of wartime would be retained into the peace, despite the widespread fears that the old, familiar, waterfront ways of the dockers and their employers would return. His determination was widely shared among union officials although the dockers themselves still had a taste for casualism, perhaps especially those of Liverpool. The employers, too, would always be opposed to joint control and, in peacetime, would press for the restoration of their claimed right to manage. But Bevin and his fellow officials were not easily deflected from the union's long-standing goals, which went back at least to James Sexton. Even at the height of war, in 1941, the Chairman of the TGWU's annual conference, commenting on Bevin's wartime measures, told the assembled delegates:

> ... to him as a docker it had been a source of great satisfaction to live and see the introduction of principles designed to abolish casual employment in dockland. He felt that they had laid down the principles which would go beyond the war and create a basis on which to build security and continuity of employment in dockland.[8]

Such euphoria was understandable, but euphoria was not enough to develop a system that would endure through to peacetime conditions. All those involved –

employers, unions and government — had much to do before an agreed, detailed scheme was on the table. Fortunately Bevin, though no longer Minister of Labour, following his move to the Foreign Office after the general election of 1945, remained closely involved as a senior member of the Cabinet. The docks had been his life's work for thirty years, and the mood of 1945 offered a golden opportunity for lasting reform which would give the docker and his family a better life. His views were clear even as the war was still in progress:

> ... the guaranteed week must not go with the war ... No one should be tempted to break it up. It was a wonderful thing for a woman to know when she was bringing up her children what her man was going to bring home and when he was going to bring it home — they never knew that under the casual system that existed before.[9]

When the war ended both the employers and the unions, encouraged by the government, moved quickly at first. In September 1945 the employers, through the National Association of Port Employers, tabled their detailed proposals for a national scheme, to be controlled by themselves. Control soon became a major issue. The unions, though welcoming a national scheme, proposed joint control, as had been the case during the war. Meanwhile, an unofficial dispute over pay, which grew to involve 50,000 port workers, was only settled in late November. It required the appointment, by George Isaacs, as Minister of Labour, of a committee of *investigation* which, as Clegg points out, was intended to be less formal and less important than a committee of *inquiry*.[10]

The failure of the employers and unions to agree in September 1945 raised the unwelcome possibility of the government imposing its own scheme under its reserve powers. It had extended the wartime scheme until July 1947 to give the parties time to find an agreed settlement, the more favoured option. But agreement was still hard to find on the fundamentals of who controlled the scheme as well as the level and form of maintenance payments. In the end it took no fewer that three committees of inquiry under three knights of the realm (Sir John Forster, Sir John Cameron and Sir Peter Hetherington) before agreement was reached and formally ratified by the employers and the unions. It became law under the Dock Workers (Regulation of Employment) Order of June 1947. It was just two weeks before the government's postponement of its powers to impose its own scheme lapsed.[11] That deadline had certainly concentrated minds, but the employers had to concede on the key issue of control. That they always found difficult to accept, and it always seemed likely that one day they would seize their chance to regain it.

Sir John Forster's recommendations were the basis of the National Dock Labour Scheme. He supported the unions on the issue of control, in the form of a central joint board much like the wartime body with parallel local boards at port level. But he recommended the employers' views on maintenance, that is a guaranteed weekly wage, '... sufficient to meet a worker's minimum needs while at the same time not being so high as to constitute a temptation to him to rely upon the guarantee rather than actual employment.'[12] The unions had pressed for a monthly payment instead.

It had taken two years, but a deal had been struck. In union circles George Isaac's Parliamentary Order was seen as a victory for the dock worker, not least by Arthur Deakin, the TGWU's General Secretary. He, like many others, spoke too soon. It would become clear that the National Dock Labour Scheme (NDLS) did not end casualism on the waterfront; neither was that a road down which many dockers were yet ready to travel. It was certainly not an end to conflict, which would get worse before it got better.

False dawns ...

It was easy to see why union officials and independent, well-informed observers should see the NDLS as path-breaking. Registration of dockers seeking work was the only way of seriously limiting casualism, if not removing it. This was strengthened by the wages guarantee which, even if set relatively low, was a major advance on the previous system, which could mean little or no pay if not called at the stand, and which also encouraged corruption. The Scheme was also established by a statutory order, controlled by a national board (complemented by local boards at the port level) with joint representation of employers and trade unions. This reflected the way earlier registration schemes had been run as, for example, in Liverpool from 1912. But the NDLS as a national, compulsory scheme was a real sharing of power and authority. The fact that the employers from the start resisted joint representation, and never liked it, revealed how radical it was: a major advance towards industrial democracy, even workers' control. It was a potential model for other industries, although the subsequent strike record on the docks did not attract imitators.[13]

The detailed powers and membership of the National Dock Labour Board (NDLB) and the local Dock Labour Boards reflected the power sharing. The NDLB had eight ordinary members: four nominated from the unions and four from the employers. The chairman and vice-chairman were independents, appointed by the Minister of Labour, who could also appoint two further independents but, in fact, never did.[14] In practice the NDLB devolved its powers as 'holding employer' to the local boards in the ports. These local, joint boards maintained the register, although its size was controlled nationally. Local employers would hire from the register. Disciplinary procedures were jointly exercised by the local boards, who could even remove a worker, or an employer, from the register. Such sanctions would clearly be difficult for a *joint* committee to put into effect. In particular, the union representatives would not wish to undermine their credibility with their members further by acting tough. That, in turn, damaged their relationship with the employer representatives in cases where sanctions were appropriate. Joint control was important for protecting a man's livelihood, for which his listing on the register was essential. But it inevitably led to major problems for the smooth running of the scheme. In that context it was fortunate that wage negotiations were outside the powers of the NDLB. This key function was left to the industry's National Joint Council.

The problems arising from the joint control of discipline pointed to the inherent design problems of the scheme, which, for good reasons, was predicated on the unions and employers working together. Yet the employers always opposed joint control, and had therefore little investment in the scheme's success. The register was a further problem. It was clearly much easier to expand it than to reduce it. Maintaining a stable level was difficult, given that trade naturally fluctuated. More efficient working also reduced the demand for labour, especially important as pallets, bulk handling and containers later profoundly influenced dockside operations. The difficulties of reducing the size of the register were well illustrated in 1949, when London dockers walked out *en masse* at the dismissal of thirty-three who were old and sick. One man, aged only 47, who had worked for one half day in forty-seven weeks, '... suffered from tonsillitis, bronchitis, rheumatism, fibrositis and had weak legs'.[15]

The inevitable outcome was that the size of the register only varied within narrow limits. In 1950 the total UK register for all dockworkers was 75,264. Ten years later it was 72,550, and on only two occasions during that decade did it reach 80,000.[16] In times of trade recession, demand for labour would fall well short of supply, with the old problem of under-employment, that is casualism. As for earnings, the guarantee was of course still available, but it fell short, in itself, of a living wage. It was usually only around 40–50 per cent of average earnings.[17] That proportion fell much further as dockers' earnings rose rapidly in the 1950s. By 1955 the total registered labour force, for the UK, was 58,000. The average number, per week, having their wages made up to the guarantee was only 335.[18] High potential earnings also encouraged non-attendance at the call or even direct hiring, by foremen, 'on the stones', away from the stands. In many ways the old ways were still intact: the scheme was not the end of casualism.

The other problem was the dockers' mistrust of union officials, perhaps most notably on Merseyside. This did not begin or end with James Sexton, although it was perhaps most acute in the years before the Great War. Sexton was identified with the attempts to remove, or at least limit, casualism; but so was Ernest Bevin and most paid officials in the TGWU. Bevin's performance at the Shaw Inquiry, the force of his personality, and his achievements as Minister of Labour during the war, earned him grudging respect. More fundamentally, the Liverpool dockers, who had formed the first viable and influential union in the NUDL, were not convinced that they had a better deal within the new general workers' union, the TGWU. There was a case for the one big general union, but there was also a case for one big national union exclusively for waterfront workers. Indeed, the Liverpool dockers, when dragging their feet over ratifying their inclusion in the TGWU, had to be given their own region as a sweetener.[19]

In 1945–47, these old problems and suspicions had not gone away and were joined in 1947 by the scheme's disciplinary procedure. Any system of discipline, however fairly administered, would always be a problem along the waterfront given its well-established traditions of solidarity, local independence, sectionalism and unofficial action. The extra, and critical difficulty with the scheme was that paid officials of the union were directly involved in both adjudicating and imposing penalties. If that led to dismissal and removal from the register, then a docker's livelihood was at stake. Furthermore, although appeals were available under the procedure, the appeals' tribunal members were appointed by local dock labour boards, that is those who imposed the penalties. Trade union members were rightly accustomed to being defended by their paid officials and not being disciplined by them, other than within their union's internal procedures.

There was also resentment over the range of offences covered. Pilfering, fighting or other 'gross' misconduct were standard offences covered under any disciplinary procedure. Other issues were seen as different. For example, refusing 'suitable' work allocated, especially if the work was not within traditional skill boundaries. 'Suitable' work meant anything the worker was physically capable of doing.[20] Thus it was even possible for the 'aristocrats' of the waterfront, the well-paid stevedores, to be allocated to dockside or warehouse portering. That, aside from the loss of earnings, was telling them that their status, skill and experience were not valued. All dockers were seen as 'labourers', even 'casual labourers'.

There was also the thorny issue of overtime. During the war compulsory overtime was acceptable as an emergency measure. In peacetime it was much less welcome, especially when pay was rising. The resentment at compulsion was widely shared across most industries. Workers saw overtime as voluntary, although employers usually preferred some element of compulsion, even going as far as including it in contracts of employment. Under the scheme refusal was a disciplinary offence subject, like absenteeism, to a fine. To the dockers compulsory overtime was an attack on traditional work habits and, along with the requirement to attend the call, and to accept allocated work, fuelled the dockers' traditional suspicion of their union officials' attitudes and commitment.

The outcome was that by the beginning of the 1950s, only a few years into the scheme that had seemed to promise so much, 15,000 dockers, 18 per cent of the workforce, had appeared before the joint disciplinary committees.[21] The other outcome, again associated with the problems of the scheme, was a rapid rise in the frequency of strike action. Nationally, the miners remained the champion strikers in terms of total man days lost, but when measured against each 1,000 employed, dockworkers were in a league of their own. Between 1947 and 1955 the average yearly number of man days lost, per thousand, was 3,134. In coal-mining it was 778. Ship-building and ship repairing, at 890, were also ahead of coal-mining.[22]

... old ways

The rise in strikes along the waterfront in the wake of the launch of the scheme in 1947 was not entirely attributable to the inherent problems of the reforms. Pay was rarely absent as an issue, though such overt 'causes', as Knowles reminds us, often tell us little about the underlying issues. One such, as we have seen, was that discipline was jointly handled, on the local dock labour boards by employers and union representatives acting together. There were also the underlying tensions between the TGWU and the National Association of Stevedores and Dockers, as well as the other source of dockers' power and influence, the unofficial movement. Resolving disputes arising out of such a complex of shifting causes would also be difficult, but were made worse by the dockers' mistrust of the procedures for resolving disputes. Nor could disputes be contained within the port of origin since sympathetic action, in other ports, was a frequent response.

Liverpool usually came out early and with strong support, notably in the two early post-scheme disputes, the zinc-oxide strike in the Port of London in 1948 and the Canadian seamen's strike in 1949. The first escalated to the point where the government threatened to send in troops and invoke emergency powers, moves not expected from a popular, Labour, administration. The second strike attracted ferocious criticism up to the Archbishop of Canterbury, who charged the unofficial leadership with being 'Communist agitators' and 'anti-Christian'. Later, in 1951, the action of the Merseyside Port Workers' Defence Committee, campaigning for the Dockers' Charter, eventually led to the arrest of four London and three Liverpool dockers on unlawful conspiracy to incite strikes, an action that escalated the dispute by provoking sympathetic action in other ports.[23]

That was far from all. The existence of well-organised port workers' committees was exacerbated by the serious, long-standing inter-union dispute between the TGWU and the stevedores' NASD. The NASD, known as the 'blue' union from the supposed colour of its membership card,[24] had its origins among the early organisations of the London stevedores in the 1880s. Though by 1922 it had about 6,000 members it refused to join the emerging new organisation of dock and transport workers.[25] That must largely explain its early and continuing rivalry with the newly formed TGWU, the 'white' union. The NASD was expelled from the TUC for 'poaching' its rival's members in London, and was not reinstated until 1945. Further conflict led to it losing its representation on the National Dock Labour Board in 1949. In 1954 the inter-union rivalry took a more serious turn when the NASD began to operate outside London, establishing branches in Hull and Birkenhead, followed by Liverpool and Manchester in 1955, ports formerly exclusive to the TGWU. The NASD was once again charged with poaching by the TUC's Disputes Committee.[26] It ruled that the NASD should cease recruiting among TGWU members in the northern ports, and should return to the TGWU the 10,000 who had been recruited during 1954–55. Following a High Court action involving the expulsion of an NASD member in arrears with his dues, the

TUC Disputes Committee ruled further that though the NASD, in law, could keep its members recruited in the northern ports, it was still forbidden to service them. That was the responsibility of the TGWU. The NASD refused to comply with the servicing ruling, although it did agree to stop recruiting. That was not enough for the TUC, which suspended the NASD in 1958 and expelled it in 1959.[27] After that the NASD's influence gradually declined along the waterfronts in the northern ports, along with its membership, as the TGWU developed a somewhat better relationship with the rank-and-file. Yet the NASD continued to make its presence felt in its London heartland, and was one of the influences in the period of Devlin's investigations and eventual final report in 1967. But small membership undermined its viability as an independent union, and it was eventually absorbed by its nemesis, the TGWU, in 1982.

Internal warfare such as that between the NASD and TGWU is always a special problem for trade union movements. Given the importance of size of membership, in maintaining power, influence and revenue, charges of 'poaching' are particularly sensitive, which explains the decisive actions of the TUC, a cautious, representative organisation not known for clear and early decision making. Perhaps more importantly, the dispute damaged trade union prestige and membership along the waterfront. Lord Devlin estimated in 1965 that in Liverpool and Hull one third belonged to neither union.[28] The rank-and-file had become deeply disillusioned. On a visit to Merseyside Jack Jones came to the same conclusion at the same time as Devlin. He was also significantly critical of those among the TGWU officials, including national officers, who,

> still tended to side with the employers rather than our members. Equally I had heard others define their role as being 'half-way between the members and the management' ... A trade union officer can be neither a policeman nor a middleman – he represents his members or he represents nothing.[29]

This also echoed the long-held views of many Liverpool dockers from the stewardship of Sexton and into recent times.[30] It compounded their problems with the administration of the scheme with which union officials were also closely identified. That also gave a boost to the NASD which, as a consistent critic of registration as well as being opposed to decasualisation, still retained popular support. It became the champion of the common man against distant bureaucrats such as Arthur Deakin, the General Secretary of the TGWU, who was no Bevin, and Lord Ammon, Chairman of the NDLB. There were also the port worker committees established in London, Liverpool, and Manchester between 1948 and 1951. These reflected the hostility to the official union organisation, which many dockers saw as betraying their interests. They also developed their own set of policies, the Dockers' Charter, which provided a national focus.

The Dockers' Charter, with deliberate echoes of the Victorian Chartists, came out of Jack Dash's Royal Docks Liaison Committee, but was also influential in the

Liverpool and Manchester port committees. In 1963 the charter's eleven demands included a 40-hour week, three weeks' paid holiday each year, a retiring age of 65 and a pension of £4 per week (average earnings were just over £18 (£255.50) in 1963),[31] as well as improved piece rates, sickness and accident pay. The scheme would be retained, with the register stabilised, and extended to every port and, in due course, nationalisation of the industry.[32]

The Dockers' Charter was primarily a list of demands to improve the dockers' terms and conditions. Its wider demands included extending the scheme to all ports and nationalising the industry. The charter was far from revolutionary. Nationalisation was also, for a time, seriously considered by the Wilson government though for government, not workers' control.[33] The charter did, however, provide a focus around which dockers could unite and resist authoritarian discipline from their employers, their union, and the disciplinary procedures and practices of the NDLB. But the *concept* of the NDLB remained important on the waterfront. It did, at least, limit employer control and, by 1989, its abolition had replaced the Charter as the issue around which the rank-and-file could rally.

In the 1960s it was, however, inconceivable that the scheme would be abolished and, if nationalisation ever came, it would be retained. The charter, as well as the NASD, were the fora for organised resistance. Less organised, even unorganised, were the many small disputes, escalating via solidarity and loyalty, to major stoppages. In that sense they were practising a raw democracy, very unlike how they saw the role of the TGWU and its officials, with perhaps some lingering, proud, nostalgic memories of 1911 when Tom Mann and the syndicalists were, for a brief period, in real control. The Liverpool waterfront of 1911 was indeed a powerful memory.[34]

By the 1960s the average number of strikes per year in Liverpool had reached 74, that is well over one per week and over twice that of London. In 1969 Liverpool experienced 97 strikes, nearly two a week. In the same year London's total was 33.[35] The authorities were worried, and for a time their focus was upon the usual suspects, the political extremists, especially Communists. The Cold War provided the backdrop, with populist, charismatic leaders, such as Jack Dash in London and Leo McGree in Liverpool, unashamed Communists, taking centre stage. But not all dissidents were Communists or even all Communists dissidents. Such confusions made it difficult to prove the existence of any organised conspiracy. Nor was there any explanation as to how such leaders could sway and lead the mass of ordinary dockers who had little sympathy for revolutionary solutions. The fact was, from their perspective, they had something to be dissident about. Few outside their own ranks could begin to understand the dockers' case, including the government and its advisers.

It required yet another committee of inquiry, under Lord Devlin.

Enter Lord Devlin

If Ernest Bevin was the 'Dockers' QC' then Lord Devlin could be termed the 'Dockers' Judge'. And judge them he did, having already chaired several earlier dock inquiries and settled disputes. Not surprisingly the dockers themselves had a different perspective on Devlin's qualifications: the unofficial leadership, for instance, noted that '… a plumber should be no more used to mend a car than a lawyer to cure the docks …'[36] More comprehensively critical was the 'Anti-Devlin Report', which demanded immediate nationalisation of the ports under a national port authority with port workers' councils sending representatives to a national port workers' council. This had more than a whiff of syndicalism about it and, given its ideological leanings, was at odds with the Communists in the ports, including Jack Dash and his Liaison Committee. They were accused of being soft on workers' control.[37]

Devlin himself gave no space, perhaps even less thought, to the ideological currents running along the Thames and the Mersey. He was more exercised with the impact of the dockers' legendary solidarity and saw their readiness to strike as 'irresponsible':

> The responsible employee in industries like the docks has to accept that the decision to work or not to work is no longer a purely personal choice … There are, in our opinion, two factors which account for the peculiar irresponsibility of the dock labourer, one being the casual system and the other being an excessive loyalty which … although deriving from the casual system has now become something to be reckoned with on its own.[38]

As we have seen, Devlin's attack on the casual system as the principal explanation for most of the ills of the waterfront was hardly new. In Liverpool it went back to well into Victorian times and was widely shared. Consistent in their opposition to the system over many years, TGWU officials at all levels welcomed Devlin's critique, albeit circumspectly. This again put them in a position potentially at odds with their members, and greatly inhibited the acceptance of reform. Successful reform also ran against the grain of dockwork, which was regulated by the fluctuations of trade, short and longer term, as well as tidal patterns and storms. Yet, despite these major constraints, reform was achieved, and casualism was finally driven from dockland in 1967.

Perhaps to his surprise, Devlin saw that it did nothing to reduce strike activity. Earlier official inquiries into the industry, those of Sir Frederick Leggett in 1951 and Lord Devlin himself in 1956, also arose from government concerns over the alleged 'strike proneness' of dockers. The inquiries considered the familiar problems including, with Leggett, the friction between the TGWU and the unofficial movement. That, it saw, as largely originating in officials serving on the Dock Boards and involved in disciplinary action. It also proposed the fashionable solution of better communications, perhaps through a special magazine for dockers, as well as more full-time officials.

In 1956 Devlin had been concerned mainly with the National Association of Port Employers' opposition to joint control of the national and local boards. That had been a fundamental issue for the employers from the beginning of the scheme. Their claimed 'right to manage' required direct and flexible responses to labour surpluses and shortages on the docks; but that conflicted with the security, for employees, of a stable register, which was seen also as the route to decasualisation. Another complication, which was a finding from Liverpool University's 1951 study of Manchester Docks, was that almost half of the dockers interviewed thought that the local Dock Labour Board was their employer rather than the Manchester Ship Canal Company.[39] The duality of the scheme was bound to lead to confusion in Liverpool as well as Manchester. The board's position as 'employer' was even confirmed on a weekly basis by the paying of wages as well as its control of the disciplinary procedure. As we have seen the procedure itself more than added to the confusion. Even if the disciplinary procedure was a joint activity, it still involved penalties, up to removal from the register, by officials who had been elected or appointed to defend their interests.

Devlin was in action again in 1964 in the resolution of another pay dispute. His report in that year formed the first stage of Devlin's work, completed by the Second Report in 1965. Devlin unequivocally denounced casualism as the root of most, if not all, evils along the waterfront. By then its eradication was also being increasingly seen as an economic as well as a social necessity, although the two were closely linked. Regular work, or at least a guaranteed income, it was contended, would help the docker to join the ranks of model, sober, responsible workers and citizens. At the same time it was held that this transformed docker would be less prone to strike and would resist the calls of unofficial leaders and troublemakers. That, in turn, would guarantee uninterrupted activity on the docks, with corresponding economic gains for the ports and an economy heavily dependent on trade.

This case and its predicted benefits were widely held. The dockers were sceptical, and the unofficial leadership was at one with the sceptics in foreseeing a major threat to jobs as employers responded to the higher labour costs of wages' guarantees after decasualisation. The port committees' alternative was to get rid of private and other forms of dock ownership and dock employers by nationalisation. Nor was that just the politics of 'pie in the sky'. It was still a political possibility as long as a Labour government was in power. Meanwhile, the unrepentant class warriors writing the leaders in the newspapers were repeating familiar attitudes: 'Giving the dockers a permanent job will be like putting a gypsy into a council house: he will expect to keep his caravan in the back garden.'[40]

The misplaced similes of *The Times*, while revealing the continuing power of ugly class perspectives that still plagued British society, did, however, carry an accurate message. The dockers did find it difficult to accept change,[41] especially when they were told it was good for them, or when their doubts, criticisms and alternatives were dismissed. Nor were they alone in their scepticism. Along the waterfront small employers were still numerous. They had long got used to the old casual system, with its limited responsibilities for employers, its low labour costs and, usually, acceptable profits. The big employers of labour had appropriately bigger concerns, including getting rid of the joint control of the NDLB, which Devlin's committee had no intention of doing. For the government Ray Gunter, Minister of Labour, was anxious to see the end of the casual system; but getting rid of the NDLB was not practical Labour government politics. Nationalisation was also, by then, well down his wish list. The employers could, at least, postpone fears for their survival. Later events and political changes would guarantee and strengthen the employers' role.

Devlin's detailed criticisms of the casual system were not new. His views were also widely shared by the TGWU officials, in spite of their continuing discomfort from the barbed criticisms of their own members and the unofficial movement. The union officials might also have shared Devlin's strictures against the 'irresponsibility' of the dockers and their waterfront solidarity. Yet despite the strong tide of opinion favouring the final removal of casualism in 1967 (two years after the report) it did not eliminate all the endemic problems of dockside employment, prevent the continuing loss of jobs and, most specifically, did not reduce the number of strikes. Other explanations and remedies were required to reduce conflict. As it turned out, the removal of casualism was perhaps not even a part of those explanations. For a time, indeed, the Devlin reforms were even a cause.

Devlin's 'giant'

Lord Devlin's experience of inquiries over ten years qualified him well to take on the task of killing what might be termed a sixth 'giant' (to complement Beveridge's five). Interestingly, his Roman Catholicism gave him some affinity among the dockers of Irish descent on the waterfront, and not only in Liverpool. But their view of 'sin' would not have been the same as Devlin's, although his moral position should not be exaggerated as Wilson points out in that he was well capable of '… separating the emotional response to casualism from the actual problems which the system generated'.[42]

His companions on the Committee of Inquiry were hand-picked. Hugh Clegg, then a fellow of Nuffield College, Oxford, was beginning to make his name.[43] He was an academic with applied, practical interests in making improving the operational effectiveness of industrial relations institutions and payment systems. They were joined by Jack Scamp, formerly responsible for General Electric's labour relations, who would clock up twenty-five more inquiries, and Sidney Ford, President of the National Union of Mineworkers, from another 'strike prone' industry which had recently replaced piecework – an issue for the Devlin

Inquiry. Witnesses were seen in private, so as to be able to speak freely, and came from right across the employer and worker spectrum. A representative from the Church of England industrial committee was also invited. That might have reflected Devlin's 'stern moral propriety',[44] but also Clegg's background as the son of a (Methodist) clergyman. The recently elected Labour government, after thirteen years out of office, was also anxious to demonstrate, at an early date, its humanitarian instincts by finally eliminating what they saw as a blight on the working lives of the dockers. More directly to the political point, it might stop them going out on strike with such regularity. That seemed also to be Devlin's thinking. Gunter moved quickly.

The committee was set up within two weeks of the 1964 election, although its first task — hence the speed — was to settle a threatened national strike by the dockers over pay. Jack Jones, who spoke frequently to Gunter, the Labour Minister, on such matters, recalls (with some irony) how rapidly government can move when under pressure.[45] The interim report was published in November 1964. The committee's longer term task was to follow its terms of reference listing decasualisation and port efficiency. Lord Devlin wrote the report himself. It was published on 5 August 1965. Many saw it as a 'blueprint' for the industry. Dissent and criticism came from the usual suspects but, within four days, Ray Gunter, the employers and the unions had agreed, in principle, to implement Devlin. That took place on 18 September 1967, Ray Gunter's 'D-Day' ('Decasualisation Day') taking from the earlier, even more historic occasion. The unofficial movement was also conscious of its own history. Jack Dash was out on the stump on D-Day. There was mixed support along the London waterfront for a strike. At its peak, over the first few weeks, 8,000 out of a labour force of 23,000 came out. Manchester and Hull dockers also struck, but the action failed to stick beyond the first week after D-Day. Liverpool, as expected, was different. The entire workforce of 12,000 struck for six weeks, although the central issue was over the levels of bonus, rather than the ending of decasualisation. It took Sir Jack Scamp,[46] heading a government inquiry, to settle it. By then the government had devalued the pound. Morale was low everywhere, except within the unofficial movement, not least along the Liverpool waterfront. Devlin found space in his report for berating the unofficial movement's behaviour and motives, developing his condemnation of 'irresponsibility' and 'solidarity'. He charged them as being against decasualisation and an improvement in working conditions, since '... anything that makes for good industrial relations is bad for wrecking'.[47] He also criticised the TGWU for allowing the unofficial movement to rival its authority.

Devlin's instructions to the TGWU to take effective action against the unofficial movement in the ports featured in the 1965 'D-Day' Report. The earlier 1964 inquiry resolved the pay dispute in that year, but was followed by the appointment of Devlin's second and third committees with their reforming terms of reference. They were to tackle the central issue of how to eliminate casualism and, just as important as later events were to prove, find ways of introducing the necessary 'modernisation'. Casualism was the province of the 1965 Report; 'modernisation', too complex and weighty, required its own report, published in 1966.[48]

The actual implementation of the 1965 and 1966 reports was a matter for negotiation by the employers and the unions on the NJC (the National Joint Council for the Port Transport Industry). It was carried out in two stages, which came to be known as Devlin Phase 1 and Devlin Phase 2, following the two reports. The unions supported this more gradual approach, but the employers (the NAPE) preferred implementation in one stage. Devlin himself went for two stages.

The employers and the unions did not come to Devlin without valuable earlier relevant experience. From 1961 to 1965 Andrew Crichton of NAPE and Frank Cousins, the TGWU's general secretary, covered the essential ground of Devlin, beginning with the 'Crichton-Cousins' Manifesto[49] in 1961. Their agreed proposals, put to the NJC, included the attachment of registered dockers to registered employers and guaranteed fallback pay. They also covered the 'modernisation' issues: the abolition of restrictive labour practices; maximum labour mobility between employers to iron out shortages and surpluses; and the introduction of systematic shift working. After five years' negotiation the NJC failed to reach agreement. The stumbling block was modernisation. The proposals were far-reaching and required persuasion and acceptance at waterfront level, where the influence of the unofficials and dockers' scepticism was strong. Acceptance would take time to achieve.

But the experience of those preparatory years influenced Devlin, who also accepted that time had to be taken over implementation, hence the two-phase approach. He also drew upon the content of the manifesto. The report sought to bring peace and greater efficiency to dockland through nine main, detailed recommendations, which came out of an exhaustive process of interviews and consultations. The nine were:

1. The elimination of casual methods by management and employers.
2. Regular employment for dockworkers.
3. Early progress towards strong and effective trade union leadership.
4. Greater labour mobility.
5. Improved welfare facilities.
6. A revised wage structure.
7. Abolition of the time-wasting labour practices.
8. Acceptance of firm discipline especially on time-keeping and recognition of the board's authority.
9. The review of manning scales to reflect increasing mechanisation and modernisation.[50]

Devlin also insisted on two necessary conditions: a drastic reduction in the number of employers, and for the TGWU to restore its authority in London, Liverpool and

Hull. Each employer would be required to be big enough to operate independently, for at least 80 per cent of the year, offering '... proper supervision, equipment and welfare facilities ...' These criteria would decide whether or not the National Ports Council, the authorising body, recommended the NDLB grant a licence. Liverpool led the field with a total of 114 employers, which Devlin saw eventually coming down to ten.[51]

On the TGWU's authority, Devlin pressed for the NASD, the 'Blues', to be brought onto the NJC, a bridge-building gesture typical of such inquiries. The TGWU also worked towards conciliation, notably in the person of Jack Jones the ex-Merseyside docker, then ranking third in the union pecking-order. From 1965 he had a special brief to supervise dock affairs. He used his old militant reputation and Liverpool connections and friends to build bridges with the NASD and the unofficial waterfront leadership.[52] He also usefully supported the principle of shop-floor democracy and influence, the TGWU introducing shop stewards on the docks for the first time. This challenged the influence of the NASD, although the Liverpool stewards were themselves later to challenge the authority of the full-time organisation in the disputes of the early 1970s.[53]

The NDLB was also given work to do. It was directed to carry out a survey of amenities in the scheme ports to see how they could be improved in cooperation with the employers and public bodies and agencies. Amenities had long been of a notoriously low standard on the docks. This requirement, along with those directed at the employers and the TGWU, related to 1, 2, 3 and 5 on Devlin's list. Recommendations 4, 6, 7, 8 and 9 were for implementation in Phase 2, except where they related to casual employment, the Phase 1 task. The revision of the wage structure (recommendation 6) was to examine all aspects of basic pay, overtime and piecework.

The third Devlin recommendation – the removal of the casual system – was the historic task under Phase 1, although there were many devils hiding in the detailed changes requiring agreement under Phase 2. The leaders of the still powerful unofficial movements were opposed to Devlin, root and branch, and the rank-and-file, including members of the TGWU, and particularly the NASD, were sceptical and wary: long experience had taught and confirmed that lesson.

The joint control of the register administered by the NDLB was retained, with labour allocated to registered employers on a permanent, weekly-paid basis. Once allocated, the direct employer in the port would carry out all employer duties. Where surpluses or shortages of labour occurred among companies, the board could transfer men between them. But not all were categorised as permanent. Temporary employment, usually comprising seasonal workers or those needed for the handling of specialised cargoes – was another category. The third category were registered workers waiting for re-allocation to another employer or awaiting a disciplinary hearing. This third group was the Temporary Unattached Register. This register was increasingly abused by employers as a backdoor means of dismissing surplus labour, a feature foreign to the principles of decasualisation and employment security. In mid-1972 the number on the TUR was 4 per cent of the total register.[54]

The abuse of the TUR was a major problem. A committee, chaired by Lord Aldington (Chairman of the Port of London Authority) and Jack Jones (then TGWU General Secretary), was set up to remove the abuse. From 4 September 1972 those on the TUR register (except for the disciplinary cases) were re-allocated to other employers. For the employers that meant they could not use the TUR for compulsory redundancy. This brake on layoffs led to the widespread allegation that working on the docks, now reasonably secure, was a 'job-for-life'. Yet this did not square with the numbers leaving the industry after 1967.[55] On 'D-Day' there were nearly 57,000 registered dockers; there were 32,000 in 1975, and just 18,000 in 1981. In the year the NDLB was abolished, the register comprised fewer than 10,000.[56]

There were clearly too many high hopes placed on the Devlin reforms. Nevertheless, except for the TUR, a loophole which was soon closed, he did succeed in decasualising the industry. That was a major achievement. It was a reform that had eluded the brightest and the best before him. But the consequences of Devlin defied analysis and confident prediction. It did nothing to reduce strikes, and seemed actually to make the problem worse. Many dockers, too, must have thought that the retention of the NDLB and the register and the guarantee of continuous work and/or fallback pay would stabilise the labour force. They were bitterly disappointed. Even if the settlements were good, they were mostly unavoidable as technological change really began to bite and jobs disappeared.

Lost jobs were for the longer term. The immediate consequence was a sharp rise in the number of strikes. Between 1960 and 1967 the average annual number of strikes was 13. Between 1968 and 1971, after Devlin, it rose to 74. Then it fell sharply to an average of 30 after 1971, that is after the negotiation of Liverpool's Phase 2 agreement in October of that year. It is also of note that Liverpool introduced piecework into its payment system in 1967, after which strike incidence increased almost sixfold. Until then it had been a time rate port.[57] Getting some order, sense and simplicity into any payment system on the docks was always going to be handicapped by having to deal with numbers of small employers with limited resources and poor motivation. Workers can also more easily pick them off, piecemeal, to win concessions. The number of employers did fall dramatically after Devlin, nationally some 470 in 1970, down from about 1,500. But of these only eleven employed more than 1,000, and eight more than 500.[58] There were fewer but most were still small. That problem remained.

The major problem for Devlin, however, which was not of its making, was that it secured permanent jobs for dockers, which were increasingly well paid, at a time when those very jobs were being undermined at an accelerating rate. The dockers must have thought, after 1967, despite their traditionally militant ways and doubts over decasualisation, that their future was bright. The pay was good, at or near the top of the British 'pay league'. The job was still varied and interesting, with some of the old freedoms intact. It was also secure. But the retention of the NDLB and modernisation to remain competitive did not bring 'jobs for life'.

Devlin, it seems, managed to achieve decasualisation mainly because the dockers' world was again turning upside down. The employers, the union, and the government all knew it, and the industry had to be ready for it. The container revolution, in the end, was unavoidable, although it had been a long time coming, originating in the United States.[59] Its impact on skills and the nature of dockwork was revolution enough, but it would also cut swathes into employment. The only defence available to save jobs, even at a much lower level, was to extend their work beyond the quayside to destinations inland where the containers were loaded and discharged, the so-called 'stuffing and stripping'. That they could tackle through their own strength, though their numbers were dwindling, by 'blacking' and 'picketing' inland operations. When that soon became unlawful, five pickets (the 'Pentonville Five') were gaoled in July 1972, although they were soon released followed by a national walk-out of 42,000 in the ports.

Strangely enough, the law almost helped the dockers' cause. In 1978 the Labour government's Dockwork Regulation Act would have extended the definition of 'dock work', for registered dockers, to include 'stuffing and stripping' containers, to half a mile (in a direct line) from a harbour. The scheme, in 1947, had limited the definition to 'in, or in the vicinity of' the port. Amendments to exclude the extension were lost in the Commons on the votes of two Labour Members voting with the opposition.

That was the last, lost defence. It would not have been enough, however. Half a mile was easily avoided by operations further inland. There was also the problem of the scheme itself. Its members were, in total, employed in about 80 ports, with about 220 outside. In 1947 that was of little account since the 80 included the biggest players, London, Liverpool, Southampton, Hull, Newcastle and Glasgow. The non-scheme ports were numerous but, individually, small and insignificant. By the 1970s that was changing, and accelerated in the 1980s. Ports such as Felixstowe and Dover were beginning to eclipse the older ports, notably Liverpool and Glasgow, as well as those holding their position well enough against others such as Southampton. Felixstowe and Southampton were also better sited, with better harbours for container ships. Dover was also geographically well placed for the growing roll-on, roll-off traffic to and from the EEC which Britain joined in 1973. Technology-led productivity allowed such ports to increase their trade, turnover and profits while drastically reducing their labour intensity as containers, machinery and the other innovations rapidly replaced the old, obsolete methods. Nor had the non-scheme ports any of the statutory regulation of their rivals, a discrepancy especially noticeable after the Devlin reforms. All of these factors put the scheme ports on the back foot compared to the non-scheme ports. At the same time, and most important for future growth and development, was the discrepancy in investment potential.

The scheme ports, perhaps notably London and Liverpool, were run by public bodies with access to capital requiring government authorisation. Government was also required to at least subsidise the long-running and expensive severance schemes in the scheme ports. These ports were also old, with inherent natural disadvantages in relation to tidal ranges, dredging, crumbling infrastructure, and geography as trade patterns continued to shift. Pound-for-pound, investing in ports such as Felixstowe, especially to capture the container trade, was a better proposition than in the scheme ports. Felixstowe's investment was also privately financed, so it was tempting for government to limit public investment in the scheme ports and let private money take the strain. It was also important that British ports should be able to meet the challenge of the big continental operators, notably Rotterdam and Antwerp. The rapidly growing non-scheme ports, such as Felixstowe and Dover, were best placed to do this. Of the old scheme ports, only Southampton had the necessary credentials.

The scheme ports' only viable options to restore their competitiveness were to press for the extension of the scheme to the non-scheme ports – a forlorn hope – or to reduce their manpower requirements. Liverpool, for all its past glories, had to accept the reality of the situation. Jobs began to go at a rapid rate, along with many of the docks themselves. Liverpool's dockland would soon become a quiet, even sad place for those who knew it years earlier. In 1989, on abolition of the NDLB, Liverpool's total of registered dockers was about 1,000. Peter Baker, with twenty-five years on the Liverpool docks (when the workforce was then over 14,000) put it somewhat poignantly:

When you walked down here at 8 a.m., it used to feel like you were going to a football match, there were so many men around you. Now you're a lonely man when you go to work.[60]

CHAPTER THIRTEEN

'The greatest game no more'

I am staggered that this Government consider the Port of Liverpool is less important than Rolls Royce.

(Councillor Cyril Carr, 1970)[1]

... the existence of a large dock labour force is no longer a viable factor in the make-up of the port.

(Francis E. Hyde, 1971)[2]

... it was never just a job – it was always more than that. Being a docker was a way of life. It was the greatest game in the world.

(Former registered docker, 1994)[3]

... we knew after the miners they were coming for us.

(Terry, a Liverpool docker, 1996)[4]

IN THE CLOSING PAGES of his economic history of Liverpool, in 1970, just three years after dock labour was finally decasualised, Professor Hyde struck an ominous note.[5] As he was writing, Liverpool was already losing a part of its Far East container trade to its old rival, Southampton. It was thought that this could be followed by further losses, such as the trade with South Africa.

Southampton was a major scheme port. Yet, even then, it was only part of the challenge to Liverpool. The other was the emerging non-scheme ports, negligible in 1947 but now an increasing threat to the old order. Trying to bring them within the scheme ports was one approach, though that was never a political starter. Another, more promising, idea was nationalisation, particularly when Harold Wilson looked certain to be re-elected in 1970. The dockers, including Jack Dash and the unofficial movement, would have welcomed public ownership. For that reason alone, it had little widespread effective political support, even within the Labour Party. But even if the docks had been taken into public ownership Hyde would still have had his doubts for the future of Liverpool '... beset with incalculable problems'. He even raised the prospect of the docks of Jesse Hartley being filled in, with Britain allowing 'her second largest port to go into a state of decline'.[6] His concluding sentences were, however, much less than apocalyptic. Although he predicted that the closure of the docks would not be Liverpool's fate, it would probably have a limited future in the bulk trades and containers.[7] This would be small consolation for the city that was once 'threshold to the ends of the earth', the 'second port of Empire'.

Hyde was, by and large, right. Within two years the operational docks would all be in the North End, with the Seaforth Docks and the newly opened Container Terminal, incorporating the Gladstone Dock Complex, forming the nucleus of the new Port of Liverpool, five miles away from the City and Mersey Docks and Harbour Board building. The link between the city and the port was, by then, visibly broken. The board was also heavily in debt. Although there had been some government support, the total investment in Seaforth was £40 million (about £430 million at today's prices). The total capital debt was £83 million (£880 million), with annual interest payments of £4.2 million (£45 million).[8] Still, Seaforth represented the future of the port. It was a modern facility with a grain terminal as well as timber, meat and deep-sea container berths. Crucially, too, the available acreage allowed space for future expansion, a wholly new feature for Liverpool with its almost endemic problems of bottlenecks and overcrowding.[9]

The South End, as well as sharing the Mersey's disadvantages, also had its own. Its ten docks had berths for 53 vessels, but rarely more than half were in use at any one time. The docks' equipment was old and obsolescent, pushing up maintenance costs to add to the prohibitive dredging costs. The South End also employed about 3,000, their jobs clearly at risk. The South End's problems had been long in the making. Over a century earlier, in Liverpool's heyday, some of its docks were already becoming obsolete, of declining use to a modern, world-beating port. Even the Albert Dock and its enclosed, fireproof warehouses, which had been state of the art in 1845, were looking antique as the age of steam gathered momentum. The other nine docks were also too small, with entrances too difficult, narrow and shallow to take the bigger steamships, a problem that got continually worse as their size increased throughout the rest of the century. However, some major reconstruction did take place, under another enabling Act (1896) notably giving Brunswick Dock a 100ft entrance, and a rebuilding of Kings and Queens Docks which, as late as the 1960s, were taking cargo liners. But the North End always had the edge, earning its living from both passengers and cargoes, the cargo liners continuing to contribute to profits. Yet the North End lost most of its passenger trade to Southampton and, after the brutal impact of the three big crises of the twentieth century – a deep depression in between two destructive world wars – Liverpool's tide began to ebb, slowly at first and almost unnoticed, then with gathering speed.

Even as late as the 1960s the Dock Board's modernisation and development plans were ambitious and optimistic.[10] But time was not on Liverpool's side. In

1966 its share of UK foreign trade, other than fuels, was still high, at 15 per cent, but falling. Then, by the early 1970s, a new factor entered the equation: Britain's entry into the EEC in 1973. That gradually shifted the balance of British trade away from the Commonwealth and North America – Liverpool's strength – towards Europe's big, deep-water harbours in Belgium and Holland. The advantage was now to the ports on the south and east coasts of England. They seized it. By 1985, Liverpool had fallen to sixth in its share of UK trade.

Nor did the political cycle favour Liverpool's survival. Labour was unexpectedly defeated in 1970, and that ruled out any lingering hopes of nationalisation,[11] which in any case had had little support beyond the waterfront. This was a critical time, when the old-style Conservative governments were transformed towards a much more free-marked orientated approach. Within a decade Edward Heath had been defeated and Margaret Thatcher came to power in 1979.

In its first two years the Heath government was not unlike its post-1979 successors. It was especially opposed to state intervention to save 'lame ducks', a mixture of simplistic ideology and nineteenth-century economic liberalism. Liverpool was one of those lame ducks, along with the flagship aero-engine manufacturer Rolls Royce. For Rolls Royce the government was helpfully inconsistent. Not so for the Port of Liverpool. It was a bitter irony that in the same month the Liverpool Corporation (whose Councillor Cyril Carr contrasted Liverpool's treatment with that of the aero-engine maker) announced the purchase of a new car, a Rolls Royce,[12] worth £13,250, for the use of the Lord Mayor. The day of the Rolls Royce announcement (4 November) was also the day that the MDHB's Interim Report revealed a loss of £3 million and an increase in port dues and other charges of 25 per cent. The acting chairman, Alderman Sir Joseph Cleary (the chairman was ill) announced on the next day that the port could survive, financially, until 31 December.[13] Within a week the acting chairman and director general, Robert Edwards, were in London seeking government aid of £6 million to repay bonds and ease the problems of the anticipated loss of £3 million. Rolls Royce won the 'lame duck' lottery, with aid of £42 million. The crisis came to a head. The next day (ominously, Friday 13 November 1970) Bessie Braddock, the fiery champion of the people of the waterfront, died. She was 71. Eric Heffer, the MP for Walton, was doing what Bessie would have done in the Commons, pointing to the loss of 3,000 jobs in the South End and the continuing paradox of Liverpool, in 1970 still handling the biggest share of the UK's vital export trade, being denied government assistance for it to survive.

Crisis and worse

The origins of most of Liverpool's problems in the 1970s were fundamental, and largely beyond the capacity of the Dock Board to handle without external assistance. There was plenty of talk about the board's its incompetence, and it could be argued that it might have acted earlier, but most of it was beyond its

The North End dock system in 1964. This aerial view was taken when the future of the port was not yet in danger, and the new non-port industries such as car and commercial vehicle manufacture were adding to trade, profits, jobs and wages. In the same year the board reported record tonnage and saw even the South End as contributing to profits. Importantly, the board was also investing £36 million, most of it for the planned new dock at Seaforth. Note in the photograph the Clarence Dock Power Station, built on the site of the infilled Clarence Dock in 1929. The power station was demolished in the mid-1990s. Jesse Hartley's clock tower, however, still stands, and can just be seen in the photograph beyond the power station.

© LIVERPOOL RECORD OFFICE.

RIGHT

Map 10.   The Mersey Dock System before the financial crisis of 1970–72 and the closure of the entire South End docks (ten from the Pier Head). The Seaforth Dock is still shown, at that time as a 'project'. The overhead railway had been demolished 13 years previously.

REDRAWN FROM PATMORE AND HODGKISS (EDS), *MERSEYSIDE IN MAPS* (LONDON: LONGMAN)

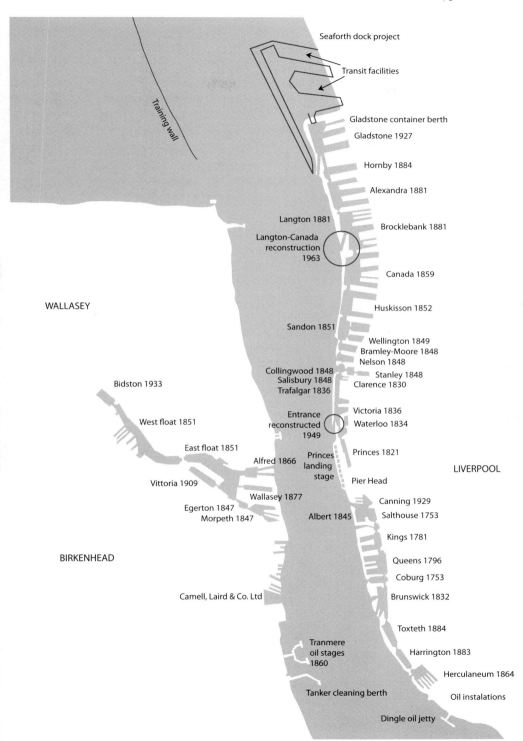

Seaforth dock project

Transit facilities

Training wall

Gladstone container berth

Gladstone 1927

Hornby 1884

Alexandra 1881

Langton 1881

Brocklebank 1881

Langton-Canada
reconstruction
1963

Canada 1859

WALLASEY

Huskisson 1852

Sandon 1851

Wellington 1849
Bramley-Moore 1848
Nelson 1848

Collingwood 1848
Salisbury 1848
Trafalgar 1836

Stanley 1848
Clarence 1830

Bidston 1933

Victoria 1836

Entrance
reconstructed
1949

Waterloo 1834

West float 1851

East float 1851

Princes
landing
stage

Princes 1821

LIVERPOOL

Alfred 1866

Vittoria 1909

Pier Head

Wallasey 1877

Canning 1929

Egerton 1847
Morpeth 1847

Albert 1845

Salthouse 1753

BIRKENHEAD

Kings 1781

Queens 1796

Coburg 1753

Camell, Laird & Co. Ltd

Brunswick 1832

Toxteth 1884

Tranmere
oil stages
1860

Harrington 1883

Herculaneum 1864

Tanker cleaning berth

Oil instalations

Dingle oil jetty

control. Other ports, such as Southampton, had all the better cards dealt by nature: its tidal range, its harbour and the space to expand. These allowed it to move quickly into the increasingly important and growing container traffic. Liverpool's Seaforth/Gladstone docks complex had room to expand away from the older docks trapped between the upwards sloping shore and river. But Seaforth's prospects were less auspicious than Southampton and, later, Felixstowe and Dover, although it did well enough. Its container traffic grew from 50,000 units in the early 1980s to 400,000 ten years later and 600,000 in 2004. But that success could not prevent Liverpool from slipping from second to sixth, between 1966 and 1986, in the UK rankings. Its container trade was also only one tenth that of Rotterdam.[14] Liverpool's location still give it an advantage in trading with Ireland and the Americas, but not with Europe. Trade patterns were shifting against the Mersey. But there were other targets easier to blame, human ones and closer to home: the Mersey Docks and Harbour Board and the dockers. Both would also blame Edward Heath's government as the crisis deepened towards the end of December 1970 and into 1971.

Following the announcement of the closure of the South End docks by the end of 1972, the board reported that the Albert, Canning and Salthouse Docks would be filled in under a £4 million scheme funded by Harry Hyams, a property developer. That would have substantially eased the board's financial burdens. However, just after Christmas reports were circulating that Hyams' 'Aquarius City' development of tower office blocks, shops, restaurants, and a maritime museum was in danger. Hyams was planning to pull out. He did so on 1 January 1971, as Liverpool was well into its New Year celebrations.

This unfortunate and suspiciously swift turnaround was not of the board's making, and in any case it made sense to try to raise money from its stock of valuable development land. In time, the three dock site was successfully developed. That would include the Albert Dock's historic warehouses to form shops, restaurants and a maritime museum, thanks largely to the otherwise little-loved Merseyside Development Corporation. Later the new 'Tate Gallery in the North' came to the site, carrying the famous name of the sugar baron who had joined the nineteenth-century exodus of Liverpool's merchants to London. His money went with him, and his successors, in 1981, were to close the famous Love Lane sugar plant. As some recompense, by the 1990s his name and fame were helping Liverpool to consolidate its new-found enthusiasm for art, culture and tourism.

The Mersey Docks and Harbour Board became the first and easy target for attack. Formed in 1857, it had been accompanied by acute controversy at its birth.[15] Its statutory origins, and membership, were not there to encourage dynamism. Its membership was designed to balance the interests of merchants, shipowners, and port users, potentially making difficult or clear-cut decisions more difficult. It was also created by Act of Parliament, which required it to seek statutory authority to make most major decisions or increase its powers. The biggest decision it did make – to close the entire South End docks by the end of 1972 – did seem to many both drastic and premature. That could be blamed on the government for refusing to rescue the port. But the resignation and replacement of the chairman and his deputy (Joseph Taylor and Alderman Cleary – both Liverpool men) by an 'industrial and City rescue-squad'[16] smacked of favouring London financial interests against the port's future and local jobs. The bondholders were indeed putting pressure on the board for the redemption of their 'paper', worth £6 million on the due date, 31 December 1970. There was also widespread criticism of the decision to raise river rates (such as those for navigational facilities and dredging aids for ships sailing to ports up the river) and dues for ships using the docks. The increases were large, 44 per cent and 25 per cent respectively.[17] This could be seen as driving essential trade away at a critical time. In its defence the board could point to its heavy capital debt to finance long-term investment.[18] But, despite the board's rescue measures, during 1971 the financial crisis continued to cloud the future for the docks, even though the dockers working under the Devlin reforms were enjoying the best times any of them had seen. But the continuing employer pressure to cut the numbers employed was ominous for the future and made worse by the financial crisis.

It was difficult in those early years of the 1970s to report any good news. In May 1971 it was even announced that the iconic New Brighton ferry was to be closed at the end of the summer season. In 1953 the ferry had carried 3 million passengers. By 1971 the forecast for the year was 250,000 – one twelfth of the 1953 figure.[19] The one bright bit of news was the opening of the second Mersey Tunnel, this time to Wallasey, on 9 June 1971. It was opened by the queen, but to be known as the 'Kingsway' Tunnel. (The first had been the 'Queensway', opened by the then king, George VI.) The two tunnels made it even easier to get to and from the Wirral by car, as car ownership continued to grow. But the tunnels did nothing for New Brighton, the 'Last Resort', as it dwindled into insignificance, overwhelmed by more sophisticated times and the lure of the overseas and exotic at no extra cost. It had been a slow death. Long before, its own tower, rivalling that of Blackpool, had to be pulled down because of disrepair. In the year the ferry closed even its landing stage collapsed, battered by ferocious waves from the estuary. It was all a cause for sadness among those Liverpudlians who remembered happy outings in difficult times. A more tangible and immediate sadness was the loss of 300 jobs in the town itself, now a negligible employer, when only six years earlier it had found work for 3,000.[20]

Meanwhile, back in Liverpool, the board was announcing its plan to sell off its historic building at the Pier Head, one of the 'three graces', for £1 million. Then, towards Christmas 1971, the dockers, unusually reticent until then, criticised the board for mismanagement. As one docker said: 'The Board are not our employers. Yet when they get into trouble we get the blame.'[21] Nor were the dockers happy, as ever, with the union, which seemed to be on the other side in the person of Harry Wall, the TGWU's regional secretary who was to keep his seat on the newly reconstituted board.

The dockers did, however, have some reasons to be satisfied, if they ignored what was taking place at the board. In March 1971 local reports were coming in that record numbers were looking for work at the docks – the most since casualism ended four years earlier. Pay was seen to be good at £40 (£425) for a 45-hour week, and there was enviable job security at a time when unemployment was ominously on the rise: in January the official rate for Merseyside, the highest in seven years, reached 4.6 per cent as Lew Lloyd, the union's district docks' secretary, reflecting on the numbers asking him about work at the docks, was telling the *Daily Post* that 'I never knew I'd got so many friends!'[22] At the same time, dockers wishing to leave the industry after 1972–73 had access to good compensation under a redundancy scheme negotiated by Lord Aldington, for the employers, and Jack Jones for the TGWU. The average age of the labour force was high and, inevitably, too many went for the scheme. Liverpool lost 2,800 dockers out of a declining labour force provoking, ironically, a labour shortage crisis, with ships being diverted from the Mersey at the rate of fifty a month.[23] The dock labour shortages even coexisted alongside company closures and redundancies. James Bibby & Son, which had been trading in Liverpool since the early part of the nineteenth century, announced the closure of its animal feedstuffs division with the loss of 400 jobs.

Some did not see the dockers as blameless for Liverpool's plight. Hyde was critical, pointing to the impact of the early post-war disputes and the disruptive effects upon the board's finances of the 1955 inter-union stoppages of the NASD and TGWU. He had equally strong words, however, for the seamen.[24] Their series of strikes in the 1950s and 1960s culminated with the big one in the summer of 1966 (the season of England's World Cup triumph) which closed nearly all the ports. The Liverpool seamen were even singled out at the time by Prime Minister Harold Wilson, local Labour MP for Huyton, as '… a band of Communist agitators holding the country to ransom'.[25] A Labour backbencher representing Toxteth, Richard Crawshaw, was targeting the dockers five years later, during the financial crisis, blaming them for driving away ships and business from the port, losing jobs and contributing to the board's already acute problems.[26]

These critics were right to point to the severe disruptive impact of strikes, especially unofficial ones, on the dockside and on shipping. Britain was also a country of many alternative ports, some of which were growing in access and size such as the non-scheme ports which began to improve their facilities and invest in new equipment. The diversion of ships was not difficult to do, even by companies that had been operating into and out of Liverpool for generations. The dockers were also undoubtedly 'strike prone', statistically well ahead of the miners, even on standardised measures.[27] Liverpool dockers were also often the most prominent, compared to other ports, in being the first out and the last to go back. In its frequency of strikes Liverpool was also often compared to London. Liverpool was ahead, even though by not much, and both were ahead of the rest.[28] London, like Liverpool, also had its own powerful unofficial workers' organisation, the Royal

Docks Liaison Committee led by the charismatic, media prominent, Jack Dash, who was involved in every dispute from 1955 until he retired in 1970. He was also influential outside London, helping to coordinate the unofficials' policies and tactics on a national basis, and he was a frequent, well-known visitor to Liverpool.

Why were Dash and his successors, and his counterparts in Liverpool, such as Jimmy Nolan,[29] so influential? They were often portrayed by the press, employers and politicians (and even by some senior fellow trade unionists) as 'agitators'. For James Sexton, no actual agitator himself, it was even used as a term of pride in the title of his autobiography.[30] But Dash, unlike Sexton, was a member of the Communist Party, then banned from holding office in the TGWU. Yet Communists, though they often attracted respect and admiration along the waterfront for their dedication to the men's interests, had little intellectual following among dockers for their ideology and politics, much like the old syndicalists before the Great War. What seemed important was that they touched a nerve, reminding the dockers of the old ways as they were being challenged by reformers, politicians, their own union and employers. Bevin, the popular hero of the Shaw Report and as Minister of Labour in war had even promised, in 1942, that the 'old ways' would be restored after the war. The war concentrated minds, but the promise was not unimportant even if Bevin had no intention of keeping it.

The old ways did not go away in 1947, and nearly twenty years later Devlin was berating them for their irresponsibility and addiction to solidarity. These, he believed, needed to be curbed in the national interest which meant, in practice, that dockers had to be mindful of the needs of the economy, which meant not going on strike, especially unofficially. This was the *economic* case for decasualisation. In reducing strikes it would help the economy. Social reformers, such as Eleanor Rathbone, pressed the *social* case. She was one of the social engineers of the waterfront who saw regular ways and regular pay as the salvation of the dockers and their families. When the union joined in, as it had done since James Sexton and Ernest Bevin before the war, seeing decasualisation as a form of liberation, the dockers were still not impressed, not least when their officials happily sat down with employers, on the local dock labour boards, to regulate and discipline their working lives and, as in Liverpool, to accept a seat on the Mersey Docks and Harbour Board. As Phillips and Whiteside put it, writing in 1985:

> In retrospect, we can see that rising rates of militancy were due less to the particular incidents sparking off a dispute than to the changing structure – and nature – of managerial authority which led to stricter discipline ... reinforced by the sense of solidarity which had long typified industrial relations on the waterfront.[31]

The old ways were also being defended by older men. The short period in the early 1970s when sons were following their fathers into good jobs on the waterfront was eventually reversed, as the proportion of dockers over 50 began to increase.

By 1978 it was over a third. Ten years later it was approaching a half.[32] The jobs had also begun to go. In 1967, the year of Devlin, total UK dock employment was 60,000. In 1970 it was 47,000, and in the abolition year, 1989, it was 18,000.[33] Liverpool followed the same path under the same influences of changing trade patterns, mechanisation and containerisation. In 1971 there were 10,500 working on the Liverpool waterfront. After the closure of the South Docks it was 7,500 and in 1989 barely topped 1,000.[34]

Containerisation was the major killer of jobs. It also largely eliminated skills that had been acquired through long experience. At its most extreme the reduction in labour requirements compared to the old methods was as high as 90 per cent. In terms of skill, a senior TGWU official responsible for docks and waterways contrasted stowage under the old methods as 'weaving a fabric of cargo'; stowing containers he saw as little different from 'stacking bricks of equal size'.[35] In terms of hours required to load and unload vessels, a conventional 11,000-ton cargo liner needed 10,584 hours to load and unload. An equivalent-sized container ship needed only 546 hours.[36] Such a dramatic undermining of jobs and skills, and its implications for costs, profits and control, was so good for employers that they could not contemplate failure to implement the new methods. The dockers fought, as they always did, but not to resist containers – they were already there to a large extent, in big ports such as Southampton and Liverpool. They struck for the right to fill the containers (i.e. 'stuff' them) and also to unpack them (i.e. 'strip' them). Stuffing and stripping were the new battleground, but this time they would lose. The employers were too determined and had willing allies in government, the courts, the media and public opinion.

Liverpool's own container revolution focused largely upon the new terminal at Seaforth.[37] That would eventually begin to turn its early losses into solid profits and largely rescue Liverpool as a going, commercial concern. But its container technology offered few jobs, and Seaforth was a long way from the old heartlands of the waterfront. There the firms supplying the insatiable needs of the big cargo liners for 'sacks, boxes, paint, rope, slings and sack hooks' as well as those offering maintenance, ship repairs and supplying food and clothing for the crews gradually went out of business. They were followed by the pubs, the 'cocoa' rooms and shops as customer numbers fell, and doors were closed reluctantly for the last time. Technological change also affected the size of crews and the time they were in port.[38] So 'sailortown'[39] went the same way as dockland, with jobs and people disappearing, their houses demolished as they moved to new houses, flats and maisonettes a long way from their old haunts. Nor was the job malaise confined to dockland. Manufacturing, Liverpool's once bright response to the decline of the port, was beginning to turn into yet another false dawn.

From boom to bust

Liverpool's economic vulnerability was understood well, even in earlier times. For many years the big profits were to be made from docks and shipping; these activities pushed alternative commercial operations away, typified by the case of the well-established Herculaneum pottery, remembered in the name of the now closed dock that had been constructed on the site.[40] Land for docks, as we have seen, was not just the first priority; it was the only priority. Ship-building hung on until the end of the nineteenth century, by which time Birkenhead had seized its chance with Laird's yard, later Cammell Laird.

Liverpool's reliance upon trade through the port was recognised as a problem. It was severe enough for shock therapy to be applied between the wars. The great port city was particularly hit by the downturn in trade unlike any time in its history and more than other UK ports. The damage and destruction of the Second World War also concentrated minds to the pressing need for Liverpool to have an industrial base, an insurance policy against the trade cycle or even secular decline in its trade. In 1945 the statistics told their own story. Fifty-two per cent of employment in the UK was in manufacturing, with 23 per cent in transport and distribution. On Merseyside the figures were 35 per cent manufacturing and 44 per cent in transport and distribution. Even the industries and firms linked to the port, including those that processed the imported raw materials such as tobacco, flour and sugar – processed by Ogden, Rank and Tate & Lyle – were essentially locked into maritime Liverpool as maritime Liverpool was locked into them, both vulnerable to the world trade cycle, shifting patterns of demand, and commodity price movements. Fortunately tobacco, flour and sugar were for long sustained by rising demand, but even that eventually turned against Liverpool. These companies, who were large employers of labour, were also mainly dockland located, their problems adding to the already dwindling demand for dock labour. Many of the alternatives for jobs, located mainly away from the river, were also linked to Liverpool's traditional, traded commodities. Flour and sugar were the raw materials for biscuits (Crawford) with sugar for sweets (Barker and Dobson) and jam (Hartley). Bryant & May's famous matches were made from timber brought from the Baltic which had been unloaded along the waterfront for at least two hundred years.[41]

In 1945 no British port had an economic structure like that of Liverpool. Even then Britain still had a lingering claim to be the 'workshop of the world'. Liverpool, meanwhile, still have ambitious plans. These came to fruition in the 1960s, with government and local authority support, at a time when the port was also doing well, further stimulated by the trade flow to and from the new industries. In the financial year 1964–65, 28.25 million tons of cargo passed through Liverpool, a record, and even the South End docks were seen by the board as a thriving part of the dock estate,[42] all justifying the total £36 million of investment for modernisation. That figure included the planned new dock at Seaforth.

The city centre map was also being redrawn by the Corporation, including new link roads and overpasses. Elsewhere, the Beatles and other bands and singers were putting Liverpool on the map in other ways. It became the celebrated focus of national, even world attention. Yet, within five years, Liverpool's existence as a major port was to be in doubt. At the same time, a second blow perhaps even more severe was the rapid, almost total collapse of Liverpool's industrial and manufacturing sector, what had only quite recently been the confident source of jobs, security, hope and optimism.

Early initiatives in the 1930s towards expanding Liverpool's manufacturing base were stimulated by government legislation. The Corporation promoted the development of suburban industrial estates such as those at Speke, Huyton and Aintree. The war added a further stimulus, with the government locating significant production, in munitions, armaments and aero-engines, in Liverpool and greater Merseyside. After the war these industries were converted to civilian use as the pre-war sites were further developed and others created, such as the large industrial and residential estate at Kirkby, formerly a large royal ordnance factory. Then there was even better news. In 1949 Merseyside was named a development area, a focus for inward investment. This in particular stimulated the manufacturing sector. The marriage of government support and corporation action was a good one. Merseyside already had some famous names, going back to between the wars, such as Littlewoods, Meccano, and Hornby. Others now joined them, such as Kodak and Albright and Wilson and, later in a 'second wave', Bird's Eye, AC Spark Plugs, English Electric, Fisher Bendix, Kraft Foods, Otis Elevator and Yorkshire Imperial Metals. Speke was an especially important area for jobs; soon it was employing about 13,000. The siting of the penicillin factory there in 1944 was the beginning of major investment by pharmaceutical firms, including Glaxo. In all there was a total gain of around 40,000 jobs on Merseyside, but this was only just sufficient to compensate for the loss of jobs along the waterfront and in port-related industries.[43] Soon things got even better as 'real' manufacturing came to the Mersey. The hard-headed bosses in the car industry, encouraged by government grants and the availability of land and local labour (at a time of national full employment) began to see Merseyside as a prime location. By 1965 'Britain's Detroit' was enjoying full employment and good times, although Liverpool was still the 'port city', the link between 'port' and 'city' not yet broken.[44]

The post-war economic boom did not endure long. As the 1960s turned into the 1970s, and the waterfront began to face acute crisis and serious decline, manufacturing industry also began to leave. The brief, golden age of full employment, economic growth and rising living standards ran out of steam as world oil prices quadrupled in 1973 under the strains of war in the Middle East. Liverpool, as always, suffered more than most cities. Between 1971 and 1984 manufacturing shed 95,000 jobs, more than half of total employment in the once booming industrial sectors. In 1978 British Leyland closed its Speke factory, putting 3,750 on the dole. The closure was preceded by a five-week strike, portrayed in the company's statements, as cause and effect. Strike-prone Liverpool workers were blamed for their own serious plight. It was obvious. Or was it?

The 'strike proneness' of the car workers ranked alongside that of dockers, coalminers and shipyard workers and, at the time, seafarers. Strikes were a general feature of the car industry, as common in Dagenham, Birmingham, Coventry or Glasgow as in Liverpool. Closure and threats of closure were just as universal, as an increasingly global industry played off one factory against another.[45] Port transport, as a whole, also had a consistently high incidence of strikes, often led by unofficial action. The roots of unofficial action were widely misunderstood and, as Jack Dash used to remind people, striking workers do not get paid. Striking was a serious matter. The seamen, too, were frequently charged with 'holding the country to ransom' as Lord Devlin was charging the dockers with 'irresponsibility' and 'solidarity'. Not all seamen were, of course, from Liverpool and the National Union of Seamen struck all ports in 1966, as Prime Minister Wilson was berating Liverpool's 'band of communist agitators'.[46] As a major exporting seaport and the 'swinging' City of Beatlemania, famous comedians, TV sitcoms and successful football teams, Liverpool attracted more than its fair share of press and media attention. For politicians, it was the seaport connection that mattered, at a time when the balance of payments, especially the export side, was a major electoral issue.

The causes of strikes are not always as obvious as they might appear. Analysis of the militancy record of dockers illustrates this well enough.[47] Some might well be triggered by the actions of the employers, who might even privately welcome them. In recessions stocks might need to be run down, while halting production, by means of a strike, might be a useful contribution. An efficiency drive, or deliberately aggressive tactics, can also provoke strikes.[48] In some circumstances, as in the 1995–98 dispute, it is easy to conclude that management's actions led to an immediate and predictable, unofficial reaction, making lawful dismissals possible and their replacement by compliant, contract labour. Detailed research on Liverpool as a whole supports these conclusions, as well as suggesting that Liverpool's strike-proneness was exaggerated.[49] Liverpool's militant image was actually no major deterrent to major movements of capital into the suburbs. So why did the industrial and manufacturing exodus out of Liverpool in the late 1960s and early 1970s match that in the opposite direction for the previous thirty years? Perhaps the most persuasive explanation lies in the dominance, among the newcomers, of manufacturing firms, the most liable to suffer from global recession. Mostly, too, these companies were trans-national and mobile, with allegiances other than in Liverpool. The Liverpool factories were branches[50] owned by companies with head offices in London, or abroad, more easily cut when recession struck. Investment could also be cut back, or delayed in local factories, so that when the market turned down, unacceptable productivity performance and lack of competitiveness could be added to poor industrial relations as the media-persuasive rationales for closure.

The loss of jobs and widespread, unfair condemnation in the media were difficult enough to bear. The new, modern, post-war houses were also failing to live up to promise. The quality of flats, in particular, came in for fierce criticism and protest, not only because people preferred houses with gardens or even the old backyards. The main targets were the high-rise tower blocks for their poor standard of workmanship and the long delays in completing essential repairs and maintenance. The tower blocks were given names such as 'Alcatraz', as the Corporation was bombarded about '... the dangers to children, ill-effects on mental health, conditions of paintwork, waste disposal, structural faults, poor landscaping and drainage of open space, vermin, lack of social facilities, transport difficulties and backlog of repairs'.[51] Alcatraz might have been better. In Liverpool the good life was literally falling apart. And soon, it would get worse.

Liverpool in free fall

In 1981 two companies, closely identified with Liverpool, closed their doors. Meccano[52] was world famous for its children's engineering construction kits as well as Hornby trains and Dinky cars. The construction kits were going out of fashion, and the toy cars went the way of their real, big brothers at British Leyland. The Liverpool factory's quality products were judged to be uncompetitive, despite the efforts of its workers, mainly women, who had probably not come across the term 'strike prone'. Earlier in the same year, on 22 January, cane sugar refining (its origins deep in Liverpool's historic though unsavoury trading relationship with the Caribbean) ceased in Liverpool. Tate & Lyle, well known for its proud, loyal, even docile workforce announced the closure of its Love Lane plant.[53] The refinery was in Vauxhall, a dockland area with a history, from the nineteenth century, of disease, poverty, malnutrition and underemployment.[54] Those days had long gone in 1981, though underemployment had made a comeback to be joined by chronic, long-term unemployment.

Meanwhile, the supposedly fearsome shop stewards at Ford's Halewood plant were unable to halt mass redundancies in the 1980s. Dunlop's workers, despite spirited resistance, saw all their jobs go in 1982;[55] but by then the reaction had already set in.

Then, in the long, hot summer of 1981, two weeks of rioting, looting and burning took place in Toxteth, an area crippled and lost beneath the socially corrosive effects of mass unemployment. Toxteth had once been a leafy suburb in the earlier part of the nineteenth century that had given its name to a dock, in the South End of the dock estate, which had opened in 1888 and closed in 1973. This eye-witness description of the 1981 rioting could have been from the Liverpool of May 1941:

> Outside the entire skyline is an angry crimson. Dense banks of black smoke hang threateningly above the rooftops ... Over by the Anglican Cathedral is

a colossal blaze ... Almost as huge is the conflagration in Parliament Street where there is a tyre factory and a couple of petrol stations ... Mass looting is taking place.[56]

By 1981 Toxteth had lost its long links with the docks and seafaring. Now it was just 'Liverpool 8', the impoverished, desperate home of unemployed black and white Liverpudlians, the focus of serious, national intervention, led by Michael (now Lord) Heseltine, from the non-interventionist Thatcher government. Other former dockland communities avoided rioting and burning, but they had already been destroyed by bulldozers rather than bare hands and flames.

Amid all the bad economic news, what of the port of Liverpool?

Limited economic activity continued in the North End docks as far as Gladstone Dock and the Seaforth Container Terminal. The Mersey Docks and Harbour Board had long owned the sands and land at Seaforth, and saw the new dock as the saviour of Liverpool's maritime fortunes. But the Seaforth Terminal, dramatically transforming the Seaforth Shore, was a long way from the heart of the old waterfront. Visitors would only see the Terminal, then as now, if they were travelling north towards Crosby and beyond to Southport. It seemed that though the Port of Liverpool, now no longer in Liverpool proper, would survive but in a truncated form, its physical and most of commercial links with the city gone for ever,[57] except for the less tangible form of its maritime and port 'heritage', developed to attract tourists and passengers from cruise liners and impress UNESCO and the judges of the European Capital of Culture award. Seaforth was, however, a bold plan and part of that long-term, strategic thinking that had characterised the construction of Liverpool's early docks. At the concept stage it was simply going to be a large, modern dock with the best facilities, but that was soon changed with the addition of a container terminal. Work began in 1967, when the port was still doing good business, even at the South End docks. The Mersey Docks and Harbour Company began its Seaforth operations in 1972 when the first ship entered the new harbour.

Before construction began, the board's officials, in the careful traditions of Jesse Hartley, had carried out preparatory surveys to predict future usage of the dock as well as a computer simulation to assess the impact on the river. The stone for the two-mile sea wall came from the purchase of a limestone quarry in Anglesey, the stone transported by sea. Gladstone Dock, built in 1927 and the last new venture before Seaforth, was incorporated into the system with an entrance cut into the Seaforth dock. The two docks were equipped with double gates, allowing water to be held at different levels, with Gladstone Dock to be used as a tidal basin. The development included a new grain terminal and silos, as well as four container berths and five new gantries specially designed for containers.[58] It was an ambitious venture, but the scale of the investment and the need to service the large interest payments kept the new dock complex long in the red. The eventual positive and major contribution to the port's revenue did not come on stream until years after the board itself had been replaced. The board's last director general was Bob Edwards. He had seen forty-three years' service and was disappointed to end his time with Liverpool in crisis. He was especially sad over the fate of the South End docks, which he saw as Liverpool's window on the Mersey. He hoped that they would be developed as housing for the people.[59]

One of the first consequences of the new régime was a steep fall in dock employment, slowly at first and then at a more rapid rate, just as Hyde had predicted in 1971.[60] In that year registered dock employment in Liverpool was 10,427. The closure of the South End docks was seen in the sharp drop, in 1973, to 7,550. At the beginning of the Thatcher era, in 1979, it stood at 5,202. Ten years later it was 1,100,[61] just before Parliament abolished the National Dock Labour Scheme. By a cruel irony, 1989 was also the centenary of the dockers' most successful industrial dispute, the Great London 'Dockers' Tanner' strike.

The 'sugar-coated bullet'[62]

From the outset the employers had only reluctantly accepted the National Dock Labour Scheme, and they had never come to terms with its requirement to share control with the unions. Under Harold Wilson the industry had perhaps come close to nationalisation, but the election of the Heath government in 1970 had buried the possibility. The idea would never again be disinterred, even after Labour returned to office in 1974. In any case Liverpool was not alone in its financial crisis, even though its problems in the 1970s were the most acute. Nationalisation meant underwriting the bills, not an attractive prospect for a government in the throes of combating rampant inflation, record levels of unemployment and, eventually, recourse to the International Monetary Fund.

The age profile of the dockers was also getting older as their numbers dwindled. Many would rather have worked, especially the older men, but accepted that the job was passing into history, including for their sons. There was also the Aldington-Jones agreement, offering voluntary redundancy settlements much better than they could have hoped for even a few years earlier. Writing in 1971 Phillips and Whiteside saw these factors at work even before Aldington-Jones: 'By the early 1970s, few men expected or wished their sons to follow them into a dying trade … The world of the dockside though it had not lost all its turbulence was more easily escaped.'[63]

The turbulence was certainly still evident in the early 1970s but, after 1975, the year of the final blacking of containers (at London and Hull) the number of strikes began to fall. Then, in 1976, came a failed attempt in Parliament to extend legally defined dockwork beyond the immediate vicinity of the waterfront. As recession hit the ports in the early 1980s, the scheme ports' profits turned into losses just as the employers were spending increasing amounts on severance payments. In 1980 the MDHC lost over £3.7 million, rising to £9.5 million in 1982. In that year the national severance scheme in the ports paid an individual maximum of £22,500.

By 1986, Liverpool and London were paying £35,000.[64] The scale of the Port of London's continuing losses throughout the 1980s was also beginning to attract predictions of possible financial collapse, as in Liverpool some fifteen years earlier. Unfavourable comparisons were also being drawn between the scheme ports and their non-scheme rivals as they continued to take increasing shares of port traffic away from the scheme ports.

The reasons for the success of ports such as Felixstowe and the decline of a port like Liverpool were many. Individual employers and the National Association of Port Employers put it down to the industrial peace along the Felixstowe waterfront compared to the always fractious, strife-ridden industrial relations on Merseyside. Some employers also believed it, and it was a widely held view beyond the industry. The truth was that if industrial peace, or its absence, is measured in terms of strikes, then the Liverpool dockers, above all, were reformed men, at peace with their employers. In the ten years up 1979, the average annual number of strikes was 43, approaching one per week. In the 1980s the annual average fell to 7, just over one every two months.[65] Nationally, in 1985 and 1986, the number of disputes at the docks was the lowest recorded for a generation. Much improved and regular pay, with a guaranteed fallback, as well as the ready availability of a redundancy package on improved terms, were significant factors in limiting the incidence of strikes. The severance money was also a route out of what now seemed, to many, a losing battle.[66] The employers also made good use of the severance option: by increasing the sums available, but with a deadline for it to be taken up, the employers found an effective tactic in both the 1989 national strike and, later, during the 1995–98 dispute in Liverpool.

Another significant factor in the lower incidence of strike action were the new employment and trade union laws enacted in the 1980s. The laws restricting trade union action were punitive and unprecedented. Even the amended Trade Disputes Act, which had followed the abandonment of the General Strike in 1926, had not seriously tampered with the original, landmark 1906 Act. In any case the Attlee government had restored trade union freedoms to the 1906 position, by legislation, in 1947. Now in the 1980s a series of new restrictions had a major impact both nationally and locally. A difficult, restrictive, staged procedure for balloting and calling strikes was introduced; these new hurdles were instrumental, in the case of the 1989 strike, in the lapse of the first mandate, requiring a repeat of the procedure. So-called secondary action was banned as strikes were confined to the place of work, while unofficial strikes, long a feature of the waterfront, were made unlawful. Furthermore, if they occurred, union officials were required to repudiate them formally, a duty enforceable by fines up to and including possible sequestration of union assets in the courts. These powerful sanctions against unofficial strikes could even be seen as tailor-made, by the government, for the waterfront. The TGWU was generally wary of being caught by the law in 1989, but far more so in 1995–98 in a local dispute that involved a complex mix of unofficial action, mass dismissals, a lock-out, and radical, new tactics by the dockers.

The government was therefore well prepared by 1989 to throw its weight behind the port employers. Before that, in 1984–85, it had used its resources and political influence to help a public sector employer, the National Coal Board, to defeat the miners. That was followed by similar treatment, though administered by private sector employers with government approval, for the printers working for the national newspapers. The dockers naturally feared that they would be next but, curiously, the government seemed to hesitate, and was even not fully convinced of the case for abolition of the scheme ports until the end of the 1980s. The government might well have paused before the latent industrial strength of the TGWU and the tradition of mass, unofficial, dockside action in the ports which, in practice, even the laws could not contain.

Meanwhile the port employers were going for broke. They saw their chance as, in a sustained, progressive campaign, they won the support of the majority of Conservative MPs for abolition. Nor could the government ultimately fail to resist temptation. Its almost messianic belief in unregulated labour markets (though of course with closely regulated trade unions) chimed closely with the NAPE's powerful call for a return to old times – for 'free' labour on the waterfront.

The arguments were initially joined at a parliamentary briefing. NAPE's detailed case for abolition was answered, largely through an effective, point-by-point written response from the Tilbury shop stewards.[67] Abolition, paradoxically, might even have been acceptable on the waterfront if a satisfactory alternative, such as locally negotiated agreements within a national framework, and bolstered by mutual trust, had been present. That alternative had never been genuinely acceptable to the employers and, from the beginning, NAPE and its predecessors had openly opposed and resented the very existence of the NDLB, culminating, in the 1980s, in local legal challenges to its authority. By the end of the 1980s the dockers saw the defence of the scheme ports as their only route towards some security of employment at a time when jobs were at a premium. Their resolve was probably increased by the dubious claims of Nicholas Finney, NAPE's director, that abolition would increase port employment, rather than reduce it.[68]

It was difficult to see where a solution could emerge. NAPE sought total abolition, not compromise. The TGWU argued for an extension of the scheme ports to all ports and a redefining of dock work to include 'stuffing and stripping' beyond port boundaries. The two sides were far apart, and a strike was now clearly inevitable. If the employers could provoke a national strike the government would most likely abolish the scheme ports. If the scheme ports was abolished, followed by a strike, then NAPE was confident that it could convince the government that it could win.[69] On 6 April 1989 the government announced its intention to abolish the National Dock Labour Scheme before the parliamentary recess three months later. On 7 April 2,800 dockers, a third of the registered labour force, walked out at eleven ports. London, Liverpool, Bristol and Southampton were among them, but not Hull. Hull's breaking of the ranks was especially disappointing, even ominous, for the strikers given its traditional militancy. Hull was later joined by a second major defector, Southampton. The unofficial action petered out within days. It was not well supported, and Rod Todd's instruction (the union's then general secretary) to return to work, was almost wholly followed. His main concern was that a national strike would be challenged by the employers in the courts as political, that is against the government's declared intention to abolish the scheme ports. The Employment Act of 1982[70] had narrowed trade union immunities during strike action, and banned 'political' action. Even the frequently dissident local leadership, the National Ports' Shop Stewards' Committee, fell into line on Todd's fears and his preference for the legal route. The employers would take note of these fears, as well as, perhaps more importantly, the emerging cracks in the dockers' legendary solidarity. The abolition Bill, meanwhile, was passing through its parliamentary stages.

The strategy of using the law, supported by the union's National Docks Committee, included deferring the proposed strike ballot. This strategy was also strongly supported by the National Ports' Shop Stewards' Committee at a delegate conference. Those ranks, at least, were firm. The employers were also now playing hardball, moving away from their earlier overtures that had seemingly favoured a negotiated, national agreement after abolition. Although they gave assurances that there would not be a return to casual labour, and they would continue with the pension scheme, they proposed that after 1989 they would withdraw from the National Joint Council and disband the National Association of Port Employers. Future negotiations would be a matter for local port employers and the unions. The High Court did, however, bring some limited cheer to the TGWU. On 27 May it ruled that the proposed strike was not a 'political' action banned by the 1982 Act, but that it would nevertheless seriously damage the 'public interest'. This mixed blessing was compounded by the Court of Appeal on 8 June. It did not overturn the 'political' strike ruling, but instead concluded that the dockers were required to work under the statutory obligations of the scheme ports. Devlin would have concurred, but for reasons of duty, rather than law.[71] Though the Appeal Court duly gave the TGWU leave to appeal to the House of Lords, that would involve considerable delay and give time for the abolition Bill to receive the royal assent. A strike, in that context, was widely seen as having limited prospects, since it would be challenging the law of the land, seeking its repeal or amendment, a forlorn prospect under any government. Todd's faith in the law was now being severely tested as the patience of the shop stewards was wearing thin. As one Tilbury shop steward put it: 'We haven't jumped the gun; we've waited for too long. We have no intention of being slaves in chains.'[72]

On Saturday 10 June the National Ports' Shop Stewards' Committee called for an immediate, all-out strike. Fourteen ports came out, totalling 3,000, a third of all registered dockers. The support was better than in April, but still too low, and further weakened by the Hull, Southampton and Manchester dockers continuing to work. With its militant history and traditions, the decision of Hull was again a special disappointment to the Shop Stewards' Committee.[73] Within a week almost all the strikers were back at work, the only resistance coming from Liverpool, Garston and Tilbury, notably ports which had witnessed, at first hand, the impact of dock closures on jobs and communities. The shop stewards, like the once powerful unofficial movement before them,[74] had lost their way. The unofficial strike was called off on 19 June, the day before the House of Lords reversed the judgement of the Court of Appeal. The way was now clear for a second, official national ballot. The first ballot, on 19 May, had expired under the legislation, given the protracted delays arising from the union's preference for the legal option. The second was held on 7 July. The first ballot recorded three to one in favour of strike action, 90.8 per cent voting. The second had a near-identical turnout of 90.3 per cent, with the same three-to-one vote supporting action. The strike was set for Monday 10 July. Meanwhile the government announced that the Act's royal assent, scheduled for 16 July, was being brought forward to 3 July, a week before the strike was due to begin. Although the law judged the strike as not being a 'political' action, the government did not share its view, and it threw its considerable weight behind the employers, including £25 million to fund a 50 per cent contribution towards individual severance payments, paid according to length of service, with £35,000 after fifteen years. These payments were the key weapon in the employers' armoury, the 'sugar-coated bullet'.

The sugar on the bullet also came with an array of 'sticks'. Faced with dismissal, including some of the local shop stewards, many opted for redundancy. Some, arriving for work, had no option, finding a letter containing their redundancy notice and cheque. For those offered work, their new contracts were usually no more than an 'on-call' system, a return to a form of casual labour. Those with ostensibly 'fair' contracts, maintaining the terms and conditions of the abolished scheme, new manning levels and disciplinary procedures, were introduced without any consultation. The employers commonly even refused to meet shop stewards. The most extreme case was the derecognition of the TGWU by the Port of London Authority and the dismissal of the shop stewards.[75]

The mass acceptance of severance payments weakened the strike in terms of the numbers actually on strike as well as the resolve of those remaining in employment. Coupled with intimidation, it was a powerful cocktail. They also had to contend with strike-breaking and the growing ineffectiveness of picketing, by then weakened further by the law. Picketing was also rare, if at all, at non-scheme ports, most of which were working normally. Hence ships could be readily diverted away from militant ports such as Liverpool and Tilbury to those where the strike was limited, or non-existent, a return to the old days. At the same time, after Jack Dash, the powerful unofficial movement had virtually disappeared. By 1989 shop stewards, one of Jack Jones' key reforms, were well established on the docks. But though they often came from the ranks of the old unofficials and developed their own national organisation, and to an extent were rivals to the official leadership, they were not so effective as the old unofficial committees had been at local and national level; their influence frequently had forced the official leadership into action and, in effect, won concessions from the employers. Furthermore, through the 1980s, legislation progressively outlawed unofficial organisation, as well as weaken official unionism. Unofficial industrial action was finally placed outside the law in the Employment Act of 1990. Even before then the rank-and-file dockers had largely lost heart as they witnessed the defeat and disarray of once proud unions, including the steelworkers, the miners and the printers. Closer to home the seamen's numbers and influence declined, with 'flagging out' and the shrinking of the British Merchant Fleet as the National Union of Seamen was absorbed into the reconstructed railway union, the RMT (Road, Maritime and Transport).

By 31 July, at the beginning of the fourth week of the strike, the number out on strike had fallen by a half from the previous week, leaving 2,745 still on strike. This number was exceeded by those – 2,812 in all – who had accepted redundancy terms. And the strikers were easily outnumbered, too, by the 3,684 dockers still working.[76] On the same day, the Hull and Southampton men voted to return to work. By then there was little left of the early resolve that had been signalled by the overwhelming votes in the two ballots. The next day, 1 August 1989, the executive met and voted, by eighteen votes to twelve, to call off the strike. Stormy meetings at the most militant ports – Liverpool, Bristol and Middlesbrough – berated Ron Todd and his colleagues for mishandling the strike and then ending it in a 'sell-out'. They were accused of calling the strike when it was essentially unwinnable. That was mainly put down to Ron Todd's insistence on going to the courts, with the inevitable delays, allowing the abolition Bill to become law. It would have been to the dockers' advantage, it was argued, if the scheme ports and the NDLB had still been in existence.

On 7 August Ron Todd and John Connolly, the national secretary of the TGWU Docks' Group, arrived in Liverpool for a mass meeting at the Liverpool Stadium. It was carefully managed to limit dissent from the floor. But some had already returned to work that morning.[77] The vote to return was inevitable; in the end it was by the big margin of two to one. Shelley's famous truism to workers that 'you are many, they are few' no longer applied with the same force on the waterfront. In 1989 there were 9,200 dockworkers. Only nine months later more than half, some 5,200, had gone. By 1991 the total leaving the industry had grown to 6,500, leaving a total dock labour force of 2,700. Liverpool and Birkenhead, their once vast army of labour sometimes exceeding 25,000, had shrunk to a combined total of 1,225. Two years later, in 1991, redundancies had taken that figure down to 520. Summary mass dismissal was also by then available, including for a refusal to work overtime, as managerial power demonstrated four years later at Seaforth. As one employer cruelly, though correctly, observed, '... The party is over'.[78] To those at the working end it undoubtedly was. But there was one battle left. Surprisingly it was a closer run thing than that of 1989.

The last stand: the 1995–98 dispute

The last stand for the dockers was a long-running, bitter dispute at Seaforth that lasted twenty-eight months, from September 1995 to January 1998. At its peak it had considerable national support from the wider labour movement (but not the unions) and, eventually, wide international support in both money and action, including from dockers in other countries stopping work, sometimes at the direct instigation of Liverpool men on their picket lines or demonstrating at dock entrances. Ships were delayed and, for a month, the important operator, Atlantic Containers Ltd, ceased sending its ships into the Mersey. The global, interdependent, maritime industry, despite its mobility, also revealed itself vulnerable to co-ordinated international action in the ports, especially those with container terminals. The first stage of such a possibility was demonstrated on 20 January 1997[79] when 100 ports around the world held rallies and marches on an international day of action in support of the Liverpool dockers. The international dimension of support was also made easier by the extensive use of the internet,[80] not for the first time in industrial relations disputes, but perhaps now essential for workers involved in actions across countries. At the first international conference, held in Liverpool for a week in February 1996, fourteen countries sent 53 delegates, and it is estimated that in the first six months of the dispute Liverpool dockers addressed 2,500 meetings, including many in other countries. It is also estimated that the average debt accumulated by each docker and his family was £20,000. Four of them also died during the dispute, stress being adjudged a contributory factor. Their wives and families were also directly involved in the campaigns for the first time, and found their own independent voice with the Women of the Waterfront[81] organisation, with close parallels, though with much fewer involved, to the Women Against Pit Closures movement during the 1984–85 coalminers' dispute.

Unless the port of Liverpool could be genuinely threatened with standstill and the diversion of its trade, none of the action or support, in the end, would prove to be enough. Atlantic Conveyors staying away for a month was only a beginning. Liverpool was able to find replacement labour throughout the entire dispute, just as the employers had done in the old days by using a depot ship of strike-breakers anchored on the river. Even so, the dockers, their wives and families had come closer to a victory than they thought possible. Yet they might also have observed, wry realists all, that even close-run things do not put hot dinners on the table. Yet although much was novel about the way the long dispute was conducted, its origins were familiar and it revealed all the ingredients which had characterised conflict on the Liverpool docks and, to a limited extent all docks, for at least a century.

The Liverpool dockers had never really accepted the verdict of 1989. The MDHC also seemed to want to try to restore a reasonable working relationship with the TGWU and the shop stewards on the waterfront. The stewards had

Marching in Stockholm. International solidarity, with Liverpool men and women travelling to ports worldwide, and with return visits to Liverpool, was made easier by the ready availability of modern forms of transport and use of the internet.

not been dismissed, as elsewhere, and trade union presence and representation remained reasonably intact. There were even the 'guarantees' of the government, in 1989, to ensure no return to the casual system and the maintenance of pay, benefits and pension rights.[82] But there were ominous signs, as early as 1989, as the National Association of Port Employers pulled out of national bargaining and dissolved itself, so ending any national bargaining. In Liverpool, the MDHC followed suit by removing any negotiating or representational roles for the Merseyside Port Shop Stewards' Committee. That decision specifically excluded Jimmy Nolan and Jimmy Davies though, in fact, the Liverpool dock employers did not refuse to meet them before and during the 1995–98 dispute.

The decentralised structure divided cargo-handling into 'five discrete business units' – containers, timber, ferries (Norse Irish and Pandoro), grain and general cargo – in each of which the TGWU had recognition, bargaining and representation rights, with each unit '... separately and independently represented'.[83] The MDHC was also anxious to stress that agreements with the TGWU gave elected shop stewards '... no right to participation in the representative structures within the Company'.[84] This structure did, of course, confine union influence within each unit, weakening it and allowing for the possibility of easier, piecemeal, derecognition. The company also maintained that the Merseyside Port Shop Stewards' Committee, which it did not recognise, had never acknowledged the abolition of the National Dock Labour Scheme. In contrast, the company claimed, the union and the 'overwhelming majority' of the workforce had accepted the reality of abolition.[85]

As we have seen, by the early 1970s the dockers had at last achieved good pay, security, benefits and some improvement in working conditions. Though there were much fewer of them by 1989, it was still important for them to try to defend the gains of a century of struggle. The Liverpool men held out in 1989 and were surely entitled to believe that they could at least salvage something from the wreckage. Nor did their actions say anything else. A series of unofficial, short stoppages, up to five days in one case, bedevilled Liverpool's industrial relations in the years up to the beginning of the big dispute in 1995. One of these, in July 1992, arose out of the transfer of employment contracts from MDHC to Pandoro, a roll-on, roll-off operation. The men wished to remain with MDHC as a right, a demand MDHC saw as trying to return informally to the old rules for former registered dock workers under the abolished scheme.[86] In that the employer was probably right.

The MDHC was, of course, not the only employer in the Port of Liverpool, even though it, and its employees, had close working relationships with the other companies. It also owned the dock estate and therefore had influence in, though it was not a party to, all contractual arrangements, a significant factor in ultimate control. By 1995 there were nineteen[87] employers listed, including three who would play a significant role in the 1995–98 dispute: Torside Ltd, PDP Services and Drake Port Services.

On abolition of the scheme in 1989 many of the smaller, non-viable companies in the port had collapsed, with the MDHC taking over their employees. Historically, the company and the board had never wished to be large employers of dockside labour. They did, of course, have their own, specialised, salaried staffs, some very senior, such as harbour masters, as well as dockgatemen and lockkeepers. Hence external companies supplying labour was seen as a necessary supplement to their own, limited, direct employment. This requirement saw the emergence of Torside Ltd in 1991, founded by Bernard Bradley[88] and Tommy Hendrick. Both had been dockers, though Bradley had worked previously for Ford where he was elected as a convenor. He also was an active trade unionist at the docks. Both took redundancy in 1989 and, supposedly, used their compensation to set up Torside. Torside's initial credibility was also helped by the status of Bernard Bradley as an ex-docker and a formerly active trade unionist. The TGWU officials saw advantages in this as a condition towards better labour relations, including the avoidance of casual employment. Torside, however, in its terms and conditions, compared unfavourably with the MDHC as well as those of the recently defunct scheme and its registered dock workers. Torside's pay levels were below those of the MDHC; nor were pensions introduced; sick pay was not available; and employment security carried limited guarantees, even though employment was regulated by permanent contracts. Nothing seemed guaranteed after 1989. So it was not surprising that a dispute began to simmer over moves for redundancy.

Total full-time employment at Torside had reached 80 when agreement was reluctantly conceded by the dockers over the employment of part-timers on the same terms and conditions. This was soon followed, as the dockers feared, by redundancy proposals for full-timers. That was inevitably resisted, with a positive ballot for strike action, although it was not actually called. Mutual distrust continued to simmer. An overtime dispute then took it to breaking point.

Overtime at Torside was conventionally worked in two-hour blocks after 4 p.m. That day, 25 September 1995, two supervisors (both from MDHC not Torside) instructed the men to stay on after 4 p.m., although the instruction was after the time set by agreement. More importantly, the extra hours were not to be paid at the usual overtime rates. Five of the twenty men in the ship refused to work under these terms, and left the ship for the canteen to change and go home. Bernard Bradley, unusually, was in the canteen. He dismissed the men summarily for refusing to return to work. The remaining fifteen supported the refusal of the five to return and they, too, were dismissed. The next day Torside's remaining employees were dismissed, bringing the total to 80. Two days later the dismissed dockers were picketing the MDHC's main gate to the Terminal. The dispute had taken on a wider, even more dangerous dimension.

The decision to picket the Terminal entrance was a difficult one, taken with much hesitation. It was made more difficult by Jack Dempsey, the union's Regional Secretary for Docks and Waterways, being unable to contact Bernard Bradley, the employer, who had reportedly left the site and was by then said to be in Bristol.

The picket at the Seaforth Terminal. In the 1980s picketing was limited, by law, to six persons and only those directly involved in the dispute. By 1995–98 picketing was, therefore, no more than a token activity.

PHOTOGRAPH: AUTHOR

At a meeting on the evening of 28 September, in the presence of the port shop stewards Jimmy Nolan and Jimmy Davies, a vote was passed to mount a picket the next morning, 28 September 1995.

MDHC employed, at that time, for all grades a total of more than 1,200, of which 390 were engaged directly on dockwork operations. Many were related to the Torside pickets. A total of 329 refused to cross the picket line on 28 September. The company's ultimatum to return to work on the 29th was refused, and dismissals followed. The Seaforth Container and Timber Terminals stopped work in consequence. The following day MDHC offered reinstatement for 200 of its employees, but was not prepared to offer work to the former Torside men, whose employer had now ceased trading. The limited offer was refused, but within a week, on 9 October, the MDHC dockers, on legal advice, voted to return to work.

The company rejected any return.[89]

Thus began the longest dispute, by far, in the history of Liverpool's dockland and perhaps its most significant, certainly its most far-reaching, in its progress. It was ultimately lost because the company was able to use two labour supply companies, PDP Services and Drake Port Distribution Services, to maintain the port's labour requirements, the former providing what was essentially casual labour, the latter, additionally, 'permanent replacements' on the US model.[90] The TGWU maintained that it did its best, throughout, offering advice and negotiating expertise at all levels. This was in default of full support on the grounds that its members at MDHC had taken unofficial action, putting the union in jeopardy of legal claims by the employers, with heavy financial penalties.[91] Somewhat paradoxically, the union had insisted on taking the legal route prior to the 1989 strike; six years later it was claiming to be in peril of the law. But the more accurate and telling contrast was with 1911. Then the strike committee could rely on solidarity throughout all the ports, as well as on Merseyside, to keep strike-breakers from delivering victory for the employers. In 1995 the world of the waterfront was very different. By the autumn of 1997 support was evaporating everywhere. The dockers were forgotten as New Labour returned to power, with drums and fanfares, after almost a generation out of office. When last in power, under James Callaghan, in 1979, it was inconceivable that anybody, even the Tories under Thatcher, could abolish the National Dock Labour Scheme, one of the pillars of the post-war settlement, and to do so within the decade.

There was still a great deal of the old about the events of the 1995–98 strike; in some ways they have a familiar, old cinematic quality, in flickering black and white. Tom Mann could have been there, albeit this time without troops on the streets or warships moored on the Mersey. There was all the old natural drama and frequent poignancy, but much had changed, including the spectacular emergence of the women as important new players, the creative use of the internet, and the remarkable extent and latent power of the wide, international support in many countries. But old fears and uncertainties still ruled men's lives. Insecurity was back on the waterfront, as it had not been in many years, as casualism was beginning to return, along with part-time and temporary work and heavy supervision. Many old things and old ways were returning to the employment agenda. Redundancy was also still being talked of despite the spectacular falls in manpower by 1989 and beyond. Even when work was not casual, employers always sought flexibility and mobility. No job seemed safe, or even its pay and conditions, as the MDHC rejected the old dock board's acceptance of its role as the 'employer of last resort' in favour of smaller, less secure firms, paying few benefits and rarely pensions. Workers had no trust in their employers in a way that they had never had before. Employers, in their turn, could not trust their employees or even their direct representatives, the shop stewards. The stewards, were also at loggerheads with the union's officials, at all levels, as the rank-and-file found it easy to support and follow those representatives who had worked with and for them, directly, along the waterfront and beyond, for up to forty years.

As an organisation and collection of full-time officers, the union did not come well out of the dispute. It had earned the opprobrium of the men, especially the general secretary, Bill Morris, whose public statements belied his actions. He might have had no option and he, and his officials, *did* try to broker reinstatement deals, although no proposal ever offered all the jobs back. Union negotiators are used to having to accept compromises which may be seen as 'shabby' to those who are not caught between resolute employers, with the whip hand, and indignant union members.

Anything less than full reinstatement, however unrealistic, was unacceptable to the men, given the length and intensity of the dispute and their tradition of solidarity. It was actually alleged that, at one point when the dispute was going in favour of the sacked dockers, Jack Dempsey, the union's Region 6 Docks and Waterways Secretary (which covered Liverpool), had been offered full reinstatement, but that had not passed this offer on. This might have been no more than a groundless rumour, but it did have some credibility, and there remained a strong belief that the union could have pressed the men's case with much greater vigour, even allowing for possible legal sanctions. Nor would sanctions necessarily follow. They would still require the employers to activate them in the courts, and it was never inevitable that that step would be taken. Winning the dispute was one thing: seriously damaging the TGWU financially was another. Yet whatever the options, the union was now a spent force on the Liverpool docks, as elsewhere in UK ports. At the time of writing the single Docks Branch (it once had five, one for each of the areas) has a reported membership of forty eight[92] out of a dockside workforce of, perhaps, fewer than a hundred. A long drawn-out legal action was also still progressing through the courts, on a no-win, no-fee basis, the sacked dockers suing the TGWU, in the person of Jack Dempsey, for misrepresentation.

The long dispute was a true 'last stand'. It touched moments of high drama, high principle, and near victory, but its end left strong and lasting feelings of bitterness and betrayal among those who had lost their jobs and, many, their futures. But what was always positive, and held to the end until broken by despair, was the traditional solidarity of the ordinary men. Though inexplicable to many, even well-meaning outsiders, it had always served them well in the past, provided it was total and enduring. It was also more than sentiment: it was often a winning hand. Lord Devlin, forty years earlier, had found fault with its enduring strength. But even the Torside dockers had themselves hesitated over the wisdom of their decision to picket the gates of the MDHC on 28 September 1995. That they did so put the onus on men, some fathers, even grandfathers, as well as uncles and brothers, to make supreme personal and family sacrifices over and above those who had loyalties to young members of their own families on the Torside picket line: 'all men being brothers', as James Sexton put it many years earlier.

It is very difficult for many to understand this kind of solidarity, and Lord Devlin was far from alone. Perhaps the last word should be that of an ex-Torside docker and shop steward, Bob Richie:

You can give nothing but praise for the men ... when they were all dismissed on that Thursday evening or afternoon when the couriers were running around with dismissal notices ... amazing we live in these nineties and they've got couriers giving out dismissal notices. I've got nothing but pride and admiration for every man who refused to cross that picket line. Because I remember that Thursday morning when we were standing there in the rain wondering, because you do, a lot of fears race through your mind: 'Are we doing the right thing?' Because don't forget what those men were giving up that day. They were giving up a severance that they refused to take in '89, a lump sum payment, the pensions, putting their job on the line for us. So what can you say? You can only say that you've got nothing but admiration for people prepared to do that for you.'[93]

CHAPTER FOURTEEN

The Leaving of Liverpool

Farewell to Lower Frederick Street,
Anson Terrace and Parkie Lane,
I'm bound for Californ-ia,
An' may never see you again.

(Sailors' song)

T H E   M E N   who in 1995–98 lost their livelihoods, financial entitlements and pensions were of all ages. Some had worked right through the transformation of dockwork over thirty years. Others had known no other than the new ways of working. The new docker is a technician, although technology dictates that there are now very few of them. He can handle cranes of all sizes, operate a variety of machines and drive an increasing number of specialised vehicles. He is younger, perhaps even fitter and stronger, relying less on experience, 'knack' and teamwork than on formal training. The old ways had passed away remarkably quickly. It took barely twenty years for the long, tried and tested methods of cargo handling, going back at least to the Phoenicians, to become obsolete. And with the dockers went many other jobs along the waterfront; the landscape changed, too, as did the way people lived. Gone are the ropemakers, the kit and tackle shops, the pubs, the cocoa rooms, the hostels, the dosshouses. Up from the Dock Road, towards Scotland Road and Stanley Road, once-crowded streets are mostly empty, rows of tightly packed terraced streets long gone under the bulldozer or the swinging steel ball. But it looks better: it *is* better. The streets down to the docks are no longer filled with belching vehicles; the air is cleaner; the houses are far more than barely fit to live in; there is more space in them; there is less reason for overcrowding ... but it is not dockland.

More enterprising Liverpudlians took their enterprise elsewhere, usually in search of work and a better life. Unlike in the sailors' song, however, relatively few would be bound for Californ-ia. Perhaps surprisingly, Liverpool's population had peaked in the depths of the Depression. In 1935 it stood at 867,000. In 1951, under post-war 'austerity', it was down to 791,000. Twenty years later, another big fall took it to 646,000. As the port and the new industries went from crisis to collapse it reached in 1981 — the year of the Toxteth riots — a new low of 510,000. It was to fall even further by 1991, to 430,000; though, in the better years to 2001, the population showed a small rise, to 439,500, In population terms Liverpool had fallen from the ranks of the big city to the medium-sized one. But by then things were beginning to look up again. They had to. Twenty years earlier plant closures, unemployment at 20 per cent, and urban dereliction on a frightening scale suggested a city '... in its death throes'.[1] Even if it survived, the common view was that '... the money-tide was going out and it was never coming in again'.[2] Liverpool people had to stop looking backwards, said one old woman, a resident of Athol Street, though she doubted if they could expect anything better:

> There's too much of the past ... we've had our lives and there's no going back is there? It's the young ones I feel sorry for, they don't even seem to have any going forward.[3]

Yet, as Liverpool entered the new millennium, the tide seemed to have turned. Employment was growing faster than in other comparable cities, and there seemed to be some prospect that Liverpool's negative image — as a city of chronic, high unemployment — was beginning to fade. The 20 per cent rate of unemployment seen in the 1980s had come down to just 4 per cent in 2003.

Liverpool began to rebuild and regenerate, in earnest, in the 1990s. The initiatives came mostly from within but, somewhat ironically, most of the investment money came from the European Union. The irony was that membership of the EU had been widely seen as one of the reasons for the decline in the fortunes of the port. Now the EU's structural funds were coming to Liverpool's aid. In 1989 the city secured Objective Two status and, from 1993, Objective One.[4] This substantial lifeline, with extra money from central government and with local government in partnership, provided a platform for major initiatives. Private finance soon followed as Liverpool was becoming an example to follow in urban regeneration and development rather than one to avoid. The process was also wide-ranging. It included cultural development in all its forms, restoring and rebuilding to housing art exhibitions, cinemas and concert venues. The Albert Dock found a new role as a home for the Maritime Museum, luxury apartments, and as a potential tourist trap. The Dock's Tate Liverpool, complementing the original gallery on London's Millbank and Tate Modern in Southwark, pointed to a new, metropolitan confidence in Liverpool as a viable, regional centre for art and the arts. It also did a little to redress the psychological shock of the closure of Tate & Lyle's Love Lane factory, even though the sugar producer still has a limited commercial presence on the waterfront. Symbols can be important. Overall, Liverpool's perhaps sustained revival is a case of a 'virtuous circle' seen elsewhere in other economies and societies. By 2003, after £700 million pump-priming from

Europe, output was rising as unemployment was falling and, on both indicators, Liverpool was out-performing the rest of the North West.[5]

At the same time, Liverpool's other assets began to reap benefits. In 2004 it became a UNESCO World Heritage Site,[6] largely for its world famous skyline of the 'three graces' which despite serious damage to two (the Cunard Building and Dock Office during the night of 2/3 May 1941), outlasted Hermann Göring and his Luftwaffe. Then, in 2005, to nearly everyone's surprise, though not apparently some optimists in Liverpool, the city beat the clear favourite, Newcastle and Gateshead, into second place to win the European Capital of Culture 2008. In 2007,it was also the time to celebrate Liverpool's 800-year history. Even the loss of the EU's Objective One funding from 2006 was not enough to deflate the euphoria. That decision was also an indicator of Liverpool's success in having kick-started regeneration and growth. More good news was that, for the first time in perhaps more than two hundred years, port employment was no higher than that for the economy as a whole. That, though, had a big downside. It reflected the collapse of jobs along the waterfront over the previous thirty years, as technology, geography and the return of employer control squeezed most of the jobs out of the industry. Liverpool would have to find its jobs somewhere else: in what was left of manufacturing, the public sector (though that had its limits) and, already and increasingly, services, hotels, tourism, retailing and leisure.

Liverpool looking forward

Visitors to Liverpool in the late 1980s who had known it only twenty years before, would have been shocked. The Albert Dock had been abandoned to the Mersey's ever-threatening silt as its once state-of-the-art warehouses, windows shattered, were reduced to the second stages of decay. Grass and weeds in the gaps between the cobbles and granite blocks were taking Jesse Hartley's work back to nature, as rust contrived to penetrate the Victorian cast-iron gates, railings and machinery. Returning a decade later, the same visitors would surely have been impressed by the transformation. Shops, cafés, restaurants and luxury apartments, as well as an impressive maritime museum and, later, the Tate in the North, opened in 1988, were revealing the tourist and leisure potential of once hard commerce. Further developments to the north and south of the Albert Dock would add more warehouses turned into apartments, hotels and car parking. On the opposite side of the road the Moathouse Hotel and bus station would disappear to be transformed into a brand-new, shining bus facility and major retail complex, all on land developed by the Duke of Westminster and funded by his countless millions.

The South End, too, was having its turn, with more converted warehouses, new bars, hotels and a casino. Earlier, in 1984, a widely acclaimed International Garden Festival had been held in Dingle, though the physical legacy of that remarkable initiative was ultimately neglected and allowed to deteriorate, ending in premature closure. By the mid-1990s, new housing developments were occupying part of the site, although more ambitious plans for a public park and sports complex had been abandoned. The actual South End waterfront did much better. The Kings Dock's transformation included luxury flats from warehouses, car parking and shops and, most spectacularly, an arena for concerts and other big events. Originally, Everton FC was going to to relocate to the dock from Goodison Park but the developers' appetite for money was to prove too large for a new, state of the art stadium. Liverpool FC, meanwhile, was developing Stanley Park with American and EU money, although financial uncertainty has now put those plans on hold, as other prestigious domestic and commercial waterfront projects suddenly have to face the consequences of economic dislocation and uncertainty.[7]

Among the other South End docks, Queen's Dock has become a watersports centre, with Coburg a marina. But the old Coburg pub has survived, in good order, to match the Baltic Fleet up the road. Brunswick Dock did even better. It has been reborn with yet another marina, an enterprise centre and business park. These docks have also had their share of warehouses becoming luxury apartments. It is all well and good, of course, and much better than dereliction and decay, even if the new facilities cater only to those who have good jobs, better prospects, high credit ratings and money to spend.

Much further upstream the coast has become a more attractive leisure location, especially at Otterspool. Beyond that, Garston Docks remains active, though still looking a bit sad, remembering the better times. Many of its buildings are ready for the demolition gangs, although one small terrace, on Garston's own Dock Road, remains upright. Its about eight, dust-flecked houses, lace curtains still intact, defiantly face their inevitable demise. Elsewhere in Garston's dockland, the usual redbrick villas have replaced the acres of Victorian terraces, as the huge, railway coal sidings have disappeared. Religion survives. St Michael's Church, seemingly marooned between gasholders, roads and a railway viaduct, still displays its notices of services, its clock telling the correct time.

Liverpool's recovery and development have had their share of mistakes, miscalculations, false starts and disappointments. Arguably it has had more than its fair share of political conflict, controversies, local political rivalries and clashes with central government. Politicians are not immune to short-sighted views. The International Garden Festival moving rapidly from extraordinary success to demoralising débâcle was the most obvious example. It gave pleasure and pride, lightening the spirits of local people when it was most needed. But it was also '… a cautionary tale to show what happens when politicians fail to think beyond the brief shelf-life of an ambitious project.'[8] Other, more recent cases are the abandonment of the new tram system, although in this case the withdrawal of government funding may move the charge of limited vision to Whitehall. The abandonment of the avant garde design for a 'fourth grace' to stand alongside the old Dock Board building, was understandable though inexplicably sudden. Its virtual replacement by the new museum of Liverpool, now nearing completion, is a perhaps more widely acceptable alternative, of good design, but it is still symptomatic of the mysterious processes by which decisions are often made on Merseyside. Older readers might also point to the total demolition of the Overhead Railway in 1957 as a mistake in the context of contemporary tourist developments, but age and maturity are as prone to hindsight as are youth and inexperience.

In 2008 Liverpool celebrated becoming European Capital of Culture. As the culture fest of 2008 drew to a close, the year was widely, and perhaps objectively, seen as a success in both presentational and popular enjoyment terms. Yet it remains very doubtful, and there are analogous cases elsewhere, whether it will have done much for the lives of the majority of Liverpool people, who have remained rightly sceptical; and who are now beginning to face very real problems – though they are far from alone. Fortunately, less now depends on the port; the burden of the city's long over-dependence is now over. At the same time, the years of absolute, even relative decline and retrenchment do now seem also to be in the past, and even the latest negative turn of the economic cycle promises to be less severe than previous trade depressions such as that between the wars. John Maynard Keynes is said to have remarked that in the long run we are all dead. Joan Robinson, almost as clever an economist, is said to have pointed out that while this might be true it was not all at once. But what long experience does tell us is that the economic cycle does turn upwards as well as downwards, so that we should still be able to see beyond the present downturn. Certainly the pattern of Liverpool's trade is different, and the economically active docks (and the life of the port), have moved several miles northwards to Bootle and Seaforth. The heart of the docks is no longer strictly in Liverpool although the entrance to the Freeport[9] and the Seaforth Container Terminal proudly proclaim themselves as the Port of Liverpool. Now it is all in the hands of its third owner. In September 2005 the Liverpool and Birkenhead docks came under the control of Peel Ports, a company with complementary assets and interests in docks, such as the Salford docks, the Manchester Ship Canal, and Liverpool's John Lennon Airport. The new owners also ambitiously envisage bringing Birkenhead to centre stage, with an ambitious complex of residential, office and retail developments, transforming both Birkenhead's prospects and self-image, as well as the view from the Liverpool side, a 'Manhattan on the Mersey'. Liverpool, too, is seen by Peel Ports' PR men as a 'portal' into and out of its old, industrial hinterland in Lancashire, Yorkshire and Cheshire, and then farther afield to Birmingham, Newcastle and London. The plans for further expansion of its container facilities at Seaforth will still continue to include trade with North America, but with a greater emphasis on Dublin, Belfast and Glasgow. Here a recent, telling comment by a Peel Ports' senior executive[10] was that any downturn in the North American economies, especially the USA, was less worrying to Liverpool's trade than a stalling in the pace of Ireland's 'Celtic Tiger' trajectory. Ireland seems to have come to the rescue of Liverpool when once its starving millions sought an unwelcoming refuge in its streets. So if Liverpool is in serious business again as a major port, its future, from its own perspective, is now tied to the progress of the British and Irish economies.

Liverpool is no longer the 'world city', on the edge of Lancashire with its back turned seaward as it looks outwards to the oceans. Both Liver Birds could now perhaps be turned to face the same way. Once again, and for the first time in perhaps 300 years, Liverpool has returned to being a town in Lancashire. The old rival Southampton has finally won the long battle for 'deep sea' supremacy. Nearly all of its container traffic, at 93 per cent, is deep sea; Liverpool trails at 44 per cent. But the story is different with the EU countries and notably Ireland, the 'short sea' trade. For those countries Liverpool's container traffic is nearly four times that of Southampton.[11] This transformation is, of course, acceptable enough: trade is trade.

Liverpool's decline from the middle of the 1970s can be partly explained by being on the wrong side of the country to benefit from rising EEC trade to compensate for the decline in Commonwealth trade. The nearness and ease of transit to the mainland were the good fortunes of Dover, with its ro-ro traffic, and Felixstowe and Southampton with their container business. Felixstowe easily leads in containers, with Southampton at about half the volume of Felixstowe. Yet Liverpool is broadly on a par with London and Medway and, on 2005 data, ranked fifth overall. More significantly, Liverpool's EU traffic in containers easily exceeded that of Southampton, as we have seen, but also that of Felixstowe and Medway, though behind London.[12]

Table 8 Trading patterns of UK container ports, 2005, in TEUs* (000s)

| | Domestic | Short sea | | Deep sea | Total container traffic[†] |
		EU	Other		
Felixstowe	78	44	223	1,809	2,760
Southampton	14	65	...	1,290	1,382
London	2	401	31	299	735
Medway	...	90	4	612	707
Liverpool	53	250	35	267	612
Total UK ports	453	2344	352	4,374	7,753

* Containers are not fully standardised except for the height and width at eight feet each. The length can be ten, twenty, thirty or forty feet. The most common is twenty which, as an equivalent, is used as the means of measuring the volume of traffic. Hence TEU is twenty-foot equivalent units.

† Includes unspecified routes (... negligible)

Source: compiled from Department of Transport (2006), 'Transport Statistics: Marine Statistics 2005', London: Department of Trade.

Change is also evident, even visibly along the Dock Road, in the cargoes passing through Liverpool. Traditional bulk cargoes such as grain, meat, animal feeds and timber remain important. These have now been joined by a new one.

Travellers and tourists, or those just going to work or home via the Dock Road, will not fail to notice the giant hills of scrap metal, at various stages of rendition, being noisily pushed and pulled by giant steel dinosaurs before being loading onto ships feeding the voracious appetites of the big world steel producers for scrap metal, now including China and India, the new additions to the ranks of super economies and super powers.

Far more glamorous, though in fact much less lucrative for the port, are the cruise ships calling at the Langton Dock terminal. The City Council has also now extended the floating landing stage at the Pier Head which, with the adjoining Prince's Dock, is able to berth the largest cruise ships, recently the *QE2* and *QM2*, as they moved into still busy 'retirement'. Big cruise liners bring trade for hotels, shops and leisure facilities when they are in port, but not many jobs, even though their growing presence on the Mersey – 19 cruise calls were counted in 2006 with further growth expected,[13] give a psychological lift to Liverpudlians, and not just those with long memories. But as a port Liverpool cannot afford to be complacent again, as it was in 1910, and even as late as 1965 when the port and the city seemed to be firing on all cylinders. Maritime and inter-port competition remains fierce as the fruits of increasing globalisation are fought over by old and new players. One old player may also be making a comeback.

The Thames as a major trade highway survived the traumas of the 1970s and 1980s by moving down the estuary to concentrate on Tilbury. Now there are ambitious plans to reverse history with a new container port, London Gateway, in Essex, four hours' sailing time from the open sea. More significantly, such a port would be in the heart of the South East, a region that consumes half of all the UK's containerised goods. However, modern container ships are big, and substantial dredging operations in the Thames upper regions will be required. There are also other container port projects being considered, under the continuing stimulus of the UK's growing imports of manufactured goods.[14] The potential threat posed to Liverpool's substantial EU and domestic container trade, about half of all its current container traffic,[15] should not be underestimated. Furthermore, all trade, especially that by sea, combined with the growing complexity, volatility and globalisation of distribution networks, is far more competitive, and more uncertain, than it was in the Empire days of 1910.

Despite the inevitable uncertainties, it is clear that the port of Liverpool has undoubtedly recovered from the point in the 1980s when its whole future seemed uncertain at best. In 1965, the tonnage passing through Liverpool, at 31.7 millions, was 9.7 per cent of all UK ports. By 1985 that tonnage had collapsed to 10.4 million and 2.2 per cent of the UK. Twenty years later, remarkably, it had surpassed the 1965 figure at 33.8 million, which was 5.8 per cent of all ports.[16] Liverpool no longer, with London, easily dominates UK trade, but it is now competing with other ports on a more level playing field. After the three front runners – Grimsby/Immingham, Tees/Hartlepool and London – it is on a par with the next group once, in 1985, well ahead of Liverpool. These include

Southampton, Milford Haven, Forth Ports and Felixstowe, as the following table shows.

Table 9   Top ten UK ports 1965–2005, by tonnage percentage share

1965*		1985		2005	
London	20.2	Sullom Voe †	12.8	Grimsby/ Immingham	10.4
Liverpool	9.7	London	11.1	Tees & Hartlepool	9.5
Milford Haven	7.8	Milford Haven	7.0	London	9.2
Southampton	7.6	Grimsby/ Immingham	6.3	Southampton	6.8
Manchester	7.6	Southampton	5.4	Milford Haven	6.4
Clyde	4.8	Liverpool	2.2	Forth	5.8
Tees Hartlepool	3.8	Medway	2.2	Liverpool	5.8
Hull	3.0	Felixstowe	2.2	Felixstowe	4.0
Bristol	2.9	Clyde	2.1	Dover	3.6
Grimsby/ Immingham	2.6	Manchester	2.1	Sullom Voe †	3.5

* Figures for 1965, Great Britain.

† Sullom Voe, in the Shetlands, emerged in the 1970s as the UK's North Sea oil port. By the 1980s, in tonnage, it became the UK's major port. It peaked in 1985 and fell in successive years as North Sea oil production declined.

Source: compiled from Department of Transport (2006), 'Transport Statistics: Marine Statistics 2005', London: Department of Trade.

But success does not always bring work. In 1910 the port had supported a lot of jobs. Before the Great War direct work at the docks, plus all the related trades and industries, had created about 60,000.[17] That was when dockwork alone could, in times of brisk trade, find work for more than 20,000. Now, with the small number of dockers, plus perhaps 2,000 indirectly created in associated and supplying companies to the docks, with the tourist and leisure activities around the central docks adding a few hundred more, a total of about 3,000 emerges. That bears no comparison to a waterfront which, even in the trade doldrums, could find work for many thousands of dockside workers alone. Such a rapid collapse in jobs is explained almost entirely by new technologies and new methods. There is no going back. The docks, as a major employer of labour, are gone for ever.

The loss of employment might be lamented, but the jobs are not missed for the working conditions that the men had to endure. The work was for long casual, in dirty and dangerous conditions, and under harsh and sometimes brutal supervision. The facilities were generally primitive, and average weekly pay was barely able to sustain the dockers and their families, even in the best of times, which were few. It was not until the 1970s that dockers' earnings became assured, and they moved to the top ten per cent of manual workers. The harsh discipline had also gone, although conditions and facilities remained inadequate, and probably still do, at least compared to other countries.[18]

Modern dock work is very different to the old ways of working, although some elements of it must remain for those cargoes that cannot be put into containers. Twelve-hour shifts are also the norm, and the work, by its nature, is more routinised and less varied and interesting. The pay is also no longer standardised through a common collective agreement throughout the port. It is decentralised to the separate areas, and there are independent companies supplying labour across the areas.[19] Peel Ports, previously the MDHC, also has its own dock labour force. The outcome is that pay is sometimes different for the same job and for the same workers who may be working alongside each other, a clear potential source of friction for management. Nor are pensions and other benefits anything like what they were, if they exist at all. Work, too, though mostly permanent as trade continues to be buoyant, can be 'on call' in slack periods, a form of casualism without the stand; and there are others who are employed on a part-time or contract basis. All this is a far cry from the way work was organised under the National Dock Labour Scheme. It is not a return to full-blown casualism, but it does amount to a move backwards in the conditions of employment. Progress, it might be argued, can move backwards as well as forwards.

But however retrograde modern dock employment may seem, it counts much less for Liverpudlians than the new occupations that are now taken by the sons, daughters, grandsons and granddaughters of former dockers. A more usual modern reality is likely to be at or little more than the minimum wage, with limited benefits and probably no pensions, in Liverpool's growing retail, service, tourist and leisure industries. More often than not these jobs are likely to be short or fixed term, part-time, and even semi-casual. Some in the informal economy will have pay and conditions less than those prescribed by law. Liverpool's unemployment rate is still above the national average, with those claiming unemployment benefit twice the national rate. Income support rates for those over 16 are also double the national rate.[20] For those in work, the better paid jobs, with better conditions and some prospects, are often only available in the public sector which became a major employer of labour as private sector and port jobs declined from the 1970s. But that route is inevitably limited, and most jobs have to be sought and taken in the newer private, post-industrial sectors. In such, trade union representation has few toeholds, and state minima are much less effective in improving pay and conditions than strong trade unions, with high and stable memberships, bargaining with employers.[21] Such a state of affairs has become an increasingly distant memory along the waterfront.

One of the inevitable consequences of Liverpool's revival was house price inflation, initially for those who could pay for rising prices in well-paid jobs in and around the central areas of the city. Speculative property development and speculative buying pushed prices up further.[22] This had wider effects as rising house and apartment prices spread beyond the central areas into the inner and outer suburbs. There developed an acute national problem of affordability for those on even average as well as low incomes. In Liverpool it was even more acute as the house price boom[23] co-existed with lower than average earnings. Now prices, mortgage finance and sales are heading rapidly in the opposite direction as repossessions rise. The cycle will, of course, turn but, for most, finding somewhere affordable and secure to live will remain.

The port and the city

What of the old waterfront communities? Is there anything left other than memories? Those who are curious could do worse than visit the old Stanley Tobacco Warehouse,[24] once serving Stanley Dock. The tobacco warehouse, dating from 1901, is a decaying, fascinating relic of the days of late Empire building. Still awesome in size, it is not as derelict as it looks from the outside, from its array of smashed window panes, an early familiar, feature of abandoned buildings and houses in Liverpool. Inside, its brick vaulted roof and walls remain intact as its rail tracks remain securely in place on the floor, though no longer in use. Yet it is still functioning, albeit not for tobacco.

Every Sunday, from 10 a.m. to 4 p.m., people flock to the old entrances in their thousands, forming a vast, noisy, vibrant, waterfront bazaar. Everything that can be carried, on foot or by car, is for sale, from carpets to cakes, bomber jackets to beef burgers. You can buy there, sell there, eat there and gossip there. It is a total experience, the old fondly remembered Paddy's Market writ very large. Many of the customers are likely to be direct descendants of the people of the old waterfront neighbourhoods, experiencing a physical recall, or just a folk memory, of the pasts of their fathers, mothers, grandfathers, grandmothers, uncles and aunts and those much farther back. Now they will, despite the uncertainties and problems of modern life, have better, more secure more prosperous lives than their forerunners. Many will be owners of their own homes. They will also live away from dockland, often many miles distant in the outer suburbs and satellite towns of Merseyside. Some, though, will still be living nearby. Not everybody left.

Stanley Dock and its giant warehouse lie in Vauxhall Ward. It was once a byword for poverty, squalor, starvation, disease and short lives. The lives and work of its poor residents were studied and catalogued by John Finch in 1842. Dr Duncan, perhaps not surprisingly, located one of his two infirmaries in Vauxhall. Vauxhall suffered heavily in the Second World War, the bomb aimers going for the docks and shipping close by. It suffered again from the decline of the docks, and then again from the closure of Tate & Lyle's big refinery there in 1981. Cane sugar refining in Liverpool went back a long way. Tate & Lyle merged in the second half of the nineteenth century, and by the twentieth the company was giving jobs to thousands. Its closure was symbolic of Liverpool's then headlong descent into joblessness, despair and riot, although the riots were in Toxteth, not Vauxhall. Vauxhall's street names are mainly still there, but they now order rows of solid, semi-detached, brick houses provided by the Eldon Gardens' Cooperative to keep the local community together with genuinely affordable housing. On that test Vauxhall has survived and even thrived.[25] So some part of dockland is still there and not just in the mind.

Vauxhall Ward's Scotland Road eastern boundary runs northwards. Just before it divides into Stanley Road and Kirkdale Road (the site of the old Rotunda Theatre destroyed by incendiary bombs in 1941) is Athol Street running straight, westwards, down to the docks.[26] But Athol Street is not what it was. It is now sealed off from traffic at its junction with Scotland Road, and ends in the same way where it once entered Vauxhall Road on its way to the Dock Road and the docks. Its Bridewell is hardly even a memory now, and the two pubs at its Scotland Road end, the Clifford Arms and the aptly named Corner House, have both been demolished. Further down, where Latimer Street crosses Athol Street, the big, white, solid three-storey building, once the Trinity Vaults, has metamorphosed into a block of luxury flats for rent.[27]

Most of the old street names parallel to Scotland Road are still there, with those going downhill to the docks now mostly inactive and the old houses long gone. Yet the layout would have still been easily recognisable to those who once lived there before the bombs and bulldozers did their work. Then, of course, as well as the docks the streets had places where men and women worked as well as lived. There were foundries, tanneries, abattoirs, mills, sugar distilleries and stables, as well as barber shops for haircuts and shaves and an array of food shops and pubs of all sizes. The jobs and nearly all the shops have gone, even most of those on Scotland Road. But so have the mean little houses with often blocked toilets in the yard and no hot running water or bathrooms. Now the residents of Athol Street, and an extensive area around it going up to Vauxhall, live as owner occupiers of smart, semi-detached houses with well-tended gardens, some with hedges and mature trees. One garden even has a sizeable, healthy palm tree!

Athol Street has almost certainly lost the old bonding of the community in the days when its residents were born, lived, worked, were bombed, married, quarrelled, shopped and died there. They also endured and survived, their community serving as an insurance against poverty and deprivation. Some common purpose may yet remain in Athol Street, but if so it now exists in the context of material lives, though still far from always comfortable and easy, at the least better than their long dead relatives, or elderly survivors, would have thought possible. It seems as though close-knit, warm communities can only survive when they are poor, and not always then.

Some will regret the passing of Liverpool's waterfront neighbourhoods, even with their poverty and squalor. It was always inevitable, just as the port could never hope to hold its dominant position for all time. Yet though the port has survived and is even prospering it is not the same. Few now work there, so that Liverpool is no longer the 'port city' as Graeme Milne has perceptively observed.[28] It has also moved, physically, to the north, away from Liverpool's old, historic core. The port and the city are now separate, as they never used to be. The return of big ships, though cruise vessels, to the Pier Head will excite old memories, but little more than that. Liverpool has reinvented itself as the city of culture, leisure and shopping on one side of the Mersey, with Birkenhead, on the other side, bidding for 'Manhattan' status.

It is not difficult to be disparaging about all this, while the current turning of the economic cycle even threatens it. Liverpool is used to unrealistic visions for its future, as in the days of Ramsay Muir before the Great War and again, in the 1920s, when it was clear that the port's future was far from assured. Even as late as 1965 Liverpool was bustling with trade and traffic, and new industries were fuelling the optimism. Within a decade optimism was sinking almost without trace.

Most of Liverpool's people have not shared at all equitably in its successful days, yet they often suffered most when its fortunes went into reverse. That may be happening once again. There are realistic fears that the transformation of the central waterfront and the city centre is for the young, prosperous, upwardly mobile. That transformation needs to 'trickle down' to those less well placed by education, training and good fortune, and then also to 'trickle out' beyond the central core into the inner and outer suburbs. Neither of these processes ever came naturally to those in power, and it is difficult to see how they could prevail without major public intervention, still anathema to those in the thrall of the liberal market economy. Yet current developments do seem to be beginning to transform those minds, if not yet hearts, as financial crisis begins to seep into Liverpool's major developments and future. The still vacant luxury flats in and around the waterfront are a dismal indicator of lost hopes as recession even threatens the future profits of the retailers in the Liverpool One development.

But we must always seek to be optimistic, and the optimists may yet have it right. Even in the dark days of 1980s' incurable unemployment, absolute poverty and riots, there were some, even ageing, romantic Lefties, who had vision and, in many ways, a remarkably accurate one at that:

> Liverpool, with its superb endowment of river and undulating terrain, its chain of parkland cutting through the city, its electric social history and its thriving cultural life will make York and Chester look as prettily twee as they actually are. Liverpool's first new future will be as one of the new cultural capitals of Northern Europe.[29]

Whatever the truth of such predictions, Liverpool's future will be forged without the contribution of its old-style waterfront communities, without the tens of thousands of dockers who tramped to the stand twice a day year after year, and above all without the character, smells or feel of a major bustling port right at the heart of the city.

Liverpool's waterfront blues are a thing, largely, of the past.

Notes and references

Author's preface and acknowledgements

1 Tony Lane, *Liverpool: Gateway of Empire* (London: Lawrence & Wishart, 1987), p. 163.

2 Ramsay Muir, *A History of Liverpool* (London: Williams & Norgate and Liverpool University Press (hereafter LUP), 1907); George Chandler, *Liverpool* (London: Batsford, 1957); John Belchem (ed.), *Liverpool 800: Culture, Character and History* (Liverpool: LUP, 2006).

3 Pat O'Mara, *The Autobiography of a Liverpool Slummy* (Liverpool: Bluecoat Press, n.d.).

4 Johnnie Woods, *Growin' Up: One Scouser's Social History* (Lancaster: Palatine Books, 1989); Terry Cooke, *Scotland Road: the Old Neighbourhood* (Birkenhead: Countyvise, 1987); Joan Boyce, *Pillowslips and Gasmasks* (Liverpool: Liver Press, 1989).

5 Bryan Perrett, *Liverpool: A City at War* (Burscough: Hugo Press, 1990).

6 Jack Jones, *Union Man: The Autobiography of Jack Jones* (London: Collins, 1986).

7 Eric Heffer, *Never a Yes Man* (London: Verso, 1991).

8 James Sexton, *Sir James Sexton Agitator* (London: Faber & Faber, 1936).

9 Jack Dash, *Good Morning Brothers! A militant trade unionist's frank autobiography* (London: Lawrence & Wishart, 1969).

10 Robert Roberts, *The Classic Slum: Salford Life in the First Quarter of the Century* (Harmondsworth: Penguin, 1980); Robert Roberts, *A Ragged Schooling* (Manchester: Mandolin, 1984).

11 National Museums and Galleries on Merseyside, Museum of Liverpool Life, *Liverpool at War: War Workers' Project.*

12 D. Caradog Jones, *The Social Survey of Merseyside* (Liverpool: LUP, 1934).

13 Sam Davies, Pete Gill, Linda Grant, Martyn Nightingale, Ron Noon, and Andy Challice, *Genuinely Seeking Work: Mass Unemployment on Merseyside in the 1930s* (Birkenhead: Liver Press, 1992).

14 Pat Ayers, *The Liverpool Docklands: Life and Work in Athol Street* (Birkenhead: Liver Press, 1999).

15 Tony Lane, *The Merchant Seamen's War* (Manchester: Manchester University Press (hereafter MUP), 1990).

16 Francis E. Hyde, *Liverpool and the Mersey: An Economic History of a Port, 1700–1970* (Newton Abbot: David & Charles, 1971).

17 Eric Taplin, *Liverpool Dockers and Seamen, 1870–1890* (Hull: University of Hull, 1974); Eric Taplin, *The Dockers' Union: A Study of the National Union of Dock Labourers,*

1889–1922 (Leicester: Leicester University Press; New York: St Martin's Press, 1986).

18 Sam Davies, Colin J. Davis, David De Vries, Lex Heerma van Voss, Lidewij Hesselink and Klaus Weinhaver (eds), *Dock Workers: International Explorations in Comparative Labour History, 1790–1970*, vols 1 and 2 (Aldershot: Ashgate, 2000).

19 Gordon Phillips and Noel Whiteside, *Casual Labour: The Unemployment Question in the Port Transport Industry, 1880–1970* (Oxford: Oxford University Press (hereafter OUP), 1985).

20 David F. Wilson, *Dockers: The Impact of Industrial Change* (London: Fontana, 1972).

21 Michael Jackson, *Labour Relations on the Docks* (Farnborough: Saxon House, 1973).

22 Ken Coates and Tony Topham, *The Making of the Labour Movement: The Formation of the Transport and General Workers' Union, 1870–1922* (Nottingham: Spokesman, 1994).

23 Michael Lavalette and Jane Kennedy, *Solidarity on the Waterfront: The Liverpool Lock Out of 1995/96* (Birkenhead: Liver Press, 1996).

24 Nancy Ritchie-Noakes, *Liverpool's Historic Waterfront: The World's First Mercantile Dock System* (London: HMSO, 1984).

25 Adrian Jarvis, *Liverpool's Central Docks: An Illustrated History* (Stroud: Sutton and National Museums and Galleries on Merseyside, 1991).

26 Frank Neal, *Sectarian Violence: The Liverpool Experience, 1819–1914* (Liverpool: Newsham Press, 1988); Frank Neal, *Black '47: Britain and the Famine Irish* (Liverpool: Newsham Press, 1998).

27 Philip J. Waller, *Democracy and Sectarianism: A political and social history of Liverpool, 1868–1939* (Liverpool: LUP, 1981).

28 Peter Turnbull, Charles Woolfson and John Kelly, *Dock Strike: Conflict and Restructuring in Britain's Ports* (Aldershot: Avebury, 1992).

Introduction: From 'Black Spot on the Mersey' to European Capital of Culture

1 The first part of the title of a detailed study of Liverpool's 'Black Spot' status in the eighteenth and nineteenth century. See Iain C. Taylor, '"Black Spot on the Mersey": A Study of Environment and Society in Eighteenth and Nineteenth Century Liverpool' (unpublished Ph.D. thesis, University of Liverpool, 1976).

2 Registrar General for England and Wales Quarterly Returns, First Quarter, 1866, p. xxxvi, cited in Taylor, '"Black Spot on the Mersey"', p. 194. With perhaps ambiguous irony, the Liverpool Mortality Sub-Committee in the same year compared Liverpool to Manchester: 'Manchester comes next and its death rate usually approximates to ours; for two years there has been ... a sort of rivalry between the two towns, sometimes one, sometimes the other, having the advantage.' Cited in Taylor, '"Black Spot on the Mersey"', p. 194. Irony aside, Liverpool's infant mortality rate (below five years) was well ahead (also in 1866) at 528 per 1,000, followed by Manchester at 510, Leeds (480), Birmingham (482) and London (408). These figures are from Dr Duncan's data, Liverpool's and the country's first Medical Officer of Health. The district where you lived also seriously affected your life (or death) chances, especially infants under one year. For Lace Street (the highest rate of infant mortality) it was 583.3 per thousand. For Rodney Street (where Dr Duncan lived) it was, unbelievably, as low as 0.5 per thousand. Your job could also put you at high risk, dictating where you lived and in what conditions. 'Labourers' (mostly dock) and 'Tradesmen' together contributed almost 85

per cent of Liverpool's deaths from fever in 1866. 'Professional and Mercantile' did much better, at 2.6 per cent. (Cited in Taylor, '"Black Spot on the Mersey"', tables 9.5 and 9.7.)

3 John Belchem, 'Celebrating Liverpool', in Belchem (ed.), *Liverpool 800: Culture, Character and History*, p. 56. Glasgow's 'urban core' has indeed witnessed a renaissance, primarily through the development of finance and banking, retailing, leisure and culture and university and college expansion. The inner suburbs such as those of the west end and south side have also continued to thrive as middle-class residential areas, as too the re-developed 'merchant city' of apartments and penthouses. Beyond those areas affluence is far more patchy. The old working class of the Gorbals and the inner core have long gone to the distant estates of Easterhouse and Castlemilk, where the older deprivations are still evident, despite the spirited and sometimes successful efforts of local people. Glasgow's 1990 slogan of 'Glasgow's miles better' was true, but only in a very limited sense.

4 Liverpool's legendary, even world-famous, 'Paddy's Market', on Scotland Road, later Great Homer Street, was a place to buy cheaply for the poor of the waterfront as well as the poor sailors of the Empire. I well remember a cherished birthday present from my grandmother, bought on its stalls, a full Apache outfit, with fringed sleeves and trouser seams plus the big chief's feathered headdress and tomahawk. The only downside was that I was always fated to die, dramatically and bloodily, by the cap-gun cowboys of the streets. Only much later did I learn that the native Americans were the truly good guys!

5 Their preference for casualism was not irrational, however. They feared that its abolition would lead to fewer jobs since work-sharing would be ruled out. See Phillips and Whiteside, *Casual Labour*, chapters 7 and 8.

6 The MDHB'S functions largely excluded the hiring of its own labour except for dock operations, maintenance etc. However, the Rochdale Report of 1962 encouraged it, to hire some dockside labour of its own, which Wilson (*Dockers: The Impact of Industrial Change*, p. 30) estimated as 'nearly a fifth' in 1972. After the abolition of the National Dock Labour Board and the collapse of many stevedoring and master porter operations after 1989, the by now MDHC took on some of the displaced labour. By the dispute of 1995–98 the company employed about 500 dockers.

7 The high-quality terraces, in and around the University and the Anglican Cathedral, formerly the houses of the professional classes (including Dr Duncan and his surgery), remain in large numbers.

8 One very readable researched account is that of Pat Ayers in her study of Athol Street off Scotland Road between the wars, to which we will return in later chapters. See, especially, chapter 9. A more faceted, academically orthodox investigation of neighbourliness for the 1950s is Madeleine Kerr, *The People of Ship Street* (London: Routledge & Kegan Paul, 1958).

9 Writing in 1980 E. P. Thompson made a similar point for coalminers who, in the national strike of 1972 '… came, at first as ambassadors of a past culture, reminding us of whom we once were'. *Writing by Candlelight* (London: Merlin Press), p. 74.

10 For the separation of the port from the city see Graeme J. Milne, 'Maritime Liverpool', in Belchem (ed.), *Liverpool 800: Culture, Character and History*, p. 257.

Chapter One: 'Something wonderful': Liverpool and Empire in 1911

1 Margaret B. Simey, *Charitable Effort in Liverpool in the Nineteenth Century* (Liverpool: LUP, 1951), p. 98. See also Lane, *Liverpool: Gateway of Empire*, p. 77.

2 This, and later maps, are reproduced here with the kind permission of Mapseeker, 'Historic maps on line' http://www.mapseeker.co.uk/major-british-cities/liverpool/?tcID=1

3 Pat O'Mara, *The Autobiography of a Liverpool Slummy*, pp. 56-7.

4 Roberts, *The Classic Slum*, p. 60.

5 John Masefield trained as a naval cadet in the Mersey on *HMS Conway*, when he was thirteen, in 1891. The *Conway* suffered a sad fate. It ran aground while being towed in April 1953, breaking its back on the rocks. In October 1956 the wreck caught fire as it was being removed. The ship's anchor is now an exhibit at the entrance to Liverpool's Maritime Museum. Among Masefield's poems of the sea two of the best known, 'Cargoes' (the last stanza quoted here) and 'Sea-Fever', remain consistently included in popular anthologies. See, for example, *The Nation's Favourite Poems* (London: BBC). (This was first published in 1996 and by 1998 had been reprinted 21 times.)

6 From an 1890 article in the *Liverpool Magazine*, cited by John Belchem, *Mersey Pride: Essays in Liverpool Exceptionalism* (Liverpool: LUP, 2000), p. 4.

7 Simey, *Charitable Effort in Liverpool*, p. 98.

8 Lane, *Liverpool: Gateway of Empire*, p. 25.

9 Muir, *A History of Liverpool*, p. 301.

10 *Liverpool Courier*, quoted in Lane, *Liverpool: Gateway of Empire*, p. 93.

11 R. Seebohm Rowntree, *Poverty: A Study of Town Life* (London: Macmillan, 1901).

12 Roberts, *The Classic Slum*, pp. 75-6.

13 Roberts, *The Classic Slum*, pp. 66-7.

14 Neal, *Sectarian Violence*, pp. 8-9.

15 Waller, *Democracy and Sectarianism*, p. 8. Coincidentally, a similar number of dockers were sacked by the Mersey Docks and Harbour Company, in 1995, triggering a three-year dispute. It could be that the MDHC were confirming their own place in the footnotes of history!

16 There were parallel developments at the same time in New York. The New York printers also downed tools in 1778, the first strike in recorded US history. In 1794 the cordwainers (shoemakers) of Philadelphia formed the new nation's first union.

17 Gent & Company is still in business but no longer in clocks. It specialises in alarm systems, related to clocks, but it is still in Leicester.

18 Cited in Nancy Ritchie-Noakes 'The Construction of Albert Dock and its Warehouses', in A. Jarvis and K. Smith (eds), *Albert Dock Trade and Technology* (Liverpool: National Museums and Galleries on Merseyside and LUP, 1999), p. 38.

19 Lane, *Liverpool: Gateway of Empire*, p. 22. Liverpool folklore has it that the cormorants are male and female. The female looks outwards waiting, in anticipation, for sailors off the ships. The male looks inwards waiting for the pubs to open. It is also said that Liverpool's days are over when the Liver Birds fly away, echoing, perhaps, the barbary apes of Gibraltar.

20 Hyde, *Liverpool and the Mersey*, appendix, pp. 235-6. Note, though, that the Bar was not a serious problem until ships increased in draught after about 1850.

21 Hyde, *Liverpool and the Mersey*, p. 2.

22 Hyde, *Liverpool and the Mersey*, p. 3.
23 Hyde, *Liverpool and the Mersey*.
24 Hyde, *Liverpool and the Mersey*, p. 27.
25 Hyde, *Liverpool and the Mersey*, pp. 27–30.
26 Hyde, *Liverpool and the Mersey*, appendix pp. 235–6.
27 From an exhibit in the Liverpool Maritime Museum.
28 Jarvis, *Liverpool's Central Docks*, p. 1.
29 Muir, *A History of Liverpool*, pp. 190–206, cited in Belchem, *Merseyside Essays in Liverpool Exceptionalism*, p. 4.
30 Jarvis, *Liverpool's Central Docks*, p. 2. One destination for respectable reinvestment of slaving profits was in banks. Heywoods Bank, founded by Benjamin and Arthur Heywood in Liverpool, in 1773, used their profits as start-up capital. The bank prospered and was later bought by the more prominent Martin's Bank, also Liverpool-based, in 1883. Martin's itself was absorbed by Barclays Bank in 1968. Recent criticisms of Barclays' links with early capital from the slave trade have not been seriously denied but the bank, in its defence, stresses its founders' historic connections with the Quakers, who supported abolition. Nick Mathiason, 'Barclays admits possible link to slavery after reparation call', *The Observer*, 1 April, 2007. This article was written in 2007, the bicentenary of Britain's abolition of the slave trade.
31 Bill Hunter, *Forgotten Hero: The Life and Times of Edward Rushton* (Liverpool: Living History Library, 2002). As for Washington, when he died he left his slaves, in his will, to his wife, Martha. Finding herself alone in a large household of slaves she went straight down to the courthouse to grant them their freedom. Fear was not as good as principle, but it often achieved quicker results.
32 See, for example, Dicky Sam, *Liverpool and Slavery: An Historical Account of the Liverpool-African Slave Trade* (Liverpool: Bowker & Son, 1884; recently reprinted by Scouse Press). Dicky Sam dedicated the book to the memory of Roscoe, his family and friends, prominent abolitionists. 'Dicky Sam', according to the late Fritz Spiegel in the foreword, was the nickname of a Liverpudlian in the nineteenth century, later 'Wacker' and now 'Scouser'. See also Belchem, *Mersey Pride*, p. 2) who notes that a true Dicky Sam, a Liverpudlian (or Liverpolitan) would have to be born within the sound of the bells of St Nicholas, on the original shoreline. The old church building was destroyed in the Second World War.
33 Waller, *Democracy and Sectarianism*, p. 2.

Chapter Two: Building the 'Pyramids'

1 Daniel Defoe, *A Tour through England and Wales* (London and New York: Dent, 1722; reprinted 1927), p. 256.
2 Muir, *A History of Liverpool*, p. 301. Muir was wrong about the 'monumental' granite. Its low quality meant it could not be quarried in large, monumental pieces, but produced a good deal of rubble, clearly seen in Jesse Hartley's walls.
3 J. A. Picton (1873) 'Memorials of Liverpool', cited in Hyde, *Liverpool and the Mersey*, p. 81.
4 Hyde, *Liverpool and the Mersey*, pp. 80–1.
5 Reproduced from *British Historic Towns: A History in Maps, 1650–1898* (http://www.

maphisteria.co.uk/)

6 Sir Edward Moore, cited in Ritchie-Noakes, *Liverpool's Historic Waterfront*, p. 18.

7 On the northern perimeter of Canning Place is Liverpool's newly built major retail, apartment and bus station complex, 'Liverpool One'. During construction, and the subsequent archaeological excavations, a good part of the brick walls of Liverpool's first dock, as well as the foundations of an area of previously unknown waterfront houses, were revealed. Part of the dock walls are now preserved for shoppers to view, through the paving, under a toughened glass cover. Running from the Liverpool One development is Paradise Street, followed by Whitechapel; these follow the line of the stream that used to drain into the Liver Pool from the then marshland to the east. Paradise Street (named by Steers, the dock engineer, after where he had lived in Rotherhithe) was to become famous as a sailor's haunt with the Old Sailors' Home in Canning Place.

8 The costs of dock development are cited throughout the text, notably in chapters 2 and 3. These, as well as data for wages, salaries and annual incomes included in later chapters, have been converted to their estimated present-day values and included in following brackets. It is estimated that the price level rose by just over threefold between 1750 and 1938 and more than fortyfold from 1938–2003 i.e. 140 times over the whole period. Author's estimates take the calculation back to 1715 (the year the Old Dock was opened) to produce index numbers used to calculate the estimates. For the method see J. M. O'Donoghue, Louise Golding and Grahame Allen, 'Consumer price inflation since 1750' in *Economic Trends*, no. 604 (London: ONS, 2004), pp. 38–46.

9 See Hyde, *Liverpool and the Mersey*, p. 15.

10 Adrian Jarvis, *The Liverpool Dock Engineers* (Stroud: Sutton, 1996), p. 4.

11 See notes, above.

12 See Appendix, table 1, note 2.

13 Adrian Jarvis, *A History of the Port of Liverpool*, manuscript.

14 'Graving' means scratching, i.e. removing rust and barnacles from the ship's hull. The graving dock, when the ship enters, has its water drained or pumped away, the vessel then resting on blocks for cleaning and repair. When completed the water can be re-admitted and the blocks removed. Note that a graving dock is also often called, confusingly, a dry dock.

15 A tidal basin, which dries out at low tide can therefore only be used at high tide. Again, confusingly, the old name was dry dock. Half-tide basins and locks use gates to control the tidal level of water within the basin or locks. Ken McCarron and Adrian Jarvis, *Give a Dock a Good Name?* (Birkenhead: Merseyside Port Folios, 1992), pp. 115–16.

16 See note 5.

17 Hyde, *Liverpool and the Mersey*, p. 77.

18 Ritchie-Noakes, *Liverpool's Historic Waterfront*, p. 46.

19 Hyde, *Liverpool and the Mersey*, pp. 80–3.

20 Hyde, *Liverpool and the Mersey*, appendix 1 (d), p. 238.

21 Taplin, *Liverpool Dockers and Seamen*, p. 14.

22 Waller, *Democracy and Sectarianism*, p. 4. For the UK as a whole, it was a similar picture, though by 1906 steam tonnage was 86 per cent, less than that of Liverpool. Some part of the explanation was Liverpool's still dominant position in the passenger trade using large liners, especially on the North Atlantic run.

23 Ritchie-Noakes, *Liverpool's Historic Waterfront*, pp. 7–8.

24 Ritchie-Noakes, *Liverpool's Historic Waterfront*, p. 98.

25 Ritchie-Noakes, *Liverpool's Historic Waterfront*, p. 5.

26 Hartley's achievement, in the number of docks and their acreage is also revealed in the statistics in the Appendix, Tables 2 and 3. For map 4, see notes, above.

27 Neal, *Sectarian Violence*, p. 2, table 1.

28 See note 5.

Chapter Three: Steam on the Mersey

1 Muir, *A History of Liverpool*, p. 240.

2 Hyde, *Liverpool and the Mersey*, p. 56.

3 £222,000 until recent years, would have been a typical salary for the head of a public corporation. For a further revealing, comparison Doctor Duncan, appointed by the Corporation in 1847, two years after Hartley's Albert Dock was opened, was paid a salary of £50,000 in today's values.

4 Sir Douglas Fox and James Henry Greathead in 1893. The concept went back even further, to 1850, when congestion on the roads along the docks was becoming acute and an overhead railway line offered a potential solution for the movement of both goods and passengers. In the end, the problems involved in lifting cargoes to an elevated track proved insoluble, and the railway opened for passengers alone, although it was pioneering in being powered by electricity rather than steam with its supposed attendant fire hazards. It was ultimately extended to seven miles, the entire docks' length, with thirteen stations from Seaforth to the Dingle. During the Second World War it proved especially useful for the movement of troops to and from ships. It also soon found an unexpected use as a shelter against Liverpool's weather for the Port's workforce, 'The Dockers' Umbrella'. It was closed in December 1956 and dismantled, a casualty of falling dock activity and lack of adequate funds for its repair and reconstruction. Fifty years later, if it had survived, even in part, it might well have found a new role as a tourist attraction. See Paul Bolger, *The Dockers' Umbrella* (Liverpool: Bluecoat Press, 1992), for an illustrated history and Ritchie-Noakes, *Liverpool's Historic Waterfront*, pp. 167–8.

5 Compare the tables on pages 49 and 55.

6 Cited in R. Bean, 'Employers' Associations in the Port of Liverpool, 1890–1914' *International Review of Social History*, vol. 21 (1976), pp. 358–82.

7 For Lyster's contribution to the dock system, see the table on page 55.

8 James Bird, *The Major Seaports of the United Kingdom* (London: Hutchinson, 1963), pp. 299–301.

9 Despite their manifest achievements and contributions to Liverpool's success and wealth as a port – on which everything else was built – neither Hartley nor Lyster are even mentioned in Ramsay Muir's *History of Liverpool* of 1907, and George Chandler's 1957 commemorative histories of King John's granting of the charter in 1207 (Chandler, *Liverpool*). Lyster is also not mentioned in the latest commemorative tome. Hartley gets just one mention, but only for his 'extraordinary pumping house' at Canada Dock. See Milne in John Belchem (ed.), *Liverpool 800: Culture, Character and History*.

10 Bird, *The Major Seaports of the United Kingdom*, p. 285.

11 Hyde, *Liverpool and the Mersey*, appendix 11, p. 241.

12 Bird, *The Major Seaports of the United Kingdom*, p. 286.

13 Hyde, *Liverpool and the Mersey*, p. 139.

14 That was an industry in itself, with its armies of energetic women, the wives, sisters and daughters of dockers and sailors supplementing mostly uncertain and mostly inadequate family budgets.

15 Liverpool's *Journal of Commerce* for 5 July 1873 listed sailings for twelve steamship companies: Cunard, National, Guion, Inman, White Star, Allan, International, Harrison, Anchor, P.S.N., Canadian Shipping and Liverpool and Baltimore. The Suez Canal had opened for ships only four years previously. Stuart Mountfield, *Western Gateway: A History of the Mersey Docks and Harbour Board* (Liverpool: LUP, 1965), p. 36.

16 Hyde, *Liverpool and the Mersey*, p. 112.

17 Between 1831 and 1835 an average of 50,000 migrants per annum was entering the United States. This doubled in ten years and from 1846 to 1850 reached 250,000 per year. In the 1880s it was just under 500,000 per year and by 1901–05 touched an annual average of a million. Between 1900 and 1920 14 million entered US ports. Most of the early migrants came from northern and, later, eastern and southern Europe. The numbers through Liverpool were bound for the eastern ports of the US, especially New York. See Herbert S. Klein, *A Population History of the United States* (Cambridge: Cambridge University Press, 2004), pp. 95–6 and Howard Zinn, *A People's History of the United States* (London: Longman, 1980), p. 373 for the immigrant population data.

18 Hyde, *Liverpool and the Mersey*, pp. 55–6.

19 Hyde, *Liverpool and the Mersey*, p. 54.

20 See chapter 1, p. 26.

21 Mountfield, *Western Gateway*, p. 47.

22 Mountfield, *Western Gateway*, p. 171.

23 Cited in Joseph Sharples, *Liverpool: Pevsner Architectural Guide* (New Haven and London: Yale University Press, 2004), p. 153.

24 Wilton J. Oldham 'The Ismay Line', cited in Lane, *Liverpool: Gateway of Empire*, p. 67. Dawpool was eventually demolished.

25 Lane, *Liverpool: Gateway of Empire*, p. 63.

26 This is not the place to enter into the controversies which have raged around his name ever since. His father's house, large and fine though not a mansion, was in Waterloo, then a small, select seaside resort just north of Seaforth sands, now the site of the Royal Seaforth Docks container terminal. The house is still there (with its blue plaque though no longer connected with the Ismay family) on Adelaide Terrace, facing the estuary, with a clear view of the container terminal, and, of course, the Mersey.

27 Klein, *A Population History of the United States* , p. 164.

28 Maggie May was the legendary, warm-hearted prostitute of the famous song: 'Oh Maggie, Maggie May / They have taken her away / And she'll never walk down Lime Street any more …' She may even have existed!

29 George and Robert Stephenson and Thomas Telford, who constructed docks as well as canals and roads, attract Smiles' special attention and admiration.

30 E. J. Hobsbawm, *Industry and Empire* (Harmondsworth: Pelican Books, 1984), p. 178.

31 The 'casual observer' comment is that of Hyde (*Liverpool and the Mersey*, p. 139) writing in 1971. Ramsay Muir writing in 1907, that is without Hyde's advantages of accumulated

subsequent knowledge and the hindsight of 1971, denied any decline: 'The tonnage of Liverpool shipping, 1,768,426 in 1835, had risen to 5,728,504 in 1870: that is to say, it had multiplied three and one-half times during the period of the unquestioned ascendancy of English trade. But in 1905 it had risen to 15,996,387. This, it is true, is less than three times as great as in 1870. But rate of increase is a very fallacious test. The important point is that the actual addition to the tonnage of Liverpool made during the period of competition was more than twice as great as the actual addition made during the period of unquestioned ascendancy. The result is, that at the end of her seventh century as a chartered borough, Liverpool finds herself among the three of the greatest ports of the world.' (Muir, *A History of Liverpool*, pp. 297–8.)

32 Hyde, *Liverpool and the Mersey*, pp. 139–41.
33 Hyde, *Liverpool and the Mersey*, p. 97.
34 Jarvis, *Liverpool's Central Docks*, pp. 220–1.
35 Jarvis, *Liverpool's Central Docks*.
36 Mountfield, *Western Gateway*, p. 96.
37 Lane, *Liverpool: Gateway of Empire*, p. 22.
38 Belchem, 'Celebrating Liverpool', in Belchem (ed.), *Liverpool 800: Culture, Character and History* p. 29.

Chapter Four: The other side of wonderful

1 Muir, *A History of Liverpool*, p. 306.
2 Anne Holt (1936) 'A Ministry to the Poor', cited in Simey, *Charitable Effort in Liverpool*, p. 18.
3 Tillett's quotation on casual employment is from Ben Tillett, *A Brief History of the Dockers Union* (1910). The 1967 reforms were presided over by the late and eminent, liberal judge, Lord Devlin. The Devlin Report and its consequences is discussed in chapter 10.
4 Strikes, especially unofficial strikes, were always a feature of dockland, though there were also some major, official, national stoppages, the last in 1989. Liverpool's reputation for more unofficial stoppages than other ports was confirmed by the statistics. However, the popular view that the supposed 'strike-proneness' of its workers explains Liverpool's decline does not do justice to the wider, much more fundamental forces at work.
5 Hobsbawm, *Industry and Empire*, esp. pp. 126–33.
6 James Larkin helped to build the National Union of Dock Labourers, described and discussed in chapter 6. His early career and formative influences in Liverpool are discussed in chapter 5. He has a street named after him off Stanley Road, near to the docks.
7 Jack Jones was later to become famous and influential as the reforming General Secretary of the Transport and General Workers' Union with major political influence in the 1960s and 1970s. He began work as a docker, was later a crane driver, and nominally a Catholic in Garston Docks in the South End. See Jones, *Union Man*. One union, the carter's union, later absorbed into the TGWU, was dominated by Protestants. Membership could be denied to Catholics.
8 Taplin, *The Dockers' Union*, p. 86.
9 See chapter 5, pp. 106–8.

10 Susan Pedersen, *Eleanor Rathbone and the Politics of Conscience* (New Haven and London: Yale University Press, 2004), p. 102.

11 Eleanor F. Rathbone, *Report of an Inquiry into the Conditions of Dock Labour at the Liverpool Docks* (Liverpool: Northern Publishing Co., 1904)

12 Eleanor Rathbone's porter's weekly average was 23s. 0d. or about £60 per annum. To put this into a wider perspective Eric Hobsbawm has estimated, for 1865–66, that a middle-class person's income would normally not be less than £300 per annum, with those higher up the income scale enjoying £1,000 to £5,000. Thirty years later these middle-class incomes would have at least been the same. Comparing them with the porter's 1899 income, in modern values (2007) we have £5,250, £26,250, £87,500 and £437,500 respectively. Note that £5,250, assuming a 40-hour week, is about half of the current national minimum wage. See Hobsbawm, *Industry and Empire*, p. 156.

13 Pedersen, *Eleanor Rathbone*, p. 19.

14 Waller, *Democracy and Sectarianism*, pp. 23–4.

15 Terry Cooke, *The Pubs of Scottie Road* (Liverpool: The Bluecoat Press, 1999), p. 15.

16 Cited in Taplin, *The Dockers' Union.*, p. 14.

17 Richard Williams, *The Liverpool Docks Problem* (Liverpool: Northern Publishing Co., 1912). See also Taplin, *The Dockers' Union*, p. 21 and Pedersen, *Eleanor Rathbone*, p. 103.

18 Also, for the first time, telephones were used to pass on information to assist deployment.

19 Graeme Milne, however, sees dockland's eastern limits as more '… a frontier than a border …' See Milne (2006) 'Maritime Liverpool', in John Belchem (ed.), *Liverpool 800: Culture, Character and History*, p. 266.

20 See chapter 1, note 1, p. 14.

21 This statistic and the other population data, including those for the Irish born in Liverpool, are drawn from Neal, *Sectarian Violence* and Neal, *Black '47*.

22 See note 21, above.

23 The hiring system and its effects are described and discussed in chapter 5.

24 Pedersen, *Eleanor Rathbone*, p. 104.

25 Pedersen, *Eleanor Rathbone*.

26 See Roberts, *The Classic Slum*, for the author's account of this dilemma in his mother's corner shop in Salford before the Great War. In my own childhood, in Liverpool in the early 1940s, I recall the familiar, terse notices in corner shops: 'Please do not ask for credit as a refusal often offends.'

27 The pawnshop was not exclusive to the poor and working class. All social classes used its convenient services, as biographical and fictional writing confirm, especially in early Victorian times when business had minimal protection against loss and bankruptcy, so that descent into poverty was common. The bailiff was an official as dreaded as the workhouse overseer. Eleanor Rathbone also had direct experience of pawn-broking, though not out of poverty. She was compelled to pawn her gold watch when she was caught without money on holiday, although she used the name of the Scottish social worker, her colleague and friend, to make the transaction. Pedersen, *Eleanor Rathbone*, p. 105.

28 Ramsay Muir, however, tells us that the Poor Law in Edwardian Liverpool was 'well managed' and, despite the exceptional problems of the city '… was one bright spot in the direction of local public affairs': Muir, *A History of Liverpool*, pp. 276–7. (It would have been instructive to hear Liverpool's paupers' views of the 'well-managed' 'bright spot' Poor Law.)

29 A frequent feature, at times of such crisis, was the immediate, direct help of neighbours, the phenomenon of 'the poor helping the poor', including generous charitable giving. Jack Jones recalls this in his own early days in Liverpool in the 1920s. Jones, *Union Man*, pp. 14–15. See also Ayers, *The Liverpool Docklands*. Such aspects of the life of the poor and working class helped them to endure lives of deprivation and partly explain why they missed their old communities when they were re-housed after demolition of the slums.

30 The density statistic was that of Doctor Duncan, cited in Anthony Miller, *Poverty Deserved? Relieving the Poor in Victorian Liverpool* (Birkenhead: Liver Press, 1988), p. 11.

31 Muir, *A History of Liverpool*, p. 305.

32 The call for special constables backfired. See chapter 1, p. 19.

33 Waller, *Democracy and Sectarianism*, p. 7.

34 Neal, *Black '47*, p. 61, table 3.7.

35 Before 1847 typhus was also often confused with typhoid. William Jenner demonstrated the difference. See Neal, *Black '47*, pp. 125–6.

36 Neal, *Black '47*, p. 150.

37 Neal, *Black '47*, p. 153.

38 Neal, *Black '47*, p. 152.

39 Muir, *A History of Liverpool*, pp. 271–2.

40 Eric Midwinter, *Old Liverpool* (Newton Abbott: David & Charles, 1971), pp. 92–3.

41 Midwinter, *Old Liverpool*, p. 92.

42 John Finch 'Statistics of Vauxhall Ward, Liverpool', reprinted, prepared and introduced by Harold Hikins as *The Condition of the Working Class in Liverpool in 1842* (Liverpool: Toulouse Press, 1986), a clear reference, from the new title, to Engels' famous study. See below, note 45.

43 Waller, *Democracy and Sectarianism*, pp. 9–10 and passim. See also J. R. Jones, *The Welsh Builder on Merseyside: Annals and Lives* (Liverpool: Liverpool University Press, 1946). Pat Ayers, in her study of Athol Street in dockland, notes the influence of Welsh housebuilders in the names of the streets (Ayers, *The Liverpool Docklands*, p. 6).

44 Friedrich Engels, *The Condition of the Working Class in England* (1845).

45 Midwinter, *Old Liverpool*, p. 87. The 'miasma' explanation for the spread of disease was then popular.

46 Midwinter, *Old Liverpool*.

47 Neal, *Black '47*, p. 21, citing from the report by J. R. Wood of the Manchester Statistical Society.

48 *Black '47*, p. 20.

49 Neal, *Black '47*, p. 18) argues that the language used by the newspapers and other commentators 'constructed' the middle-class views of the poor. He cites terms such as 'teems' and 'swarms' that were used to describe overcrowding, as well as 'lairs' and 'dens' when referring to their homes. The *Liverpool Mercury* also used the word 'herd'. More muted, though similar terms, have featured in recent debates in the UK on immigration.

50 Simey, *Charitable Effort in Liverpool*, p. 39.

51 Simey, *Charitable Effort in Liverpool*, p. 137.

52 Pedersen, *Eleanor Rathbone*, p. 54.

53 Simey, *Charitable Effort in Liverpool*, p. 39.

54   Nicholas Timmins, *The Five Giants: A Biography of the Welfare State* (London: Harper Collins, 1996), p. 12.

55   A well-known charity activist, mainly working in and around Scotland and Vauxhall wards was Lee Jones. In 1893 he founded the Liverpool Food Association, distributing soup and other food to school children for a modest charge. It became the Food and Betterment Association and later the League of Welldoers. The league is still active in Liverpool but now works for the needs of the old. The CRS, in contrast, gradually lost its way. In 1932 it was disbanded and its functions taken over by the City Council.

56   Simey, *Charitable Effort in Liverpool*, p. 11.

57   Frank Neal, *Black '47*, pp. 20–1.

58   Muir, *A History of Liverpool*, p. 315.

59   The Council also used a well, in Green Lane (off Brownlow Hill) for sewer flushing, street cleansing and fire-fighting.

60   Muir, *A History of Liverpool*, p. 318.

61   Newlands' achievements, but not his name, easily rank with these of Duncan. Note that Joseph Bazalgette, responsible for his historic removal, through his sewers of London's 'Great Strike' in 1858, has recently received major media publicity through his descendants.

62   Midwinter, *Old Liverpool*, p. 114.

63   Larkin was recalling his early life in Liverpool in an interview in 1920. See Emmet Larkin, *James Larkin: Irish Labour Leader, 1876–1947* (London: Routledge and Kegan Paul, 1965), p. 9. The street was even a venue for entertainment with a circus from 1795, later a theatre and a cinema from 1911 until 1841. Larkin would have observed this further evidence of the two Liverpools (see Harold Ackroyd, *Picture Palaces of Liverpool* (Liverpool, Bluecoat Press, 2002), p. 32). Christian Street is still there, now behind Liverpool John Moores University's Byrom Street building.

Chapter Five: Working on the old waterfront

1   Jones, *Union Man*, p. 31.

2   Sexton, *Sir James Sexton Agitator*, p. 67.

3   Jack Jones also fought with the Republicans in the Spanish Civil War.

4   The NUDL was originally founded in Glasgow in 1889 and had members in other northern ports. Though its focus, and central administration, was soon established in Liverpool, it changed its name in 1919 to the National Union of Dock, Riverside and General Workers. Yet it remained an exclusively dockers' union and was generally known as the 'Liverpool Union'. When it became part of the TGWU in 1922 its special status and importance was recognised (and as an inducement to a vote in favour) it was given 'area' status within the new union. For a comprehensive analysis see Coates and Topham, *The Making of the Labour Movement*.

5   E. J. Hobsbawn, *Labouring Men: studies in the history of labour* (London: Weidenfeld & Nicholson, 1968), p. 208.

6   For example in Manchester, in the 1950s, a case of twelve bottles of whisky for export could be carefully and skilfully dropped on a corner without visible damage. The whisky could then be drained off, the one broken bottle remaining inside the case.

7   For example, James Larkin, when a foreman on the docks, was a highly respectable

family man, teetotal, ambitious and hard-working. See chapter 6, pp. 113, 137–8.

8 An excellent, affectionate account of the closing days of the horses on the docks is Harry Wooding, *Liverpool's Working Horses* (Liverpool: Print Organisation Ltd, 1991).

9 B. G. Orchard, 'The Clerks of Liverpool', cited in Waller, *Democracy and Sectarianism*, p. 5.

10 R. Bean, 'Custom, Job Regulation and Dock Labour in Liverpool, 1911–39', *International Review of Social History*, vol. 27, part 3 (1982), p. 274.

11 As, for example, Glasgow's now famous historical landmark, the giant Finniston Crane, though not a cargo crane.

12 Taplin, *The Dockers' Union*, pp. 9–10.

13 An unsuccessful 1876 petition to the MDHB, signed by 19,000 dock labourers, requested the prohibition of steam engines on the quays. See R. Bean, 'The Liverpool Dock Strike of 1890', *International Review of Social History*, vol. 18 (1973), p. 52.

14 In London job demarcation was not as clear as in Liverpool, although the stevedores sought, and succeeded for a time, to monopolise 'shipwork', restricting 'dockers' to the quays and warehouses. Other ports had their own distinctions. In New Orleans, until the early years of the twentieth century, the cotton bales, largely destined for Liverpool, were loaded by 'screwmen', specialists in packing the maximum number of bales into holds. See Daniel Rosenberg, *New Orleans Dockworkers: race, labour and unionism, 1892–1923* (New York: SUNY Press, 1988). In San Francisco the stevedores loaded and unloaded in the days of sailing ships, the 'longshoremen' moving goods to and from the dockside, much as Liverpool's quay and warehouse porters. However, over time, all dockworkers came to be known as longshoremen. In New York, where there were as many as 30,000 working on the docks before containerisation, they were all called longshoremen, hired in gangs of twelve or thirteen, divided by task – hatch, deck and dock. See Colin J. Davis, 'New York City and London, 1945–60' in Davies *et al.* (eds), *Dock Workers*, p. 214. In Western Australia, dockworkers were undifferentiated 'lumpers' (a term once used in Liverpool for those 'breaking out', i.e. unloading cargo) or, more commonly now, 'wharfies'.

15 Taplin, *The Dockers' Union*, pp. 12–13.

16 Taplin, *The Dockers' Union*, p. 18.

17 Bean, 'The Liverpool Dock Strike of 1890', p. 59.

18 London, too, had some permanent employees, known as 'perms', though that was often a misnomer.

19 Caradog Jones, *The Social Survey of Merseyside*, pp. 130–1.

20 The term gained further currency beyond the docks in the Second World War when clothes, goods and foodstuffs were rationed. Shopkeepers were widely believed to favour the 'blue eyes' with extra rations beyond the allowances kept 'under the counter'.

21 That is according to Sexton (*Sir James Sexton Agitator*, p. 201). Sexton is not necessarily a reliable source given his deep differences with Larkin, especially in Larkin's early years at the NUDL. Emmet Larkin's 1965 biography confirms Sexton's account (Larkin, *James Larkin*, p. 8), though he may have been drawing on Sexton's autobiography.

22 See chapter 8, pp. 161–3.

23 See wage rate table, p. 99.

24 Roberts (*The Classic Slum* 1980), reports his personal experience in Salford, as a boy, in the 'wave of industrial unrest' of the years from 1910 to the outbreak of war. In that

year, 12½ million days were lost, compared to an average annual loss from 1900 to 1909 of 1½ million (pp. 90–1). Over the same period (1900–10) union membership in the UK rose from just over 2 million to over 2½ million. It reached its peak, at 8.3 million, ten years later. See George Sayers Bain and Robert Price, *Profiles of Union Growth: A Comparative Statistical Portrait of Eight Countries* (Oxford: Basil Blackwellm 1980), Table 2.1, p. 37. Roberts did not, however, see any sign of revolutionary tendencies, despite the widespread militancy and unrest in that period.

25 Bean, 'The Liverpool Dock Strike of 1890', p. 54.

26 Employers, such as Cunard, shared work among the men. It was practised at maintaining a readily available labour surplus.

27 Bean, 'The Liverpool Dock Strike of 1890'.

28 Hobsbawn, *Labouring Men*, pp. 225–6.

29 Ministry of Labour: Employment Department, *Report on an Inquiry into the Conditions of Boy Labour on the Docks at Liverpool* (London: HMSO, 1920).

30 Bean, 'Custom, Job Regulation and Dock Labour in Liverpool, 1911–39', p. 280.

31 Henry Mayhew, *London Labour and the London Poor*, selected by Victor Neuberg (Harmondsworth: Penguin, 1985).

32 Peter Razzell (ed.), *The Morning Chronicle Survey of Labour and the Poor: the Metropolitan Distress*, vol. 1 (Firle, Sussex: Caliban Books, 1980).

33 Cited in Wilson, *Dockers: the impact of industrial change*, p. 23.

34 Wilson, *Dockers: the impact of industrial change*, p. 22.

35 Peter Razzell, *The Morning Chronicle Survey of Labour and the Poor*, p. 96.

36 Sexton, *Sir James Sexton Agitator*, pp. 71–2. Robert Tressell in the *Ragged Trousered Philanthropists* also observed that the rich's greatly superior graves to those less blessed with wealth confirmed that the inequities of the class system were not removed even by death.

37 The need for the trust of the men was eventually recognised in industries such as coal-mining where tonnage was the standard measure of earnings. The 'checkweighman', responsible for weighing the coal, became a key union official, the best way of gaining the men's confidence. The miners did, of course, normally trust their union officials, in contrast to the dockers.

38 Sexton, *Sir James Sexton Agitator*, p. 72.

39 Quoted in Taplin, *The Dockers' Union*, p. 56.

40 Taplin, *The Dockers' Union*, p. 56.

41 Taplin, *The Dockers' Union*, p. 60. Note, too, that under the legal principle, 'The Defence of Common Employment' the Engineer-in-Chief (or other senior figure) could be considered a 'workmate' whose negligence would invalidate a claim against the board.

Chapter Six: 'All men being brothers …'

1 Sexton, *Sir James Sexton Agitator*, p. 114.

2 Taplin, *The Dockers' Union*, p. 51.

3 Sexton, *Sir James Sexton Agitator*.

4 Sexton, *Sir James Sexton Agitator*, pp. 74–5.

5 The story of the 1775 riot is well told by Harold Hikins, in 'Origins of working-class

politics: Liverpool, 1756–91', in Hikins (ed.), *Building the Union: Studies on the growth of the workers' movement: Merseyside, 1756–1967* (Liverpool: Liverpool & Toulouse Press, 1973), pp. 16–21.

6 In Manchester itself the dragoons were used, infamously, in St Peter's Fields in 1819, the 'Peterloo Massacre'. Back in Liverpool they were deployed on three occasions – the strikes of 1879, 1890 and 1911 – but only as a show of strength and as escorts for convoys of goods from the docks and to protect strike-breakers. In 1911, however, there were deaths and violence involving the police and armed infantry. Mounted and infantry battalions in 1890 and 1911 were also accompanied by the threatening presence of warships on the river, shades of the Kronstadt sailors on the Aurora in 1917, but with a reactionary rather than a revolutionary intent.

7 There were 246 port employers in Liverpool as late as 1914. See Bean, 'Custom, Job Regulation and Dock Labour in Liverpool, 1911–39', vol. 27, part 3, p. 274.

8 For a good, summary account of the Knights of Labor and their early origins in the United States see Melvyn Dubofsky and Foster Rhea Dulles, *Labor in America: a history* (Illinois: Harlan Davidson, 1999), pp. 116–37.

9 Taplin, *The Dockers' Union*, p. 100.

10 Taplin, *Liverpool Dockers and Seamen*, p. 18.

11 Taplin, *Liverpool Dockers and Seamen*, pp. 19–20.

12 Taplin, *Liverpool Dockers and Seamen*, p. 35.

13 Taplin, *Liverpool Dockers and Seamen*, p. 41.

14 Taplin, *Liverpool Dockers and Seamen*, p. 39.

15 Taplin, *Liverpool Dockers and Seamen*, p. 42.

16 Taplin, *Liverpool Dockers and Seamen*, p. 49.

17 As James Sexton, although he did not become active until some years later.

18 Taplin, *Liverpool Dockers and Seamen*, p. 50.

19 Taplin, *Liverpool Dockers and Seamen*, p. 50.

20 Taplin, *Liverpool Dockers and Seamen*, p. 51.

21 Taplin, *The Dockers' Union*, p. 56.

22 Taplin, *The Dockers' Union*, p. 58.

23 Muir, *A History of Liverpool*.

24 For the seamen, major grievances remained and especially in times of war. As late as 1943 a seaman's pay, and hence the payment to his wife ('allotments'), ceased at the time his ship sank. A merchant seaman was also, technically, a 'non-combatant', although his service from the First World War, was known as the Merchant Navy with a cap badge and uniform for the officers. Overall, the relative non-recognition of their contribution was widely resented, especially given the heavy naval casualties at sea. In the Second World War estimates of between 28,000 and 35,000 died in the Battle of the Atlantic. Not surprisingly, 'capsizing' the MN badge to 'NW' ('Not Wanted') was a widespread form of protest. See Richard Woodman, *The Real Cruel Sea: The Merchant Navy in the Battle of the Atlantic, 1939–1943* (London: John Murray, 2004) and Lane, *The Merchant Seamen's War*, p. 12. Grievances and resentments over pay and their treatment relative to the Royal Navy were still in evidence from those manning the troop transporters and supply ships during the 1982 Falklands War.

25 Other organisations did, however, remain active. The coal-heavers, for example, were powerful enough to impose most of their own terms and conditions on employers. The

carters also survived as well as the South End Association. Of the essentially benefit societies the Clarence Dock Club, for those working in the coastal trade, was the best-known survivor.

26 In the UK votes at mass meetings were made unlawful during the 1980s and replaced by the secret postal ballot. Mass meetings and demonstrations have always alarmed governments. In the USA union meetings in semi-public places such as shopping malls are also banned, despite employers invariably refusing to sanction any union meetings on their premises.

27 He became Liverpool's third archbishop in 1873. Waller judged him to be a '… solid, rather retiring figure but Tory inclined …' (*Democracy and Sectarianism*, p. 504). He contrasts him with his older contemporary, and superior in the Catholic Church, Henry Manning, who was Archbishop of Westminster and a Cardinal, during Liverpool's 1879 strike. Manning was closely linked to London's Great Dock Strike of 1889. He was seen by his enemies as a dangerous radical, even revolutionary, who had written on the socially destabilising effects of gross inequalities of wealth. His unquestioning support for the London dock communities (along with the other religious denominations and activists) significantly influenced the outcome of the strike. He was so popular on London's waterfront that a union lodge was named after him, and his image was sewn into the lodge banner! See Waller, *Democracy and Sectarianism*, p. 504; and Terry McCarthy (ed.), *The Great Dock Strike, 1889* (London: Weidenfield & Nicholson, 1988), pp. 75–6 and passim.

28 Eric Taplin provides a lively account of the tramwaymen's 'agitation' and its outcome (they would be 'out' again in 1911) in 'The Liverpool tramwaymen's agitation of 1889' in Hikins (ed.), *Building the Union*, pp. 55–76.

29 That was the *Liverpool Citizen's* term, cited in Bean, 'The Liverpool Dock Strike of 1890', p. 51.

30 Bean, 'The Liverpool Dock Strike of 1890', pp. 59–60.

31 Sexton, *Sir James Sexton Agitator*, pp. 111–12. Forty-five tons of two hundredweight (224 lbs) sacks meant the moving of 450 sacks per day. That would be at a rate of up to 50 an hour, assuming some breaks in a long working day. However, though piecework was 'job and finish' so that a 'normal' working day was not always worked, this example provides an illustration of how hard waterfront work could be for 'good' pay, especially if based upon piecework.

32 Wearing the union 'button' was a practice that probably originated in the USA where it served as a badge of resistance. It may have been brought to Liverpool by the Knights of Labor, but introduced to the NUDL by Richard McGhee, who also designed it.

33 Bean, 'The Liverpool Dock Strike of 1890', pp. 60–1.

34 Bean, 'The Liverpool Dock Strike of 1890', p. 62.

35 The sailing ship companies in the South End remained separate members of the Shipowners' Association.

36 R. Bean, 'Employers' Associations in the Port of Liverpool, 1890–1914', *International Review of Social History*, vol. 21 (1976), p. 364.

37 Bean, 'Employers' Associations in the Port of Liverpool, 1890–1914', pp. 364–5.

38 Bean, 'The Liverpool Dock Strike of 1890', pp. 64.

39 Sexton, *Sir James Sexton Agitator*, pp. 107–8.

40 Taplin, *The Dockers' Union*, pp. 28–30.

41 Sexton, *Sir James Sexton Agitator*, p. 10.

Chapter Seven: 'All the King's horses ...'

1 Tom Mann, *Tom Mann's Memoirs* (London: Macgibbon & Kee, 1967 edition), p. 223.
2 Waller, *Democracy and Sectarianism*, p. 15.
3 Mountfield, *Western Gateway*, p. 120.
4 The grey, menacing shape of the warships would have been alarming in themselves. The name of one of them, the *Antrim*, would have made it perhaps more so to the predominantly Irish Catholic dockers of Liverpool's North End.
5 The Liverpool police also had their own grievances against their employers which drove them to their own strike action in 1919. See pp. 170–2. The police were from Birmingham and Leeds. The Birmingham force, in particular, had a reputation for vigorous policing.
6 Philip Gibbs, quoted in Eric Taplin, *Near to Revolution: The Liverpool General Transport Strike of 1911* (Liverpool: The Bluecoat Press, 1994), p. 12.
7 Margaret Postgate, later Margaret Cole the wife of G. D. H. Cole, was the sister of the historian Raymond Postgate. She was prominent in her own right as a socialist, pacifist and feminist. See Taplin, *Near to Revolution*, p. 12.
8 Waller, *Democracy and Sectarianism*, p. 255.
9 H. A. Clegg, *A History of British Trade Unions since 1889, vol. 2, 1911–1933* (Oxford: OUP, 1985), p. 568.
10 H. R. Hikins, 'The Liverpool General Transport Strike, 1911', *Transactions of the Historic Society of Lancashire and Cheshire, 1961* (1962), p. 169.
11 After 1911 the NUDL was universally recognised by employers along Liverpool's waterfront. The surge in union membership in London after the triumph of 1889–90, under favourable economic conditions, turned to decline as the trade cycle reversed itself in the 1890s. See John Lovell, *Stevedores and Dockers: A Study of Trade Unionism in the Port of London, 1870–1914* London: Macmillan, 1969), p. 120.
12 Wilson, *Dockers: the impact of industrial change*, p. 72.
13 Joseph White, *Tom Mann* (Manchester and New York: MUP, 1991), p. 178. Sexton was also to write a play, 'The Riot Act', a 'fictional' account of the strike, which included himself and performed by the Liverpool Repertory Theatre in 1914. The three main characters are Maddocks (Mann?), Waring (Larkin?) and Cunliffe (Sexton?). Cunliffe berates Maddocks for his fanaticism and obsession with solidarity but without discipline (reflecting Mann's Industrial Workers of the World connections?). Waring (Larkin) is one of the 'irresponsibles', and the men, in Cunliffe's (Sexton's) view, are '... the mob ... a bigger tyrant and a greater despot than the Capitalist system which it so vigorously denounces ...' At the close of the play he reflects on the fact that his efforts are not appreciated, and he needs to find work that would quadruple his salary. Sexton did become an MP in 1918. Lord Derby, the 17th Earl, who was Secretary of State for War from 1916 to 1918 admired Sexton as a 'very straight little man and not at all the sort to countenance Bolshevism'. See Waller, *Democracy and Sectarianism*, pp. 252–3 and 510–11.
14 This account, including the metaphor, draws upon the vivid depiction of the Great Strike in Coates and Topham, *The Making of the Labour Movement*, pp. 51–77.
15 Coates and Topham, *The Making of the Labour Movement*, p. 55.
16 Coates and Topham, *The Making of the Labour Movement*, pp. 45–50. See Ann Stafford, *A Match to Fire the Thames* (London: Hodder & Stoughton, 1961).

17 See Gareth Stedman Jones, *Outcast London: A Study in the Relationships Between Classes in Victorian Society* (Oxford: OUP, 1971), chapter 17, pp. 315–36, 'The Impact of the Dock Strike'.

18 Quoted in Coates and Topham, *The Making of the Labour Movement*, p. 61.

19 The Australian dockers ('wharfies') gave similar support to the Liverpool dockers more than eighty years later in their 1995–98 dispute.

20 Mann, *Tom Mann's Memoirs*, pp. 129–99.

21 Jonathan Schneer, *Ben Tillett: Portrait of a Labour Leader* (London and Canberra: Croom Helm, 1982), pp. 111–12.

22 Taplin, *The Dockers' Union*, p. 75.

23 Taplin, *The Dockers' Union*, p. 67.

24 Taplin, *The Dockers' Union*.

25 See H. A. Clegg, Alan Fox and A. F. Thompson, *A History of British Trade Unions since 1889, vol. 1, 1889–1910* (Oxford: OUP, 1964), passim.

26 White, *Tom Mann*, p. 173.

27 Taplin, *The Dockers' Union*, p. 81.

28 Taplin, *The Dockers' Union*, p. 100.

29 White, *Tom Mann*, pp. 75–82. See also Mann, *Tom Mann's Memoirs*, pp. 85–97.

30 White, *Tom Mann*, pp. 83–9.

31 White, *Tom Mann*, pp. 105–10.

32 The syndicalists, like most parties of the left, fought bitter ideological battles among themselves. Seizing power by way of a general strike was the main ideological strand, the other being the winning of democratic control of Parliament. Mann, under the influence of the IWW, had taken the revolutionary line. Yet in Liverpool in 1911, though his speeches were stirring, his actions were pragmatic and his aims limited.

33 Taplin, *The Dockers' Union*, p. 83. For a lively account of the women's role in 1870 Paris see Gay L. Gullickson, *Unruly Women of Paris: Images of the Commune* (Ithaca and London: Cornell University Press, 1996).

34 This account of the 1911 Strike relies for its detail on the 1962 account of Hikins, 'The Liverpool General Transport Strike, 1911'. It also draws upon contemporary press reports mainly in the *Liverpool Daily* Post and *Liverpool Courier* which gave major coverage to the events as they unfolded. For an excellent collection of the many photographs taken in 1911 and an overview see Taplin, *Near to Revolution*.

35 Hikins, 'The Liverpool General Transport Strike, 1911', pp. 176–7.

36 By 1911 the code, enhanced, was the White Book Agreement.

37 The Strike Committee co-opted him.

38 Set up when Lloyd George was at the Board of Trade in 1907.

39 It was also known, at the time, as 'Red Sunday'.

40 Hikins, 'The Liverpool General Transport Strike, 1911', p. 188.

41 Mann, *Tom Mann's Memoirs*, p. 214.

42 Mann, *Tom Mann's Memoirs*, p. 212.

43 Taplin, *The Dockers' Union*, p. 95. Waller, *Democracy and Sectarianism*, p. 255 put it at 90,000.

44 Mann, *Tom Mann's Memoirs*, p. 222.

45 Waller, *Democracy and Sectarianism*, p. 255.

46 White, *Tom Mann*, p. 176.

47 White, *Tom Mann*.

48 Hikins, 'The Liverpool General Transport Strike, 1911', p. 195.

49 Taplin, *The Dockers' Union*, pp. 102–3.

50 Hikins, 'The Liverpool General Transport Strike, 1911', p. 195.

51 Clegg, *A History of British Trade Unions since 1889*, vol. 2, table 1, p. 26.

52 Taplin, *The Dockers' Union*, pp. 100–1, drawing on R. Holton, 'Syndicalism and Labour on Merseyside, 1906–14 in Harold R. Hikins (ed.), *Building the Union: Studies on the growth of the workers' movement, Merseyside, 1756–1967* (Liverpool: Toulouse Press, 1973).

53 Taplin, *The Dockers' Union*, p. 252.

54 Taplin, *The Dockers' Union*, p. 100.

55 Taplin, *The Dockers' Union*, p. 251.

56 White, *Tom Mann*, p. 179.

Chapter Eight: War, peace and the union

1 Phillips and Whiteside, *Casual Labour*, p. 33.

2 This is an extract from a letter sent, in 1917, 'to every British household'. Cited in full in Richard van Emden and Steve Humphries, *All Quiet on the Home Front: An Oral History of Life in Britain during the First World War* (London: Headline Book Publishing, 2004), p. 194.

3 Coates and Topham, *The Making of the Labour Movement*, pp. 834–5.

4 Clegg *et al.*, *A History of British Trade Unions Since 1889*, vol. 1, *1889–1910*, Oxford: OUP, 1964), pp. 374–5 and table 5.

5 Henry Pelling, *A History of British Trade Unionism* (London: Macmillan, 1972), p. 122.

6 The Employment Act of 1982 narrowed the immunities of the 1906 Act, greatly limiting the scope for industrial action. The term 'immunities', used in a legal sense, was seemingly required in 1906 to circumvent the special peculiarities of the English common law. It was turned to political advantage in the debates of the 1980s. A positive 'right' to strike, as in other countries, would have been less easy to attack. Immunities suggested 'privileges'. Later legislation, under Margaret Thatcher, also completely removed the immunities for unofficial action. This proved especially significant in determining the course and outcome of the 1995–88 Liverpool docks' dispute, as discussed in chapter 13.

7 Phillips and Whiteside, *Casual Labour*, p. 76.

8 Phillips and Whiteside, *Casual Labour*, p. 88–9.

9 He was commissioned as Captain Williams, adjutant to the Battalion under Lord Derby's command. In April 1916 his experience was used in a more direct role in the war on his appointment to the army's transportation staff in France. See K. R. Grieves, 'The Liverpool Dock Battalion: Military Intervention in the Mersey Docks, 1915–1918', *Transactions of the Historical Society of Lancashire and Cheshire*, vol. 131 (1982), pp. 140–58.

10 Taplin, *The Dockers' Union*, p. 128.

11 The paper was published in the same year (Williams, *The Liverpool Docks Problem* (Liverpool: Northern Publishing Company, 1912)).

12 See p. 103.

13 Williams, *The Liverpool Docks Problem*.

14 See pp. 71–2. Williams also cites from Eleanor Rathbone's 1904 report in his paper: '…
    the present irregularity of employment is much greater than is arithmetically necessary
    to balance the irregularity of the amount of work in the Port taking it as a single labour
    market.'

15 Taplin, *The Dockers' Union*, p. 111.

16 Taplin, *The Dockers' Union*, p. 7.

17 Taplin, *The Dockers' Union*, pp. 108–10.

18 Phillips and Whiteside, *Casual Labour*, pp. 92–5.

19 Phillips and Whiteside, *Casual Labour*, p. 93.

20 This was a national problem. Glasgow and Manchester dockers took the same stance
    and Tillett rejected 'Labour Exchange methods' for the London docks. Clegg *et al.*, *A
    History of British Trade Unions Since 1889*, vol. 1, p. 104.

21 Clegg *et al.*, *A History of British Trade Unions Since 1889*, vol. 1, p. 92.

22 Clegg *et al.*, *A History of British Trade Unions Since 1889*, vol. 1, p. 93.

23 Clegg *et al.*, *A History of British Trade Unions Since 1889*, vol. 1, p. 95.

24 Williams addressed the Liverpool Economic and Statistical Society for the second time
    in November 1913 where he presented the developing ideas recorded here. His lecture
    was also published, as before. See R. Williams, *The First Year's Working of the Liverpool
    Docks Scheme* (London: P. S. King, 1914), p. 123.

25 The Shaw Inquiry is discussed later in the chapter. Williams, in his 1913 publication
    (*The First Year's Working of the Liverpool Docks Scheme*), had also referred to Eleanor
    Rathbone and W. Grisewood who had proposed similar ideas as early as 1886. He also
    acknowledged his friend Frederick Keeling, the academic economist (Williams, *The First
    Year's Working of the Liverpool Docks Scheme*, p. 134). Keeling was very explicit: 'if the
    employers of a port state that they require a certain normal maximum of men, they
    should pay for their labour at such a rate and in such a manner that the total sum of
    wages is sufficient to provide a fair wage all the year round for each of the men.' See
    F. Keeling, 'Towards the Solution of the Casual Labour Problem', *Economic Journal*,
    vol. 23, March (1913), pp. 6–10.

26 For good accounts of the Dockers' Battalion, drawn upon here, see Taplin, *The Dockers'
    Union*, pp. 125–37 and Grieves, 'The Liverpool Dock Battalion', pp. 139–58.

27 Grieves, 'The Liverpool Dock Battalion', p. 143.

28 Taplin, *The Dockers' Union*, p. 126.

29 Taplin, *The Dockers' Union*, p. 127.

30 Grieves, 'The Liverpool Dock Battalion', p. 142.

31 Taplin, *The Dockers' Union*, p. 129.

32 From a leading article in *The Times* calling for reprisals. Waller, *Democracy and
    Sectarianism*, p. 272.

33 Sydney Bond in van Emden and Humphries, *All Quiet on the Home Front*, pp. 73–4.

34 Cited in O'Mara, *The Autobiography of a Liverpool Slummy*, p. 166. This account in the
    Liverpool Echo was similar to that of both Pat O'Mara and Sydney Bond.

35 O'Mara, *The Autobiography of a Liverpool Slummy*, p. 163. The concentration of
    seamen's homes in a few districts of Liverpool was also a factor in the Second World
    War. Johnnie Woods (Woods, *Growin' Up: One Scouser's Social History*, chapter 9) was
    brought up in Bostock Street, off Scotland Road.

36 Waller, *Democracy and Sectarianism*, p. 272.

37 Waller, *Democracy and Sectarianism*.

38 Jeremy Black, *The British Seaborne Empire* (New Haven and London: Yale University Press, 2004), pp. 269–70.

39 van Emden and Humphries, *All Quiet on the Home Front*, p. 190.

40 van Emden and Humphries, *All Quiet on the Home Front*.

41 van Emden and Humphries, *All Quiet on the Home Front*.

42 van Emden and Humphries, *All Quiet on the Home Front*, p. 197.

43 See, for example, Flora Thompson, *Lark Rise to Candleford* (Oxford: OUP, 1939).

44 Waller, *Democracy and Sectarianism*, p. 284.

45 H. A. Clegg, *A History of British Trade Unions since 1889, vol. 3, 1911–1933* (Oxford: OUP, 1985), p. 195.

46 Waller, *Democracy and Sectarianism*, p. 284.

47 Waller, *Democracy and Sectarianism*, p. 284.

48 O'Mara, *The Autobiography of a Liverpool Slummy*, pp. 169–70.

49 Waller, *Democracy and Sectarianism*, p. 284.

50 Waller, *Democracy and Sectarianism*, p. 285. See also Coates and Topham, *The Making of the Labour Movement*, pp. 719–20.

51 See Sexton, *Sir James Sexton Agitator*, p. 264, on his support for the war.

52 Coates and Topham, *The Making of the Labour Movement*, table 18.1, pp. 681–2. These figures are from TUC Annual Reports. Even the low point of 1922 (31.6 per cent) was higher than the present figure (2008) for union density for trade union membership. For long-term historical data see G. S. Bain and R. Price, *Profile of Union Growth: A Comparative Statistical Portrait of Eight Countries* (Oxford: Blackwell, 1980).

53 Taplin, *The Dockers' Union*, p. 138.

54 Taplin, *The Dockers' Union*, pp. 141–2.

55 Following the Shaw Inquiry the employers came together in their own national negotiating body, the National Council of Employers of Dock and Riverside Labour.

56 This Act provided the basic foundation for subsequent third-party, independent arbitration. Modern examples, among others, are ACAS (with its wide, though now changed remit) and the Central Arbitration Committee (which now mainly examines and adjudicates claims for trade union recognition).

57 There had been failed attempts in the 1890s to amalgamate the London and Liverpool dockers' unions. Ben Tillett came to Liverpool in 1890 to propose a merger. McHugh, of the NUDL, opposed it, and it came to nothing. The second attempt, in 1894, was at a joint conference which passed a supportive resolution. Sexton was also in favour, but the sectionalist branches were against. See Taplin, *The Dockers' Union*, pp. 438–63.

58 Coates and Topham, *The Making of the Labour Movement*, pp. 736–7.

59 Coates and Topham, *The Making of the Labour Movement*, p. 648.

60 Taplin, *The Dockers' Union*, p. 144. Also notable, diligent team members were Bevin's secretary, Mae Forcey and George Milligan, the Liverpool District Secretary, who was well thought of by Bevin.

61 Bowley was also well known among several generations of university and other students of statistics (including the author!) for his best-selling textbook.

62 Coates and Topham, *The Making of the Labour Movement*, p. 732. See pp. 126–7 for the Liverpool grain bushellers.

63 Coates and Topham, *The Making of the Labour Movement*, p. 733.

64 Taplin, *The Dockers' Union*, p. 147.

65 Taplin, *The Dockers' Union*, p. 150.

66 Coates and Topham, *The Making of the Labour Movement*, p. 322.

67 In the first six months of 1921 unemployment climbed from 691,000 to 2,171,000.

68 Taplin, *The Dockers' Union*, pp. 151–2.

69 Coates and Topham, *The Making of the Labour Movement*, p. 723.

70 Taplin, *The Dockers' Union*, p. 154.

71 Taplin, *The Dockers' Union*, p. 155.

72 Taplin, *The Dockers' Union*, pp. 154–6.

73 Taplin, *The Dockers' Union*, p. 156.

74 Sexton, *Sir James Sexton Agitator*, pp. 268–9.

75 *Liverpool Daily Courier*, 24 January 1921, p. 8. Cited in Taplin, *The Dockers' Union*, pp. 146–7.

Chapter Nine: 'Send it down, J.C.': life and labour between the wars

1 Cited in D. E. Baines and R. Bean, 'The General Strike on Merseyside, 1926', in J. R. Harris (ed.), *Liverpool and Merseyside: Essays in the economic and social history of the port and its hinterland* (New York: Augustus M. Kelley, 1969), p. 242.

2 Cited in Davies *et al.*, *Genuinely Seeking Work*, p. 8.

3 Davies *et al.*, *Genuinely Seeking Work*, p. 22.

4 Woods, *Growin' Up: One Scouser's Social History*, p. 20.

5 Baines and Bean in Harris (ed.), *Liverpool and Merseyside*, p. 245. One of the leaders was an ex-policeman who had lost his job and pension when on strike, in 1919. He was one of those 'swathed in bandages', in the dock. For an activist/writer's contemporary account of the Walker Art Gallery demonstration and the emergence of Liverpool's contingent in the National March on London in the winter of 1922 see George Garrett, *The Collected George Garrett* (Nottingham: Trent Editions, 1999), pp. 185–239.

6 Garrett, *The Collected George Garrett*, p. 245.

7 Caradog Jones, *The Social Survey of Merseyside*, pp. 78–9, cited in Davies *et al.*, *Genuinely Seeking Work*, p. 13.

8 Gordon Philips and Noel Whiteside, *The Unemployment Question in the Port Transport Industry, 1880–1970* (Oxford: OUP, 1985), p. 179.

9 Philips and Whiteside, *The Unemployment Question*, p. 180.

10 Davies *et al.*, *Genuinely Seeking Work*, p. 19.

11 Baines and Bean in Harris (ed.), *Liverpool and Merseyside*, p. 246.

12 See chapter 13, pp. 290–7.

13 The major landmark was, of course, the Trade Disputes Act, 1906. See below, note 26.

14 Clegg, *A History of British Trade Unions Since 1889*, *vol. 2*, pp. 470–1.

15 Henry Pelling, *A History of British Trade Unions* (London: Macmillan, 1963), p. 171.

16 Somewhat paradoxically the miners saw public ownership – that is *state* control of the mines – as their only real salvation. That was recommended by the Sankey Commission as early as 1919 and achieved in 1947 under the post-war Attlee government. The rank-and-file welcomed nationalisation enthusiastically, though mistakenly, as *their* ownership of *their* industry. The state was, however, still firmly in control. That was

clearly demonstrated when the political pendulum moved sharply to the right after Mrs Thatcher's election in 1979.

17 The impact of 'overvaluing' the pound via the return to the gold standard was probably exaggerated. Coal had been facing exporting difficulties since 1921. Churchill's action may have been used as a welcome pretext to cut wages and increase hours. See also Clegg, *A History of British Trade Unions since 1889*, vol. 2, pp. 386–7 for an assessment.

18 See also Clegg, *A History of British Trade Unions since 1889*, vol. 2, p. 387.

19 Although the General Council was a representative body and responsible to Congress, it was given authority to conduct negotiations over the now locked-out miners' pay and hours with the Government and, if necessary, to call a national strike. The special conference delegates voted overwhelmingly to '… place their powers in the hands of the General Council from time to time, both regarding the conduct of the dispute and financial assistance'. (See also Clegg, *A History of British Trade Unions since 1889*, vol. 2, pp. 400–1.) It was remarkable that independent trade unions should give the TUC such authority, even on a one-off basis.

20 Baines and Bean in Harris (ed.), *Liverpool and Merseyside*, p. 239.

21 See also Clegg, *A History of British Trade Unions since 1889*, vol. 2, pp. 403–6.

22 Pelling, *A History of British Trade Unions*, p. 176.

23 See also Clegg, *A History of British Trade Unions since 1889*, vol. 2, p. 405.

24 See also Clegg, *A History of British Trade Unions since 1889*, vol. 2, p. 406.

25 See also Clegg, *A History of British Trade Unions since 1889*, vol. 2, pp. 406–7.

26 Pelling, *A History of British Trade Unions*, p. 177. The TUC was at pains to conduct the strike as an industrial dispute within the terms of the 1906 Trade Disputes Act. Nor was sympathetic action prohibited by the Act. Those aspects re-emerged in 1984–85 when the miners were again seeking the support of the TUC and individual unions. By then the scope of the Trade Disputes Act had been narrowed in the spate of legislation from 1980, and sympathetic (i.e. 'secondary') actions had been outlawed. It is interesting to note that in industrial relations and trade union terms, the 1920s were a more liberal era than the 1980s, and a national strike called by the TUC would clearly be unlawful today. For a recent assessment of the 1906 Act and proposed legislation to restore the trade unions' earlier rights see K.D. Ewing (ed.), *The Right to Strike: From the Trade Disputes Act 1906 to a Trade Union Fairness Bill* (Liverpool: Institute of Employment Rights, 2008).

27 Baines and Bean in Harris (ed.), *Liverpool and Merseyside*, p. 254.

28 Baines and Bean in Harris (ed.), *Liverpool and Merseyside*, p. 248.

29 See chapter 7, pp. 150–1.

30 Baines and Bean in Harris (ed.), *Liverpool and Merseyside*, p. 250.

31 Baines and Bean in Harris (ed.), *Liverpool and Merseyside*, p. 252.

32 Here the special dispensation for dock gatemen was similar to the measures keeping the coal mines safe and protected from flooding during strikes. Miners' deputies, as supervisors, were also traditionally required to ensure health and safety precautions at such times, in practice inhibiting their freedom to strike.

33 Baines and Bean in Harris (ed.), *Liverpool and Merseyside*, pp. 254–5.

34 Baines and Bean in Harris (ed.), *Liverpool and Merseyside*, p. 258.

35 For example David Logan, the long-serving MP for Kirkdale who lived on Scotland Road all his life. See also Baines and Bean in Harris (ed.), *Liverpool and Merseyside*, p. 260.

36 Baines and Bean in Harris (ed.), *Liverpool and Merseyside*, p. 261.

37 This raises the question as to the meaning of 'win' and what can be expected of a 'defeated' government. Such important questions were again rarely asked, let alone answered, in 1984–85 concerning the strike aims (formally against pit closures) of the National Union of Mineworkers.

38 Baines and Bean in Harris (ed.), *Liverpool and Merseyside*, p. 263.

39 Caradog Jones, *The Social Survey of Merseyside*, p. 133.

40 Caradog Jones, *The Social Survey of Merseyside*, p. 142.

41 See Timmins, *The Five Giants*, and chapter 11 in this volume.

42 Davies *et al.*, *Genuinely Seeking Work*, p. 33.

43 John Stevenson (1984), 'British Society, 1914–45', Harmondsworth: Penguin, p. 206, cited in Davies *et al.*, *Genuinely Seeking Work*, p. 33.

44 Margery Spring Rice (1939), 'Working-Class Wives: Their Health and Conditions', Harmondsworth: Penguin, p. 167, cited in Davies *et al.*, *Genuinely Seeking Work*, p. 35.

45 This was the author's own childhood experience. However, the husband and father did work that was usually heavily physical and arduous. Meat was seen by wives as an essential food for such work.

46 Cited in Davies *et al.*, *Genuinely Seeking Work*.

47 See pp. 106, 174–5.

48 Sam Davies, '"Three on the hook and three on the book": dock labourers and unemployment insurance between the wars', *Labour History Review*, 59: 3 (Winter 1994), p. 34.

49 Davies, '"Three on the hook and three on the book"', p. 35.

50 Cited in Davies, '"Three on the hook and three on the book"', p. 35.

51 Phillips and Whiteside, *Casual Labour*, p. 185.

52 O'Mara, *The Autobiography of a Liverpool Slummy*, pp. 217–18.

53 Davies, '"Three on the hook and three on the book"', pp. 37–41.

54 Making toffee apples and selling them in the back yard, customers entering through a gate in the wall, was another steady trade if the apples were of good quality. There was plenty of competition, but having a gate in the back yard was rare, which must have limited entry into the toffee apple selling market! (Author's own childhood experience.)

55 Cited in Davies *et al.*, *Genuinely Seeking Work*, p. 25.

56 In similar circumstances another woman managed to extract some extra income from her work, with some satisfaction: 'One man told us how his mother would walk from Edge Hill to Mossley Hill at the beginning of the week, collect some washing from a large house there, pawn it later in the day, take it out of pawn on Thursday, wash it on Friday and walk back to Mossley Hill on Saturday morning.' Davies *et al.*, *Genuinely Seeking Work*.

57 Davies *et al.*, *Genuinely Seeking Work*, p. 27.

58 According to Jim Mottram, a railway worker, cited in Davies *et al.*, *Genuinely Seeking Work*, p. 23. It is interesting that in 2006 the French government sought to legislate a similar age limitation on employment in the interests of a more 'flexible' labour market for young people. Adverse expert opinion and, more importantly, street demonstrations and riots, forced its abandonment.

59 Davies *et al.*, *Genuinely Seeking Work*, p. 23.

60 Davies *et al.*, *Genuinely Seeking Work*, p. 24.

61 See, for example, F. F. Ridley, 'Youth on Merseyside', *The Political Quarterly*, vol. 52, 1 (1981), pp. 16–27.

62 See, for example, Roberts, *The Classic Slum*. His Salford slum, before the Great War, was bounded by two railway systems, north and south, a furlong apart; bonded warehouses to the east; and the middle classes to the west '… bay-windowed and begardened. We knew them not.' (p. 16).

63 Heffer, *Never a Yes Man*, pp. 94–7 and passim.

64 This anecdote, though not about football *per se*, does not portray the boys' game as divided on sectarian lines, at least for these two Catholic schools (also the author's experience). At the highest, professional level, Everton and Liverpool, there is also no evidence that the teams were divided on sectarian lines, even though it is commonly believed, even in Liverpool. The original team, Everton, began in Protestant Liverpool (a Methodist chapel team in St Domingo Vale) but when a boardroom row led to the formation of Liverpool FC, the motives were the usual ones of power, ambition and money – not religion. Everton even lost their ground, Anfield, to the new club. They then acquired a ground in Goodison Road. For a good, accurate concise history see Tony Mason (1985), 'The Blues and the Reds: A history of Liverpool and Everton Football Clubs', *Historic Society of Lancashire and Cheshire*, pp. 17–20. Johnnie Dodds, in his memoir, p. 63, also strongly argues that the intense football rivalry between the two clubs was a force for unity rather than division and helped to break down sectarianism.

65 John Belchem (ed.), *Popular Politics, Riot and Labour: Essays in Liverpool History, 1790–1940* (Liverpool: LUP, 1992), puts it well as '… the character, culture and welfare networks of the old slums' (p. 18).

66 Ayers, *The Liverpool Docklands*, p. 2.

67 Many years later it was found that head lice did not necessarily flourish in the unkempt, often dirty hair of the children in the slums. It seems that the lice prefer clean hair, a conclusion much to the chagrin of middle-class mothers and headteachers.

68 The clog was also unsuitable for street football, an important factor in Liverpool. It made running very difficult and flew off when the ball was kicked. The plimsoll, light, flexible and cheap, was the widely worn 'football boot' of the streets.

69 Woods, *Growin' Up: One Scouser's Social History*, pp. 23–4.

70 Woods, *Growin' Up: One Scouser's Social History*, p. 3.

71 During the Second World War the clocks went forward a further hour for Double Summer Time.

72 For the Liverpool Police Strike, see pp. 170–2.

73 Ayers, *The Liverpool Docklands*, p. 61.

74 Ayers, *The Liverpool Docklands*, p. 68.

75 Woods, *Growin' Up: One Scouser's Social History*, pp. 52–3, gives a detailed description of the game.

76 Ayers, *The Liverpool Docklands*, p. 63. As also labour dissidents on the run, such as Leo McGree (see chapter 11, pp. 236–7) and his comrades. See Lane in Hikins (ed.), *Building the Union*, pp. 166–70.

77 See Linda Cooke Johnson, 'Criminality on the Docks', in Davies *et al.* (eds), *Dock Workers*, pp. 721–45, for an analytical, sociological, and sympathetic approach to pilfering.

78 Cooke Johnson in Davies *et al.* (eds), *Dock Workers*, p. 724.

79 Cooke Johnson in Davies *et al.* (eds), *Dock Workers*, p. 724.

80 Ayers, *The Liverpool Docklands*, p. 65.

81 Ayers, *The Liverpool Docklands*, p. 65.

82 Robert W. Cherry, 'San Francisco Bay, 1849–1960', in Davies *et al.* (eds), *Dock Workers*, p. 117.

83 Davies *et al.*, *Genuinely Seeking Work*, p. 49. Belchem, however, cites a lower proportion (15 per cent) rehoused: Belchem (ed.), *Popular Politics, Riot and Labour: Essays in Liverpool History*, p. 18.

84 Davies *et al.*, *Genuinely Seeking Work*, p. 51.

85 The term 'condemned' must also have been difficult for those, however poor, who had good family memories of their homes.

86 O'Mara, *The Autobiography of a Liverpool Slummy*, p. 218.

87 Caradog Jones, *The Social Survey of Merseyside*, p. 139. He also argued, in the same study, for the reform of the employment system at the docks, focusing, like most reformers, on decasualisation.

88 Jim Mottram in Davies *et al.*, *Genuinely Seeking Work*, pp. 51–2.

89 Davies *et al.*, *Genuinely Seeking Work*, p. 52. See also Pedersen, *Eleanor Rathbone*, chapter 17, pp. 359–78 for a detailed treatment of Eleanor Rathbone's success in achieving legislation – the Family Allowances Act. But she had to accept that the advance was paid to the father. It would have been a concession too far for most MPs.

90 Davies *et al.*, *Genuinely Seeking Work*, p. 52.

91 Davies *et al.*, *Genuinely Seeking Work*, p. 54. Father Michael O'Ryan was speaking in 1929. His parishioners in Gerard Street would, in a few years, be rehoused in Gerard Gardens, one of the new tenement blocks. The tenement was a great improvement on earlier conditions, but fell well short of the original ideal in terms of amenities.

92 Davies *et al.*, *Genuinely Seeking Work*, p. 60.

93 Davies *et al.*, *Genuinely Seeking Work*, p. 56.

Chapter Ten: Dockland under siege: the Second World War

1 John Hughes, *Port in a Storm: The Air Attacks on Liverpool and its Shipping in the Second World War* (Liverpool: National Museums and Galleries on Merseyside and Countyvise, 1993), p. 159, and p. x.

2 Cited in Janet Menzies, *Children of the Doomed Voyage* (Chichester: Wiley, 2005), p. 69.

3 The commander of U-boat 48, Heini Bleichrodt, was tried for war crimes for the sinking of the *Benares*, but was acquitted after two days. His first officer, Rolfe Hilse, maintained that they did not know the *Benares* was carrying children and, if they had, they would not have torpedoed it (Menzies, *Children of the Doomed Voyage*, pp. 69, 201).

4 C. B. A. Behrens, *Merchant Shipping and the Demands of War* (London: HMSO and Longmans Green, 1955), p. 10, note 2, cited in Mountfield, *Western Gateway*, p. 169.

5 Mountfield, *Western Gateway*.

6 Hyde, *Liverpool and the Mersey*, p. 179.

7 Mountfield, *Western Gateway*, p. 169.

8 Calculated from Hughes, *Port in a Storm*, p. 160.

9 Cited in Mountfield, *Western Gateway*, p. 165.

10 Cited in Hughes, *Port in a Storm*, p. 88.

11 Hughes, *Port in a Storm*, p. 160.

12 A Medical Research Council estimate, published in 1956, was 46.3 per cent. Cited in Woodman, *The Real Cruel Sea*, p. 679.

13 Woodman, *The Real Cruel Sea*, pp. 726–7, note 9; Lane, *The Merchant Seamen's War*, p. 12.

14 'Lascars' (from the Hindi, 'lascari', for soldier), were a familiar sight on the waterfront. They also crewed the *Benares*. The children, as they boarded, were welcomed by '... magnificent Indian men wearing huge turbans and beautiful clothes with shoes that turned up at the ends. They looked like something out of the *Arabian Nights*. And they bowed to us, called us little ladies, little gentlemen. They said "welcome to our ship". And we felt as if we were in heaven!' Bess Walder, cited in Menzies, *Children of the Doomed Voyage*, p. 38.

15 Lane's sources (*The Merchant Seamen's War*, pp. 25–6) reveal that Liverpool and London each provided 17 per cent of all merchant seamen serving in 1941. Taking even the lowest estimate of total British losses (Lane's at 28,000) that gives, proportionally, Liverpool and London's at nearly 4,800 in each case. For Liverpool, that figure exceeds the number of those killed in the bombing raids on the city or even Merseyside as a whole. The deaths at sea were also mainly those of men from a small number of localities in Liverpool, as were the air raids. For example, the *Ceramic*, sunk in December 1942, went down with all hands. Of the crew of 288 half were from Merseyside, mainly from the Scotland Road, Kirkdale, Toxteth and Walton areas, Birkenhead and Wallasey. Lane, *The Merchant Seamen's War*, pp. 25–6. The same was true of the Great War. *Lusitania*'s losses of seamen were heavily concentrated in a few streets.

16 Juliet Gardiner, *Wartime Britain, 1939–45* (London: Headline, 2004), p. 402.

17 Including Vera Brittain and her two children.

18 Angus Calder, *The People's War: Britain, 1939–1945* (London: Pimlico, 1992), p. 36.

19 Churchill was against the scheme, seeing it as defeatist. However, even after the government subsidy was withdrawn, having sent 2,500 abroad, private arrangements continued with 4,200 going to the USA and some 13,000 to Canada. See Gardiner, *Wartime Britain*, p. 404.

20 Calder, *The People's War*, p. 36.

21 Gardiner, *Wartime Britain*, p. 18.

22 Gardiner, *Wartime Britain*, p. 21.

23 Boyce, *Pillowslips and Gasmasks*, p. 7.

24 Boyce, *Pillowslips and Gasmasks*, p. 8.

25 Boyce, *Pillowslips and Gasmasks*, p. 35.

26 See chapter 9, p. 197.

27 Ayers, *The Liverpool Docklands*, p. 74.

28 A 1939 study by Liverpool University reported two-thirds of its sample of 570 children leaving from the city centre on one day were bound for Chester. The sample was unlikely to be representative, although Chester was clearly an important and attractive destination, well known to at least some of the evacuees. Cited in Boyce, *Pillowslips and Gasmasks*, p. 15.

29 Boyce, *Pillowslips and Gasmasks*, p. 403.

30 Boyce, *Pillowslips and Gasmasks*, p. 13.

31 Boyce, *Pillowslips and Gasmasks*, p. 11.

32 Boyce, *Pillowslips and Gasmasks*, p. 14.

33 One bizarre placement (in Kent and not involving a Liverpool child) was that of a 17-year-old member of the Young Communist League, billeted in a rectory. The rector's wife had difficulty with Doreen who wanted to know what the maid was paid. She also refused to go to church on Sunday, the last straw. She had to go! (Gardiner, *Wartime Britain*, p. 43). For Liverpool children there was an even more fundamental problem; in the more remote parts of north Wales the only spoken language was Welsh.

34 Gardiner, *Wartime Britain*, pp. 37–8. Orwell's account of his own childhood experience of the 'shame' of bed-wetting reiterates the conventional attitudes of the time. See George Orwell, 'Such, Such were the Joys' in '*A Collection of Essays* (New York: Harcourt, Brace, Jovanovich, 1953).

35 Boyce, *Pillowslips and Gasmasks*, p. 21.

36 Gardiner, *Wartime Britain*, pp. 40–3.

37 Brian Marsh and Sue Almond, *The Home Port: Bootle, the Blitz and the Battle of the Atlantic* (Liverpool: Sefton Council, 1993), p. 56.

38 Lane, *The Merchant Seamen's War*, p. 265; Richard Vivien, *The Unfree French: Life under the Occupation* (London: Allen Lane, 2006), p. 77.

39 Clegg, *A History of British Trade Unions since 1889, vol. 3*, pp. 239–40.

40 Clegg, *A History of British Trade Unions Since 1889, vol. 3*, pp. 253–4.

41 Clegg, *A History of British Trade Unions Since 1889, vol. 3*, p. 243. The *Liverpool Daily Post* reported another Belfast dispute in April 1943, over a traditional 'bread and butter' issue, when overtime rates should be paid. Sixty-five walked out demanding the payment of Sunday rates, on a Monday, after the partial discharge of the cargo by the military the day before. 'New Dock Dispute at Belfast', *Liverpool Daily Post*, 6 April 1943, p. 1.

42 *Liverpool Daily Post*, 20 August 1943, p. 4. This dispute, over the application of overtime rates, was always common along the docks. Overtime pay was also the trigger for the dispute over fifty years later, though in very different circumstances. It was also followed by a sympathy strike. By 1995, however, dismissal rather than suspension was the action taken, and sympathy strikes were unlawful.

43 Perrett, *Liverpool: A City at War*, p. 111.

44 Hughes, *Port in a Storm*, p. 6.

45 Marsh and Almond, *The Home Port*, p. 43.

46 Perrett, *Liverpool: A City at War*, p. 115.

47 Hughes, *Port in a Storm*, pp. 152–3.

48 Hughes, *Port in a Storm*, p. 103.

49 Churchill once remarked that '… the only thing that ever really frightened me was the U-boat peril'. Marsh and Almond, *The Home Port*, back cover.

50 There were, of course, many other 'turning points'. El Alamein (1942), Stalingrad (1942) and Kursk (1943) would have strong claims. For Liverpool it was undoubtedly May 1941.

51 Marsh and Almond, *The Home Port*, p. 38, quoting Churchill in November 1939.

52 Marsh and Almond, *The Home Port*, pp. 37–8.

53 Woodman, *The Real Cruel Sea*, p. 487.

54 Woodman, *The Real Cruel Sea*, p. 576.

55 'Sloop' might have been a more accurate description, although 'corvette' was in common use. Monsarrat's *Compass Rose* was a corvette.

56 Perrett, *Liverpool: A City at War*, pp. 157–8.

57 Marsh and Almond, *The Home Port*, p. 58.

58 *Kite* had left the battle, having used up all her depth charges. *Woodpecker* was hit by an acoustic mine and taken in tow but sank, in heavy seas, off the Scillies. See Perrett, *Liverpool: A City at War*, p. 158.

59 Perrett, *Liverpool: A City at War*.

60 Martin Gilbert, *The Day the War Ended: VE Day 1945 in Europe and Around the World* (London: Harper Collins, 1996), p. 118. The US merchant fleet also suffered heavy losses in men and ships, mainly alongside the British in the Atlantic and with the convoys to Murmansk. As the British, their proportionate fatal casualties exceeded those of their armed forces.

61 Woodman, *The Real Cruel Sea*, p. 681. Canada's part in the war has been given little credit in the British literature, even the vital role its troops played on the Normandy beaches and after. Its naval and merchant fleets were also important combatants in the Battle of the Atlantic. The Canadian Pacific line lost two of its liners in the war after they had been requisitioned as troopships. The *Empress of Britain*, a big fast ship of 42,000 tons was bombed and torpedoed in the North Atlantic in October 1940. All on board were evacuated by warships. *The Empress of Asia*, at 17,000 tons, was a veteran of the Liverpool, Hong Kong and Tokyo run. It left Liverpool on 12 November 1941 to be bombed and set on fire off its destination, Singapore, on 2 February 1942. Many of its 2,235 troops and 431 crew were taken prisoner to work on the infamous Thailand–Burma railway. Limited evidence points to the possibility that my uncle, a deckboy on the *Empress of Asia*, was one of these. He died of dysentery in 1943. Source: Registry of Shipping and Seamen (20 August 1996), Cardiff.

62 Lane, *The Merchant Seamen's War*, p. 19.

63 World War II casualties, Wikipedia (http://en.wikipedia.org/wiki/World_War_II_casualties_by_country), 13 May 2007. These cited 'official' data remain, at best, subject to wide margins of error, given that they include the inevitable 'estimates' of casualties and may even be enhanced for purposes of exaggerating a nation's contribution to victory. A recent source, using an earlier German study takes a broader, comparative perspective. This is, perhaps, as good as we can get given the passing of the years: '… for every Briton or American who died, the Japanese lost seven people, the Germans twenty, and the Soviets eighty-five.' J. D. Barber and M. Harrison, *The Soviet Home Front, 1941–45: A Social and Economic History of the U.S.S.R. in World War II* (London: Longman, 1991).

64 By January 1947, a month in which nearly 49,000 were released, the cumulative total was 4.3 million. The highest in any one month was January 1946 when 445,000 were released. See Barry Turner and Tony Rennell, *When Daddy Came Home: How Family Life Changed Forever in 1945* (London: Hutchinson, 1995), Appendix, pp. 231–2.

65 Gilbert, *The Day the War Ended*, p. 407.

66 Turner and Rennell, *When Daddy Came Home*, p. 137.

67 Turner and Rennell, *When Daddy Came Home*, pp. 56–7.

68 John Stevenson, 'The Jerusalem that Failed: The Rebuilding of Post-war Britain', in Terry Gourevish and Alan O'Day, *Britain since 1945* (London: Macmillan, 1991), pp. 97–8.

69 Hughes, *Port in a Storm*, p. 140.

70 However, bombing raids were usually at night when the dockers were not normally at work.

71 Alan Bullock, *Ernest Bevin: A Biography* (London: Heinemann, 2002), pp. 262–3; Hyde, *Liverpool and the Mersey*, p. 180.

72 Hyde, *Liverpool and the Mersey*, p. 179.

Chapter Eleven: Peace, politics and giant-killing

1 Bertolt Brecht, 'Epistle to the Augsburgers' in Hugh Aughton (ed.), *Second World War Poems* (London: Faber & Faber, 2004).

2 Cited in Peter Hennessy, *Never Again: Britain, 1945–51* (London: Jonathan Cape, 1992), p. 174.

3 Cited in Ayers, *The Liverpool Docklands*, p. 76.

4 It certainly had earlier competition for infamy: the Great War, the wars against Napoleon for close on twenty years, and the Thirty Years' War (1618–48), which took most of the ravaged German states back fifty years and killed off perhaps a fifth of the population.

5 Graeme J. Milne, 'Maritime Liverpool', in John Belchem (ed.), *Liverpool 800: Culture, Character and History*, p. 309.

6 In contrast, the Great War ended at a specific time on a specific day. See Gilbert, *The Day the War Ended*, pp. 87–98, for a good account of the difficulties of making a definitive announcement.

7 The Homer Cinema, on Great Homer Street, down from St Anthony's, was showing an afternoon film at the time of the official announcement broadcast by Churchill at 3 p.m., on 8 May. The film was stopped and all the lights put on as the manager took to the stage, in front of the blank screen, to announce that the war was officially over. The audience left quickly, en masse, skipping and shouting into the streets. No film could compete with such good news. (Author's personal recollection.)

8 Liverpool's street air-raid shelters, brick built with thin, flat, concrete roofs, virtually unused since 1942 as shelters, soon found alternative uses.

9 One especially large bonfire was on an extensive, cleared site on Doncaster Street, off Scotland Road. The open space faced onto Aintree Street which ran into Athol Street. The flames, at its peak, reached well beyond the rooftops. (Author's personal recollection.)

10 Penicillin was widely publicised as the wonder drug, although at first too expensive to produce in large quantities. That this drug would soon be available, free on prescription, seemed to many too good to be true. The National Health Service was far and away the most popular innovation in the years 1945–51. It has remained so.

11 *Liverpool Echo*, 4 July 1945, p. 3.

12 *Liverpool Echo*, 10 May 1945, p. 3.

13 There were reports, as late even as the 1980s, of Japanese soldiers, found hiding in impenetrable jungle, not knowing the war was over, waiting for orders.

14 At that time the lasting and wider impact of atomic radiation was not known to the public or even the armed forces. The two bombs were viewed simply as dwarfing anything before, causing massive destruction and loss of life on an unprecedented level. The newsreel films of Hiroshima and Nagasaki were shocking, but perhaps no more

that those of German cities as heaps of rubble and less than the horrific films that were emerging of Heinrich Himmler's death camps.

15 These 'rifles', the wooden stocks of 303s (British Army issue) with the barrels but without the steel firing mechanisms, were being sold to eager boys on Liverpool's streets. Street trading, with no questions asked, was common at that time, especially in port cities.

16 *Social Insurance and Allied Services*, Cmd 6404 (London: HMSO, 1942).

17 The title of one of C. P. Snow's novels, bestsellers in the 1950s and 1960s. Snow's 'New Men' were the British scientists and politicians competing with the Americans in 1944–45 to produce and test the first atomic bomb. The British test took place towards the end of the 1945–51 Attlee administration but without the knowledge of the full Cabinet.

18 Major Attlee, as he was affectionately known in Limehouse from his rank in the war, also liked his comforts, to the wry amusement of local people. At weekends he escaped to his mother's house in middle-class Putney. His house in the East End, a 'barracks of a place' but with an over-painted Adams fireplace, he shared with his manservant/housekeeper, Charlie Griffiths, who prepared his breakfast and ran his bath. Griffiths was at his bedside when he died in 1967. See Kenneth Harris, *Attlee* (London: Weidenfeld & Nicholson, 1982), pp. 44–5, 563.

19 *Liverpool Echo*, 5 July 1945, p. 3. The *Echo's* response was haughtily restrained, calling Braddock's charges 'irresponsible': the same as Devlin, over twenty years later, of the dockers.

20 See also Alan Bullock, *Ernest Bevin: a Biography* (London: Politico's Publishing, 2002), p. 383.

21 Waller, *Democracy and Sectarianism*, p. 387 and p. 467, note 6.

22 That was the case during his address to a large crowd on a cleared bombed site on the lower end of Hopwood Street, at which the author was present. These raucous gatherings reflected the political excitement of those days, laced with a perhaps naïve optimism. McGree did not, in the end, stand in the election, perhaps because Scotland Division was largely populated by Irish Catholics.

23 Colin G. Pooley, 'Living in Liverpool: The Modern City', in Belchem (ed.), *Liverpool 800: Culture, Character and History*, p. 252, table 3.12.

24 See p. 234.

25 Jim Griffiths, *Pages from Memory* (London: Dent, 1969), p. 81. Cited in Hennessy, *Never Again*, p. 130.

26 See p. 188.

27 Timmins, *The Five Giants*, p. 25.

28 Timmins, *The Five Giants*, p. 23.

29 Cited in Hennessy, *Never Again*, p. 123.

30 'Social Insurance and Allied Services', cited in Timmins, *The Five Giants*, p. 24.

31 Pooley, in Belchem (ed.), *Liverpool 800: Culture, Character and History*, pp. 224–5 and p. 248, table 3.2.

32 Pooley, in Belchem (ed.), *Liverpool 800: Culture, Character and History*, p. 225.

33 Pooley, in Belchem (ed.), *Liverpool 800: Culture, Character and History*.

34 Boundary Street, off Scotland Road, had twenty or so good houses with railings and steps up to the front doors: Scotland Road's own 'Rodney Street'. These doctors worked hard among the poor for relatively modest rewards, often waiving fees for the

very poorest. One, who wrote my grandmother's prescriptions, at every visit to his surgery always seemed the worst for drink. He was almost certainly not alone, given the exceptional stress of their work. He and his Boundary Street colleagues would have been enthusiastic supporters of the National Health Service.

35 In the 1930s survey Caradog Jones studied the occupations of the sons and daughters of waterfront workers. This showed that seventy per cent of sons were dock labourers or other 'unskilled' workers. Only seven per cent were in skilled occupations. For the daughters, over 40 per cent were factory workers, with nearly 20 per cent clerks, shop assistants, dressmakers, etc. Almost a quarter stayed at home to help with the domestic chores. See Caradog Jones, *The Social Survey of Merseyside*, p. 141, table xxi.

36 Recent research, using library borrowing data and library tickets, provides a more factual basis for measuring such variations in working-class communities' attitudes to education and reading. See Jonathan Rose, *The Intellectual Life of the British Working Classes* (New Haven and London: Yale University Press, 2001).

37 Ayers, *The Liverpool Docklands*, p. 27.

38 Woods, *Growin' Up: One Scouser's Social History*, pp. 7–12.

39 Hennessy, *Never Again*, pp. 160–1. Much of this provision was for returning ex-servicemen and women whose education had been interrupted or postponed by the war. Some started from scratch with special, two-year degrees. Many recall the excitement and optimism of those times. Others harboured different memories. One, the late Karl Stadtler (known to the author) was a refugee from Hitler's annexation of Austria in 1938; he stayed on after the war to take a two-year history degree at Bristol University. Many years later, though a British citizen and by then a senior academic historian, he was offered a professorship at the University of Linz. His wife encouraged him to accept. Linz was, of course, Hitler's birthplace. A few years before his death, at a public lecture at the University of Nottingham, he denounced Kurt Waldheim (the Austrian former Secretary General of the UN) for his involvement in war atrocities, as an officer in the Wehrmacht, in the Balkans. It was a kind of revenge.

40 Hennessy, *Never Again*, p. 158.

41 Crossland's historic circular (10\65) to local authorities 'requested' them to set up comprehensives.

42 Sir Toby Weaver, cited in Hennessy, *Never Again*, p. 158.

43 Hennessy, *Never Again*, pp. 161–2.

44 As in the author's own school, St Sylvester's. The opponents of any form of selection, enjoyed a little *Schadenfreude* many years later when Sir Cyril Burt, the famous educationalist and the begetter of selection at eleven, after his death was found to have falsified his research data to demonstrate the accuracy and value of intelligence tests.

45 Pay beds remained an issue, especially when Barbara Castle was at the Department of Health, twenty years later.

46 See Timmins, *The Five Giants*, p. 115.

47 The National Insurance Scheme, with unemployment, pensions and accident benefits all became law on the same day, 5 July 1948.

48 *Liverpool Daily Post*, 5 July 1968, p. 8 on the twentieth anniversary of the founding of the NHS.

49 *Liverpool Daily Post*, 5 July 1968, p. 2.

50 *Liverpool Daily Post*, 5 July 1968.

51 *Liverpool Daily Post*, 12 July 1950, p. 4. See also Alice Law, page 232, earlier.

52 *Liverpool Daily Post*, 5 July 1949, p. 4.

53 *Liverpool Daily Post*, 5 July 1949.

54 Pooley, in Belchem (ed.), *Liverpool 800: Culture, Character and History*, pp. 232–3.

55 Pooley, in Belchem (ed.), *Liverpool 800: Culture, Character and History*.

56 A retired miner, Fred Thompson of Mansfield, in the 1980s told the author of the time, before the NHS, when he made an incubator for his two prematurely born sons out of a stretched blanket, on hoops across a low-sided tangerine box, with a 100 watt lamp rigged up on a board at one end, 'like an American pioneer's covered wagon'. When the NHS actually came in, he and all the others he lived among couldn't believe it.

57 The author's grandmother was prescribed the drug to treat a chronic leg ulcer. Also, before the ready availability of drugs and medications, people were obsessed with 'being regular'. George Beecham, with his famous pills, built a fortune upon it. After 5 July 1948 Beechams' Pills sales began to take a downwards path. See T.A.B. Corley: *Beechams, 1848–2000: From Pills to Pharmaceuticals* (Lancaster: Crucible Books, forthcoming, 2011).

58 See Timmins, *The Five Giants*, pp. 261–2.

59 See p. 201.

60 Home ownership in Liverpool has always lagged behind the national average, itself an indicator of higher levels of poverty, lower incomes and insecure employment. It did not become the largest form of tenure until 1991. See Pooley in Belchem (ed.), *Liverpool 800: Culture, Character and History*, p. 220 and p. 253, table 3.13.

61 Pooley in Belchem (ed.), *Liverpool 800: Culture, Character and History*, p. 220.

62 R. Bradbury, 'Post-war housing in Liverpool', *Town Planning Review*, 27 (1956/57), pp. 145–63.

63 Pooley in Belchem (ed.), *Liverpool 800: Culture, Character and History*, p. 220.

64 Bradbury, 'Post-war housing in Liverpool', p. 153.

65 M. Cormack and K. Cook, 'Liverpool housing: facts and figures', in D. Morley (ed.), *Liverpool: Liverpool Council for Voluntary Service* (1981), p. 30.

66 Ayers, *The Liverpool Docklands*, pp. 78–81.

67 Peter Townsend, *The Family Life of Old People* (London: Routledge & Kegan Paul, 1957), p. 196. See also Young and Willmott's famous study of London's East End and its 'successor' work published nearly fifty years later. This separation in time vividly illustrates decline, change and transformation in the work, life and population of another waterfront community. Michael Young and Peter Willmott, *Family and Kinship in East London* (London: Routledge & Kegan Paul, 1957); Geoff Dench, Kate Gavion and Michael Young, *The New East End: Kinship, Race and Conflict* (London: Profile Books, 2006).

68 See also John Finch's 1848 Survey, pp. 82–3.

69 Pooley in John Belchem (ed.), *Liverpool 800: Culture, Character and History*, p. 221.

70 Pooley in John Belchem (ed.), *Liverpool 800: Culture, Character and History*, p. 223.

71 Another from the same mould was Lord Donovan. His Royal Commission ranked more highly than Devlin's Inquiry and had a wider remit, including the seeming breakdown of the once stable and orderly industrial relations system. It began work in 1965. It would report in 1968, a year after Devlin. For Donovan see *Royal Commission on Trade*

Unions and Employers' Associations, 1965–68: Report presented to Parliament by Command of Her Majesty, cmnd 3623 (London: HMSO, 1968).

Chapter Twelve: High hopes, false dawns … old ways, and Devlin

1   Wilson, *Dockers: the impact of industrial change.*

2   Dash, *Good Morning Brothers!*

3   Phillips and Whiteside, *Casual Labour.*

4   Hennessy, *Never Again*, p. 273. The severe winter of 1947 essentially brought the economy to a halt. Weather, historically, has often been a significant factor in military victories and defeats, usually bad weather and defeats. Fortunately, for Britain, the winters of 1940–42 were not so severe.

5   Hennessy, *Never Again*, p. 284.

6   Jackson, *Labour Relations on the Docks*, p. 10.

7   In his 1970 memoirs Albert Speer comments on the mobilisation of labour in 'authoritarian Germany' compared to 'democratic England', in that 'It remains one of the oddities of this war that Hitler demanded far less from his people than Churchill and Roosevelt did from their respective nations'. Speer, and Hitler, did of course make a significant use of imported slave labour to maintain the production of armaments at a high level almost to the end of the war. See Speer, *Inside the Third Reich: Memoirs by Albert Speer* (New York and Toronto: The Macmillan Company, 1969), pp. 256–69.

8   Jackson, *Labour Relations on the Docks*, p. 37 (citing a *London Times* editorial).

9   Jackson, *Labour Relations on the Docks*, pp. 30–1.

10 Clegg, *A History of British Trade Unions since 1889, vol. 3*, pp. 340–1.

11 Wilson, *Dockers: the impact of industrial change*, p. 93.

12 Jackson, *Labour Relations on the Docks*, p. 33. Any guaranteed payment for not working was still anathema for the still influential old school of employer on the NDLB with memories going back to inter-war mass unemployment (See Wilson, *Dockers: the impact of industrial change*, p. 157). But too low a guarantee, especially if less than unemployment benefit, would limit attendance with a 'three on the hook, two on the book' effect as between the wars. That would not meet the scheme ports' search for stable earnings and employment on the docks. In the event, dockers' earnings rose steadily in the post-war period, climbing ahead of national average weekly earnings though remaining unstable (Jackson, *Labour Relations on the Docks.*, pp. 104–6).

13 Wilson, *Dockers: the impact of industrial change*, pp. 98–101.

14 Wilson, *Dockers: the impact of industrial change.*

15 Wilson, *Dockers: the impact of industrial change*, p. 117.

16 Jackson, *Labour Relations on the Docks*, p. 106, table 5.

17 Jackson, *Labour Relations on the Docks*, table 4.

18 Phillips and Whiteside, *Casual Labour*, p. 246.

19 See p. 177.

20 Phillips and Whiteside, *Casual Labour*, pp. 248–9.

21 *Casual Labour*, p. 246.

22 Jackson, *Labour Relations on the Docks*, p. 42, table 1. Simplistic explanations for stike-proneness were widely accepted by public opinion, led by the media. The first wise words, and possibly still the best are by Knowles in his seminal study

of British experience between 1911 and 1947: '... before considering [the statistics of strike causes] we must clear the ground by making two points: (a) that strikes are only one of many possible manifestations of industrial unrest, and (b) that the statistics of strike causes, relating only to immediate causes, may not adequately reflect their underlying causes'. K. G. J. C. Knowles, *Strikes – A Study in Industrial Conflict* (Oxford: Blackwell, 1952), pp. 209–10. A later study for the period thirty years after that of Knowles, soberly countering the now commonplace national hysteria when workers strike, concludes, 'The occurrence of strikes is unfortunate, in that they usually impose some costs on all concerned. From time to time these costs may be extremely severe, and may well cancel out the gains, even to those who appear to have won. Nevertheless, they are an unfortunate necessity in that, on some occasions, their benefits – which are indispensable to a democratic society – could not be secured in any other way.' J. W. Durcan, W. E. J. McCarthy and G. P. Redman, *Strikes in Post-War Britain: A study of stoppages of work due to industrial disputes, 1946–73* (London: Allen & Unwin, 1983), p. 432.

23 For the detailed origins and course of these and other disputes see Jackson, *Labour Relations on the Docks*, pp. 51–4.

24 Interestingly, as Wilson maintains, the NASD card was not always 'blue'. It issued different coloured cards each quarter as a way of checking on members in arrears with their dues. Wilson, *Dockers: the impact of industrial change*, p. 81.

25 See Coates and Topham, *The Making of the Labour Movement*, passim, for a detailed account of the conflict between the 'blues' and the 'whites'. At its height, post-Devlin, Jack Jones (then still a senior officer in the TGWU) used his contacts and influence to try to end the rivalry. See also below, note 53.

26 This important TUC committee was set up following the TUC's Bridlington Congress in 1939. It soon became known as the 'Bridlington Committee'. Chairing this important committee would later make the reputation of John Monks, who went on become the TUC's General Secretary.

27 For a full account see Jackson, *Labour Relations on the Docks*, pp. 61–6.

28 Jackson, *Labour Relations on the Docks*, p. 66.

29 Jones, *Union Man*, pp. 61–6.

30 See p. 277.

31 Jackson, *Labour Relations on the Docks*, p. 105, table 4.

32 Wilson, *Dockers: the impact of industrial change*, p. 169; Dash, *Good Morning Brothers!*, chapter 7.

33 The Wilson government seemed intent on bringing the industry within the public sector for a mix of reasons – its importance, and some lingering commitment to socialism as a route towards limiting conflict. That died with the loss of office in 1970 and the earlier commitment, in opposition, amounted to little.

34 The author's grandmother, who lived off Scotland Road for a good part of her life, in the late 1950s still had a vivid recall of soldiers 'with fixed bayonets' marching down Scotland Road.

35 Turnbull *et al.*, *Dock Strike*, p. 24, table 1; Wilson, *Dockers: the impact of industrial change*, p. 295, table 3.

36 Wilson, *Dockers: the impact of industrial change*, p. 172.

37 The Institute of Workers' Control, its principal advocate still based in Nottingham,

was then a well-funded, activist organisation with considerable influence among shop stewards, unofficial movements and in some unions. It published a large quantity of accessible books and pamphlets at a time when, in universities and the WEA, day release and other educational programmes for industrial workers (including dockers and miners) and shop stewards were funded by employers along with government support and subsidies.

38 Devlin, *Final Report of the Committee of Inquiry under the Rt. Hon. Lord Devlin into certain matters concerning the Port Transport Industry*, cmnd 2734 (London: HMSO, 1965), p. 4. Turnbull *et al.*, almost thirty years later, points to Devlin's devout Roman Catholicism and '... strong sense of "right and wrong"'. That morality judged both casualism and striking as sins, but in practice linked together so closely that the removal of casualism would, at the same time, remove the cause of strikes along the waterfront (Turnbull *et al.*, *Dock Strike*, p. 19). Devlin was not alone in his stern view of casualism, from Eleanor Rathbone onwards. But she, and those who thought like her, were concerned with the *social* impact of casualism, not the *economic*.

39 University of Liverpool, Department of Social Science, *The Dock Worker: An Analysis of Conditions of Employment in the Port of Manchester* (Liverpool: LUP, 1956).

40 Jackson, *Labour Relations on the Docks*, p. 87 citing a leading article in *The Times*.

41 American academics were, at the time, deeply interested in the failings of the British economy, for which they commonly laid the blame on British workers and their trade unions. In their 1968 contribution to the debate the economists of the prestigious Washington-based Brookings Institution concluded: 'Does economic advice here overstep into social imperative? Are we not propounding growth and change in a society where don and docker alike prefer tradition, leisure and stability? This may be. But many segments of British society have declared for growth, or at least the fruits of growth. Their aspirations can be satisfied – at a price – and they should know the price they pay.' Richard E. Caves *et al.*, *Britain's Economic Prospects* (London: Brookings Institution/Allen & Unwin, 1968), p. 495. It is of some note that, forty years later, that 'price', in terms of 'change' has been paid but the long-term trend rates of productivity and economic growth have remained much the same.

42 Wilson, *Dockers: the impact of industrial change*, p. 172.

43 Immediately after Devlin he made his mark on the Royal Commission on Trade Unions and Employers' Associations, set up by the Wilson government chaired by another judge (Lord Donovan) in 1965, to find out what ailed the once well-functioning industrial relations system and the proposed remedies. The famous 'two systems' diagnosis was essentially his (aided by his Nuffield College colleague Allan Flanders and the labour law academic Otto Kahn Freund) as well as the main remedy of legitimising and strengthening the role of shop stewards within collective bargaining. The problems in the 'strike prone' industries, including the docks, the Commission saw as behind much of this. See *Royal Commission on Trade Unions and Employers' Associations, 1965–68*. His last public policy contribution was as Chair of the Pay Comparability Commission until sacked in 1981 by Margaret Thatcher. Clegg was, undoubtedly, not 'one of us', as she might have said.

44 Wilson, *Dockers: the impact of industrial change*, pp. 172–3.

45 Jones, *Union Man*, p. 163.

46 Wilson, *Dockers: the impact of industrial change*, pp. 187–8.

47 Cited in Vernon H. Jensen, *Decasualization and Modernization of Dock Work in London* (Ithaca, New York: Cornell University, 1971), pp. 16–17.

48 Ministry of Labour, *Report of the Committee of Inquiry into the Wages Structure and Level of Pay for Dockworkers*, cmnd 3104 (London: HMSO, 1966).

49 Andrew Crichton, later knighted, was Chair of the National Association of Port Employers; Frank Cousins was the General Secretary of the TGWU. See Wilson, *Dockers: the impact of industrial change*, pp. 158–62.

50 These are listed in Jensen, *Decasualization and Modernization of Dock Work in London*, p. 17, drawing on *Final Report of the Committee of Inquiry under the Rt Hon. Lord Devlin into certain matters concerning the Port Transport Industy*, cmnd 2734 (London: HMSO, 1965), note 38 above.

51 See Wilson, *Dockers: the impact of industrial change*, pp. 178–9.

52 Jack Jones' role as conciliator (Jones, *Union Man*, pp. 163–5) was at variance with the public and media's perception of him as a militant thorn in the side of government. His conciliation also had some success, although in that he had no support from his senior colleagues. He helped to bring the NASD in from the cold by influencing the employers' willingness to include their representatives on Devlin's National Modernising Committee, but not the NJC, as Devlin wished. The NASD did, however, leave the Modernising Committee in 1969 over its rejection of an agreement on shiftwork. By then, its membership was down to 6,381. At its peak, in 1955, it had 14,383 (Wilson, *Dockers: the impact of industrial change*, p. 208). Jones' conciliatory stance was evident, again, under the Wilson/Callaghan government from 1974. He is widely credited with being the driving influence behind the setting up of the Advisory, Conciliation and Arbitration Service in 1974–75. See also note 25 above.

53 Wilson, *Dockers: the impact of industrial change*, pp. 192–211, gives a good account of the emergence of shop stewards at the docks. See also Jack Jones' own account (Jones, *Union Man*, pp. 191–224).

54 Turnbull *et al.*, *Dock Strike*, pp. 24–5.

55 Turnbull *et al.*, *Dock Strike*, pp. 24–5.

56 Lavalette and Kennedy, *Solidarity on the Waterfront*, p. 21.

57 Turnbull *et al.*, *Dock Strike*, pp. 22–4. A study of post-Devlin strikes in the London docks also pointed to the influence of piecework, which persisted even after the Phase 2 reforms. Piecework systems have always tended to increase conflict in virtually all occupations. On the docks piecework had an historic reputation for causing trouble. Those being paid by the piece need to be able to trust those who control the system. That trust was rarely present. For the London, post-Devlin study see Michael Mellish, *The Docks after Devlin: A study of the recommendations of the Devlin Committee on industrial relations in the London docks* (London: Heinemann, 1972), pp. 134–5. A later paper accepted that piecework, especially its introduction in Liverpool, had some influence on the post-Devlin increase in strikes, but for the docks as a whole the primary explanation was neither casualism nor the industry's pay system but rather '... the competitive, unplanned nature of port transport and the chaotic structure and conditions forced on it by outside interests such as the shipping companies'. Peter Turnbull and David Sapsford, 'Why Did Devlin Fail? Casualism and Conflict on the Docks', *British Journal of Industrial Relations*, vol. 29, 2 (1991), p. 255.

58 Turnbull and Sapsford, 'Why Did Devlin Fail?', pp. 42–3.

59 Early users of containers were the British railway companies' 'freight boxes' and Jacobs' biscuits (a Liverpool firm) 'cubic boxes', both in the 1920s. But the real pioneers were the US Army's 'military boxes' for shipping armaments in the Second World War. By 1956 cargo containers were being placed on conventional vessels for trade along the east coast of the USA, followed by special container ships, and container gantries in the ports, on runs to South America and the Pacific. The first all-container transatlantic vessel arrived in Rotterdam in 1966 as containers began to enter London's Royal Docks.

60 *Financial Times*, 8 April 1989, cited in Turnbull *et al.*, *Dock Strike*, p. 47.

Chapter Thirteen: 'The greatest game no more'

1 *Liverpool Echo*, 27 November 1970, p. 5.
2 Hyde, *Liverpool and the Mersey*, p. 207.
3 Peter Turnbull and Victoria Wass, 'The Greatest Game No More: Redundant Dockers and the Demise of "Dock Work"', *Work, Employment and Society*, vol. 8, 4 (1994), pp. 487–500.
4 Lavalette and Kennedy, *Solidarity on the Waterfront*, p. 25.
5 Hyde, *Liverpool and the Mersey*, p. 210.
6 Hyde, *Liverpool and the Mersey*.
7 Hyde, *Liverpool and the Mersey*.
8 *Liverpool Daily Post*, 1 December 1971, p. 7.
9 Southampton, for many years Liverpool's direct rival, enjoyed major geological advantages. It has a double high tide and its tidal range is minimal, about two feet compared to Liverpool's thirty. It has a natural, deep water harbour – Liverpool had to construct accessible berths to minimise its disadvantages; and it has ample land for expansion, notably and later, for container traffic.
10 The Board even reformed itself, reducing its numbers from 24 to 16 and setting up a small executive committee of 7 or 8.
11 Cammell Laird had been rescued by the Wilson government, although the shipyards were not nationalised.
12 The luxury car manufacturer has no corporate connection with the aero-engine maker of the same name, although they share historical origins. Yet the irony of the same name loses none of its force. It was also seen as extravagant in very difficult times.
13 *Liverpool Echo*, 5 November 1970, p. 1.
14 Milne in John Belchem (ed.), *Liverpool 800: Culture, Character and History*, p. 204.
15 See pp. 54–7.
16 *Liverpool Echo*, 14 November 1970, p. 1.
17 *Liverpool Echo*, 18 December 1970, p. 1.
18 *Liverpool Echo*, 1 December 1970, p. 7.
19 *Liverpool Echo*, 5 September 1970, p. 7.
20 *Liverpool Daily Post*, June 1971, p. 9.
21 *Liverpool Daily Post*, 1 December 1971, p. 7.
22 *Liverpool Daily Post*, 24 March 1971, p. 1.
23 Sidney Gilman and Sharon Burn, 'Dockland Activities: Technology and Change' in W. T. S. Gould and A. G. Hodgkiss (eds), *The Resources of Merseyside* (Liverpool: LUP, 1982), p. 32.

24 Hyde, *Liverpool and the Mersey*, pp. 191–2.

25 In Belchem (ed.), *Liverpool 800: Culture, Character and History*, p. 432.

26 *Liverpool Daily Post*, 1 December 1971, p. 7.

27 See chapter 12, p. 259.

28 Turnbull *et al.*, *Dock Strike*, p. 24.

29 Jack Dash retired just as Jimmy Nolan was emerging into prominence. Nolan was a co-founder of the 1968 National Port Shop Stewards' Committee which, in the early 1970s, offered a clear challenge to the official authority of the TGWU, even under official stoppages as in 1989 (see later in the chapter). Nolan was still going strong during the 1995–98 dispute in Liverpool. For a short biography see Lavalette and Kennedy, *Solidarity on the Waterfront*, p. 8. Jack Dash has his own autobiography (Dash, *Good Morning Brothers!*).

30 Sexton, *Sir James Sexton Agitator*.

31 Phillips and Whiteside, *Casual Labour*, p. 251.

32 For the early, rapid increase in waterfront jobs for dockers' sons, see, for example, Turnbull and Wass, '"The Greatest Game No More"'. For the reversal of this process see Turnbull *et al.*, *Dock Strike*, p. 100, and Phillips and Whiteside, *Casual Labour*, p. 26 and footnote 63 later in the chapter.

33 Calculated from British Ports Federation data and Lavalette and Kennedy, *Solidarity on the Waterfront*, p. 21.

34 Lavalette and Kennedy, *Solidarity on the Waterfront*.

35 John Connolly, Docks and Waterways Secretary, TGWU, cited in Turnbull *et al.*, *Dock Strike*, p. 57.

36 Milne in Belchem (ed.), *Liverpool 800: Culture, Character and History*, pp. 430–1.

37 For the new Seaforth Dock see p. 283.

38 Milne in Belchem (ed.), *Liverpool 800: Culture, Character and History*, p. 431.

39 Liverpool's 'sailortown' originally in the area of Paradise Street, and later Union Street at Prince's Dock, was still very much alive as late as the 1950s. Liverpool was the favourite port of many seafarers, from Herman Melville to Tony Lane (the sailor turned academic and author who even stayed here). They always received a warm welcome, with ready solace for all their physical, even spiritual needs – if that were required. They were also very welcome for their pay, burning holes in their pockets, to be preyed upon by the owners of cheap lodgings ('crimps') and prostitutes. In contrast, their commercial instincts often involved them in informal businesses in goods, animals and birds, including monkeys and parrots. Park Lane (a street listed in the seafarers' song 'Leaving of Liverpool') was the main street for parrots which could still be bought there in the 1950s, Amazon Greens bought for £1 going for £10. For a colourful account see Lane, *Liverpool: Gateway of Empire*, pp. 105–6; also Stan Hughill, '*Sailortown*' (London: Routledge & Kegan Paul, 1967). Tony Lane, on his first shore leave, which was in Liverpool in 1956, saw Liverpool as '… a sailor's city like no other' (*Liverpool: Gateway of Empire*, p. 10).

40 Liverpool's Maritime Museum has on display a few surviving pieces from Herculaneum pottery.

41 This brief account and what follows draws specifically upon John Murden in Belchem (ed.), *Liverpool 800: Culture, Character and History*, pp. 404 et seq. See also Trever Cornfoot, 'The Economy of Merseyside, 1945–1982: quickening decline or post-industrial change?', in Gould and Hodgkiss (eds), *The Resources of Merseyside.*, p. 31.

42 Murden in Belchem (ed.), *Liverpool 800: Culture, Character and History*, p. 404.

43 Murden in Belchem (ed.), *Liverpool 800: Culture, Character and History*, pp. 408–9.

44 See Milne in Belchem (ed.), *Liverpool 800: Culture, Character and History*, p. 257.

45 A practice known by US workers as 'whipsawing', from the two-man, alternating log saw.

46 Murden in Belchem (ed.), *Liverpool 800: Culture, Character and History*, p. 432.

47 See Phillips and Whiteside, *Casual Labour*, pp. 237–68, for a demythologising analysis of the deeper causes of waterfront unrest.

48 See, for example, R. Bean and Peter Stoney, 'Strikes on Merseyside: A Regional Analysis', *Industrial Relations Journal*, vol. 17, 1 (1986), pp. 9–33. The national miners' strike of 1985–86 is also a case of employer provocation inducing a strike at a time unfavourable to the National Union of Mineworkers, that is, in the summer when coal stocks are normally high and electricity demand at a low level. See, among others, Brian Towers, 'Posing larger questions: the British miners' strike of 1984–85', *Industrial Relations Journal*, vol. 16, 2 (1985), pp. 8–25.

49 Bean and Stoney, 'Strikes on Merseyside: A Regional Analysis'.

50 See Murden, in Belchem (ed.), *Liverpool 800: Culture, Character and History*, pp. 435–6.

51 Murden, in Belchem (ed.), *Liverpool 800: Culture, Character and History*, p. 415.

52 Some suggest that the toy construction kit encouraged the early development and skills of later engineers. For an excellent, recent history of Meccano Ltd see K.D. Brown, *'Factory of Dreams': A History of Meccano Ltd* (Lancaster: Crucible Books, 2007).

53 A powerful image of Tate & Lyle's demolition featured in Alan Bleasdale's famous TV series *Boys from the Blackstuff*, broadcast in 1982.

54 See p. 82.

55 Murden in Belchem (ed.), *Liverpool 800: Culture, Character and History*, pp. 436–7.

56 John Cornelius, cited by Murden in Belchem (ed.), *Liverpool 800: Culture, Character and History*, p. 440.

57 Milne in Belchem (ed.), *Liverpool 800: Culture, Character and History*, p. 257, for a brief discussion.

58 *Liverpool Daily Post*, 21 July 1971, p. 2.

59 *Liverpool Daily Post*, 31 July 1972, p. 6.

60 Hyde, *Liverpool and the Mersey*.

61 Lavalette and Kennedy, *Solidarity on the Waterfront*, p. 21, table 1; see also, Gilman and Burn, in Gould and Hodgkiss (eds), *The Resources of Merseyside*.

62 This graphic epithet was used by a Liverpool shop steward to describe the redundancy payments offered during the strike and in the wake of the 1989 return to work. See Turnbull *et al.*, *Dock Strike*, p. 172.

63 Phillips and Whiteside, *Casual Labour*, p. 268. Jack Jones was rightly proud of his efforts to secure permanent work on the docks, but it was an achievement built on sand, as one docker reminded him: 'As I left Transport House that day one of the shop stewards came up to me. He was holding his little son by the hand. "What about my future?" he asked. "You've got a permanent job as a result of this agreement [Aldington-Jones]," I replied. "Ah," he said, "but what about the boy?"' Jones, *Union Man*, p. 253.

64 Phillips and Whiteside, *Casual Labour*, p. 31 and p. 49, table 2.1.

65 Phillips and Whiteside, *Casual Labour*, p. 24, table 1.5.

66 Traditionally, those opting for redundancy were accused by those remaining of 'selling

their jobs'. That charge lost much of its force given the increasing numbers involved and the industry's deteriorating prospects.

67 Turnbull *et al.*, *Dock Strike*, p. 100.

68 Turnbull *et al.*, *Dock Strike*, p. 96.

69 Turnbull *et al.*, *Dock Strike*, pp. 108–9.

70 The Thatcher legislation was a 'step-by-step' approach in six Acts of Parliament, with five directly limiting the ability of trade unions to conduct and win strikes. The first, the Employment Act of 1980, regulated picketing, in terms of numbers involved as well as outlawing 'flying pickets', used effectively in the disputes of the 1970s, especially by the miners. The 1982 Employment Act, among a number of changes and reforms, narrowed the definition of a trade dispute established by the 1906 Trades Disputes Act, ruling out strikes with 'political' aims. The third piece of legislation, the Trade Union Act 1984, made majority support for industrial action mandatory, via secret ballots, if it was to be within the law. The ballots themselves had to be conducted within strict time limits, as did the implementation of a vote to strike. 1988 saw the passage of a further Employment Act that allowed limited scope for secondary action (that is, 'sympathy' strikes). The last statute, the Employment Act of 1990, saw the final stage of outlawing unofficial strikes. All immunities were removed. Union officials (on pain of sanctions against the union's assets) were required to repudiate unofficial strikes. The strikers themselves were also liable to dismissal. For a detailed analysis and discussion of the Thatcher government's legislation see Brian Towers (ed.), *A Handbook of Industrial Relations Practice* (London: Kogan Page, 1992). For the 1906 *Trade Disputes Act* see K. D. Ewing (ed.), *The Right to Strike: from the Trade Disputes Act 1906 to a Trade Union Freedom Bill 2006* (London: Institute of Employment Rights, 2006).

71 Turnbull *et al.*, *Dock Strike*, pp. 124–7.

72 Mickey Fenn in the Communist Party's newspaper, the *Morning Star*. See Turnbull *et al.*, *Dock Strike*, p. 129.

73 Turnbull *et al.*, *Dock Strike*, pp. 129–33.

74 For a comment on the life of Jack Dash see Turnbull *et al.*, *Dock Strike*, p. 23. Unofficial leaders of his stature by this time had vanished from the waterfront.

75 Turnbull *et al.*, *Dock Strike*, pp. 141–74.

76 Turnbull *et al.*, *Dock Strike*, p. 169.

77 Turnbull *et al.*, *Dock Strike*, p. 182, table 6.2. See also Lavalette and Kennedy, *Solidarity on the Waterfront*, p. 21, table 1.

78 Turnbull *et al.*, *Dock Strike*, p. 175.

79 A second was held on 8 September 1997.

80 See Chris Carter, Stewart Clegg, John Hogan and Martin Kornberger, 'The Polyphonic Spree: The Case of the Liverpool Dockers', *Industrial Relations Journal*, vol. 34, 4 (2003), pp. 290–304.

81 The leaders of WOW soon became national figures and platform speakers, often to their own surprise. They also developed their own, unique tactics in their confrontations of senior port managers, both face-to-face at their homes and by letter. For brief biographies of most of the leading members (Doreen McNally, Sue Mitchell, Joan Bennett, Pat Walker, Irene Campbell and Cathy Dwyer) and an account of WOW, see Lavalette and Kennedy, *Solidarity on the Waterfront*, chapter 3, pp. 45–66.

82 These 'guarantees' were cited by Jimmy Nolan, of the Merseyside Port Shop Stewards

Committee, in the House of Commons Report on the dispute. It had also, by then, been referred to ACAS. Nolan had first come to work on the docks in 1964 at the age of 19, and was first involved in the post-Devlin strike of 1967. Jimmy Davies also figured prominently at the parliamentary hearing and in the report. He had followed a path parallel to that of Nolan, starting work on the docks at 18 in 1960. He first became a steward in 1969 and both he and Nolan were prominent members, over many years, of the Merseyside Port Shop Stewards Committee. Another long-serving activist was Terry Teague, who started on the docks in the same year as Jimmy Nolan, 1967, at age 15, becoming a registered docker at the minimum age, three years later. The fourth to give evidence at the hearing was Mike Carden, from a family of dockers, who first came to work on the docks, in the clerical section, when he was 18 in 1972. He was one of a number of energetic, able, articulate 'office dockers' who played a prominent part in disputes up that of 1995–98. See Education and Employment Committee, *The Employment Implications of the Industrial Dispute in the Port of Liverpool*, HC 413 (London: HMSO, 1996), paras 104–7, pp. 10–16, 27–38, 43–5, for their evidence and memoranda on behalf of the Merseyside Port Shop Stewards Committee.

83 'Further memorandum submitted by the Mersey Docks and Harbour Company', *The Employment Implications of the Industrial Dispute in the Port of Liverpool*, HC 413, paras 2–9, pp. 45–6.

84 *The Employment Implications of the Industrial Dispute in the Port of Liverpool*, HC 413, para. 10, p. 46.

85 *The Employment Implications of the Industrial Dispute in the Port of Liverpool*, HC 413, para. 8, p. 46.

86 *The Employment Implications of the Industrial Dispute in the Port of Liverpool*, HC 413, para. 23, p. 24.

87 MDHC was not 'involved' in all the operating companies. It had a 100 per cent interest in five, 50 per cent in four and 33 per cent in one. In one other, it had a 'landlord' relationship. For the others, its involvement was 'none', including Torside Ltd and PDP Services. See *The Employment Implications of the Industrial Dispute in the Port of Liverpool*, HC 413, para. 6, pp. 42–3.

88 Bernard Bradley also had two sons. One of them, James, worked for a time as General Manager of Torside, his father as Managing Director.

89 The record of the events leading up to the final dismissals of the 329, taking the total to 409, has several versions. The account here draws on those of the MDHC, Lavalette and Kennedy, *Solidarity on the Waterfront*, pp. 1–2, the Merseyside Port Shop Stewards (Employment Committee, *The Employment Implications of the Industrial Dispute in the Port of Liverpool*, and an interview with Bob Richie, an ex-docker and former Torside shop steward, in January 2007. The author also had a discussion in December 2006 with Eric Leatherbarrow, Head of Peel Port's Corporate Affairs (the successor to the MDHC) who was closely involved in the 1995–98 dispute and attempts to find solutions.

90 Close questioning of Bernard Cliff, the then Port Operations Director, by the Commons Committee made it clear that PDP contracted its employees on a casual, no guaranteed work basis (*The Employment Implications of the Industrial Dispute in the Port of Liverpool*, paras 63 and 64, p. 8). It was also clear that Drake Port Distribution Services provided a permanent, trained, replacement workforce to handle cargo at the Container Terminal.

91 Legal and other arguments raged within union and labour movement circles as to how

far the union could support the dockers without falling foul of draconian penalties. The dockers themselves, and others, argued that after they were dismissed, actions for unofficial action did not apply. Bill Morris, the then TGWU General Secretary, was in any case accused of making solemn promises, in rank-and-file meetings, which he did not keep.

92 From a confidential source.

93 From an interview transcript. The interview was conducted early in the dispute by Bill Hunter, an author and activist based in Liverpool.

Chapter Fourteen: The Leaving of Liverpool

1 Murden, in Belchem (ed.), *Liverpool 800: Culture, Character and History*, p. 429.

2 P. Du Noyer, cited in Murden, in Belchem (ed.), *Liverpool 800: Culture, Character and History*, p. 436.

3 Cited in Ayers, *The Liverpool Docklands*, p. 80.

4 EU Regional Policy identifies those regions most in need of economic assistance from the EU's Structural Funds. The highest, Objective One, is for regions with Gross Domestic Product below 75 per cent of the EU average. Objective Two is for regions with less serious problems but perhaps with high and permanent levels of unemployment. Liverpool was given Objective Two status in 1986 and then Objective One in 1993 when GDP per capita was at the 73 per cent average. Amid growing prosperity, it lost Objective One status in 2006.

5 Nick Mathiason, 'Liverpool finds the formula for success', *The Guardian*, 7 September 2003; Murden, in Belchem (ed.), *Liverpool 800: Culture, Character and History*, pp. 470–85 describes Liverpool's recovery in local detail.

6 The UNESCO accolade was briefly in some danger in the autumn of 2006 when the UN agency publicly voiced its doubts about the threat, from inappropriate and large buildings, to Liverpool's world famous skyline. The threat did not materialise.

7 The old rivalry is as strong as ever. Everton had originally sought Stanley Park but were denied by the council. The case for the retention of the historic park as a public space remains strong. Everton are still seeking another ground. At the time of writing, a site in Kirkby aided by funding from Tesco for an adjacent supermarket, is being sought subject to a public inquiry, but not without opposition from those supporters who wish to remain within the city. Liverpool FC is now owned by Americans, but has announced postponement of its plans to build a new stadium in Stanley Park.

8 C. Couch, 'City of Change and Challenge: Urban Planning and Regeneration in Liverpool', pp. 50–1, cited in Murden, in Belchem (ed.), *Liverpool 800: Culture, Character and History*, p. 463.

9 Cargoes within the Freeport are only liable for the payment of EU import duties and VAT when they leave. This cuts costs for importers, in a way similar to goods held in bonded warehouses such as alcoholic spirits and tobacco.

10 Eric Leatherbarrow, Head of Corporate Affairs, Peel Ports Group.

11 See table, p. 303.

12 See table, p. 303.

13 Port of Liverpool *Handbook and Directory 2005* (Liverpool: Mersey Docks and Harbour Company, 2005) p. 70.

14 London Gateway is owned by DP World based in Dubai, the world's fourth largest container port by volume, which took over P&O, the iconic British company in 2006. For that and the London Gateway project see R. Wright, 'Port plan "will change" distribution', London: *Financial Times*, 10 January 2007, p. 4.

15 See table, p. 303.

16 See table, p. 305.

17 This is Lane's estimate. See *Liverpool: Gateway of Empire*, p. 42.

18 Devlin had been demanding action in 1965, and the abolition of the scheme ports after 1989 did little to improve conditions. Bob Richie, the Torside shop steward who was working at Seaforth from 1991 to 1995 observed that, '… even in the 1970s the conditions were an outrage … on the dock estate in Liverpool I think the conditions are disgusting, the facilities just don't compare … back to Sweden again. We walked into it [i.e. the facilities for the dockers] like a five-star restaurant … subsidised meals, subsidised canteen, beautiful set-up, saunas for the men to come out to. They actually employ a guy in an overall room who's an ex-docker, who had an accident and now all he does is look after the men's overalls, to clean their overalls every day … in Liverpool you'd be walking around in the same pair of overalls for twelve months without them getting washed.' See chapter 13, note 92.

19 The Port of Liverpool *Handbook and Directory* (2005) lists six stevedoring companies, including Drake Port Distribution Services which was being used by the MDHC during the 1995–98 dispute.

20 Pooley in Belchem (ed.), *Liverpool 800: Culture, Character and History*, p. 206.

21 The trade union 'wage premium', the average difference in wages between unionised and non-unionised workers, once substantial, has now virtually gone. There is no need here to list the likely reasons.

22 Within hours of the announcement, in early June 2003 that Liverpool had won the European Capital of Culture award for 2008, the prices of city centre apartments began to rise, reportedly '… some by around 15%'. In January 2003 a speculative purchase of apartments was made by a London-based director of recruitment for £95,000 each. They were worth £110,000 within six months. This was seen as good news for Liverpool since it was likely that the average price of a house, then £63,000, would also rise. It did. For Merseyside, in January 2007, it reached just under £131,000. By January 2005 it was ahead of the North West as a whole, although there were signs of it weakening in 2007. This doubling of the cost of finding a home would, of course, not be paralleled by rising earnings, especially in Liverpool. See Helen Carter, 'Culture means cash for housing market', *The Guardian*, 18 June 2003, p. 10; Land Registry, *House Price Index January 2001 to January 2007* (Cymraeg: Land Registry, 2007).

23 One 'solution', widely adopted by lenders, was to extend the house price earnings multiple as high as six so that high prices could be met on low earnings. With a low deposit houses could then be 'affordable'. One recent poster campaign in Liverpool guaranteed moving into a new house with 'only £99.00 deposit'. [Editor's note: Professor Towers wrote this section before the financial crisis of 2008.]

24 The warehouse is just up from the entrance to the Clarence Dock, now filled in. On the wall, on the right-hand side of the former entrance gate, is a fresh looking, appropriately green, plaque commemorating a 150th anniversary and which reads: 'Through these gates passed 1,300,000 Irish migrants who fled the Great Famine and

"took the ship" to Liverpool in the years 1845–1852. Remember the Great Famine.'
25 See p. 248.
26 See pp. 197–9 for an account of life in Athol Street between and just after the Second World War .
27 Though seemingly a good conversion it perhaps fails the usual location test even though Athol Street is perhaps now a fully law-abiding neighbourhood!
28 Milne in Belchem (ed.), *Liverpool 800: Culture, Character and History*, p. 257.
29 Lane, *Liverpool: Gateway of Empire*, p. 163.

Select bibliography

This book, has drawn upon a variety of sources. These necessarily include both serious, general histories and specialist, research based explorations and analyses of those different periods and aspects which make up the colourful, and frequently turbulent, long history of the City and its waterfront. Also cited throughout, and quoted from, are a number of biographies and autobiographies which personalise and enliven the more sober, prosaic sources. There are also the, regrettably too few, graphic stories and accounts from the direct experience of those who had to do other things than enjoying the privilege of writing for a living. All have their place but busy people, who wish to read further, may need some guidance.

The following is a brief list of books chosen from those cited in the text which readers may find useful and interesting. There are also detailed general histories of the Second World War with copious references to Liverpool, such as those of Angus Calder, Juliet Gardiner and Martin Gilbert. Some are directly available in libraries and bookshops, others may require more effort to locate. The local and national library networks remain important. These are now supplemented by the very useful web pages which give easy access to the stocks of a large number of new and secondhand bookshops. There is also now considerable access, via computer, to mountains of factual detail. This, however, more than other sources, has to be used with great care.

Aughton, Peter, *Liverpool: A People's History*, 3rd edn (Lancaster: Carnegie, 2008)

Ayers, Pat, *The Liverpool Docklands: Life and Work in Athol Street* (Birkenhead: Liver Press, 1999).

Belchem, John (ed.), *Liverpool 800: Culture, Character and History* (Liverpool: LUP, 2006), esp. Colin G. Pooley (chapter 3), Graeme J. Milne (chapter 4) and Jon Murden (chapter 6).

—— (ed.), *Popular Politics, Riot and Labour: Essays in Liverpool History, 1790–1940* (Liverpool: LUP, 1992)

Boyce, Joan, *Pillowslips and Gasmasks* (Liverpool: Liver Press, 1989).

Coates, Ken and Tony Topham, *The Making of the Labour Movement: The Formation of the Transport and General Workers' Union, 1870–1922* (Nottingham: Spokesman, 1994).

Cooke, Terry, *Scotland Road the Old Neighbourhood* (Birkenhead: Countyvise, 1987)

Dash, Jack, *Good Morning Brothers! A Militant Trade Unionist's Frank Autobiography* (London: Lawrence & Wishart, 1969).

Davies, Sam, Colin J. Davis, David De Vries, Lex Hœrma van Voss, Lidewij Hesselink and Klaus Weinhaver (eds), *Dock Workers: International Explorations in Comparative Labour History, 1790–1970*, vols 1 and 2 (Aldershot: Ashgate, 2000).

Davies, Sam, Pete Gill, Linda Grant, Martyn Nightingale, Ron Noon and Andy Challice,

Genuinely Seeking Work: Mass Unemployment on Merseyside in the 1930s (Birkenhead: Liver Press, 1992).

Heffer, Eric, *Never a Yes Man* (London: Verso, 1991).

Hughes, John, *Port in a Storm: The Air Attacks on Liverpool and its Shipping in the Second World War* (Liverpool: National Museums and Galleries on Merseyside and Countyvise, 1993).

Hughill, Stan, *Sailortown* (London: Routledge & Kegan Paul, 1967).

Hunter, Bill, *Forgotten Hero: The Life and Times of Edward Rushton* (Liverpool: Living History Library, 2002).

Jarvis, Adrian, *Liverpool's Central Docks: An Illustrated History* (Stroud: Sutton and National Museums and Galleries on Merseyside, 1991).

——, *The Liverpool Dock Engineers* (Stroud: Sutton, 1996).

Jones, Jack, *Union Man: The Autobiography of Jack Jones* (London: Collins, 1986).

Lane, Tony, *Liverpool: Gateway of Empire* (London: Lawrence & Wishart, 1987).

——, *The Merchant Seamen's War* (Manchester: MUP, 1990).

Emmet Larkin, *James Larkin: Irish Labour Leader, 1876–1947* (London: Routledge and Kegan Paul, 1965).

Lavalette, Michael, and Jane Kennedy, *Solidarity on the Waterfront: The Liverpool Lockout of 1995/96* (Birkenhead: Liver Press, 1996).

Mann, Tom, *Tom Mann's Memoirs* (London: Macgibbon & Kee, 1967 edition).

Marsh, Brian and Sue Almond, *The Home Port: Bootle, the Blitz and the Battle of the Atlantic* (Liverpool: Sefton Council, 1993).

Menzies, Janet, *Children of the Doomed Voyage* (Chichester: Wiley, 2005).

Midwinter, Eric, *Old Liverpool* (Newton Abbott: David & Charles, 1971).

Miller, Anthony, *Poverty Deserved? Relieving the Poor in Victorian Liverpool* (Birkenhead: Liver Press, 1988).

Muir, Ramsey, *A History of Liverpool* (London: Williams & Norgate and Liverpool University Press, 1907).

Neal, Frank, *Black '47: Britain and the Famine Irish* (Liverpool: Newsham Press, 1998).

——, *Sectarian Violence: The Liverpool Experience* (Liverpool: Newsham Press, 1988).

O'Mara, Pat, *The Autobiography of a Liverpool Slummy* (Liverpool: Bluecoat Press, n.d.).

Perrett, Bryan, *Liverpool: A City at War*, Burscough: Hugo Press, 1990).

Phillips, Gordon, and Noel Whiteside, *Casual Labour: The Unemployment Question in the Port Transport Industry, 1880–1970* (Oxford: OUP, 1985)

Ritchie-Noakes, Nancy, *Liverpool's Historic Waterfront: The World's First Mercantile Dock System* (London: HMSO, 1984).

Sexton, James, *Sir James Sexton, Agitator* (London: Faber & Faber, 1936).

Taplin, Eric, *Liverpool Dockers and Seamen, 1870–1890* (Hull: University of Hull, 1974).

——, *Near to Revolution: The Liverpool General Transport Strike of 1911* (Liverpool: Bluecoat Press, 1994).

——, *The Dockers' Union: A Study of the National Union of Dock Labourers, 1889–1922* (Leicester: Leicester University Press; New York: St Martin's Press, 1986).

Turnbull, Peter, Charles Woolfson and John Kelly, *Dock Strike: Conflict and Restructuring in British Ports* (Aldershot: Avebury, 1992).

Waller, Philip J., *Democracy and Sectarianism: A Political and Social History of Liverpool* (Liverpool: LUP, 1981).

Wilson, David F., *Dockers: The Impact of Industrial Change* (London: Fontana, 1972).

Woods, Johnnie, *Growin' Up: One Scouser's Social History* (Lancaster: Palatine Books, 1989).

Index

compiled by Ali Stewart